Minor Marriage in Early Islamic Law

Studies in Islamic Law and Society

VOLUME 41

The titles published in this series are listed at *brill.com/sils*

Minor Marriage in Early Islamic Law

By

Carolyn G. Baugh

BRILL

LEIDEN | BOSTON

Library of Congress Cataloging-in-Publication Data

Names: Baugh, Carolyn, author.
Title: Minor marriage in early Islamic law / by Carolyn G. Baugh.
Description: Leiden ; Boston : Brill, 2017. | Series: Studies in Islamic law and society ; volume 41 | Includes bibliographical references and index. |
Identifiers: LCCN 2017021552 (print) | LCCN 2017022380 (ebook) | ISBN 9789004344860 (E-book) | ISBN 9789004344839 (hardback : alk. paper)
Subjects: LCSH: Marriage age (Islamic law)—History—To 1500. | Child marriage—Law and legislation—Islamic countries—History—To 1500.
Classification: LCC KBP543.955 (ebook) | LCC KBP543.955 .B38 2017 (print) | DDC 346/.167016—dc23
LC record available at https://lccn.loc.gov/2017021552

Typeface for the Latin, Greek, and Cyrillic scripts: "Brill". See and download: brill.com/brill-typeface.

ISSN 1384-1130
ISBN 978-90-04-34483-9 (hardback)
ISBN 978-90-04-34486-0 (e-book)

This book is printed on acid-free paper and produced in a sustainable manner.

Contents

Introduction 1

PART 1
The Early Formative Era

1 Contextualizing and Conceptualizing Minor Marriage 25

2 The Early Compendia 59

3 Early Ḥanafī Thought 78

4 Early Mālikī Thought 103

5 Al-Shāfiʿī 122

PART 2
Consensus, Consensus Writing, Post-Formative Era Writing, and Whether Consensus Matters

6 Consensus 143

7 Writing Consensus 167

8 Post-formative Scholars 206

Conclusion: Does Consensus Matter? 225

Appendix: Excerpts from the Early Compendia 239
Bibliography 257
Index 263

Introduction

A Global Challenge

The phenomenon of minor marriage is by no means limited to the Muslim world. The United Nations Children's Fund has described minor marriage as a global challenge requiring multiple fronts of action to protect the rights of children. Both boys and girls married prior to maturity are by definition victims of gross violations of their human rights. The right to free and full consent to a marriage is recognized in the Universal Declaration of Human Rights (1948) with the recognition that consent cannot be 'free and full' when any of the parties involved is not sufficiently mature to make an informed decision about a life partner.[1] In nations across the world activists struggle to implement the recommendations of both the Universal Declaration of Human Rights (1948) and the Convention on the Elimination of all Forms of Discrimination against Women (1979); one such recommendation is that there be a minimum marriage age of eighteen. Child brides are more often prey to domestic violence and sexual violence, and are exposed to premature pregnancy and a vast range of sexually-transmitted diseases.[2] A 2014 United Nations Population Fund report declares that within the next decade some 140 million girls will marry prior to the age of eighteen.[3]

Each year, fourteen million adolescents give birth, an age group that suffers twice the mortality rate in childbirth as women in their twenties.[4] UNICEF calls on governments to educate their people on human rights and health issues and to enforce minimum ages of marriage as well as the registration of marriages and births. To achieve this, however, cultural attitudes and

1 http://www.unicef.org/policyanalysis/files/Child_Marriage_and_the_Law(1).pdf, last accessed on 7/19/16.

2 http://www.unicef.org/policyanalysis/files/Child_Marriage_and_the_Law(1).pdf, last accessed on 7/19/16. See also: http://www.data.unicef.org/corecode/uploads/document6/uploaded_pdfs/corecode/Child-Marriage-Brochure-HR_164.pdf. Last accessed on 7/19/16.

3 http://www.equalitynow.org/sites/default/files/Protecting_the_Girl_Child.pdf, last accessed 7/19/16.

4 Ibid. Note one Yemeni Shaykh's furious refutation of what he refers to as the conspiracies of "Organizations" such as UNICEF. These, he claims, portend to fear for the reproductive health of children while being behind the parliament's "worthless decision" (*qarār lā wazn lahu walā qīma*) to raise the Yemeni marriage age to seventeen. http://www.ahlalhdeeth.com/vb/showthread.php?t=228599, last accessed on 7/21/16.

© KONINKLIJKE BRILL NV, LEIDEN, 2017 | DOI 10.1163/9789004344860_002

traditions that foster acceptance of prepubescent and child marriage must be approached through dialogue and open discourse.

Minor marriage knows few borders; it is most prevalent in Sub-Saharan Africa and South Asia. A recent study has detailed the pervasiveness of the phenomenon in countries of Central and Eastern Europe as well as those of the Former Soviet Union.[5] In the United States, it occurs among certain Christian denominations, most famously the Fundamentalist Church of Jesus Christ of Latter Day Saints (FLDC), or United Effort Plan (UEP). This denomination also tenaciously insists on preserving the practice of polygyny.[6] Its president/ prophet, Warren Jeffs, spent time on the Federal Bureau of Investigation's "most wanted" list for his role in forced minor marriages and was prosecuted for statutory rape of his twelve-year-old wife.[7]

Nor has minor marriage escaped the notice of the United States Congress, which passed in 2013 the Violence against Women Reauthorization Act. Not only does the Act affirm the commitment of the United States to fighting the issue of child marriage domestically, but it also gives a mandate to the Secretary of State to compel each embassy to give an accounting of human rights violations. Investigation into forced marriage and minor marriage has become an essential component of such reporting.[8]

While widespread globally, marriages of minors are also pervasive in certain regions of the world that claim an Islamic religious identity. Although some countries such as Jordan and Syria have enshrined eighteen as the legal age at which to marry, and Libya institutionalized a marriage age of twenty-one, Egypt's minimum age remains only sixteen and Sudan's is only eleven.[9] Of the Sub-Saharan African countries where Muslim populations exceed one million, seven have determined no minimum age, while three have a minimum age of

5 http://www.un.org/womenwatch/daw/egm/vaw_legislation_2009/Expert%20Paper%20EGMGPLHP%20_Cheryl%20Thomas%20revised_.pdf, last accessed on 7/16/2016.

6 See John Krakauer, *Under the Banner of Heaven* (New York: Anchor Books, 2004). Note the stories of Mary Ann Kingston, pp. 18–20 and Linda Kunz Green, pp. 20–24. See Carolyn Jessop, *Escape* (New York: Broadway Books, 2007) and Elissa Wall, *Stolen Innocence* (New York: William Morrow, 2008), both focused on the abuses of women and children within the FLDS sect.

7 Ben Winslow, "Jeffs seen in Arizona?" *Deseret News*, June 13, 2006.

8 http://www.girlsnotbrides.org/new-law-makes-ending-child-marriage-a-us-government-priority/, last accessed 7/15/2016.

9 Ibrahim, Barbara and Abdalla, Alyce, "Child Marriage: Arab States," in Encyclopedia of Women and Islamic Cultures, General Editor Suad Joseph. Consulted online on 16 July 2016, http://proxy.library.upenn.edu:2146/10.1163/1872–5309_ewic_EWICCOM_0162a.

fifteen for girls (eighteen for boys) and one, Chad, allows girls aged fourteen to marry. Saudi Arabia has not set a minimum age.[10]

Even where minimum marriage ages are legislated, enforcement remains difficult, particularly in rural areas where state authority is lacking and in areas where there is a cultural assumption that early marriage is a religiously-sanctioned institution. In Egypt, for example, the Law on Marriage Age (no. 56/1923) set the minimum age of marriage and stipulated that legal claims cannot be heard by married parties under that age. No punishments or legal consequences are stipulated for the early marriages. Thus it remains a common practice in rural areas of Egypt to marry off girls at the age of thirteen and delay registration of the marriage until age sixteen, creating serious legitimacy issues for any offspring born in the interim.[11] In Syrian refugee camps in Jordan, Iraq, Egypt, Lebanon and Turkey, where there is no recourse to any sort of state authority, there have been dramatic increases in child marriage since 2011.[12]

In Islamic law, marriage is a contractual relationship. As with any contract, it requires the consent of the involved parties. As a contractual relationship, marriage imposes on the parties mutual rights and obligations.[13] The act of marriage causes husband and wife to inherit from each other and affirms any paternity claims. Wives receive the full range of financial maintenance in exchange for providing sex. Accordingly, husbands may restrict the movements of their wives in order to fully benefit from their sexual availability.[14] While

---

10 Although the *Encyclopedia of Women and Islamic Cultures* asserts that the marriage age in Yemen is 14 (art. "Child Marriage: Arab States"), elsewhere Yemen has been grouped with Saudi Arabia as not yet having determined a minimum age for marriage. A report from Human Rights Watch details that some 14% of Yemeni girls are married before the age of fifteen, while 52% are married prior to the age of eighteen. http://america.aljazeera.com/articles/2014/1/19/rights-group-lawfailingtoprotectchildbrides.html.

11 See *Women Living Under Muslim Laws: Women, Family, Laws and Customs in the Muslim World*, International Solidarity Network (New Delhi: Zubaan, 2006), 129. See also the important study of Shaham, Ron, "Custom, Islamic Law, and Statutory Legislation: Marriage Registration and Minimum Age of Marriage in the Egyptian Sharīʿah Courts," in *Islamic Law and Society*, Vol 2, no. 3, *Marriage, Divorce and Succession in the Muslim Family* (1995), pp. 258–281. See also *Expert Witness*, 122–123.

12 http://www.savethechildren.org/atf/cf/%7B9def2ebe-10ae-432c-9bd0-df91d2eba74a%7D/TOO_YOUNG_TO_WED_REPORT_0714.PDF, last accessed 7/25/2016.

13 Kecia Ali, "Marriage in Classical Islamic Jurisprudence," in Asifa Quraishi and Frank Vogel, eds., *The Islamic Marriage Contract: Case Studies in Islamic Family Law* (Cambridge: Harvard University Press, 2008), 12.

14 For more on marriage laws of Egypt, and how Egyptian women can circumvent the husband's legal ability to prevent them from studying or working outside the home via

procreation is typically deemed an added benefit, the main purpose of marriage is to create a framework in which sex can take place licitly.[15]

The debate over setting a minimum marriage age in Saudi Arabia is an area where early Islamic legal thought is often invoked.[16] Saudi Arabia has famously abstained from adopting the Universal Declaration of Human Rights, citing Article Sixteen's description of marriage rights[17] as one of the principle reasons

clauses in the marriage contract, see Zulficar, Mona, "The Islamic Marriage Contract in Egypt," in *The Islamic Marriage Contract,* 231–265.

15 For an extensive discussion of the benefits of marriage with regard to taming the passions see (the Shāfiʿī) al-Ghazālī (d. 1111), *Iḥyāʾ ʿulūm al-dīn*, Chapter on the Ethics of Marriage (*Adāb al-nikāḥ*), 2:32–77. Although the gist of the chapter is generally that marriage is for those who cannot otherwise control their passions, particularly given that marriage involves intensive preoccupation with worldly affairs such as earning a living, all of which distract from God, he spends some time on the issues of women's sexuality, particularly the benefits of foreplay and simultaneous orgasm (74–75), admonishing the man through a Prophetic hadith (deemed false, see fn. 6) not to "satisfy his need for her before she has satisfied her need for him" (74). Unsatisfied passion in the woman is considered "harmful for her" (75). Further, he should increase, if necessary, the every-four-night rule with regard to her sexual needs, "according to her need for being rendered chaste" (*bi-ḥasb ḥājatihā fī al-taḥṣīn*) (75). See additionally, pps. 43–44 for insights into the concept of exhausting one's (i.e., the man's) physical passions in order to empty the heart to better focus on God. While espousing a typically Sufi perspective, al-Ghazālī still includes culturally-enlightening reports, some encouraging sex in order to enhance focus, some encouraging abstinence for the same reasons. The reports are of varying authenticity, regarding such companions as Ibn ʿUmar who would reportedly break his fast by having sex before the sundown prayer, or the report of Ibn ʿAbbās that "the best among you is the one with the most women." Conversely, a telling maxim illustrating the perspective of disdain regarding marriage reads, "Whoever has gotten used to the thighs of women achieves nothing!" (51).

16 It is expedient, although perhaps unfair, to focus sole attention on Saudi Arabia. This issue is of major importance in Sub-Saharan Africa, as mentioned, where marriage age debates are taking place on the tribal and regional level, as seen in Kenya. Personal correspondence with John Kunyuk, magistrate who used my article, "An Evolution in Early Juristic Thought on Prepubescent Marriage," *Comparative Islamic Studies*, vol. 5.1 (2009) 33–92, to press the case for marriage age with resistant local leaders.

17 Article 16 reads: (1) Men and women of full age, without any limitation due to race, nationality or religion, have the right to marry and to found a family. They are entitled to equal rights as to marriage, during marriage and at its dissolution. (2) Marriage shall be entered into only with the free and full consent of the intending spouses. (3) The family is the natural and fundamental group unit of society and is entitled to protection by society and the State. Universal Declaration of Human Rights, http://iipdigital.usembassy.gov/st/english/pamphlet/2012/06/201206026702.html#axzz4EVXdSZK9, last accessed 7/15/2016.

for dissent.[18] In a recent case of compelled minor marriage in Saudi Arabia, the legal arguments used appeared more traditional than text-based,[19] and their resolution was purely the result of prudential calculations on the part of the Saudi government. After international outcry, a member of the Saudi royal family paid the husband to renounce his right to his bride.[20] It had been, in the final analysis, a marriage arranged to settle the debt of the bride's father, a scenario which is historically familiar,[21] but which nonetheless obviates the inherent right of the bride alone to her bridal gift. Although both the Ministry of Justice and the Shūrā Council have proposed measures to set one, the concept of a minimum age for marriage, particularly one that aligns with internationally-accepted norms, has remained a highly contentious issue.[22]

The Early Legal Tradition's Relevance

What exactly is at stake? For many Saudi Arabian jurists, the issue of minor marriage is inextricably tied to consensus (*ijmāʿ*), one of the four sources of Sharīʿa law.[23] Consensus is deemed to be binding; disagreeing with a perceived consensus is posited as disagreeing with Islam itself and a sin. Thus consensus has acquired a mystique of unassailability. However, when pressed, modern Muslim scholars struggle to explain consensus. Does the term refer to the

18 http://ccnmtl.columbia.edu/projects/mmt/udhr/article_16.html, last accessed on 7/15/2016.

19 A Saudi judge in 2008 refused to annul the marriage of an eight year-old girl to a fifty-eight year-old man. See Black, Ian, "Marriage of Saudi Arabian girl, 8 annulled," *The Guardian*, Friday, 1 May, 2009 http://www.theguardian.com/world/2009/may/01/saudi-arabian-child-marriage-annulled, last accessed 1/26/15. See also Black, Ian, "Saudi girl, 8, married off to 58-year-old is denied divorce," *The Guardian*, Tuesday, 23 December 2008 http://www.theguardian.com/world/2008/dec/23/saudi-arabia-human-rights last accessed 1/26/15. The same case appears in other news outlets as being between an eight-year-old girl and a 47-year-old-man. http://www.cnn.com/2009/WORLD/meast/01/17/saudi.child.marriage/, last accessed, 1/26/15.

20 http://www.theguardian.com/world/2009/may/01/saudi-arabian-child-marriage-annulled, last accessed, 1/26/15.

21 Ottoman sources detail many such marriages, as we shall see in Chapter 8.

22 http://america.aljazeera.com/articles/2014/1/19/rights-group-lawfailingtoprotectchildbrides.html, last accessed, 7/19/16.

23 The Qurʾān, the Sunna (the "way"/"practice" of the prophet, or prophetic tradition), consensus and analogy all provide the building blocks of Islamic law. They are considered the *uṣūl*, literally the sources or roots. Positive law derived from these sources is known as the branches, the *furūʿ*.

consensus of the community at large? The Companions of the Prophet? All of the qualified early scholars? If so, of which generation exactly? How were their opinions assessed? What if one scholar disagreed? What if one only tacitly agreed? What if one agreed and then changed his mind? How many voices of disagreement could nullify a consensus? When pressed further, many are able to articulate that the consensus existed to ascribe certainty to a particular prophetic tradition. But what if there is consensus about a tradition's content but not about its interpretation? What if there is consensus about its interpretation but not about its content? Such debates have swirled on since very early in Islamic legal history.

How does consensus factor into modern legal debates? First and foremost it is an invocation of early authority. Early authority matters for Muslims, particularly that of the earliest scholars of Islam who attempted to distill the divine will into righteous practice. Often this sort of authority matters far more than current international norms.

But authority is not vested only in those earliest jurists, or the earliest community, but stretches along a vast continuum of pious men engaged with the law and its texts.[24] That it has been a largely male enterprise is evidenced by the fact that "women's basic rights are often sacrificed when dominant modes of argument press claims into their extreme form."[25] The sources of law, when dealt with selectively, can submit easily to an "authoritarian hermeneutic"[26] that preserves male power when it comes to the realms of divorce, sexual access, the right of a father to contract marriage for his daughters, and many other issues.

What, then, is the process undertaken to cull guidance from the sources of law? In formulating responsa to modern issues, Saudi jurists often look to a multi-volume work of positive law called *al-Mughnī*. Composed by the thirteenth-century Ḥanbalī jurist Muwaffaq al-Dīn Ibn Qudāma al-Maqdisī (d. 620/1223),[27] *al-Mughnī* is one of the six jurisprudential works around which

---

24 This is not to suggest that no women undertook this task. *Al-Muhaddithat*, Mohammad Akram Nadwi (Interface Publications, 2013), is but the preface to a forty volume biographical dictionary detailing the lives of women scholars of Islam.

25 Kecia Ali, "Just Say Yes: Law, Consent, and Feminist Epistemologies," in *Jihad for Justice* (48Hrs), 133.

26 Khaled Abou el Fadl, *Speaking in God's Name: Islamic Law, Authority and Women* (Oxford:Oneworld, 2001), 5.

27 Ibn Qudāma was born outside of Jerusalem in 541/1147 and left with his family for Damascus after persecution by the Franks. He studied in Baghdad with the great Ḥanbalī scholar ʿAbd al-Qādir al-Jīlī but eventually returned to Damascus where he remained except for the period in which he took part with Saladin in the conquest of Jerusalem in 583/1187.

the Saudi legal system is shaped. Not only is it a useful legal history, but it incorporates many now-lost Ḥanbalī legal sources alongside a commentary on an important fiqh work of Abū al-Qāsim al-Khiraqī (d. 334/945).[28]

On the topic of minor marriage, the claim of consensus features prominently in Ibn Qudāma's position on the subject of compulsion in minor marriage. Most fascinating about his approach is that Ibn Qudāma invokes an early consensus claim *first* in his arguments regarding minor marriage, prior even to any invocation of the Qurʾān or the Sunna.[29] The latter two sources are accorded a higher status than consensus, because they are understood to emanate from the divine, while a perceived consensus only takes on a stamp of divine approval retroactively. In contrast to Ibn Qudāma's position, it is worth noting that a modern Saudi mufti, Ṣāliḥ al-Fawzān (b. 1935),[30] reverses the order as he argues his case for prepubescent marriage. He looks to Quranic evidence (65:4[31]), then to the model of the prophet's marriage to ʿĀʾisha,[32] at age six with the marriage consummated at age nine,[33] and then to the consensus of the scholars.

28 Susan Spectorsky, *Chapters on Marriage and Divorce: Responses of Ibn Ḥanbal and Ibn Rāhwayh* (Austin: University of Texas Press, 1993), xi.

29 http://www.ahlalhdeeth.com/vb/showthread.php?t=254364, last accessed 7/21/16.

30 See also al-Fawzān's media presence via his website, http://www.alfawzan.af.org.sa, or a popular television show, https://youtu.be/qoIi9trRFwg. Of additional interest is his position teaching judges in al-Maʿhad al-ʿĀlī lil-Qaḍāʾ.

31 "Now as for your women as are beyond the age of monthly courses, as well as for such as do not have any courses, their waiting-period—if you have any doubt [about it]—shall be three [calendar] months; and as for those who are with child, the end of their waiting term shall come when they deliver their burden. And for everyone who is conscious of God, He makes it easy to obey His commandment." Muhammad Asad, *The Message of the Qurʾān* (Gibraltar: Dar al-Andalus, 1993), 873.

32 ʿĀʾisha bint Abī Bakr was renowned as a relater of hadith, and has some three hundred traditions in the canonical hadith collections. She died in 58/678, and her birth date is debated. Watt gives it as ca. 614; further, he says she could not have been more than ten at the time she was transferred into the prophet's house. Watt, W. Montgomery, "ʿĀʾis͟ha Bint Abī Bakr", in: *Encyclopaedia of Islam, Second Edition*, Edited by: P. Bearman, Th. Bianquis, C.E. Bosworth, E. van Donzel, W.P. Heinrichs. Consulted online on 04 August 2016 <http://proxy.library.upenn.edu:2146/10.1163/1573-3912_islam_SIM_0440>. (Designated hereafter as EI2.)

33 The *Encyclopedia of Women and Islamic Cultures* suggests, without citing a source, that her age was twelve. Ibrahim, Barbara and Abdalla, Alyce, "Child Marriage: Arab States," in Encyclopedia of Women and Islamic Cultures, General Editor Suad Joseph. Consulted online on 16 July 2016, http://proxy.library.upenn.edu:2146/10.1163/1872-5309_ewic_EWICCOM_0162a .

Al-Fawzān practices the art of the jurisconsult in a post-colonial world where, for all intents and purposes, there is no Islamic legal system. Lacking the processes, institutions, and instructional methodologies of the past, Islamic law exists in the "present age as a set of *aḥkām* (rules) and not as a process of *fiqh*."[34] Even the self-proclaimed model of the Muslim state, Saudi Arabia, has resorted to codification which is, at its heart, anathema to the epistemologies and methodologies of *fiqh*. For al-Fawzān, relying on the "sources" of Islamic law is tantamount to safeguarding the Muslim community. The Sharīʿa does not define a girl's marriage age, he writes, and it is not up to those who want to impose one to legislate anything for which God did not grant permission. Doing so, he warns, will lead to communal destruction (*halāk*) and untold suffering (*ʿadhāb*). In his 2011 internet *fatwa*, he defends the lack of an established marriage age by adducing no less than four claims of Ijmāʿ about the licit nature of marrying off prepubescents. He also extracts the entirety of Ibn Qudāma's opinion from the *Mughnī*.

What, then, was Ibn Qudāma's opinion?

It is possible to parse the statements made by Ibn Qudāma in such a way that his words open pathways into each discrete topic of this study. His arguments may be outlined here as follows:[35]

1. A father may contract marriage for his mature or prepubescent virgin daughter against her will, as long as he has made for her a suitable match.[36]
2. There is no difference of opinion over the father's ability to compel the prepubescent virgin. Ibn Qudāma then cites the consensus claim of Ibn al-Mundhir (d. 318/930).[37] Accompanying this claim is the caveat that the match must be one that is "suitable."[38]

---

34 Khaled Abou El Fadl, *Speaking in God's Name*, 171. Abou el Fadl defines fiqh as "lit., the understanding. Islamic law: the process of jurisprudence by which the rules of Islamic law are derived. The word is also used to refer generally to law" (300).

35 See *al-Mughnī*, 9:200–202.

36 *Idhā zawwaja al-rajul ibnatahu al-bikr fa-waḍaʿhā fī kifāyah fa-l-nikāḥ thābit wa-in karahat kabīra kānat aw ṣaghīra.*

37 Abū Bakr Muḥammad ibn Ibrāhīm ibn al-Mundhir al-Nīsābūrī. For more information on Ibn al-Mundhir see the introduction to Ibn al-Qaṭṭān al-Fāsī, *al-Iqnāʿ fī masāʾil al-ijmāʿ* ed, Fārūq Ḥammāda, (Damascus: Dār al-Qalam, 2003), pp. 64–70 See also *Kitāb al-Awsaṭ*, ed. Abū Ḥammād Ṣaghīr Aḥmad, 11–18 and 47–51; the latter is also the preeminent source on Ibn al-Mundhir's works and their abridgments, see especially 19–46.

38 *Ammā al-bikr al-ṣaghīra fa-lā khilāf fīhā. Qāla Ibn al-Mundhir: ajmaʿa kull mān naḥfaẓ ʿanhu min ahl al-ʿilm anna nikāḥ al-ab ibnatahu al-bikr al-ṣaghīra jāʾiz idhā zawwajahā min kufūʾ wa yajūz lahu tazwījuhā maʿa karāhiyatihā wa-imtināʿihā.*

3. Prepubescent marriage is licit because of Q65:4.[39] The waiting period (*ʿidda*) does not become mandatory unless an actual divorce from a consummated marriage has taken place; Ibn Qudāma states unequivocally that this verse proves that the prepubescent female can be married and divorced/repudiated without consideration of her opinion.[40]
4. He then cites the report of ʿĀʾisha's early marriage, noting that it is "agreed upon," and that ʿĀʾisha at the time of her marriage, being six (at the time of the contract) and then nine (at the time of consummation), had no opinion to give.[41]
5. Next, he cites as precedent the early marriages of Qudāma ibn Maẓʿūn and Umm Kulthūm bint ʿAlī ibn Abī Ṭālib.
6. Finally, he discusses the difference of opinion over the licit nature of marrying off virgins in their majority without their permission.

From the outset, it is necessary to point out that Aḥmad ibn Ḥanbal (d. 241/855) himself, eponymous founder of the school to which Ibn Qudāma belonged, left a rather equivocal legacy. In one mention of this issue he states clearly that a virgin should not be given in marriage without her express permission, and then refused to speak about whether or not her marriage would stand if she did not consent. In another rescension of his opinions, he was asked if a man could marry off his virgin daughter without consulting her; he conceded that it was possible, but that he preferred she be consulted.[42] This lack of clarity from the eponym could partially explain why Ibn Qudāma resorted quickly to the authority of Ibn al-Mundhir.

Three major issues present themselves within Ibn Qudāma's first assertion. He is convinced of the valid role of the *walī mujbir*, the *walī* (marriage guardian) who has the ability to compel[43] his virgin daughter. This first point

---

39 *Wa-allāʾī yaʾisna min al-maḥīḍ min nisāʾikum in artabtum fa-ʿiddatuhunna thalāthatu ashhur wa-allāʾī lam yaḥiḍna....*

40 *Wa-qad dalla ʿalā jawāz tazwīj al-ṣaghīra qawl Allāh taʿālā "wa-allāʾī yaʾisna min al-maḥīḍ wa-allāʾī artabtum fa-ʿiddatuhunna thalāthatu ashhur wa-allāʾī lam yaḥiḍna" fa-jaʿala lillāʾī lam yaḥiḍna ʿiddata thalāthata ashhur wa-lā takūn al-ʿidda thālāthatu ashhur illā min al-ṭalāq fī nikāḥ aw faskh fa-dalla dhālik ʿalā annahā tuzawwaj wa-tuṭallaq wa-lā idhn lahā yuʿtabar.*

41 *Wa qālat ʿĀʾisha raḍī Allāh ʿan-hā tazawwajanī al-nabī ṣallā Allāh ʿalayhi wa sallam wa-anā ibnatu sitt wa banā bī wa-anā ibnatu tisaʿ. Muttafaq ʿalayh. Wa-maʿlūm annahā lam takun fī tilka al-ḥāl mimman yuʿtabaru idhnuhā.*

42 Susan Spectorsky, *Chapters on Marriage and Divorce*, 63 and 143.

43 In the case of the minor (prepubescent), Kecia Ali points out that *ijbār* (compulsion) "gives a false impression of constraint; though occasionally the jurists discussed the

has major implications with regard to the marriage contract and the concept of consent which validates it. Second, through his use of terms such as "*bikr*" (virgin)[44] and "*kabīra/ṣaghīra*" (mature/prepubescent), we see that he predicates legal capacity upon lack of virginity, while indicating that he recognizes on some level a point at which females mature physically. This invites the question of when childhood ends and when maturity begins. Third, the concept of suitability (*kafā'a*) is factored into Ibn Qudāma's justification of a father's right to compel: *the father's ability to compel is limited to his ability to place his daughter in a socially and legally appropriate match.*

In his second assertion, we encounter the consensus statement that will be explored throughout Part Two of the present study. This consensus is the *first* legal support that Ibn Qudāma adduces to bolster his position, before any recourse to what he considers to be Qur'ānic or Sunnaic evidence. Its invocation prior to the Qur'ān or Sunna is the essence of the statement's importance for this project.

Within his third assertion we find Ibn Qudāma's position that prepubescent virgin females can be married and divorced without taking their opinions into consideration. Of major importance here is Ibn Qudāma's insistence that divorce can only occur after consummation, which clearly reveals that he believes that prepubescents can engage in sexual intercourse (or, as we will see that the language of juristic discourse indicates, "have it performed upon them"[45]). In other words, these are not marriages that exist merely on paper

permissibility of contracting such a marriage over a son or daughter's objections, for the most part minors were presumed too young to have any opinion," Kecia Ali, *Marriage and Slavery in Early Islam.* (Cambridge, Mass: Harvard University Press, 2010), 31.

44 It is important to note that the word "*bikr*" and the concept of virginity could easily enjoy comprehensive treatment in a monograph. For the purposes of this study we will use the word "virgin" to mean *bikr*, with some reference throughout to the fact that its semantics have varied with context, and jurists themselves could recognize the need to qualify the term in certain circumstances, particularly where they required it to mean "never married" as opposed to "never having experienced intercourse". See also Mohammad Fadel, "Reinterpreting the Guardian's Role in the Islamic Contract of Marriage: The Case of the Mālikī School," *The Journal of Islamic Law*, 3:1, Spring/Summer, 1998, esp. note 9, pp. 5–6.

45 Almost invariably, as jurists consider the legal parameters of sex with prepubescents, ("at what point is the minor female able to tolerate the sexual act upon her"/*matā tuṣliḥ lil-waṭ'*) the word used when describing sexual relations with a prepubescent female is *waṭ'*. This is a word that I have chosen to translate as "to perform the sexual act upon her." This translation, although unwieldy, seems to convey the lack of mutuality in the sexual act that this word suggests (unlike, for example, the word *jimā'*). It is worth noting that the semantic range of the word includes "to tread/step on;" indeed this is given as the primary meaning of the word. See Ibn Manẓūr, *Lisān al-'Arab* (Beirut: Dār Ṣādir, 1955), 2:195–197.

until such a time as the female matures sexually. The issue of when a prepubescent female becomes sexually viable and when the maintenance payments her sexual availability requires become due are topics of serious legal discussion. Finally, with regard to divorce, it is noted here that Ibn Qudāma implies that a female can be divorced against her will, just as she can be married against her will. He makes no mention here of the minor male, or the doctrine of the right of rescission (*khiyār al-bulūgh*, the "choice of [annulling a marriage upon reaching] puberty").[46]

By invoking the report of ʿĀʾisha, and noting that it is "agreed upon," Ibn Qudāma has in many ways appealed to consensus again. In this case, the consensus claim effectively functions as a shortcut. There is no accompanying chain of transmission (*isnād*), and consensus here is used to "elevate" a presumptive source to the level of certainty.[47] There would have been, during Ibn Qudāma's era, little doubt that those considered to have agreed on the veracity of the hadith would have been the famed hadith compilers al-Bukhārī and Muslim.[48] Even so, it is al-Shāfiʿī's[49] introduction of the report into these discussions which is of most interest and perhaps of most enduring influence, as will be discussed extensively. Ibn Qudāma's use of this report, and the fact that he delays reference to the other major text[50] on the subject until his discussion

46 He does reference this later in the chapter, 9:204–5, but he believes the proper context for the discussion to revolve in the main around the rights of orphans.

47 Aron Zysow, *The Economy of Certainty* (Atlanta: Lockwood Press, 2013), 114–115.

48 For more information, see Jonathan Brown, *The Canonization of al-Bukhāri and Muslim, the Formation of the Sunni Hadith Canon* (Leiden: Brill, 2007).

49 For further information on the life of Muḥammad ibn Idrīs al-Shāfiʿī see Kecia Ali, *Imam Shafiʿi, Scholar and Saint* (Oxford: OneWorld, 2011). See El Shamsy, *Canonization*, and also the editor's introduction to *Kitāb al-Umm*, ed. Dr. Rifʿat Fawzī ʿAbd al-Muṭṭalib, (al-Manṣūrah: Dār al-Wafāʾ, 2008). See also Lowry, Joseph E., "Muḥammad ibn Idrīs al-Shā¯fiʿī," in M. Cooperson and S. Toorawa, eds. *Arabic Literary Culture, 500–925* (Detroit: Thomson Gale, 2005), pp. 309–317. See also E Chaumont, "Al-Shāfiʿī" in *EI2*, IX, 181–5 and Schacht, Joseph, "Shāfiʿī's Life and Personality," *Studia Orientalia Ioanni Pedersen* (Copenhagen: Einar Munksgaard, 1953), 318–326. Finally, there is a brief discussion in the introduction to Lowry, Joseph E., *Early Islamic Legal Theory, The Risāla of Muḥammad ibn Idrīs al-Shā¯fiʿī* (Leiden: Brill, 2007), pp. 6–7. For the primary sources on the subject, consult Sezgin, Fuat, GAS, volume I, 485.

50 The *ayyim/bikr* hadith is found most famously in Mālik's (179/795) *Muwaṭṭaʾ*. The hadith occurs (somewhat earlier) in al-Awzāʿī with the wording *thayyib/bikr: Lā tunkaḥ al-thayyib ḥattā tustaʾmar wa lā tunkaḥ al-bikr ḥattā tustaʾdhan wa idhnuhā al-ṣumūt.* ("The non-virgin is not married until she is consulted, and the virgin is not married until her permission is sought, and her permission is silence.").

of the virgin in her majority, indicate the preeminence that the ʿĀʾisha report had acquired by this time in Islamic legal thought.

Ibn Qudāma pointedly refrains from referring to any of the many early anecdotes regarding the compelled marriages of prepubescent males. He instead advances his argument for compelling a female prepubescent by relying on two anecdotes that discuss only females.

In his sixth assertion, he proceeds into the argument that the physically-mature level-headed virgin (*al-bikr al-bāligha al-ʿāqila*) can also be compelled to marry. This is a reprise of point one, for we have already encountered his position that virgins both prepubescent and pubescent can be compelled. He adds to this discussion, however, by invoking texts that will appear throughout the early discourse on this subject, as we shall see.

As a whole, this section of the *Mughnī* is cited repeatedly in modern discourse on the subject of minor marriage.[51] As such, those reading his fatwa are confronted with Ijmāʿ as a powerful rhetorical device for mustering authority on a given topic. Scholarly consensus is clear that prepubescent girls may be married off. Not only this, but they can be married off against their will. Therefore, no minimum marriage age for little girls can be determined. All calls for one, says al-Fawzān, have been instigated by "media interference."

Is the consensus to which he refers the same as that to which Ibn Qudāma refers? Whose consensus, after all, could be so potent as to become a legal end-point after which silence must reign? Modern scholars cite Ibn Qudāma. Ibn Qudāma, in turn, cites Ibn al-Mundhir. Ibn al-Mundhir is adduced in ways very similar to the way that the Qurʾān and the Sunna are adduced; there is no doubt that Ibn Qudāma regards Ibn al-Mundhir's opinions on consensus as a source of binding legal authority (*ḥujja*).[52]

51 In addition to al-Fawzān's fatwa cited above, see the following lengthy Yemeni opinion on the marrying off of minor girls. When adducing Ijmāʿ ʿAlī al-Ḥudhayfī, who possesses an internet following but no solid credentials, resorts to Ibn al-Mundhir and then Ibn Qudāma, clearly using Ibn Qudāma's quotation from Ibn al-Mundhir without looking to Ibn al-Mundhir's actual works or reviewing any contexts used by him in his extensive discussions. http://www.ahlalhdeeth.com/vb/showthread.php?t=228599, last accessed 7/21/16.

52 Ibn Qudāma is not alone. Ibn Ḥajar al-ʿAsqalānī quotes Ibn al-Mundhir some 590 times in *Fatḥ al-Bārī*, while Ibn Humām said of him that Ibn al-Mundhir "was among those whose transmission (*naql*) and conclusions (*taḥrīr*) are relied upon," (Citing *Fatḥ al-Qadīr*, 5:260 in Abū Ḥammād Ṣaghīṟ Aḥmad, ed., *K. Al-Awsaṭ*, (Riyāḍ: Dār Ṭayba, 1993) 1:18. Ibn al-Mundhir seems often to be treated as a *muḥaddith* (ḥadīth relater), hence his inclusion in a book like al-Dhahhabī's *Tadhkirat al-ḥuffāẓ*. In this latter, he is referred to as Shaykh al-Ḥaram and "an independent scholar who imitated no one (*mujtahid lā*

The following investigations of Ibn al-Mundhir and other jurists who wrote on consensus in the early tenth through mid-eleventh centuries show that they also cited earlier scholars. Investigations of *those* early scholars prove that the consensus on a father's ability to compel his prepubescent virgin daughter is but "the lowest common denominator"[53] of agreement on a tangled and multi-faceted legal issue. The consensus is, in other words, a surface scholarly agreement masking multiple layers of disagreement and dissent. This project highlights certain lacunae in the legal arguments related to the marriages of prepubescents that suggest that jurists encountered many challenges in attempting to reconcile an underlying cultural practice with what came to be understood in the early formative period as basic precepts of the Islamic legal system. Moreover, writing on prepubescent marriage was originally concerned with both genders and evolved into an almost exclusive concern with females. The culture of dissent that characterized early efforts to articulate a legal structure from the loose framework of Sharīʿa was eventually to lose ground to trends toward consolidation, uniformity, and abridgment. Such a journey has made it possible for scholars like al-Fawzān to rely on claims of Ijmāʿ that affirm the power of the father to marry off his minor daughter. Such claims never mention the minor son or the myriad issues related to prepubescent marriage about which there was simply no consensus at all.[54]

When opinions like that of al-Fawzān refer to consensus, it is put forward in a way that would suggest that because the early scholars (those charged with making sure the human and divine could meet in the realm of language[55]) agreed on a rule, its authoritativeness is therefore unquestionable. Consensus, however, "cannot be identified with the simple fact of agreement."[56] It requires a basis. Ibn Qudāma's second invocation of consensus is closer to the way that consensus functioned for jurists like Ibn al-Mundhir. But the jurists in general did not use the same texts to reach their conclusions about the basis for the

---

yuqallidu aḥadan)." Al-Dhahabī, *Tadhkirat al-Ḥuffāẓ* (Hyderabad: Majlis Dāʾira al-Maʿārif al-Niẓāmīya, 1915), 3:45. Still, Ibn al-Mundhir's juridical opinions, far more than his hadith, are what seem to have been most commonly passed down.

53 I have taken this term from Joseph E. Lowry. See *Early Islamic Legal Theory*, Brill: Leiden, 2007, Chapter 7, "*Ijmāʿ* in the *Risāla*."

54 http://www.ahlalhdeeth.com/vb/showthread.php?t=254364, as well as http://www.ahlalhdeeth.com/vb/showthread.php?t=228599 last accessed 7/21/2016.

55 Paul R. Powers, "Finding God and Humanity in Language: Islamic Legal Assessments as the Meeting Point of the Divine and Human," in *Islamic Law in Theory* (Brill: Leiden, 2014), 223.

56 Zysow, *Economy*, 156.

rule in question. This study will expose the different approaches and proof texts and widely varying vocabulary that early Muslim jurists used.

Methodology and Sources

Part One

I have organized this book into two parts. Part One is organized in two ways. First, it presents the thought of the earliest scholars of Islam in the earliest legal manuals. Second, each chapter is organized conceptually around the several topics implicit in the words "minor marriage," inspired in part by Ibn Qudāma's above-mentioned discussion points. How did other late antique cultures conceptualize maturity, and how did it come to be discussed in an Islamic historical-legal context?[57] If marriage is entered into via contract, then who may contract it for one who does not yet have legal capacity? Can a party to such a contract be compelled, and if so, what does this do to the validity of the contract? What, after all, is marriage, and what are the rights and duties of spouses—and can they be fulfilled by children? What happens when one whose marriage was contracted prior to attaining legal capacity then attains that state—what makes it possible to rescind some contracts of marriage while others can only be sundered through repudiation?[58] If a groom's "suitability" (*kafāʾa*) is the only possible check on a father's power to compel his minor daughter, then what renders someone "suitable"? Lineage? Class? Race? Profession? Piety?

Each of the above issues has within it many layers which challenge the notion that the permissibility of marrying off minor girls was a firmly-rooted

57 Hodgson, Hallaq and, following them, Azam argue for strong levels of cultural interaction and interreligious literacy forged by trade between Arabia and the surrounding societies. See Marshall S.G. Hodgson, *The Venture of Islam: Conscience and History in a World Civilization*, 3 vols,(Chicago: University of Chicago Press, 1974), 1:103–104, and Hallaq, *Sharia*, esp. 27–34, and Hina Azam, *Sexual Violation in Islamic Law: Substance, Evidence, and Procedure* (Cambridge: Cambridge University Press, 2015), esp. 22–23. See also Fisher, Greg, ed. *Arabs and Empires before the Sixth Century*, Oxford: Oxford University Press, 2015, pp. 66–67. See also the chapter on "Arabs and Christianity and the Christianization of Arabs," pp. 276–372, and pages 370–371 for similarities between pre-Islamic Arabs, called Ishmaelites or Saracens, and their Jewish neighbors.

58 I have, for the most part, chosen to emphasize the unilateral nature of *ṭalāq* by translating it as "repudiation" instead of divorce. A clearer translation would be "unilateral male repudiation of the wife." However, it is sometimes more awkward than it is worth to attempt this, and I have, in a few places, resorted to the word "divorce."

doctrine of Islamic law guaranteed by consensus instead of a topic fraught with contingencies and competing viewpoints. My approach to the legal manuals and compendia discussed below[59] has been historical, doctrinal, and philological. Language, and the legal theoretical issues it presents, is key.[60] For although the jurists' task is to explore the sources for legal indicants and then to generate rules,[61] inherent in this task is discovering and communicating a stable lexicon able that can encompass discussions of the divine will for the community. The jurists must "discern, to de-code as it were, the meanings of divine speech and to minimize (and otherwise come to terms with) the problems of completeness and certainty."[62] This study attempts to expose some of the instability of the lexicon used by jurists to discuss minor marriage. Words matter: Marriage, which is at the heart of this investigation, is a contractual agreement requiring binding verbal pronouncements. Consent is expressed through verbal pronouncements. Yet crucial texts declare that silence, for certain categories of females, can express consent or that certain females, due to age or inexperience, have no actual consent to give and can be compelled.[63]

---

59 This is not without an awareness of the instability of the texts themselves, both from the standpoint of paleographical issues and editorial misinterpretations and from the standpoint of the textual fluidity of an oral culture transforming itself to a writerly culture. For questions about the authenticity and polyvocality of early legal texts see Schacht, Joseph, *Origins* (306–310) and *Introduction to Islamic Law* (45) Calder, Norman, *Studies in Early Muslim Jurisprudence* (Oxford, Clarendon Press, 1993) and Mubārak, Zakī, *Kitāb al-Umm lam yu'allifhu al-Shāfiʿī innammā allafahu al-Buwayṭī wa taṣarrafa fīhi al-Rabīʿ ibn Sulaymān* (Cairo: Maktabat Miṣr, 1991) . For additional thoughts on polyvocality of early texts, see J. Lowry, review of Muranyi, Miklos, "*Die Rechtsbucher des Qairawāners Saḥnūn b. Saʿīd: Entstehungeschichte und Werkuberlieferung*," Journal of the American Oriental Society, Vol. 123, No. 2 (April–June, 2003), pp. 438–440, and also J. Lowry, review of Berg, Herbert, ed. *Method and Theory in the Study of Islamic Origins* (Islamic History and Civilization. Studies and Texts. No. 49.) in *Journal of the Royal Asiatic Society of Great Britain & Ireland* (*Third Series*), 2005 15, pp. 104–107.

For an intriguing study of the shift from the oral to the writerly culture see Toorawa, Shawkat, *Ibn Abī Ṭāhir Ṭayfūr and the Arabic Writerly Culture* (London: Routledge Curzon, 2005).

60 For al-Shāfiʿī's discussion of language and its role see El-Shamsy, *Canonization*, esp. 72–75.

61 Wael Hallaq, *The Origins and Evolution of Islamic Law* (Cambridge: Cambridge University Press, 2005), 131.

62 Powers, "Finding God and Humanity," 206–207. Note that for al-Shāfiʿī, "certainty is not a prerequisite for religiously sanctioned judicial decisions." El Shamsy, *Canonization*, p. 58.

63 For extensive discussions of silence and consent in Islamic Law, see: ʿAbd al-Raḥīm, Muḥammad, *Aḥkām idhn al-insān fī al-fiqh al-Islāmī*, Damascus: Dār al-Bashā'ir, 1996, and ʿAbd al-Qādir Muḥammad Qaḥṭān, *al-Sukūt al-muʿabbir ʿan al-irādah wa atharuhu fī*

Given these many considerations, this study should yield information that is of general interest. First, it provides a historical survey of Islamic legal doctrine on minor marriage and several related areas of the law pertaining to capacity, guardianship, maintenance, suitability, and termination of marriage through rescission or repudiation or divorce. Second, it provides an example of an investigation of the practical implications of consensus claims on positive law. Although subordinated to the larger inquiry concerning minor marriage, this inquiry into the contours of a particular consensus offers new and substantive methodological implications for the field of Islamic law that should resonate beyond the current study.

Chapter One, "Contextualizing Minor Marriage," attempts to locate the ensuing legal discussions of minor marriage in their Near Eastern contexts as well as in the early history of the Islamic community as it transitioned away from a purely Arabian identity. Such an approach prevents the temptation to suggest that certain practices show either "Islamic exceptionalism" or can lead to "Islamic ghettoization."[64] It is in this chapter as well that the importance of the lexicon comes to light: how were majority and minority, pubescence and prepubescence, and adulthood and childhood discussed by early writers, with what vocabulary and what possible shades of meaning? How are we to interpret the deep and abiding ambiguities in these discussions? As God's speech the Qurʾān must provide these "stable signifiers and their assigned signifieds,"[65] and so an exploration of exegesis shines some light on the concept of maturity and its various implications. What then of the Sunna, that "auxiliary" of divine communication?[66]

Most of the juridical methodologies included in this study revolve around Sunnaic indicators and attempts to determine their meaning and applicability. Chapters Two through Five present the vast ranges of differing opinions held by Muslim scholars of the eighth and ninth centuries.[67] Chapter Two is devot-

---

al-taṣarrufāt, Cairo: Dār al-Nahḍah al-ʿArabiyyah, 1991. For a comparative look at consent in other legal systems, see Qarah Dāghī, ʿAlī Muḥyī al-Dīn ʿAlī, *Mabda' al-riḍā fī al-ʿuqūd: dirāsah muqāranah fī al-fiqh al-Islāmī wa al-qanūn al-madanī: al-Rūmānī wa al-Faransī wa al-Injlīzī wa al-Miṣrī wa al-ʿIrāqī*, Beirut: Dār al-Bashā'ir, 1985 .

64 Azam, *Sexual Violation*, 240.

65 Powers, *Finding God*, 204–205.

66 El Shamsy, *Canonization*, 5.

67 With Hallaq, I am comfortable designating this period the "formative period" of Islamic law, the period which saw the birth and development of a complete judiciary, fully-elaborated positive law doctrine, interpretive methodologies and doctrinal schools. Schacht's notion that this period of formation ended in the mid-ninth century does not account for these four "essential attributes." Most periodizations refer to formative, founding, or

ed to mining the compilations of Abū ʿAmr ʿAbd al-Raḥmān ibn ʿAmr al-Awzāʿī (d. 158/774), ʿAbd al-Razzāq ibn Hammām ibn Nāfiʿ al-Ṣanʿānī, al-Yamanī al-Ḥimyārī (d. 211/826), and Abū Bakr ʿAbd Allāh ibn Muḥammad ibn Ibrāhīm Ibn Abī Shayba (d. 235/849). It then proceeds to the early and oft-invoked foundational-era luminaries. These include the major representative of the early Ḥanafī school, Muḥammad ibn al-Ḥasan al-Shaybānī (d. 189/805), in Chapter Three. Chapter Four presents the thought of Mālik ibn Anas (d. 179/795), eponymous founder of the Mālikī school. His work is expounded and elaborated upon by Saḥnūn ibn Saʿd al-Tanūkhī (d. 240/854). Chapter Five presents the thought of Muḥammad ibn Idrīs al-Shāfiʿī (d. 204/820), eponym of the Shāfiʿī school and jurisprudential revolutionary.

Each of these chapters attempts to locate for each scholar or set of scholars the opinions that pertain to the issues inherent in minor marriage, using as a launching pad the famous opinion of Ibn Qudāma because of its modern relevance.

It was not, of course, possible to explore the juristic thought of every early scholar of Islamic law. This study has readily-acknowledged limitations which should serve to inspire future studies on, for example, early Shiʿī scholarship in this area, or a wider exploration of the Ḥanafī school, or a deeper plunge into exegesis. Ḥanbalī ideas are more coherently explained in the book's final chapter, which deals with later scholars and whether or not consensus held for them much impact. It would have been ideal to work from manuscripts instead of editions in which misprints abound. Even more ideal would have been reliance upon court records across regions and periods, as the Ottoman specialists in these pages have done, to attempt to construct the real-life ramifications of the juridical opinions herein. Alas, these for the most part do not exist for the formative era.

Still, the early formative-era scholars whose work is here considered represent a vigorous sampling of the oft-quoted crew whose names still spill off the tongues of muftis, shaykhs, specialists, students, and laypeople. Importantly, when consensus claims hinge on the collective opinion of "the scholars," where no names are given at all and the implicit meaning is the founding intellectuals

classical periods. I will mostly refer to early formative (for the eighth and ninth centuries) and late formative for the late ninth through early eleventh centuries. (I have included Ibn ʿAbd al-Barr among the late formative-era scholars because of the role he played as "foundational" for jurists like al-Subkī) (see Chapter Six, below). Thereafter, I will refer to the post-formative eras. See Hallaq, *Origins*, 2–3, which contains his refutation of Joseph Schacht's periodization schema. For a different view, see Intisar Rabb's discussion of this in *Doubt in Islamic Law* (Cambridge: Cambridge University Press, 2015), 8 and fn. 15.

rather than the Companions of the prophet, then it is entirely logical to turn to these, as we shall see in Part Two of this work.

Not every scholar discussed in Part One will deal with each of the issues at hand or discuss the issue in a way that allows it to be disentangled from an umbrella topic. For example, there is no clear passage on suitability in Mālik's *Muwaṭṭa'*; meanwhile, his thoughts on rescission are best inserted into the larger topic of the legal capacity of slaves, although the entire topic is best treated by exploring the way al-Shāfiʿī approached and refuted Mālikī positions (in Chapter Five). Some scholars will add new nuance to the discussions (for example, investigations of the legal capacity of slaves in comparative discussions on the legal capacity of minors). But as we will see, some common concerns appear throughout these very different texts.

Al-Shāfiʿī's approach to prepubescent marriage differs from earlier scholars. However, much that is unique to his approach begins to appear in the writings of jurists who follow him, and most particularly in the writings of the scholars discussed in Part Two—those explicitly concerned with matters of consensus.

Part Two

Given the extensive debates on so many issues tied to minor marriage, this study suggests that the practice is in many ways incompatible with the structures of legal marriage as articulated by jurists in the early formative period. As with Jewish law,[68] the basic tasks of sexual intercourse and procreation, viewed as cornerstones of a valid marriage, cannot be accomplished when the participants in the marriage are children. Thus there is much to suggest that minor marriage was an underlying cultural practice that became enshrined, however shakily, as law.[69]

The "purely juristic tool"[70] of consensus served the tenth century's attempts at streamlining, delineating, and consolidating the juridical enterprise well.

68 For this reason, interpreters of Jewish *halakhah* rejected the talmudic statement "commending a parent who gives his children in marriage when they are close to the age of puberty (*samukh lefirkan*) and [instead interpreted it as meaning that] *samukh le-firko* meant just after his reaching the full age of 13." The *mitzvah* (good deed) of marriage (with its implicit goal of procreation) only becomes applicable at the age of 18. (Schereschewsky, "Child Marriage," 616; for more on this topic see also Satlow, 105).

69 Shaham, "Custom, Islamic Law and Statutory Legislation," 261. Shaham also notes that juristic opinion did not hold with the Qur'anic (4:6) recommendation "that the desired age at marriage is the age of maturity of mind (*rushd*)." The verse to which he refers reads: *Ḥattā idhā balaghū al-nikāḥ fa-in anastum minhum rushdan* ... This verse concerns when an orphan should take control over any assets in his or her name.

70 Hallaq, *Origins*, 129.

Much has been written about the doctrine of Ijmāʿ, its modalities, and its theoretical underpinnings.[71] This project focuses on the practical implications of writings on consensus, particularly those from a crucial period in development of Islamic legal thought, the late formative era.

Where the understanding of consensus was such that it constituted a determination of the implications of a hadith, it could not, in the early period, be distinguished from Sunnaic practice.[72] For all intents and purposes, that practice emerged from the consensus of the Companions. And yet the deeply inconsistent Sunnaic practices were what "hadith protagonists" such as al-Shāfiʿī sought to replace with a carefully delineated textual corpus of hadith.[73]

Where—much later—the understanding of consensus was such that it was the unanimous agreement of the scholars of a given age, the sheer impossibility of assessing their opinions loomed as the ultimate hurdle. In order to have weight, the consensus had to be transmitted as a textual source that could be, like the Qurʾān and Sunna, referred to and studied. To this end, the nonexistence of works disseminating those issues upon which there was an established consensus was a lacuna in the juridical enterprise.[74]

Some scholars did, however, attempt to compile issues of consensus, and Part Two of this study intends to bring some of them to light. In pointing out the vast differences between "early" (early tenth through mid-eleventh century) and "late" (thirteenth-century to modern) presentations of consensus, this work insists there has been a change. The polyvocality and pluralism of legal thought and reasoning strategies around compelling the minor female to marry have gone missing, allowing for more simplistic discussions.

Thus Part Two of this work focuses on consensus itself, with the ultimate goal being: if minor marriage is a test case for juristic claims of consensus, and the consensus in this case proves quite rickety, how sturdy is any given consensus claim? In Chapter Six, I will explore some of the legal-theoretical issues

---

71 For the theoretical background of consensus, see Hallaq, Wael, "On the Authoritativeness of Sunni Consensus," *International Journal of Middle East Studies*, Vol. 18, No. 4, (Nov. 1986), (Cambridge University Press), pp. 427–454; Weiss, Bernard, *The Search for God's Law: Islamic Jurisprudence in the Writings of Sayf al-Dīn al-Āmidī*, (Salt Lake City: University of Utah Press, 1992), Chapter Five, "The Ijmāʿ"; and Lowry, Joseph E., *Early Islamic Legal Theory*, (Leiden: Brill, 2007), Chapter 7, "*Ijmāʿ* in the *Risāla*.". See also Aron Zysow, *The Economy of Certainty*, 198–262.

72 Hallaq, *Sharīʿa*, 48.

73 Ibid. See also Ahmed El Shamsy, *The Canonization of Islamic Law: A Social and Intellectual History*. (New York: Cambridge University Press), 2013, esp. pp. 5–6, 12.

74 Bernard Weiss, *The Spirit of Islamic Law* (Athens: The University of Georgia Press, 2006), pp. 122–123.

regarding consensus, and the beginnings of what can loosely be called "consensus writing" (some writers, after all, titled their books with the vocabulary of "disagreement writing").[75] Who were the consensus writers and how did they understand consensus? In the 13th century, Ibn al-Qaṭṭān al-Fāsī (d. 628/1230) took the trouble to compile a consensus manual. It is not always accurate, and it is almost entirely devoid of any contextualizing discussions. But it contains the consensus statements of these very writers.

Chapter Seven then presents the writings of each of these major early consensus writers. It asks what they gleaned from the oft-cited jurists whose discussions comprise Part One. What did these tenth- and eleventh-century discussions of minor marriage look like and how did they differ from those that preceded them in the eighth and ninth centuries? How did the consensus writers cope with the instability of the early lexicon of minor marriage and how did they attempt to provide certainty for a community requiring rules?

Finally, Chapter Eight considers how the works of these early consensus writers were used or even ignored by other jurists. Ibn Qudāma, ever on the minds of modern muftīs, is featured prominently as this chapter looks to the thought of post-formative and Ottoman-era scholars. It investigates their stances and sources, with the question being, Did discussions of minor marriage change substantially because of a claimed consensus on the matter? Was anything resolved, or did disagreement and debate continue?

This work's concluding chapter asks, Does consensus matter? What value are consensus manuals and consensus claims today? Consensus is seen by some as the primary tool for resurrecting and codifying Islamic law in Muslim majority countries?[76] Is this a workable solution moving forward, or is consensus nothing more than a rhetorical device projecting authority onto a particular legal position?

The ensuing discussions of minor marriage and its intertwined legal issues are complex. The many differences of opinion coupled with the great variety of early proof texts show that there is a profound lack of resolution on the topic. Could the lack of resolution on this issue of claimed consensus have implications for other topics within Islamic law? Such a conclusion may well bring into question how many complex and tangled issues in Islamic legal history have come to acquire a veneer of resolution through the engine of consensus.

75 It should be noted that these writers were also often deemed writers of "*Ikhtilāf*". Indeed Ibn al-Mundhir, perhaps the most enduringly famous of consensus writers, is classified in Sezgin as one who wrote on *ikhtilāf*. GAS, 1:495–496. Also Tāj al-Dīn al-Subkī in *al-Ṭabaqāt al-Shāfiʿīya* (citing al-Dhahabī)(Maṭbaʿat ʿĪsā al-Bābī al-Ḥalabī, 1964), 3:102, entry 117.

76 See Zysow, *Economy*, 157.

What is clear is that for the prepubescent virgin female, whose opinion is considered to be no opinion, and whose voice is quite literally considered to be no voice, the full weight of fourteen hundred years of patriarchal authority can still be brought to bear by simply saying, "They have agreed …" For, as the introduction to one consensus manual states, anyone deciding an issue contrary to a prior consensus ("of the Companions and the scholars of the garrison cities") is a deviant sinner (*fāsiq*).[77]

77 *Kitāb al-Iqnāʿ*, 6–7, citing Abū Isḥāq al-Shīrāzī's *Lumaʿ*, 347–348.

PART 1

The Early Formative Era

CHAPTER 1

Contextualizing and Conceptualizing Minor Marriage

In his study on minor marriage in the Ottoman Levant, Harald Motzki describes the practice as having been both "common" and "licit" throughout the ancient and pre-modern world. Locales as disparate as China and Rome engaged in it.[1] Yet despite its historical prevalence, scholarship on the subject of child marriage has approached it with certain levels of distaste. Classicists, for example, struggled to reconcile their admiration for Roman achievements with the realities of marriage practices they considered to be "savage."[2]

This chapter discusses minor marriage in the adjacent legal cultures of the Near East, hoping to shed some light on the early and late formative era discussions of Muslim jurists that comprise the bulk of this book. The chapter will also explore some of the early narrative evidence for the practice in Muslim sources. Finally it will address concepts of maturity as they appear in the work of exegetes and in legal theory. The outstanding feature to note is the early lack of resolution regarding definitions of maturity, majority, or minority.

The Near-Eastern Milieu

Unlike Islamic law, which, as we will see, is divided on when majority occurs, Jewish *halakha* has assigned very specific ages to the onset of majority: for boys, one is a minor until the end of the thirteenth year, while girls are legal minors until the end of the twelfth year.[3] Rabbinic law was concerned with

1 Harald Motzki, "Child Marriage in Seventeenth-Century Palestine," in *Islamic Legal Interpretation, Muftis and their Practices*, ed. Masud et al., (Harvard: Harvard University Press, 1996), 129.

2 M.K Hopkins, "The Age of Roman Girls at Marriage," *Population Studies*, Vol. 18, no. 3 (Mar. 1965), 310.

3 Ben Zion Schereschewsky and Menachem Elon, "Child Marriage," in *Encyclopedia Judaica*, Ed. Michael Berenbaum and Fred Skolnik. Vol. 4. 2nd ed. (Detroit: Macmillian Reference USA, 2007), 616. *Katan* is the word for the male minor; *gadol* is the major. *Ketannah* is the female minor; *gedolah* is the major female. An intermediary phase for girls is also noted, from age 12 to 12.5 she is deemed *na'arah* (newly matured); from the age of 12.5 and one day she is called *bogeret* (mature). See also E. Neufeld, *Ancient Hebrew Marriage Laws* (London: Longmans

 | DOI 10.1163/9789004344860_003

how best to bring peace and order to society. Controlling sexual desire was part of this, and the resulting scholarly opinions encouraged early marriage. Similar to Islamic law, the age of majority is also related to issues of when to instruct the maturing child on fasting.[4] In additional accord with Islamic law, the rabbis investigated questions of legal capacity of minors to contract marriage independently and of their guardians to give them in marriage.

Some scholars of the Talmudic era[5] stated their opposition to child marriages, forbidding the father to marry the minor girl until she had attained an age at which she could give her informed consent.[6] Jewish marriage practices require consent of the parties, although the bride's consent was often negotiated with her after the families had negotiated the details of the marriage contract. Actual consent might have differed in substantive ways from formal consent.[7] Social conventions dictating that daughters submit to the contracts arranged by parents were very strong. Moreover, silence was understood to be consent.[8]

Post Talmudic-opinions reverted to support for early marriages. Jewish communities of the Near East and North Africa typically married off girls at the age of twelve or before, while the age for males was higher.[9] Diasporic life was uncertain, and delaying marriage until adulthood was perceived as imperiling

---

Green and Co, 1944) 254, fn. 1, where he points out that none of these terms possessed legal implications in the Bible. Bogeret does not exist at all in the Hebrew Bible. As a late Hebrew word it "is connected with the Hebrew verb b-k-r, 'made a firstling,' and with the Arabic bikr 'to do something early' (Akkadian: bukru is 'firstborn')."

See also Aharon Gaiman, "Marriage and Divorce Customs in Yemen and Eretz Israel," in *Nashim: A Journal of Jewish Women's Studies and Gender Issues*, No. 11, Yemenite Jewish Women (Spring, 5766/2006), pp. 43–83; the article cites the Talmud and decisions of Maimonides (d. 1204) as institutionalizing child marriage for the Yemenite Jewish community.

4 See Satlow, 105 and fn. 31 p. 307.

5 C. 50–500 CE. With Mishnah and Halakhic Midrash the key productions of the Tannaitic era, c. 50 CE to 220 CE, the Palestinian Talmud, Aggadic Midrash, and Babylonian Talmud were productions of the early 3rd to early 6th centuries (the Amoraic era). Redactions of the Babylonian Talmud did continue thereafter, however.

6 Schereschewsky, 616. An opinion of the scholar/philosopher Maimonides appears to be based on these earlier opinions. See also Satlow, 108 and 121 for elaboration on this early opinion and its source and Rachel Biale, *Women in Jewish Law: An Exploration of Women's Issues in Halakhic Sources* (New York: Schocken Books, 1984), p. 65, quoting Kuddushin 41a: "A man is forbidden to betroth his daughter while she is a minor, [he should wait] until she grows up and says: I want so-and-so."

7 Suzanne Stone, "Jewish Marriage and Divorce Law," in *The Islamic Marriage Contract*, 81.

8 Biale, *Women in Jewish Law*, 57–58.

9 Ibid., 65–66.

a daughter.[10] This point is borne out well into the later Middle Ages when incidences of child marriage among Jews were quite high, particularly in the Levant.[11] Later figures from Europe seem to indicate that only the elite tended to marry quite young, as it was an expensive undertaking for most families to support non-earning couples.[12]

In this vein, elite minor marriages in Rome were common. Some examples include Octavia (d. 62), daughter of the emperor Claudius (r. 41–54), who was married at the age of eleven; the mother of Nero, Agrippina, who married at twelve; and the daughters of Cicero, Quintilian, and Agricola.[13] The lack of attention these early marriages received in primary sources was due to the fact that child marriage, being thoroughly unremarkable, did not garner the early historians' interest.[14]

Revisionist notions assert that typical Roman marriages took place for girls above the age of eighteen, while numerous studies detail prepubescent marriages of Roman girls and their early consummation.[15] The Greek Plutarch (d. 120) assumed the cultural phenomenon of child marriage to lie in "the Roman desire for an unformed character and an untouched body."[16] Further, he notes early advice of the Greek doctor Soranus (fl. 1st/2nd c. CE), who, practicing in Rome, advised against prepubertal consummation of marriage and resulting premature conception, and instructed the Romans to keep the intent of marriage, "children and succession," in mind, rather than the pursuit of pleasure. As far back as the reign of Augustus (r. 27 BCE To 14 CE), Roman law cited a legal minimum marital age: twelve for girls and fourteen for boys.

10 Schereschewsky, "Child Marriage," 616.

11 See Ruth Lamdan, "Child Marriage in Jewish Society in the Eastern Mediterranean during the Sixteenth Century," in *Mediterranean Historical Review* 11 (1996): 49–50, pp. 41–42. While Lamdan points out that rabbis and judges typically discouraged marriages of minors, fathers were authorized to give their daughters in marriage even as infants and the marriages were valid; and indeed the practice was quite common as supported by the responsa literature. See also Grossman, Abraham, "Child Marriage in Jewish Society in the Middle Ages," *Peamim*, 45 (1990), 108–125 (Hebrew).

12 Lowenstein, "Ashkenazic Jewry," 156. Lowenstein speculates that Jewish adoption of later marriage ages in the 18th and 19th centuries was due to a combination of governmental restrictions on Jewish populations and acculturation of Jews with the dominant Christian model.

13 Hopkins, 313–317.

14 Ibid.

15 Ibid., pp. 309–310. He cites in particular the multiple articles of M. Durry on Roman prepubescent marriage and consummation; see fn. 8, p. 309.

16 Ibid., 314.

The law was one of that category known as *leges imperfectae*, "laws which neither threatened their violators with penalties nor invalidated their transgression. The sole limitation placed on illegal early marriages was that none of the legal consequences of marriage followed until the girl was twelve."[17]

The average age of Pagan girls at marriage was between twelve and fifteen.[18] While the average marital age of girls in the Christian Roman population was higher than that of Pagan girls, typically between fifteen and eighteen, still, some 19.44% were married between the ages of ten and fourteen.[19] Overall, inscriptions, moral precepts, and textual evidence of social commentary, give the impression that prepubescent marriage was quite common in Roman society, and remained so for quite some time.[20] Augustus' law of twelve as the minimum age for girls stayed "on the books" until as late as 530.[21]

Byzantine law required that a girl attain the age of thirteen before contracting a marriage. Whether she would have consented to the marriage or not prior to this age is deemed immaterial as she would have no legally viable consent to give.[22] All parties to a marriage needed to issue consent, including the groom, the bride, and her parents. In cases where a girl consented to intercourse prior to marriage it was assumed that she consented to the marriage itself and the families would then arrange it. However, if that intercourse occurred prior to the age of thirteen, the groom would meet with the law's most serious punishments due to the girl's assumed legal inability to consent.[23]

Although investigation into Sasanian-era (224–651 CE) child marriage practices unearths scant information, the age of twelve is again important for girls. According to the Avesta, the age of majority was clearly set at fifteen for boys as well as girls; Middle Persian civil law allowed marriage at age nine, provided

17 Ibid., 313–314. Note that this situation now obtains in Egypt (and other countries) where the legal minimum age of marriage is subverted by marrying off younger children and then postponing registration until the child reaches the age of 16. See above p. 3.

18 Ibid., 319.

19 Ibid.

20 The recent study by Brent Shaw challenges some of Hopkins' conclusions, particularly those in which he has relied solely on middle class epigraphy. See "The Age of Roman Girls at Marriage: Some Reconsiderations," in *The Journal of Roman Studies*, Vol. 77 (1987), pp. 30–46. Shaw concludes that most Roman women married in their late teens.

21 Ibid., 313.

22 Angeliki Laiou, "Sex Consent, and Coercion in Byzantium," in Angeliki Laiou, ed., *Consent and Coercion to Sex and Marriage in Ancient and Medieval Societies* (Washington D.C.: Dumbarton Oaks, 1993), 123. This is a phrase used often by Muslim jurists when discussing the minor and specifically prepubescent female.

23 Laiou, 122–123.

that consummation wait until age twelve.[24] In the case of physical maturity, one juristic opinion suggests the marriage can be consummated at the age of nine years for the girl. Under this system, if she reached the age of fifteen and refused marriage, "she had committed a capital sin," while if her father or guardian failed to arrange a marriage for her at that age, he too had sinned.[25]

While little is to be gleaned on minor marriage per se, the fact that a father had control over his daughter's choice is clearly found in the phenomenon of consanguineous (*xwēdōdah*) marriage. The uptick in such unions has been marked in three periods: during the third century CE's rivalry with Manichaeanism to be the official state religion, during the sixth century CE's conversion efforts by Nestorian Christians, and in the eighth and ninth centuries following Arab Muslim conquest.[26] The father, in arranging the daughter's marriage in such circumstances was charged by the priests to consolidate the community through preservation of racial and religious purity. The perceived benefits of keeping wealth within the family and preventing a daughter from being converted by an exogamous spouse were high.[27] The sort of "family superstructure" resulting from such unions is also one in which the father could exert power over the daughter's spouse—in order, perhaps, to assure her safety and societal position.

Indeed, it is quite conceivable that securing an early match for a minor was, in the early Muslim consciousness, the best possible guarantor of that child's protection and security. In particular, for those females whose only social move was a linear journey from the home of the father to the home of the husband, and given the postulate (supported by early reports[28]) that "women were many," it could have been a wholly proper—not to mention protective—undertaking for a father to provide early marital arrangements for his daughters.[29]

---

24 Mansour Shaki, "Children iii. Legal Rights of Children in the Sasanian Period," *Encyclopaedia Iranica*, Online Edition, 20 July 2005, available at www.iranicaonline.org/articles/zoroastrianism-i-historical-review, last accessed 7/26/2016.

25 Ibid.

26 Daryaee, "Marriage, Property, and Conversion," 93–94.

27 Ibid.

28 See the *Muṣannaf* of Ibn Abī Shayba ¶18245–6:

"I asked Ibrāhīm about the divorce of a boy, and he said, 'The women are many.' Ibrāhīm said regarding the divorce of a boy, 'It means nothing (*laysa bi-shay'in*), and the women are many.'"

29 This notion, too, would not have been dissimilar to Jewish thought on the subject:

"This absolute legal right of a father to betroth his daughter is related to the rabbinic assumption that women were so desperate for marriage that they would be happy with

Paternal Power

By peering into other early legal systems, it becomes apparent that Islamic conceptions of paternal power embodied in the doctrine of the guardianship of compulsion, the *walī mujbir*, are often quite limited in comparison. In other systems, coming of age did not terminate the father's power over his children. Moreover the father's authority extended to the wife and household at large, none of whom had individual rights.[30]

This concept was a feature of Roman jurisprudence well into the sixth century. Arjava notes that it is probable that many citizens of the western Roman empire did not fully fathom the extent to which the father's power was designed to render his descendants powerless: "It is quite possible that many of them did not perfectly understand the legal definition of *potestas*: they may have regarded it as a kind of guardianship rather than an absolute domination."[31] Regarding males, Roman law stipulated the consent of the son and the father to a contract of marriage, although cultural production of second century Rome, such as early plays, often depicted fathers exercising force in the form of pressure.[32]

It would seem that as time progressed, the latent power of the *patria potestas* would surface unevenly. Fifth century legal codes did not contain provisions for guardianship of females, just as a wife had to grant authorization for a husband's economic interference in her affairs.[33] The Lombards, meanwhile, "placed women perpetually under male power (*mundium*) of either the husband or a blood relative or the king."[34] This list is very reminiscent of many we will encounter in Islamic law with regard to who is the appropriate guardian for a woman, with the word "king" replaced by the word "*sulṭān*."

---

anyone that their parents chose. An adult woman who was unmarried, the rabbis thought, felt 'shame'" (Satlow, 121).

30 Patricia Crone, *Roman, Provincial and Islamic Law* (Cambridge: Cambridge University Press, 1987), 77. For more on the doctrine of *patria potestas*, see Westrup, C.W., *Family Property and Patria Potestas* (London: Oxford University Press, 1936), esp. pp. 24–28. See also Richard P. Saller in "The Social Dynamics of Consent to Marriage and Sexual Relations" in *Consent and Coercion to Sex and Marriage in Ancient and Medieval Societies*, ed. Angeliki Laiou (Washington D.C.: Dumbarton Oaks, 1993) n. 42, p. 99, quoting Dumont, "L'imperium," 493–494, that paternal power would not have been "arbitrary or unrestrained" but would have been held in check by social constraints based on tradition.

31 Arjava, Antti, "Roman Family Law after Barbarian Settlements," in *Law, Society and Authority in Late Antiquity*, Ed. Ralph Mathisen (Oxford: Oxford University Press, 2001), 42.

32 Saller, "Evidence of Roman Comedy," 94–95.

33 Arjava, "Roman Family Law," 47.

34 Ibid.

The concept of *patria potestas* was widespread among "Semites" generally and the Hebrews of antiquity in particular. The culmination of this point lies in the right of *ius vitae necisque* which the father retained over his children, supported by Biblical precedents of Lot and his offer of his daughters' honor, Abraham and his attempted sacrifice of Isaac, and Jephthah's sacrifice of his daughter.[35]

That a Jewish father had full authority over his daughter's marriage was, therefore, only natural. His power over her, perhaps suspended by her transfer to a husband's authority, resumed upon her widowhood.[36] Insofar as a daughter (or son) was in "the father's house," the father had complete authority. Indeed, scholars held that "a woman with a living father need not be asked for her opinion" with regard to marriage.[37] Mishnaic law even allowed fathers to sell their minor daughters into slavery, a right that ceased upon their attaining age twelve.[38] His power over her was absolute, and she was in actuality his property, but only until her "majority/attainment of personhood."[39]

Although *patria potestas* dissipated only gradually, the Talmud did serve to modify parental authority, particularly by stipulating an ideal age for marriage. Still, the father's power over his prepubescent daughter sparks a question that is particularly pertinent for the coming discussions. What is the status of the prepubescent non-virgin (in Islamic law, *al-thayyib al-ṣaghīra*)?[40] Because the Jewish father who contracts marriage for a prepubescent daughter forfeits his guardianship of her permanently, he cannot contract any other marriage for her. She cannot contract for herself according to biblical law because of her legal incapacity prior to majority. She is, for all intents and purposes "an orphan

35 Neufeld, *Ancient Hebrew Marriage Laws*, 252–253. Neufeld further claims that the *ius vitae necisque* existed so strongly among the pre-Islamic Arab Semites that they considered it quite within their rights to bury unwanted baby daughters alive.

36 Ibid., 253.

37 Satlow, *Jewish Marriage*, 124.

38 Judith Romney Wegner, *Chattel or Person: The Status of Women in the Mishnah* (New York: Oxford University Press, 1988), p. 34.

39 Ibid.

40 Satlow makes a pertinent observation: "The tannaim discuss the marriage of female minors at length precisely because they are so legally problematic and interesting, not because they [the tannaim] necessarily are consumed with a set of real problems." His study of Jewish marriage in antiquity emphasizes that the relationship between rabbinic law and actual Jewish societal practice can rarely be substantiated, while opinions offered in the law are often designed to communicate an ideal. That ideal is, of course, deeply linked to the personae of those offering the legal opinions. In both past and present, this is a useful point to recall when approaching Muslim jurisprudence.

in her father's lifetime." And so the rabbis allowed through a *takkanah* (legislative enactment) permission for her to contract her own marriage or empower a mother, brother, or even, in one opinion, the father to do so—although this is technically outside the pale of biblical law.[41]

Another modification of paternal authority was that fathers could not contract marriages for minor Jewish males without their consent under any circumstances; halakhic law deems a father's contract of marriage for a male before the age of majority to be "prostitution and forbidden."[42] In the case of minor females, however, fathers need not secure the consent of their daughters, and neither is their age of importance. "A father is entitled to arrange the *kiddushin* [change in personal status to "married"[43]] of his daughter, whether she is a *ketannah* (minor) or a *na'arah* (newly-major), without her consent."[44] In those instances wherein the jurists evidenced a concern for a female's consent, it was not consideration for the rights of women on the part of the rabbis: "An unhappy wife who commits adultery brings shame upon her father, and one who ultimately divorces and returns to her father's house could become an economic liability."[45]

Although a father could unilaterally betroth and marry off his daughters, Rabbinic thought also considers the case of the girl who betroths herself, deeming this to be outside the pale of legal possibility. Says the Tosephta, "A minor who betroths herself and marries herself in the life of her father—her betrothal is no betrothal, and her marriage is no marriage."[46]

Likewise, minor Byzantine females were deemed "legally incapable" prior to the age of thirteen. Legal codes considered her consent a legal impossibility and any union contracted to be moot.[47]

---

41 Schereschewsky, "Child Marriage," 616.

42 Ibid. See however, Satlow, Michael, *Jewish Marriage in Antiquity*, p. 307 fn. 32, where he states that the Mishnah establishes the "minimum male legal age of marriage" as nine, with the minimum being three for girls. "Some Palestinians ... do advise a man to marry his son when he is still a *qaṭan* (*ketan*/minor). In these sources, the word most likely means 'young,' and denotes no specific or legal age."

43 Biale translates this in more detail below, p. 37.

44 Ibid. Satlow, however, points out that there were differences of opinion about when a girl should be betrothed and married (p. 108).

45 Satlow, *Jewish Marriage*, 121.

46 Satlow, Ibid., 122.

47 Laiou, "Sex, Consent, and Coercion," 123.

Sex, Maintenance, and Sexual Maturity

In Islamic Law, while attainment of majority is the single most important change in legal status that a Muslim can undergo (other than the journey from slavery to manumission), what constitutes the shift is a subject of some disagreement. For many jurists, the terms *al-ḥulum* and *al-bulūgh* are synonyms for pubescence. *Al-ḥulum* is semantically linked to *al-iḥtilām*, meaning nocturnal emission.[48] But most jurists recognized that pubescence and maturity were very different things. Maturity included the development of reason. Juristic discussions reveal attempts to determine at what point prepubescence (*al-ṣighar*) ends and when the legally accountable Muslim (*al-mukallaf*) emerges. For this reason, we find debates over the age of maturity amidst discussions of anything from fasting to the management of financial assets. Jurists were aware, for example, that the true meaning of fasting would be lost on the child, and the exercise would be an empty one. Nowhere are these discussions more fraught than in the jurists' treatment of the maintenance due a female who submits to and provides sex.

Other Near Eastern systems witnessed similar concerns. Maintenance was a part of the social consciousness of antiquity. In the Code of Hammurabi, if a husband—considered the literal owner of the wife—was taken prisoner without having provided for his wife, and the wife committed adultery with a man who took on the role of her provider, she was considered to have been free from blame.[49] There was some question in Roman and, later, Byzantine society as to the true telos of marriage. Was marriage without sex possible? It is possible to trace one answer to Byzantine laws that linked marriage age to the onset of puberty and divorce to a man's impotence.[50] Authorities even advised against the pious withholding sex from each other. When a rather different answer was put forward by other authorities, that intent alone was key to union, this proved a difficult assertion to maintain.

In Jewish marriage contracts[51] the male was likewise expected to provide food, clothes and sex for his wife. The wife's obligations, although

48 Despite the use of the term *bulūgh al-ḥulum* in largely male contexts, females are acknowledged as having nocturnal emissions from which lustration is necessary. See al-Bukhārī, *Saḥīḥ*, 1:60.

49 Neufeld, *Ancient Hebrew Marriage Laws*, 157.

50 Laiou, "Sex, Consent, and Coercion," 182.

51 For an example of the earliest known Jewish marriage contract see Neufeld, *Ancient Hebrew Marriage Laws*, 156. Neufeld discusses the *mōhar*/bridal gift as "the value of the husband's *jus mariti* (marital rights) over the girl, but not the price of the girl's person" (96). For details on the concept of *mahr*, and, more controversially, on the concept of *pretium pudicitiae* in Hebrew law, see Neufeld, pp. 94–117. For a critique of Neufeld's

numerically more, and included cleaning, did not actually include sex.[52] Still, in practice, being sexually available was viewed as essential to her duties as a wife, and there was a direct link between sexual obligations and economic responsibilities in Jewish contracts of marriage. Withholding sex resulted in punishments such as having sums subtracted from her marriage settlement.[53] Withholding of sex was depicted as rebelliousness and the women in question as rebels.[54]

But what of the prepubescent bride? At what point could she be compelled to participate in sexual encounters? For the period of antiquity, there is little information from Jewish sources on how to deal with a wife's minority or lack of sexual maturity; consummated prepubescent marriages certainly existed.[55] Still there are debates from the *amoraim* that support early betrothals and show reticence over when actual marriage (i.e. consummation) should take place. Some opinions said that the minor female's opinion about when she wanted to marry should be heard, other opinions said minors should not have wedding celebrations, while still others cited cases of females betrothed as minors and married only after having attained legal majority.[56]

While marrying off children close to the "coming of age" (defined as the "reaching of puberty and sexual maturity") was on the one hand deemed to engender societal peace, it was still conceived as legally problematic because "sex with no potential for conception whatsoever is analogous to masturbation and 'wasting seed'."[57] Those marriages which were contracted prior to maturity were often forged from economic uncertainties. When a dowry could be

assertions, see T.M. Lemos, *Marriage Gifts and Social Change in Ancient Palestine: 1200 BCE to 200 CE*, Cambridge: Cambridge University Press, 2010), esp. pp. 6–7 .

52 Satlow, *Tasting the Dish*, 283.

53 Ibid., 286.

54 This topic, too, would be worthy of lengthy comparative study, as the doctrine of *nushūz*, based on interpretations of Q4:34, provides for similar discussion of sexuality and rebelliousness. See in particular Ibn Taymīya, *Fatāwā al-nisā'*, ed, Sa'd Yūsuf Abū 'Azīz (Cairo: Dār al-Fajr lil-Turāth, 1999), 213.

55 We do, however, have access to information in the early Middle Ages in the form of responsa of the Eastern Mediterranean Jewish communities. For conclusive evidence indicating the prevalence of child marriage and the proof of early, often violent consummation, see Ruth Lamdan, "Child Marriage in Jewish Society in the Eastern Mediterranean during the Sixteenth Century," in *Mediterranean Historical Review* 11 (1996).

56 Satlow, *Jewish Marriage*, 108. Of note here is the legal capacity accorded the minor female, to whose wishes her guardians should defer.

57 Biale, *Women in Jewish Law*, 66.

amassed, the marital bond was pursued because assets could vanish. A socially and economically secure match dispelled some of the peril of an otherwise opaque future.[58] Instability, war, persecution, and fear increased incidences of early marriage.[59]

Suitability and Termination of Marriage

Suitability is one of the least determined of the requirements when a father arranges or compels a marriage in Islamic Law. Perhaps its lack of clear regulations indicates to what extent arranging socially compatible unions was a deeply ingrained cultural assumption and therefore needed no elaboration. Alternatively, it could have been so highly variable that it was by definition undefinable. Whether racially or religiously or economically motivated, other early cultures had similar doctrines and attempted to construct a consistent way of legislating their concerns.

According to the *Lex Burgundionum*, Roman women suffered a diminution of rights for joining of their own accord with Burgundian men: "he will have power not only over the wife herself but in a like manner over all her property, too."[60] Still, Romans are not perceived as having too many qualms over the concept of intermarriage. Both the Greeks and the Jews are said to have been irked by Roman disregard for racial purity. (The Greeks in particular were partial to endogamous unions, particularly between uncles and nieces; this was banned by the Romans.[61])

In Judaism, when priests became for all intents and purposes irrelevant after the Temple's destruction, there arose a nostalgic longing for the purity of descent from the priestly line. Marrying a daughter from a priestly lineage to a non-priest was seen as defiling her.[62] Still, alongside this inclination, the rabbis were pushing for a reevaluation of lineage. For them, knowledge was of greatest value in a match, and a case was made for "Torah descent" over priestly descent.[63]

Peculiarly, however, it was these very rabbis who argued for a "marital caste system"[64] within Jewish society. The Mishnah details ten marital "castes" from

58 Ibid.

59 Ibid., 68. This relates to the uptick in modern incidences of minor marriage among Syrian refugees. See the introduction above, p. 3.

60 Arjava, "Roman Law after the Barbarian Settlements," 47.

61 Satlow, *Jewish Marriage*, 143.

62 Ibid., 147.

63 Ibid.

64 Ibid., 148.

which the Rabbinic marital restrictions are extracted.[65] Marrying outside of a given group was thus forbidden.

Prior to the legal articulation of this classification system (considered to be in the last half of the first century CE), both Greek and Roman values were shown to be influential factors upon Jewish ideals for the male selection of a bride. The best mates were "virgins, freeborn, and of good parents." Slaves were reviled as lowly members of society, and therefore entirely unsuitable.[66] Only after the institution of this system, however, would slavery be perceived to be a genealogical issue.

Although of far less concern than the Jewish male's spouse, Jewish women also had to contend with strict ideas of who is suitable and who is not. The resultant child of a union between a Jewish woman and a "Gentile or slave" is defined as *mamzer*, even though this term should refer only to children born of incest.[67] It is particularly interesting to see how both Gentile and slave were deemed to be equally polluting to the Jewish woman.

Satlow complains of this "marital caste system" as a "strikingly unbiblical enterprise,"[68] a position that certain Muslim jurists would echo in considering attempts to base marital suitability on such issues as lineage, tribe, and wealth. And yet social and economic factors continued to play an enormous role in determination of the ideal Jewish spouse. It was an issue of particular importance for men: men could be degraded by marrying women of lowly or "boorish" origin,[69] and tannaitic sources speak of "supernatural punishments" for a man marrying an "unfit bride."[70]

Here, then, emerges an issue that does appear to be quite at odds with the Muslim approach to suitability. Muslim men could not be diminished by their choice of spouse. Only Muslim women suffered from uneven matches. Slavery was debated as being an impediment to matches for Muslim women. Many

65 Ten genealogical classes (yoḥasin) came up [with Ezra to the Land of Israel] from Babylonia: priests, levites, Israelites, "profaned" (ḥalale), gere, ḥarure, mamzere, netine, shetuke, and foundlings. Priests, levites, and Israelites are permitted to marry each other. Gere, ḥarure, mamzere, netine, shetuke, and foundlings are permitted to marry each other. *Mishnah Qiddushin* (tractate), 4:1 (ed. H. Albeck, Jerusalem: Bialik Institute, 1952–58, 3:325) cited in *Jewish Marriage*, 148.

66 Ibid., 149.

67 Michael Satlow, *Tasting the Dish: Rabbinic Rhetorics of Sexuality* (Atlanta: Scholars Press, 1995), 85. Note that there is no controversy over the child born of a Jewish man and a Gentile woman, for this child is, by Mishnaic definition, a Gentile (92).

68 Satlow, *Jewish Marriage*, 149.

69 Ibid., 153. The term is *'am ha'areṣ*.

70 Ibid., 152.

Muslim jurists had an ideological insistence on spiritual piety as preeminent, although this was often in conflict with patterns of deep social stratification. Still, a failure of suitability was (and remains) one legal justification for a female's refusal or annulment of a compelled match.

Another form of marriage termination is the "choice upon maturity" (*khiyār al-bulūgh*) wherein prepubescents can reject a match upon gaining the legal capacity usually, though not always, imbued by pubescence. Such a system, in which a marriage ends without the necessity of the *ʿidda* waiting period necessary for establishing paternity, seems to be a relic of a time when marriage was a multi-phase process marked by a period of betrothal.

Such a multi-phase process was part and parcel of Rabbinic law. Although it is clear that "betrothal by intercourse" was de rigeur in early Jewish communities, after the Mishnaic period, the rabbis insisted on phases that would more properly involve parental approval and the community's endorsement. Many opinions are offered decrying "betrothal by intercourse" and lauding betrothal following engagement. Intercourse came to be understood as the culminating phase of a long marriage process.[71]

The word for betrothal, *kiddushin,* is semantically related to the word for being holy or sanctified[72] and is used because the female in question will enter into an exclusive sexual relationship with the male and become forbidden to all others. (No such restriction applies to the man.)[73]

Under this system, a minor female who is betrothed by someone other than the father (in the case of his death, for example) could reject that match upon maturity.[74] The consummation phase of marriage seems to have been delayed until the girl enters her "early to mid-teens." Rights of refusal were often brought to bear in the tannaitic period, possibly indicating that the *amoraim* had more reservations about prepubescent unions.[75]

It is possible that something resembling the Jewish manifestation of the practice of formal betrothal was in play in early Islam. It is even possible that cultural assumptions were in place that prepubescent unions would remain unconsummated until pubescence. Certainly a more rigorous exploration of early texts, including literary works, could provide a firmer understanding of

71 Biale, *Women and Jewish Law*, 56.

72 Cf. the Arabic root q-d-s.

73 Biale, *Women and Jewish Law,* 48–49.

74 See Satlow, *Jewish Marriage*, 73–83.

75 Ibid., 108.

the difference between *zawāj* and *nikāḥ*.[76] From our present vantage point, however, it is possible to hypothesize that one had initially meant "betrothal" in the earliest period, and with time, and perhaps with shifts from the oral/aural to the written transmission of texts, the two terms became blurred.[77] It is not at all clear from the language of legal manuals and hadith compendia whether a term like *dakhala ʿalā* is meant to signify solely cohabitation, cohabitation with consummation, or perhaps simply "visiting."[78] Several *fiqh* books speak of periods in which a bride had a lengthy stay in her husband's house but remained a virgin. In some cases, the contract would precede consummation by many years. In some cases consummation would never occur, and in some cases there would be cohabitation without consummation.

Muslim jurists had very mixed opinions on whether rescission, when the right is granted at all, could take place after consummation or not. A simple perusal of the chapter on consensus writing (Chapter Seven) will amply illustrate the point that it is highly likely that rescission was designed for an unconsummated, betrothal-phase of marriage. Imagining such a phase might also be helpful when considering the early narratives on minor marriage.

Early Anecdotes

The following anecdotes detail some examples that remained, and remain, in the juristic consciousness regarding early marriage. It is perhaps useful to point out that early anecdotes served the function of legal precedent for early jurists, because the behavior of noteworthy individuals was, and remains, normative.[79] Thus when Ibn Qudāma discusses child marriage in the thirteenth century he refers specifically to two stories from the first Islamic century, that of Qudāma ibn Maẓʿūn and that of the daughter of ʿAlī ibn Abī Ṭālib, Umm Kulthūm.[80] This section presents these and similar anecdotes. What is consistent in the earliest texts is that the practice of prepubescent marriage applied

76 Muhammad Fadel asserts that minor marriages were actually only betrothals and that consummation occurred at puberty. See "Reinterpreting the Guardian's Role," p. 6 note 10. For more on the language of marriage and its evolution see Hallaq, *Sharīʿa*, pp. 273–274 and note 13.

77 Byzantine marriages also had a blurred line between betrothal and marriage; often one was equated with the other. See Laiou, "Sex, Consent, and Coercion," 122.

78 See also Chapters Four and Five, below.

79 See Hallaq, *Origins and Evolution*, 47. This is, of course, why the Sunna (the "way" or practice) of the Prophet is of such importance.

80 *Al-Mughnī*, 9:201.

equally to boys and girls; importantly, when Ibn Qudāma chose anecdotes for inclusion in the *Mughnī,* none of the stories involved boys.

In Ibn al-Mundhir's *Kitāb al-Ishrāf* we find the following anecdote: "Ibn ʿUmar contracted marriage (*zawwaja*) for his prepubescent son, and he and his son fought over this, taking the case to Zayd,[81] who allowed it."[82] An earlier source, ʿAbd al-Razzāq's *Muṣannaf,* indicates that ʿUrwa ibn al-Zubayr[83] contracted a marriage for his six year old son to the daughter of Muṣʿab[84] (ibn al-Zubayr; thus ʿUrwa's niece) when they were five and six years old.[85] This incident is also mentioned in the *K. al-Istidhkār* of Ibn ʿAbd al-Barr.

ʿAbd al-Razzāq's *Muṣannaf* includes a lengthy narrative about the marriage of ʿUmar ibn al-Khaṭṭāb[86] to Umm Kulthūm, the daughter of ʿAlī and the Prophet's daughter Fāṭimah.[87] It was, according to the texts, a marriage by

81 Zayd ibn Thābit, died anywhere from 42/662–3 to 56/675–6. A major figure in both the collection of the Qur'ān and the organization of and overseeing of the treasury, he was famed for his literacy in both Arabic and Hebrew (or possibly Syriac). It is not clear that he held a post that would allow him to make judicial decisions such as the one mentioned above, but he was an adviser to Muʿāwiyah (r. 41/661 to 60/680) and then-governor Marwān ibn al-Ḥakam (64–5/684–5). Lecker, M. "Zayd b.Thābit." EI2.

82 *Al-Ishrāf,* 27. I did not find this story about ʿAbd Allāh Ibn ʿUmar ibn al-Khaṭṭāb (d. 73/693) elsewhere in any of the early sources at my disposal.

83 ʿUrwa ibn al-Zubayr, died 94/713. Son of the Companion al-Zubayr and Asmāʾ bint Abī Bakr, he remains a major source of Prophetic traditions and early social history. For more information see Ṭāhir, Salwā Mursī, *Bidāyat al-kitābah al-tārīkhīyah ʿinda al-ʿarab: ʿUrwa ibn al-Zubayr ibn al-ʿAwwām* (Beirut: al-Muʾassassah al-ʿArabīyah lil-Dirāsāt wa-l-Nashr, 1995).

84 Muṣʿab ibn al-Zubayr, known for his womanizing and iron hand as a governor for his brother the counter-caliph, ʿAbd Allāh ibn al-Zubayr (d. 73/692), died in 71/690 in battle against Marwanid forces. Lammens, H. "Muṣʿab b. al-Zubayr, Abū ʿAbd Allāh or Abū ʿĪsā." *EI2.*

85 ʿAbd al-Razzāq, *Muṣannaf,* ¶¶s 10397 and 10398, 6:132. The first version is related by al-Zuhrī, while the second is related by Hishām Ibn ʿUrwa; both of these also relate ʿĀʾisha's report from ʿUrwah in the *Muṣannaf* (¶¶s 10388 and 10389, respectively). See also *al-Istidhkār,* 5:405.

86 The Second of the "Rightly-Guided" Caliphs, ʿUmar ibn al-Khaṭṭāb initially opposed Islam, but eventually became one of its most passionate defenders; reigned as Caliph from 13/634 until his death in 23/644. See G.Levi DellaVida-[M.Bonner]. "ʿUmar (I) b. al-Khaṭṭāb." EI2. For additional information see Haykal, Muḥammad Ḥusayn, *Fārūq ʿUmar* (n.p., 1963–1964).

87 See also the Appendix.

which ʿUmar sought to link himself to the lineage of the Prophet. Importantly, though, it was a marriage that ʿAlī initially protested:

> He [ʿAlī] said, "She is young (*innahā ṣaghīra*)." And it was said to ʿUmar, "He means by that to prevent her [from marrying]."

Caught in an attempt to keep his peer from marrying his daughter, ʿAlī sends the girl to ʿUmar, saying, "If you are content with her, she is your wife." When ʿUmar attempts to lift her dress to look at her leg, she threatens to slit his throat.[88] Another early story is preserved in the *Aḥkām al-Qurʾān* of al-Jaṣṣāṣ[89] (d. 370/981) wherein the Prophet married Salama (the son of Umm Salama) to the daughter of Ḥamza when they were two small children (*wa humā ṣabīyān ṣaghīrān*). Al-Jaṣṣāṣ notes that they never actually cohabited before both died (*fa-lam yajtamiʿān ḥattā matā*).[90]

The *Ḥujja ʿalā Ahl al-Madīna* of Muḥammad ibn al-Ḥasan al-Shaybānī (d. 189/805) contains two relevant stories. The first is the marriage of Qudāma ibn Maẓʿūn[91] to the newborn daughter of al-Zubayr ibn al-ʿAwwām. While the latter was visiting the ill Qudāma ibn Maẓʿūn, al-Zubayr was given the news of the birth of a baby girl (*bushshira al-Zubayr bi-jāriya*). Qudāma said, "Marry me to her!" Al-Zubayr replied, "And what would you do with a prepubescent girl (*jāriya ṣaghīra*) while you are in this condition?!" So he said, "If I survive, she is the daughter of al-Zubayr [i.e., a good catch], and if I die, she will be the most-beloved of my beneficiaries (*aḥabbu man warathanī*)."[92]

88 *Fa-kashafa ʿan sāqihā fa-qālat, "Arsil. Fa-law lā innaka Amīr al-Muʾminīn la-ṣakkaktu ʿunuqaka."* The reports number 10390–10393, pp. 130–131.

89 Aḥmad ibn ʿAlī Abū Bakr al-Rāzi, he was a famous Ḥanafī scholar, student of Abū al-Ḥasan al-Karkhī and al-Ḥākim al-Nīsābūrī, he has an especial role in this project as the abridger of al-Ṭaḥāwī's *Ikhtilāf al-ʿulamāʾ*. See also Spies, O. "al-D̲jaṣṣāṣ, Aḥmad b. ʿAlī Abū Bakr al-Rāzī." *EI2*.

90 Al-Jaṣṣāṣ, *Aḥkām al-Qurʾān*, 2:52.

91 It is interesting that al-Qurṭubī's (d. 671/1272) proof text on marriage of orphans also involves Qudāma ibn Maẓʿūn and another possible ʿAbd Allāh (besides that of Ibn al-Zubayr) as related by al-Daraqūṭnī: ʿAbd Allāh ibn ʿUmar. In that story, ʿAbd Allāh was married by his maternal uncle, Qudāma ibn Maẓʿūn, and the female in question (the orphaned daughter of Qudāma's brother) rejected the match on the grounds that al-Mughīra ibn Shuʿba was more suitable because of his wealth. See Abū Abd Allāh Muḥammad al-Qurṭubī, *Tafsīr al-Qurʾān* [*Jāmiʿ al-Aḥkām*] (Beirut: Dār al-Kutub, 2000), 5:11.

92 Muḥammad ibn al-Ḥasan al-Shaybānī, *al-Ḥujja ʿalā ahl al-madīnah*, ed. Mahdī Ḥasan al-Kīlānī (Beirut: ʿĀlam al-Kutub, 2006), 2:290.

The second story also involves a newborn girl, given hastily in marriage by an exuberant father to his female cousin for her son.[93] Although the father claimed to have been joking afterwards, the marriage was made to stand by the local legal scholar, in this case ʿAbd Allāh ibn al-Mubārak.[94]

Of the earliest stories, these are the ones that appear relatively frequently in the juridical literature. Their implications are used variously, depending on the context in which they appear. For example, Ibn al-Mundhir includes the story of Ibn ʿUmar to buttress his stance on the licit nature of contracting marriage for minor sons. Ibn ʿAbd al-Barr relies on the story of ʿUrwa ibn al-Zubayr marrying his son to his niece; he strikes, in fact, rather a defensive tone as he justifies the right of the father to contract for the prepubescent,

> And people were all about at the time [i.e., as witnesses]. And who, after all, is ʿUrwa?[95]

Ibn ʿAbd al-Barr's inclusion of this last statement ("And who, after all is ʿUrwa?") would seem to mean, because ʿUrwa's status as Companion renders him an exemplar, how could anyone criticize his decision to marry off his child? Regardless, the 11th century scholar Ibn ʿAbd al-Barr himself gives very little treatment indeed to this story in the context of his own discussion of child marriage, and even less to the concept of contracting marriage for minor males.

For Ḥanafīs, the story of the exuberant father and the joking marriage serves to affirm their doctrine that there is no joking in matters of marriage, divorce and the freeing of slaves,[96] while also proving the ability of mothers to participate in marriage contracts as the guardians of their minor children.[97]

93 See also the treatment of this story by Kecia Ali in *Marriage and Slavery in Early Islam* (Harvard: Harvard University Press, 2010), 29–31.

94 *Al-Ḥujja*, 2:74. Probably the anecdote is designed to emphasize that unserious uses of legal language will be strictly construed against the user of that language.

95 *Al-Istidhkār*, 5:405.

96 This concept is based on the oft-appearing hadith, "There are three things in which there is no joking (*hazluhunna jadd*), divorce, manumission of slaves, and marriage," see *al-Ḥujja*, 2:106–110. See also, *al-Muwaṭṭa'*, 2:67: "There are three things in which there is no joking (*laysa fīhinna laʿib*), marriage, divorce, and manumission of slaves," and ʿAbd al-Razzāq, ¶10281–10291.

97 This facet of Ḥanafī doctrine remains into the Ottoman period. See Tucker, Judith E., "Contracting a Marriage In Ottoman Syria and Palestine," in Quraishi, Asifa and Vogel, Frank, eds, *The Islamic Marriage Contract: Case Studies in Islamic Family Law* (Cambridge: Harvard University Press, 2008), 125. The case to which Tucker refers on this point is one

Although al-Shaybānī never explicitly links Qudāma ibn Maẓʿūn to the issue, the latter's intention to marry and confer inheritance upon his newborn bride in the event of his death might well explain the Ḥanafī stance that brides from a non-consummated marriage should still inherit—a stance deemed contradictory by the Mālikīs.[98]

Interestingly, both these stories contain textual indications of protest on the subject of early marriage. Al-Zubayr is dumbfounded by the idea of his sick friend marrying his tiny daughter, while ʿAlī clearly does not want to marry his daughter to ʿUmar. Still, he sends her, making the marriage conditional upon ʿUmar's being "content" with her. The report gives ʿAlī's primary reason for protest as being his daughter's minority.[99] The report further shows how he bowed to cultural pressure not to offend his peer by subsequently sending his daughter to him for an "interview" of sorts, one that might reasonably have been deemed *designed* to displease the Caliph. That the Caliph was amused and insisted on going ahead with the marriage is evidence of his strong desire to link his bloodline with that of the Prophet's, or his strong desire for the girl, or both. We are not given the details as to the actual age of Umm Kulthūm upon consummation, i.e., if she were allowed to reach pubescence beforehand, or if she entered ʿUmar's household while still a prepubescent.

This detail is in fact missing from all of these stories; there is little indication that any of the early marriages discussed were more than unconsummated contractual unions. Significantly, this holds true as well for the most famous of the early stories of prepubescent marriage, that of ʿĀʾisha bint Abī Bakr.

> Muḥammad ibn Yūsuf related to me that Sufyān related to him from Hishām from his father from ʿĀʾisha that the Prophet married her when she was a girl of six and she was taken to him when she was a girl of nine, and she stayed with him nine years.[100]

---

in which a mother acting as legal guardian for her orphaned daughter married her to "a suitable man with a fair *mahr*." The fact of a mother contracting a marriage is also a feature of Ḥanafī thought on the subject of marriage; other schools do not permit women to contract marriages. See below, Chapter Three, "Early Ḥanafī thought." Note that Kecia Ali, in referencing this anecdote again on p. 75 of *Marriage and Slavery*, reverses the sexes of the children in question, which would diminish the power established by the text for the mother's ability to contract marriage for her prepubescent son.

98 See below, pp. 99–100.

99 The *Muṣannaf* is not clear as to when the marriage was consummated, but does mention that Umm Kulthūm had a child from ʿUmar and that both mother and son were murdered by ʿAbd al-Malik ibn Marwān out of his fear of a challenge to the caliphate.

100 Al-Bukhārī, *Ṣaḥīḥ*, Hadith #5188, chapter 39, Marriage, vol. 3. Ḥadīth #5213 is related by Qabīṣa ibn ʿUqba, with a variance in wording. The latter reads "*banā bihā*", he

This story will figure prominently in the history of early marriage within the Islamic legal system. Numerous debates still swirl about the authenticity of the narrative as well as its implications for the law.[101] Because so few indicators are provided regarding maturity or any firm age given for the onset of sexual readiness or maturity, a compelling case can be made for considering how the exegetes interpret what the Qur'ān has to say about marriage and maturity.

Exegetical Discussions

Several Qur'ānic verses directly or indirectly refer to an age at which one is still a child. Where the subject is the groups who are allowed to view "the adornments (*zīna*) of women", we find in (24:31) that children (*al-ṭifl*, collective) have that privilege. *Ṭifl* is also used in 22:5 as the Qur'ān delineates the phases of life; in context, it would seem to mean infants. Where the subject is leave-taking to enter a room, among those required to ask it are *alladhīna lam yablughū al-ḥulum*, (those who have yet to attain pubescence, 24:58). In 24:59, leave-taking is still required from "the children who have attained pubescence" (*idhā balagha al-aṭfāl minkum al-ḥulum*).

There is an age at which one matures, such as in 12:22: *Lammā balagha ashuddahu*, "when [Joseph] reached his peak [or, 'full manhood'[102]]". The same terminology is used for Moses in 28:14, and in 22:5. Note that there is no middle

"consummated the marriage with her"; the former reads, "*udkhilat ʿalayh*", literally, "she was taken to enter his home" at the age of nine. See Chapter 5 on al-Shāfiʿī for varying understandings of the word *dakhala ʿalā* versus *dakhala bi-*. While it is not impossible, in light of jurists' writings with regard to lengthy stays for brides without consummation, that the bride's entry into the Prophet's house was not in fact accompanied by immediate consummation, the majority understanding of the text's meaning in modern debates is that the consummation indeed occurred at the age of nine.

101 Some of these issues include: The relater, Hishām ibn ʿUrwa, was alleged to have been senile at the time of his narration. Although it is not impossible that Mālik would have accepted the content of the report given early practice, Mālik is one of many jurists who did not rely on this text, which does not in fact occur in any of the early books of jurisprudence except for that of al-Shāfiʿī and, shortly after him, ʿAbd al-Razzāq's *Muṣannaf*. Even later jurists such as Ibn Taymīya and Ibn al-Qayyim shy away from it, although it is used by Ibn Qudāma before them. Presuming its authenticity (it occurs in Bukhārī and Muslim), questions occur such as, was ʿĀ'isha in fact compelled against her will? Can we assume that Abū Bakr did not consult her? Had she, at age nine, entered her majority or was she still prepubescent?

Note the invocation of this event in the recent story of the Yemeni child divorcee, *I am Nujood*, Nujood Ali with Delphine Minoui (New York: Three Rivers Press, 2010), 54.

102 Asad's translation.

ground in 22:5 between being an infant (*ṭifl*), or newly emerged from the womb and attaining one's peak.

These phases and this vocabulary for the attainment of maturity are reprised in 40:67, with the addition of "attaining reason": *li-tablughū ajalan musammā wa-laʿallakum taʿqilūn*. In 6:152, "reaching the peak" is juxtaposed with the state of being an orphan (*al-yatīm*); this is repeated in 17:34, with both instances being injunctions against stealing an orphan's money or assets.

And yet the interest of the scholars was most often piqued by Q4:6. Particularly with regard to assets, fascinating discussions revolve around the meaning of this verse—which focuses on the timing of when an orphan may take possession of his or her inheritance:

> *Wa-btalū al-yatāmā ḥattā idhā balaghū al-nikāḥ fa-in anastum minhum rushdan fa-dfaʿū ilayhim amwālahum.*
>
> And test the orphans [whose affairs you direct] until they reach the age of marriage; and if you detect in them a mature mind, give them their assets.

The verse mentions that there is an age of marriage (*ḥattā idhā balaghū al-nikāḥ*); more importantly it refers to seeking evidence of a mature mind (*in anastum minhum rushdan*). Jurists and exegetes alike wrote extensively on the indicators of *rushd* and the proper age of marriage. In both discussions of fasting and wardship, many different solutions are offered as indicators of when one ceases to be a child and reaches the age of responsibility.

There are a vast range of opinions on the topic. Those who link it invariably to pubescence are countered by those who recognize that pubescence in its physical manifestation (the beginning of emissions for males or the onset of the menstrual period for females) might come late. Another writer of early consensus/disagreement, the Shiʿī scholar al-Ṭūsī (d. 455 /1067), engages in a survey of early legal opinions, concluding that the age of maturity is nine for girls and fifteen for boys, based on the report of ʿĀʾisha[103] and the *jihād* hadith of ʿAbd Allāh ibn ʿUmar, respectively.[104] Additionally, al-Ṭūsī is sure that the growth of pubic hair is an indicator of pubescence.[105] Further, for boys,

103 He does not specify whether it is the report that refers to her own age at marriage or the one that says a "young girl who reaches nine years of age is a woman."

104 In this report, ʿAbd Allāh ibn ʿUmar is said to have repeatedly requested to serve the Prophet in battle, but was turned away until he reached the age of 15.

105 Al-Ṭūsī, *al-Khilāf*, 121.

pubescence might not come at all: there is a Ẓahirī opinion recorded in al-Thaʿlabī (d. 427/1035)[106] which states that a male is never considered to be mature until such a time as an emission occurs, even if he is forty years of age.[107] There are Ḥanafī positions which state that maturity is reached by a female, if she has not yet menstruated, at age seventeen, and for a male at age nineteen.[108] These are then considered the outer limits after which the law presumes maturity. In those rare instances where determination of *bulūgh* is not linked to nocturnal emissions or menstruation (i.e., their failure to appear is not the determining factor in legal classification), we encounter opinions of both Abū Ḥanīfa and the early scholar Zufar to the effect that the age of eighteen is legally sufficient for becoming an adult.[109]

Building on the Ḥanafī position, al-Zamakhsharī (d. 538/1144)[110] notes that it is only at the age of *iḥtilām* (nocturnal emission) that the boy becomes suitable for marriage, "and to seek that which is [marriage's] intention, procreation and the extending of bloodlines (*al-tanāsul*)." He avers that it is possible that one might attain this age without giving any indication of *rushd*, which he defines as "propriety in religion and intellect." In such a case, al-Zamakhsharī invokes Abū Ḥanīfa's conclusions with respect to age: eighteen being the age of puberty, plus an added seven in which to pass through adequate amounts of life-experience for the age of twenty-five. He points out, however, that other Ḥanafīs refuse to cede financial capacity unless indications of *rushd* are evidenced, even if the age of twenty-five is reached.[111] The Shāfiʿī position is variously given as the age of fifteen and the onset of pubic hair, while Mālik is cited as locating maturity in the deepening of the voice of the boy.[112]

---

106 Aḥmad ibn Muḥammad ibn Ibrāhim al-Thaʿlabī was an exegete and a collector of stories of the Prophets. See Rippin, A. "al-Thaʿlabī, Aḥmad b. Muḥammad b. Ibrāhīm Abū Isḥāḳ al-Nīsābūrī." *EI2*.

107 *Al-Kashf wa al-bayān*, 3:255.

108 Al-Ṭaḥāwī, *Ikhtilāf al-ʿulamā'*, 2:6.

109 Ibid., 2:5.

110 Maḥmūd ibn ʿUmar al-Zamakhsharī, a Muʿtazilī scholar and author of an authoritative grammar of the Arabic language, the *Mufaṣṣal fī ṣinʿat al-iʿrāb*, ed. Muḥammad Muḥammad ʿAbd al-Maqṣūd (Cairo: Dār al-Kitāb al-Miṣrī, 2001). For more information see Lane, Andrew, *A Traditional Muʿtazilite Qur'ān Commentary: The Kashshāf of Jār Allāh al-Zamkhsharī* (Leiden: Brill, 2006).

111 *Al-Kashshāf*, vol. 1, p. 500. It is worth emphasizing that the current international designation of the age of eighteen as the age at which one is no longer a child could well enough be a Ḥanafī opinion.

112 Al-Ṭūsī, *al-Khilāf*, 121.

These discussions reveal more than a concern to assess surface indications of physiological changes. There is much to suggest that pre-modern scholars were interested in deepening the definition of maturity to include the attainment of mental maturity (*rushd*). Exegetical discussions on the meaning of Q4:6 find jurists wrestling with what it means to reach the age of marriage, and questioning the wisdom behind its linkage with a mature mind. The two elements in concert made for a larger concept of "coming of age." The scholars struggled to delineate intangibles such as *rushd* in order to resolve debates over when an orphan should be given his or her property; as we will see below, Mālik even applied this thinking to when a woman should be allowed her marriage gift. No unmarried female, in his opinion, could possibly attain the state of *rushd*. Al-Thaʿlabī suggests various methods of testing for *rushd*.[113]

"A group of scholars," says al-Thaʿlabī, "has found that the prepubescent (*al-ṣaghīr*) is one of two things: either a boy or a girl." After this intrepid beginning, he goes on to explain that if the prepubescent is a boy, then the way he is assessed is in how he deals with a monthly allowance; if he is seen to deal with the money responsibly (i.e. spending and disbursing), then he can be given his property. If a girl, she is assessed as one would a housewife, how she deals with running a household (i.e. weaving, cleaning, etc). If she is found to possess a mature mind, then her property can be given to her. If [either] is found to be unfit, the assets should remain under someone else's administrative control until the youth is seen to have become mature-of-mind. Meanwhile, "al-Ḥasan al-Baṣrī,[114] Mujāhid,[115] and others have suggested that they should be tested

113 See also Abū ʿAbd Allāh Muhammad al-Qurṭubī, *Al-Jāmiʿ li-aḥkām al-Qurʾān*, ed. Sālim al-Badrī (Beirut: Dar al-Kutub al-ʿIlmīya, 2000) 5:24. Al-Qurṭubī includes a few more scholarly discussions by way of elaboration. Important among them are the following: a report that no *ḥadd* should be enacted unless both *inbāt* and *bulūgh* are present—indicating that he considered the two to be separate entities. The separation of the two is supported by Abū Ḥanīfa who insists that, "no ruling (*ḥukm*) is established by the growth of hair (*inbāt*); it is neither *bulūgh* nor an indicator of *bulūgh*" (*Tafsīr* 5:25). For al-Zuhrī and ʿAṭāʾ, Shāfiʿī and Mālik (once), and some of the latter's companions, no criminal punishments can be applied to those who have not had an emission. He closes this section with the statement that "it would seem that [the issue] should not take hair and age into consideration (*ẓāhiruhu ʿadam iʿtibār al-inbāt wa al-sinn*).

114 Died 110/728, he was perhaps the most-quoted of the "successor" generation, famed for his sermons and rhetoric, he was also an outspoken political critic. See Mourad, Suleiman Ali, *Early Islam between myth and history: al-Ḥasan al-Baṣrī* (Leiden: Brill, 2006).

115 Mujāhid ibn Jabr, d. 104/722, one of the earliest known exegetes of the Qurʾān. For more information see Ismāʿīl, Aḥmad, *Mujāhid al-mufassir wa-l-tafsīr* (Cairo: Dār al-Ṣafwa lil-Ṭibāʿa wa-l-Nashr wa-l-Tawzīʿ, 1990). See also GAS, 1:29.

with regard to their intellects, their religion, and how they might develop their assets (*tanmiyat amwālihim*)."[116]

Al-Thaʿlabī, like many before him,[117] equated *bulūgh al-nikāḥ* (reaching [the age of] marriage) with *bulūgh al-ḥulum* (reaching pubescence). But is there an argument that the Qurʾān might be unequivocal about marriage age? In discussing 2:237, al-Ṭabarī (d. 310/923) allows us a major semantic insight. The previous verse [Q2:236: "There is no blame upon you if you divorce women (*al-nisā'*) before you have touched them"] directly influences the understanding of the pronoun "*hunna*" in both the words "*ṭallaqtumūhunna*" (you divorced them) and "*tamassūhunna*" (you touch them) in 2:237. The verse 237 cannot therefore possibly be talking about the *walī* who is making decisions for a prepubescent because the word "women" (*al-nisā'*) does not include children.

> Children are not called women (*al-ṣabāyā lā yusammāyna nisā'*), rather they are called children or little girls (*jawārī*). *Nisāʾ* (women) in Arabic is the plural of *imrāʾa* (woman), and the Arabs do not refer to the female infant or child or prepubescent (*al-ṭiflah wa-l-ṣabiyyah wa-l-ṣaghīra*) as "woman," just as they do not say to the male prepubescent child "man" (*kamā lā taqūl lil-ṣabī al-ṣaghīr rajul*).[118]

This in turn allows for several unequivocal statements by al-Qurṭubī (d. 671/1272), who often lifts directly from al-Ṭabarī. Al-Qurṭubī copies this reasoning almost verbatim in declaring that 4:3 ("marry those women whom you consider good"—*ankiḥ mā ṭāba lakum min al-nisā'*) cannot be referring to the marriages of those who are yet prepubescent, for only those who have reached pubescence are called women.[119] Al-Qurṭubī is clear. One marries from among women, and if the female in question is not yet a woman, she is not marriageable.

This discussion would be remiss without some reference to 65:4, the Qurʾānic locus cited by Ibn Qudāma as proof positive that prepubescent marriage is affirmed by the Qurʾān. Al-Ṭabarī offers multiple interpretations suggesting that "those who have not menstruated" could be those whose menstrual cycle has

116 *Al-Kashf wa al-bayān*, 3:254–55.

117 See, for example, *Tanwīr al-Miqbās*, 85. Al-Ṭabarī also includes *al-ḥulum* as the definition for when *bulūgh al-nikāḥ* takes place. Al-Ṭabarī does not refer to any Qurʾānic verse, merely citing several early opinions without offering any contradictions. The early opinions he cites are those of Mujāhid, al-Suddī, Ibn ʿAbbās, and Ibn Zayd. (See *Jāmiʿ al-bayān ʿan taʾwīl āyy al-Qurʾān*, ed. ʿAbd Allāh al-Turkī (Giza: Dār Hijr, 2001), vol. 6, 404.).

118 Al-Ṭabarī, *Jāmiʿ al-bayān*, 4:335.

119 Qurṭubī, *Tafsīr*, 5:11–12. *Lā yuqāl nisāʾ ilā li-man balagha al-ḥulum.*

been disrupted (i.e., for a medical or psychosomatic reason, not pregnancy) and therefore do not conveniently menstruate when the *ʿidda* requires (and therefore not, obviously, children).[120] Ibn al-ʿArabī is definitive in his opinion that the verse applies to *al-ṣaghīra* and that in it is proof (*dalīl*) that a man may contract marriage for his prepubescent daughter because God "made the *ʿidda* of the non-menstruating female three months, and the prepubescent female does not menstruate."[121] Al-Qurṭubī takes elements from both Ibn al-ʿArabī and al-Ṭabarī, but cites Mujāhid as being among those who believe the verse's best explanation lies in the now-suspended cycle of a previously-menstruating woman.[122] This is not a tack that any of our formative era scholars will take in approaching child marriage in the coming pages. I have inserted it here only for the sake of showing that certain interpretations of the text—al-Qurṭubī is, of course, late and his region distant in many ways from the 8th and 9th century Arabian Peninsula—find it to be unequivocal. For others, the Qur'anic text provides no solid indicator as to what the age of marriage truly is, and so jurists are reluctant to specify.[123]

In Legal Theory

At this point, the thought of al-Jaṣṣāṣ, who wrote prolifically on both exegesis and legal theory, is useful. His ideas regarding the crucial concept of orphanhood have implications for understanding early thought generally and Ḥanafī thought in specific, both with regard to minor marriage and in regard to minor marriage. Al-Jaṣṣāṣ attributes to the Prophet the words, "No orphans after pubescence" (*lā yutm baʿd bulūgh al-ḥulum*). His source is surely al-Shaybānī's

120 *Tafsīr al-Ṭabarī*, 23:54. See also al-Jaṣṣāṣ, *Aḥkām al-Qurʾān*, 3:456–457.

121 Ibn al-ʿArabī, *Aḥkām al-Qurʾān li-Ibn al-ʿArabī*, Tafsīr sūrat al-Ṭalāq (Beirut: Dār al-Kutub, 2006), 528.

122 *Tafsīr al-Qurṭubī*, 18:107.

123 Compare Jewish *halakha*, which assigns the age of maturity at 13 for boys and 12.5 for girls, also stipulating the existence of the growth of "two hairs" for the girl. See Ruth Lamdan, "Child Marriage in Jewish Society in the Eastern Mediterranean during the Sixteenth Century," in *Mediterranean Historical Review* 11 (1996): 49–50, pp. 41–42. While Lamdan points out that rabbis and judges typically discouraged marriages of minors, fathers were authorized to give their daughters in marriage even as infants and the marriages were valid. The responsa literature often covers this topic, although, as noted, incidences of a topic's occurrence in the response literature did not necessarily reflect social practice. See also Abraham Grossman, "Child Marriage in Jewish Society in the Middle Ages," *Peamim*, 45 (1990), 108–125 (Hebrew).

discussion in the *Ḥujja*, (1:87–92) which is geared toward destroying the Mālikī position that only fathers may marry off prepubescents; the Ḥanafi position, in turn, is that any guardian may do so, and their argument for this centers on 4:3[124] and the definition of (*yatīm*).

According to the majority of opinions in *Lisān al-ʿArab*, the idea that there are no orphans after pubescence is true for males but not for females. The female remains a *yatīma* forever: "Abū Saʿīd said, The woman is addressed as orphan, and the name of "orphan" is never lifted from her (*wa yuqāl lil-marʾa yatīma wa lā yazūlu ʿanhā ism al-yutm abadan*)." Abū ʿUbayda says that this name applies to the female before marriage, and after marriage the name no longer applies. One unattributed opinion reads, very similarly to al-Jaṣṣāṣ, that "If they (dual) reach pubescence, the name orphan is lifted literally (*ḥaqīqatan*), although it might be applied metaphorically after pubescence, as they used to call the Prophet as an adult 'the orphan of Abū Ṭālib.'"

Further, the *Lisān* explains the hadith which will figure so prominently in the jurists' discussions about consulting females *istiʾmār* refers to the orphan girl:

> And in the hadith, "The female orphan is consulted with regard to herself, and if she is silent, this is her permission." He meant by *yatīma* the mature virgin whose father died before her maturity, so the name of 'orphan girl' stuck with her and she is called by it, despite her maturity, metaphorically (*duʿiyat bihi wa hiyya bāligha majāzan*). And in al-Sha'bī's hadith: A woman came to him and said, "I am an orphan woman (*innī imrāʾa yatīma*)," whereupon he laughed and his companions laughed and said, "All women are orphans," meaning weak (*ḍaʿāʾif*).[125]

Al-Jaṣṣāṣ is quite faithful to the range of interpretations of 4:3. None of these mentions children specifically, but all mention orphans. Where the very definition of orphan *is* the prepubescent, the verses become proof texts for the contracting of marriages for prepubescents, particularly by other than the father or grandfather (contrary to the views of Mālik and al-Shāfiʿī). As in al-Shaybānī's *Ḥujja*, this section in *Aḥkām al-Qurʾān* of al-Jaṣṣāṣ has been titled "The Chapter on Marrying Prepubescents" (*Bāb tazwīj al-ṣighār*). Al-Jaṣṣāṣ then enters into

---

124 "And if you have reason to fear that you might not act equitably towards orphans (*al-yatāmā*), then marry from among [other] women such as are lawful to you (*mā ṭāba lakum min al-nisāʾ*)—[even] two, three, or four: but if you have reason to fear that you might not be able to treat them with equal fairness, then [only] one—or [from among] those whom you rightfully possess ..." Asad, *Message of the Qurʾān*, 101.

125 *Lisān al-ʿArab*, 53:646.

discussion of 4:3, including the interpretation of ʿĀʾisha and Ibn ʿAbbās, which refer to orphans (*yatāmā*) without referencing prepubescents (*ṣighār*), and then he includes two other interpretations which serve to contradict these. He then invokes multiple early companions and successors to support the position that other than the father and grandfather can marry off the prepubescent.[126]

Al-Jaṣṣāṣ is already aware of the objection to tying the exegetical interpretations of 4:3 attributed to ʿĀʾisha and ʿAlī to the marriages of children.

> It is said that this verse refers to the mature female (*al-kabīra*), because ʿĀʾisha said that people had gone seeking a decision from the Prophet after this verse was revealed and God Most High sent down: {They seek a decision from you with regard to women, say: God gives you a decision with regard to them and what is given to you in the Book with regard to orphan women (*yatāmā al-nisāʾ*)} [4:127] … Thus when He said, {orphan women} this signified that the intent was the mature ones of them (*al-kibār min-hunna*), not the little ones because the little ones are not called women (*al-ṣighār lā yusammayna nisāʾ*).

Al-Jaṣṣāṣ's response, then, is to invoke the *ḥaqīqa/majāz* dichotomy. 4:3 speaks literally of orphans, and mature orphans, he claims, are only called orphans metaphorically. Moreover, 4:3 speaks of women, and both prepubescent females and mature women are included in the genus of women (*al-ṣighār wa al-kibār dākhilāt fīhinna*).[127]

Al-Jaṣṣāṣ further supports his opinion by adducing the story wherein the Prophet married Salama to the daughter of Ḥamza when they were two small children (*wa humā ṣibyān ṣaghīrān*). That Umm Salama allowed the Prophet to contract the marriage for her son is the source of al-Jaṣṣāṣ's claim that other than the father or grandfather has this right over small children. Not only can the judge do it, as one who has taken on the legal position in the community of the Prophet himself, but any of the relatives who inherit, including the mother, if no one else can be found who is closer.[128]

Thus language leads this scholar to a very specific place as he attempts to explore the landscape of vocabulary on minor marriage. A different focal point

126 Al-Jaṣṣāṣ, *Aḥkām*, 2:51–55 .

127 Ibid., 2:52. See al-Qurṭubī's opposite opinion on both this interpretation and the meaning of *nisāʾ al-Jāmiʿ*, 5:11, a position in consonance with al-Ṭabarī, *Jāmiʿ al-bayān*, 4:335.

128 Al-Jaṣṣāṣ, *Aḥkām*, 2:52.

can be found with al-Jaṣṣāṣ's slightly earlier fellow Ḥanafī. The legal theorist al-Shāshī (d. 344/955) considered the issue of financial *rushd* to be vital to the discussion of minor marriage and consent. He bases the father's contracting marriages for children on the latter's need for financial guardianship (*walāya*), which logically entails personal guardianship.[129]

For al-Shāshī, emergence from a father's guardianship comes with the attainment of mature intellect. It is a stage as applicable to and attainable for girls as for boys:

> The state of being a child is the *ratio legis* for the father's guardianship for a child. The ruling with regard to the female child is due to the existence of this *ratio legis*. The attainment of a mature intellect (*al-bulūgh ʿan ʿaql*) is the *ratio legis* for the removal of a father's guardianship with regard to the boy (*al-ghulām*). This ruling applies [equally] to the girl due to this *ratio legis* (*fa-yataʿaddā al-ḥukm ilā al-jāriya bi-hādhihi al-ʿilla*).[130]

In keeping with his project of elaborating legal theory, the part of al-Shāshī's discussion which concerns us actually occurs in his exposition on analogy (*al-qiyās*). There is that which has a *ratio legis* (*ʿilla*) found in the Qur'an, and that which has its *ratio legis* in the Sunna, and finally that which has its *ratio legis* in a decision emanating from consensus. The example given for this last is the state of being prepubescent (*al-ṣighar*).

> The state of being prepubescent (*al-ṣighar*) is the *ratio legis* for the guardianship of the father with respect to the prepubescent male (*fī ḥaqq al-ṣaghīr*). The ruling is also established with regard to the prepubescent female (*fī ḥaqq al-ṣaghīra*) due to the existence of the same *ratio legis*. And the reaching of mental maturity (*al-bulūgh ʿan ʿaql*) is the *ratio legis* for the lifting of guardianship with regard to the prepubescent boy; the ruling with regard to the prepubescent girl is also applied on this basis.[131]

---

129 Aḥmad ibn Muḥammad Niẓām al-Dīn al-Shāshī, Uṣūl al-Shāshī, ed. Muhammad Akram Nadvi (Beirut: Dār al-Gharb al-Islāmī, 2000), 329.

130 Ibid., 231.

131 Ibid. The father's power is here conceptualized as being limited by his children's attainment of majority; *patria potestas* disallowed any capacity for children of either sex throughout the lifetime of the father (see Westrup, C.W., *Family Property and Patria Potestas* (London: Oxford University Press, 1936), esp. pp. 24–28. See also Arjava, Antti, "Roman Family Law after Barbarian Settlements," in Mathisen, ed, *Law, Society and Authority in Late Antiquity* (Oxford: Oxford University Press, 2001), 41–45.

There are, he informs us, two types of analogy. One has to do with the transfer of the ruling (*al-ḥukm al-muʿdā*) from a kind of ruling which is originally established in the underlying case (*min nawʿ al-ḥukm al-thābit fī al-aṣl*). The second is when the new case is of the same kind (*an yakūn min jinsihi*).

> Thus, for example, there is union of species (*al-nawʿ*) … in that the state of being a child is the *ratio legis* for marriage guardianship with respect to the young boy. The marriage guardianship with respect to the young girl is established due to the existence of the *ratio legis* in her. In this way, the ruling is established with respect to the prepubescent non-virgin.[132]

The classification of females for al-Shāshī is not according to their virginity or lack thereof, but according to their age.[133] Al-Shāshī continues, although under the heading now of "The *Ratio legis* Emanating from Consensus," by offering another example of *ratio legum* of the same kind:

> The state of being prepubescent is the *ratio legis* for the guardianship of a father's managing the finances (*walāyat al-taṣarruf lil-ab fī al-māl*), thus it establishes the guardianship of the person through the ruling based on this *ratio legis*. And a girl's reaching intellectual maturity (*bulūgh al-jāriya ʿan ʿaql*) is the *ratio legis* for the *removal* of the guardianship of the father with regard to money and it (also) removes his guardianship with respect to the person based on this *ratio legis*.
>
> Further, it is necessary in this type of analogy from the same kind of *ratio legis* for us to say: The guardianship of the father with regard to the property of the prepubescent girl is due to her inability to manage by herself. Thus the Law has established his guardianship in order that her financial benefits related to that not be hindered (while) she is unable to manage herself; thus it is necessary to acknowledge the father's guardianship of her.[134]

132 Ibid.

133 I must draw attention here to the work of Kecia Ali in her outstanding study of early rulings on marriage and slavery. Slavewomen, however, were not classified in this way, due to either the presumed unlikelihood of their having retained virginity or to the *irrelevance* of their sexual status: the status of being enslaved obviated any consent to marriages. See *Marriage and Slavery*, 32.

134 Al-Shāshī, *Uṣūl*, 333.

Finally, al-Shāshī typifies early Ḥanafī thought on this subject as he insists that the male and the female are dealt with equally under the law:

> A boy's reaching intellectual maturity (*bulūgh al-ghulām ʿan ʿaql*) is the *ratio legis* for the removal of the marriage guardianship upon him, thus removal of that guardianship upon the girl (*al-jāriya*) is also by means of this *ratio legis* (*bi-hukm hādhihi al-ʿilla*).[135]

While this typifies early Ḥanafī thought, al-Shāfiʿī's exposition of similar ideas could perhaps be cited as a precedent for certain aspects of this discussion, as we shall see.

The concept of an "age of marriage" is alluded to in much of the *fiqh* literature and indeed in exegesis due to its mention in 4:6.[136] This concept is closely intertwined with *rushd*, levelheadedness or maturity of mind, and thus caused some jurists to look closely at what constituted a marriageable person, and even to develop criteria for assessing such a state. *Rushd*, however, being ultimately highly subjective and intangible, was of significantly less legal value than *bulūgh*, a verbal noun denoting the attainment of sexual maturity.

Both participial terms *bāligh* and *ṣaghīr/ṣaghīra*, are quite polyvalent, as the impending discussion will illustrate. Beginning with the case of the word *bāligh*, the more appropriate term might be "mature." Jurists did not neglect investigations of questions spurred by the concept of maturity—at what point is one deemed mature, and what does maturity entail? It is a complex subject upon which much hinges. Mere majority makes religious obligations and criminal punishments applicable. Disposing of property and managing assets required the *rushd* mentioned in 4:6; how was it exhibited and how was it tested? The Mālikīs would not allow virgin females into the category of mature until they had acquired life experience outside of the father's home, while the Ḥanafīs assigned an outer limit for which to withhold assets from a maturing subject, perhaps inspired by the *legitima aetas* in Roman Law, of twenty-five years.

Marriage, in the opinion of many jurists, did not necessarily require the condition of *rushd*.[137]

---

135 Ibid.

136 "And test orphans until they reach [the age of] marriage (*ḥattā idhā balaghū al-nikāḥ*), then if you detect levelheadedness in them (*fa-in anastum minhum rushdan*), give them their assets."

137 *EI2*, art. Bāligh, v. 1:993.

Witness Abū Yūsuf's response to al-Awzāʿī's claim that a *ṣabī* (child) could have a share of the spoils of war: he is definite that such a position is completely unknown and the prophet would never have distributed to a child. He then invokes the opinion of Ibn ʿAbbās who was responding to a written inquiry over "when a child ceases to be an orphan and is allotted a portion of the spoils."

> He emerges from the state of being an orphan if he has a nocturnal seminal emission. At that time he is allotted a portion [of the spoils].
>
> *Yakhruju min al-yutm idhā aḥtalam wa-yuḍrab lahu bi-sahm.*[138]

Poring over the word *yutm* in early Arabic lexicons provided no added nuance—no indication that it could mean "childhood," or the state of being a minor. The only possible conclusion must be that, because of the axiom that there are no adult orphans, the state of being an orphan is another way of saying minority. The transition itself from minority to majority (for males) thus hinges on attaining puberty, through the onset of nocturnal emissions.

As we saw in the Qurʾānic verses mentioned, there is no word put forward in the Qurʾān for adolescence. The concept of "adolescence" seems to be a later legal development: Islamic law envisages a gradual transition from the status of minor to that of major, as exemplified by the *mumayyiz*, the "discerning minor", and the *murāhiq*, the "minor on the point of reaching puberty,"[139] but neither of these terms is mentioned in the pre-eleventh century sources we consulted. It has been proposed that the institution of late marriage itself resulted in the "separate state of adolescence," and it is not until Tucker's work on the Ottoman period that we find juristic references to a solid middle ground of adolescence. This adds a certain nuance to the later discourses on the subject that is lacking early on; these early texts speak only of the *ṣaghīr* versus the *bāligh*, and, rarely, the *kabīr*.

Childhood as discussed in medieval Islamic texts[140] was closely linked to multiple phases. Ibn Qayyim al-Jawzīya, in *Tuḥfat al-mawdūd fī aḥkām al-mawlūd*, details twelve phases of childhood, while an earlier scholar, Ibn

138 Abū Yūsuf, *al-Radd ʿalā siyar al-Awzāʿī*, 42–43.

139 *EI2*, *Bāligh*, v. 1:993 .

140 See also Reynolds, Dwight, ed. "Childhood in 1,000 Years of Arabic Autobiography." *Edebiyât: A Journal of Middle Eastern Literatures*—Special Issue on Arabic Autobiography. NS Vol. 7, no. 2 (1997): 379–392.

al-Jazzār al-Qayrawānī (4th/10th century), relies on Greek schematics in delineating four phases of childhood:

1. Infancy proper from birth to dentition (*sinn al-wildān*)
2. Second infancy from dentition to age of seven (*sinn al-ṣibyān*)
3. Childhood from the age of seven to fourteen (*sinn ibn sabʿ sinīn*)
4. The age of transition from childhood to puberty starting at the age of fourteen.[141]

Ibn al-Jazzār's schemata do not include what later jurists refer to as the age of *tamyīz*, discernment. The word *ṣabī*, "child," is by far the most common term found in the earliest texts, after the word *ṣaghīr*. *Tamyīz* is rarely mentioned early, but al-Ghazālī (d. 504/1111), for one, refers to it as the phase in which "discernment rounds off the development of the sense, ushers in the 'stage of intellectual grasp' and presages the perfection of mental and moral qualities in adolescence."[142] It may prove a useful comparison to note that adolescence as a concept did not appear in Western European societies until after the shift began to later marriages. Western Europe had shared medieval marriage patterns with the majority of world cultures until the seventeenth century. Indeed, what has been termed the "European marriage pattern"[143] is a comparatively recent phenomenon, and one which was initially anomalous. Delaying marriage until well after physical maturation, a practice linked to widespread increases in private property ownership, helped to bring into being the separate state of adolescence.[144]

Still, it must be noted that such phases were not well delineated in the centuries of scholarship considered here. What, then, of the word *ṣaghīr*? I have translated it in al-Jaṣṣāṣ's opinions and also in al-Shāshī's exploration of guardianship as "prepubescent." Lane cites both the *Qāmūs* and the *Ṣiḥāh* as sources indicating that the word means indeed prepubescent.[145]

But is the word *ṣaghīr/ṣaghīra* synonymous for the jurists with "minor"? In some respects yes, and in some respects no. The debates among the scholars we

141 Giladi, A. "Ṣaghīr." *EI2*.

142 Giladi, citing al-Ghazālī, *al-Iḥyā'*, iii:22, 72, 92 and Motzki, *Das Kind*, 421–423.

143 Lowenstein, Steven M. "Ashkenazic Jewry and the European Marriage Pattern: A Preliminary Survey of Jewish Marriage Age," *Jewish History*, Vol. 8, No. 1/2. The Robert Cohen Memorial Volume (1994), p. 155.

144 Ibid.

145 William Edward Lane, Arabic-English Lexicon, London: Williams and Norgate, 1863), vol. 1:1692, http://www.tyndalearchive.com/tabs/lane/, accessed 7/26/16.

shall soon encounter indicate clearly that their jargon includes the prepubescent virgin (*al-bikr al-ṣaghīra*) and the pubescent virgin (*al-bikr al-bāligha*[146]). There is even the prepubescent non-virgin (*al-thayyib al-ṣaghīra*). However, because many jurists, particularly the Shāfiʿīs and Mālikīs believe that majority is itself imbued through sexual intercourse and not the onset of pubescence, a female could thus be minor perpetually, no matter her age.[147] As we have seen in Ibn Qudāma's arguments, even the physically-mature, level-headed virgin (*al-bikr al-bāligha al-ʿāqila*) is still not considered to have attained majority, and her father can compel her marriage. However, Ibn Qudāma does not even approach the most challenging juristic quandary. When the status of prepubescence is coupled with the status of sexually-experienced (*thayyib*), deep inconsistencies in juristic logic are exposed. By definition now her consent *must* be attained, and yet she is not in her majority.[148]

The vocabulary is unavoidably troubling and clumsy. Every effort has been made in the direction of terminological precision, even if the result, at times, may prove taxing to the reader's patience. Indeed, it is much easier to say (and write) "minor" instead of "prepubescent." However, the legal category "minor," while often correct and applicable, does not always possess the requisite level of nuance. In these juristic discussions, the pubescent virgin had none of the legal capacity that a pubescent non-virgin might have, or, for that matter, the prepubescent non-virgin. Not every minor was prepubescent, but every prepubescent was a minor, unless the loss of her virginity had catapulted her into

---

146 Rarely (al-Jaṣṣāṣ himself is alone in my sources) do jurists use the term: *al-bikr al-kabīra*. Ibn Qudāma does, although he embeds the term in a longer phrase (*al-bikr.... kabīra kānat aw ṣaghīra*, Mughnī, 9:200).

147 It is significant that slave women were not classified in this way, due either to the presumed unlikelihood of their having retained virginity or to the *irrelevance* of their sexual status: the status of being enslaved obviated any consent to marriages. See Ali, *Marriage and Slavery*, 32.

148 Al-Ghazālī, for example, lists women whom it is not possible to marry. He includes "the sexually-experienced minor" who should not be married until after she reaches her majority (*al-Iḥyā*, 2:56). He offers no explanation for this rule, the reasons of which will become clear within the pages of this project, These center on the fact that Shāfiī law, like Mālikī law, predicates legal capacity on sexual experience instead of the attainment of sexual maturity (i.e., a father can compel a virgin daughter, but he cannot compel the non-virgin). Once sexually-experienced, it is evident from al-Ghazālī's thought, a girl cannot be given in marriage without her consent, and yet she will possess consent only upon attaining majority.

It is to be noted that Giladi quotes al-Ghazālī as designating the age of sixteen as the age of marriage. (Cit. in *Ṣaghīr*, *EI2*).

early maturity. The state of being a minor thus was an abstract legal category, while the state of prepubescence anchored the female in a particular realm of that category. For all but the Ḥanafīs, the vocabulary has many layers of complexity.

In the coming pages, I will attempt to consistently translate the word *ṣaghīr*[149] as "prepubescent" and the word *bāligh* as "physically mature," or simply "pubescent," with an awareness that the words *rashīd* and *ʿāqil* convey the concept of intellectual or emotional maturity much better. It may well be that the jurists themselves could only find common ground on the definition of prepubescence, which is how part of this story might have begun.

Conclusion

This chapter has explored multiple contexts for the legal discussions found in the coming chapters. It provided, in an albeit limited way, legal contexts that might have been easily accessible to neighbors and trading partners in the Near Eastern milieu. It has offered some of the anecdotes key to early conceptualization of minor—indeed, prepubescent—marriage. These involved stories of both boys and girls. The narratives in question also neglected to give clear information about determining sexual maturity. Finally the chapter presented discussions of maturity in the contexts of exegetical and theoretical discussions which, rather than clarifying, serve to cement a divide in perspective over female minority and majority.

What is clear is that Muslim Arab fathers, like other Near Eastern fathers, could and did contract for and compel children to marry. Guardianship (*walāya*) is etymologically related to the concept of being a protector and an intimate friend. Thus it is possible to assume motivations of benevolent intent born of "discretion and compassion."[150] Whether or not the decisions of fathers have always emanated from discretion and compassion is not within

149 Giladi suggests *Ṣaghīr* means "infant, child, or minor" when it is in apposition to the word "bāligh" while it means prepubescent when in apposition to "kabīr". I suggest that these definitions are not nuanced enough, and that legal minority is not, as he notes, categorically ended by physical maturity unless one is a boy, and perhaps, if Qur'anic and juristic considerations come into play, not even then. Giladi, A., "Ṣaghīr", EI2.

150 Ibid.

the scope of this project. Rather, this project is concerned with the legal mechanisms by which a father, or any other guardian, compels marriage and how the legal capacity necessary to reject or refuse such compulsion is attained.

Thus modern incidences of the phenomenon of minor marriage have solid historical and legal precedent. Yet it is quite possible that the history of minor marriage in Islamic law is in essence the story of juristic struggles to reconcile existing cultural practices with the doctrine of consent and the teleological exigencies of marital union. These concerns propel us into the coming chapters.

CHAPTER 2

The Early Compendia

The *Sunan* of al-Awzaʿī and the Two *Muṣannafs*: A Wealth of Conflicting Attitudes

Some of the earliest legal sources at our disposal are the *Sunan* of al-Awzāʿī (158/774),[1] the *Muṣannaf* of ʿAbd al-Razzāq (211/826)[2] and the *Muṣannaf* of Ibn Abī Shayba (235/849).[3] Standard methods of hadith criticism[4] have caused many of the reports in these collections to be deemed weak; as such, they are often used selectively or neglected altogether by Muslim scholars. Yet Harald Motzki finds, at least in the case of ʿAbd al-Razzāq's *Muṣannaf*, much of value:

> [The reports therein] supply a firm and extensive textual basis for delineating the state of the development of law towards the end of the first and the beginning of the second/eighth century.[5]

1 Abū ʿAmr ʿAbd al-Raḥmān ibn ʿAmr, he was the leader of the Syrian school of law. Born in Damascus, he may have held a government position in Yamāmah, then lived for a time in Beirut, where he died. Schacht, J. "al-Awzāʿī, Abū ʿAmr ʿAbd al-Raḥmān b. ʿAmr." *EI2*. See also his biography in *Sunan al-Awzāʿī, aḥadīth wa athār wa fatāwā*, Beirut: Dār al-nafāʾis, 1993), 1–9. For more information see Judd, Steven, *al-Awzāʿī* (Leiden: Brill, 2009).

2 ʿAbd al-Razzāq ibn Hammām ibn Nāfiʿ al-Ṣanʿānī, al-Yamanī al-Ḥimyārī. The leading scholar of Yemen, ʿAbd al-Razzāq studied with some of the most famous names of jurisprudential history, including, Maʿmar b. Rā<u>sh</u>id (d. 153/770) Ibn Jurayj (d. 150/767), Sufyān b. ʿUyayna (d. 198/813–4) and the Kūfan Sufyān al-<u>Th</u>awrī (d. 161/778), as well as al-Awzāʿī (d. 157/774) and Mālik b. Anas (d. 179/795). Motzki, H. "al-Ṣanānī, ʿAbd al-Razzāḳ b. Hammām b. Nāfiʿ, Abū Bakr al-Yamanī al-Ḥimyarī." *EI2*. See also, Motzki, Harald, *The Origins of Islamic Jurisprudence* (Leiden: Brill, 2002), Chapter Two; see also *al-Muṣannaf*, ed. Ayman Naṣṛ.a̤l-Dīn al-Azharī (Beirut: Dār al-Kutub al-ʿIlmiyyah, 2000), vol. 1.

3 Abū Bakr ʿAbd Allāh ibn Muḥammad ibn Ibrāhīm, the Iraqi jurist who died in Baghdād after having established himself as a great scholar. His book (originally entitled *K. Al-Musnad*) was considered canon in Muslim Spain and the west until the 7th/13th century. Pellat, Ch. "Ibn Abī Shayba, Abū Bakr ʿAbd Allāh b. Muḥammad b. Ibrāhīm (= Abū <u>Sh</u>ayba) b. ʿU<u>th</u>mān al-ʿAbsī al-Kūfī." *EI2*. See also *al-Muṣannaf*, ed. Muḥammad ʿAwwāmah, (Beirut: Dār Qurṭubah, 2006).

4 On complaints from Muslim hadith scholars regarding ʿAbd al-Razzāq see Harald Motzki, *The Origins of Islamic Jurisprudence* (Leiden: Brill, 2002), 66–71.

5 Motzki, *Origins*, xiv.

 | DOI 10.1163/9789004344860_004

Motzki is even further convinced that the reports in the *Muṣannaf* are capable of shedding a reasonable amount of light on the first/seventh century; some may indeed have been the actual sayings of the Prophet.[6] The reports provide not only fascinating glimpses into social history, but often, due to sheer volume, give a sense of the prevailing jurisprudential opinions. Due to their combination of Prophetic and non-Prophetic reports and the opinions of major scholars, the two *Muṣannaf*s "can thus better be compared to the compilations of the second/eighth century such as the *Muwaṭṭa'* of Mālik and the *Āthār* of Abū Yūsuf than with the classical Ḥadīth collections of the third/ninth century."[7] Above all, however, they provide solid evidence of the range of opinions still circulating prior to the rise of consensus writing. For each issue reviewed in this study these compendia contain differing, contradictory opinions.

Further, it is of great interest to note the differences in the *number* of reports and opinions provided by the texts. Although there is a mere seventy-five years at most between the two *Muṣannaf*s and the *Sunan* of al-Awzāʿī (fifty years in the case of the *Muṣannaf* of ʿAbd al-Razzāq), the *Sunan* contains far fewer reports than the two *Muṣannaf*s. The *Kitāb al-Nikāḥ* of al-Awzāʿī has some forty-six reports, very few going back to the Prophet himself. Forty-six reports would comprise but a few tiny sub-chapters of the massive works of the *Muṣannaf* compilers.

These scholars presented a wealth of proof texts on prepubescent marriage and compulsion; this chapter deals with those most commonly found on the subject. It also considers their approaches to reconciling the right of a father to determine his child's affairs with the necessity of the parties' consent to a valid marriage contract. Issues of capacity, as well as sex and maintenance, appear frequently.

The early compendia are particularly concerned with the issue of prepubescent divorce, especially with regard to the minor male. There is a comparative wealth of material in these early sources. That later sources contain fewer reports on this topic suggests that, as the law evolved, the minor male garnered less attention in discussions of prepubescent marriage.

Proof Texts

This section explores the universe of proof texts that can be found in these early sources for discussions of prepubescent marriage and consent in marriage generally. One goal is to show how, according to early sources such as the two *Muṣannaf*s, the practice of prepubescent marriage was universal with

6 Ibid.

7 Ibid., 51.

regard to gender. Another goal lies in illustrating to what extent the jurists' conversations revolved around texts *other* than the report of ʿĀʾisha which will figure so prominently in later discussions. One such proof text is the *ayyim/bikr* report that has so often changed wording, now featuring orphans, now shifting from *ayyim* to *thayyib*, and so on.

As we will see, only the *Muṣannaf* of ʿAbd al-Razzāq (d. 211/826), approximately contemporaneous with al-Shāfiʿī (d. 204/820), includes the report of ʿĀʾisha. The evolution of this proof text, from its occurrence in a minority of early compendia and legal manuals to its becoming the preeminent text is a key part of the story of minor marriage in Islamic legal history. In order to fully contextualize that report's appearance, it is useful to revisit the earliest proof texts as they appear in these earliest compendia.

As mentioned, Mālik dealt with the *ayyim/bikr* hadith in his *Muwaṭṭaʾ*, but its first recorded incarnation comes in the compendium of al-Awzāʿī with the wording *thayyib/bikr*:

> *Lā tunkaḥ al-thayyib ḥattā tustaʾmar wa lā tunkaḥ al-bikr ḥattā tustaʾdhan wa idhnuhā al-ṣumūt.*
>
> The non-virgin is not married until she is consulted, and the virgin is not married until her permission is sought, and her permission is silence.[8]

The variant of this hadith found in the *Muwaṭṭaʾ* uses the word *ayyim* rather than *thayyib*, and it occurs thus in all of the other primary sources consulted in this study, except, as noted in Chapter One, where it uses the vocabulary of the orphan. In the version presented in the *Sunan* of al-Awzāʿī, the chain of transmission goes back to Abū Hurayra. The translation of the word *ayyim* is a subject for debate. *Ayyim* evidences Qur'anic roots: *wankiḥū al-ayāmā minkum* ('marry the single persons from amongst yourselves;' Q24:32). But the hadith is also often found with the word *thayyib* (previously-married person) substituted for *ayyim*. The debate centers on whether this substitution is semantically proper or an interpolation that led to classification of women based on their sexual experience or lack thereof.[9]

With regard to anecdotal proofs, the report of ʿĀʾisha is one of several that ʿAbd al-Razzāq offers. We have already discussed the stories of ʿUmar Ibn

8 *Sunan*, p. 323, ¶1047, and see the Appendix.

9 For further insight into the language of the report, especially with regard to a woman's authority over herself, see Ali, *Marriage and Slavery*, 37.

al-Khaṭṭāb and the daughter of ʿAlī, as well as that of ʿUrwa ibn al-Zubayr with his son and niece.[10] This chapter opens with the report of ʿĀ'isha:

> ʿAbd al-Razzāq [heard] from Maʿmar[11] [who heard] from al-Zuhrī[12] [who heard from] ʿUrwa who said, "The Prophet married ʿĀ'isha when she was a girl of six, and she was given to him (*uhdiyat ilayh*) when she was a girl of nine; her toys were with her. She became his widow (*māta ʿanhā*) when she was a girl of eighteen.[13]

There is, in the text itself, nothing to suggest that her father compelled her to marry, or that if she had wished to rescind upon pubescence she would have been denied the right to do so. Nor is there any mention of Abū Bakr. The legal implications of the story are thus obscure. As though to heighten the obscurity, different reports emphasize different aspects of the rights of children in the face of a father's contract. One of these declares it legal for a father to contract marriage for "prepubescents" (*al-ṣighār*);[14] another says that "only fathers can compel marriage;"[15] finally, it is related that prepubescents married off by their father can rescind upon majority.[16] If it is implicit in these first two reports that rescission can occur upon pubescence, all three reports can be harmonized. If the assumption is, as many jurists would express, that the father's contract cannot be annulled, there is contradiction.

The Walī Mujbir

The reasoning behind this justification of the father's right to compel is mentioned to some degree in the early compendia, particularly in the section on divorce. The two main sources of a father's power over his children are to be

10 See also ʿAbd al-Razzāq, *Muṣannaf*, 6:131–132.

11 Maʿmar ibn Rashīd (d. 153/770), the primary teacher of ʿAbd al-Razzāq, a scholar of Basran origin who had settled in Ṣanʿāʾ.

12 The second version of this, ¶10389, has Hishām ibn ʿUrwa in place of al-Zuhrī. Al-Zuhrī is Abū Bakr Muḥammad b. Muslim b. ʿUbayd Allāh b. ʿAbd Allāh b. Shihāb, d. 124/742, he was a major early traditionist, known for being close to the Umayyad ruling family. See Schacht, *Origins*, 245–246, and Lecker, M. "al-Zuhrī, Ibn Shihāb." *EI2*.

13 ʿAbd al-Razzāq, *Muṣannaf*, 6:130, ¶10388.

14 Ibid., 131, ¶10394.

15 Ibid., ¶10395.

16 Ibid., ¶10396.

found in the combination of an extrapolation of his financial capacity and in Qur'ānic notions of righteousness as linked to obedience to the parents.[17]

In contrast to the materials preserved in ʿAbd al-Razzāq's *Muṣannaf*, the *Muṣannaf* of Ibn Abī Shayba contains a very clear picture of the permissibility of marrying children before the age of maturity. In particular, Ibn Abī Shayba has an entire chapter addressing the marriages of young boys ("With regard to the man contracting marriage for his prepubescent son, and those who allow this").[18] There is in the subheading at least the negative implication that some disagreed. The reports themselves, however, insist on the lack of rights of the male child in the face of a father's decision. Two of these reports, ¶16262–¶16263 pertain to both children.

> Shurayḥ said, "If a man marries off his son or daughter, both have no choice if they mature (*idhā shabbā*)."[19]
>
> Al-Zuhrī, al-Ḥasan and Qatāda ... said: "If fathers marry off prepubescents, the marriage is binding."[20]

Three others reports pertain only to sons,[21] and one is general with regard to the father being the only one capable of compelling marriage (*lā yujbiru ʿalā al-nikāḥ illā al-ab*).[22] In the next section, we will see how the generally accepted nature of the father's power to compel is manifested in the context of constructing a valid marriage contract.

Within the early compendia of al-Awzāʿī and the *Muṣannafayn* there are several reports which directly or indirectly indicate a lack of concern with female consent, prepubescent or otherwise. Yet the vast majority of texts affirm and reaffirm a right to protest and overturn a father's contract, even for the virgin (no age specified).

In the *Sunan* of al-Awzāʿī we find two reports affirming the view that a virgin's silence is considered as acceptance; these occur just after the *thayyib/bikr* reports. In all, eleven reports affirm the requirement of female consent

17 See *al-Umm* 6:47. See also Qur'ān 19:14, 32; 17:23, 46:17. Note also the opinion of Ibn Taymīya, *Majmūʿat fatāwī shaykh al-islām*, 33:16: "It is permissible for a father to order his son to divorce if he sees that there is benefit in it for him as Ibn ʿUmar was ordered by his father."

18 Ibn Abī Shayba, *Muṣannaf*, 9:59.

19 Ibid. The chain is: Ibn Abī Shayba > Muṭarraf > al-Ḥakam.

20 Ibid. The chain is: Ibn Abī Shayba > ʿAbd Allāh ibn al-Mubārak > Maʿmar.

21 ¶16261, ¶16264, ¶16266.

22 Ibid. The chain is: Ibn Abī Shayba > Sharīk > Jābir > ʿĀmir.

generally. Of these, five specifically support the virgin's right to consent. No age is specified, nor is majority or minority mentioned. All the reports supporting a virgin's consent are versions of a report transmitted by ʿAṭāʾ ibn Abī Rabāḥ in which the Prophet dissolved the marriage of a virgin whose father married her against her will (*wa-hiya kāriha*).[23]

There are many reports of this nature in the two *Muṣannaf*s. In the *Muṣannaf* of ʿAbd al-Razzāq, we find multiple chapters dealing specifically with consent. The chapters entitled "Seeking Women's Orders with Regard to Themselves," "On Consulting the Orphan with Regard to Herself," and "On Issues of Marriage Compulsion that Render it Non-binding," contain some forty-three reports in all.[24] Sixteen of these confirm the necessity of consent generally, for both virgins and non-virgins.[25] Eleven address only the *thayyib*'s right to consent, while just two address only the consent of the virgin. Seven speak only of the orphan.[26] Only five reports specifically deny the virgin's right to consent/choose. In all of these, no age or stage of physical development is mentioned whatsoever.[27] The remaining two reports address the need for mothers to be involved in decisions concerning their daughters' marriages, rather than it being a unilateral decision on the part of the father.[28]

The same range of views that predominantly uphold female consent regardless of age or virginity is found in the *Muṣannaf* of Ibn Abī Shayba: Of twenty-four reports, six support the necessity of female consent generally, one speaks in a limited way about the consent of the *thayyib*, while two focus on the virgin's right to consent without compulsion.[29] Two reports suggest that a father

---

23 Ibid., 324 ¶¶1056–1059.

24 For these and the chapters on consent of al-Awzāʿī and Ibn Abī Shayba, please see the Appendix.

25 The compilers may have considered prepubescents to be outside the pale of women generally: in other words, prepubescents may constitute a separate category altogether, and thus any reference to female consent, even that of virgins, may implicitly exclude prepubescents. Also in the Appendix are the small chapters addressing prepubescents: In ʿAbd al-Razzāq's *Muṣannaf*, his "Chapter on marrying two prepubescents" (¶¶10388–10398) and for Ibn Abī Shayba, "On the man who contracts marriage for his prepubescent son: who allows it" (¶¶16261–16266). Each contains reports to the effect that the father can compel either male or female; each contains contradictory reports as to whether said children can rescind.

26 One of these, ¶10337, has adapted the language of the *ayyim/bikr* report exactly, substituting the word *yatīma* for *bikr*.

27 ʿAbd al-Razzāq, *Muṣannaf*, 6:117–122. ¶¶10338–10358.

28 Ibid., ¶¶10348–10349.

29 Ibn Abī Shayba, *Muṣannaf*, ¶¶16229–16230.

can compel marriage regardless of his daughter's status, and two deny the virgin choice outright;[30] a final report declares the father's right to compel any of his dependents to marry. The remaining ten reports all support an orphan's right to reject or assent to any union.[31]

Most significantly, all of these reports rephrase the language of the *ayyim/bikr* (or *thayyib/bikr*) report by stating that each female must be consulted or asked permission. The wording varies in a way that makes it plausible that they are responding to or elaborating upon that report.

Typical of such reports are the following two:

> *Al-ayyim aḥaqq bi-nafsihā dūn walīhā wa-l-bikr tusta'dhan.*
>
> The single woman has more legal capacity than her marriage guardian (with regard to herself), and the virgin must be asked permission.[32]
>
> *Yasta'miru al-rajul ibnatahu fī al-nikāḥ, al-bikr wa-l-thayyib.*
>
> A man must consult his daughter with regard to [her] marriage, the virgin and the non-virgin.[33]

One of the versions of the famed hadith surrounding Khansā' bint Khidām is found in the *Muṣannaf* of ʿAbd al-Razzāq.[34] This version shows that it was the spouse who was a *thayyib*.

> Khidām Abū Wadīʿ contracted marriage for his daughter to a man and she went to the Prophet and complained that she was married against her will, so he removed her from her husband and said, "Do not compel them." After that, she married Abū Lubāba, who was previously married (*kāna thayyiban*).

30 Ibn Abī Shayba, *Muṣannaf*, ¶16225–16226. The latter includes ʿAṭā's opinion that it is far better for her to marry whom she loves (*hawāhā*) rather than he whom her father prefers. This occurs in ʿAbd al-Razzāq, *Muṣannaf*, ¶10351. An additional three reports in AR speak of love and the licit nature of marrying whom one loves. ¶¶10353, 10355, 10357.

31 Ibn Abī Shayba, *Muṣannaf*, ¶¶16231–16241.

32 ʿAbd al-Razzāq, *Muṣannaf*, 6:114 ¶10320.

33 Ibn Abī Shayba, *Muṣannaf*, 9:47 ¶16222.

34 ʿAbd al-Razzāq, *Muṣannaf*, 6:119, ¶10346: *Khidām Abū Wadīʿ ankaḥa ibnatahu rajulan fa-atat al-nabī fa-ishtakat ilayhi annahā unkiḥat wa hiya kāriha fa-intazaʿhā min zawjihā wa qāla, "lā tukrihūhunna". Fa-nakaḥat baʿda dhālika Abā Lubāba al-Anṣārī wa kāna thayyiban.*

This text is significant in regard to later discussions. Throughout the later corpus of texts and juridical discussions on the subject of women and consent Khansāʾ will be held up as the woman whom the Prophet allowed to reject her father's contract. As it is usually claimed that she was previously married, the jurists have almost always rushed to emphasize her status as previously married. This, they aver, was the primary reason behind the Prophet's decision. The possibility that the previously married person in question was the spouse (Abū Lubābah) and not Khansāʾ would tend to undermine the logic of those later discussions of this report, particularly for those scholars who, based on this text, tied the lack of virginity to legal capacity.

Legal Capacity of Females

We have seen that the majority of reports in these early compilations indicate that women generally had the ability to refuse a father's attempt to compel them to enter into a marriage. In a similar vein, women could challenge the decisions of guardians generally. One report even affirms the ability of a mother to intervene as a guardian on her daughter's behalf.

Even if, according to some reports, she has a right to reject marriage contracts made on her behalf, certain early reports emphasize her inability to contract the marriage for herself. Al-Awzāʿī includes a report that originates with Abū Hurayra:

> A woman cannot marry off another woman, and a woman cannot contract her own marriage. The adulteress is she who contracts her own marriage.[35]

In another report included by Ibn Abī Shayba, however, a woman's capacity with regard to another woman (in this case, her daughter), is affirmed. In this report, which appears among a group of reports dealing with conflicts between guardians and their female wards, the mother's rights with regard to her daughter's marriage are discussed:

> A woman came to Shurayḥ with her mother and her (paternal) uncle. The mother wanted [to marry her to one] man and the uncle wanted [a different] man. Shurayḥ gave the woman a choice, so she chose the man her mother had chosen. Shurayḥ said to the uncle, "Do you give your permission?" He replied, "No, by God, I do not give my permission." Shurayḥ rejoined, "Do you give your permission, before there is no

35 Al-Awzāʿī, *Sunan* 327, ¶1061. See also ʿAbd al-Razzāq, *Muṣannaf*, 6:158, 160: ¶¶ 10522, 10535.

> permission left for you to give?" The uncle responded, "No, by God, I do not give my permission." Shurayḥ said [to the mother], "Go and marry your daughter to whomever you wish."[36]

ʿAbd al-Razzāq includes a report from ʿAlī allowing a woman to marry pursuant to the permission of her mother and maternal uncle.[37] He also includes several other reports holding that the marriage contracted without a *walī* could not stand unless consummation had already occurred.[38] Only one report allows a woman to contract her own marriage;[39] another validates a marriage without guardian approval only if the spouse is "suitable."[40]

That said, we now turn briefly to the issue of slaves, oft-compared to females in their minority with respect to legal capacity. In the chapter on suitability we will encounter the story of the freed slave woman Barīra. Jurists debate whether her ability to rescind her marriage was based on her new status as a free woman, whose slave husband was unsuitable, whether her husband was indeed a slave, or whether her husband's status was immaterial and her freedom simply resulted from the attainment of legal capacity. This last situation seemed most closely to resemble that of the prepubescent female coming into her majority.

Legal Capacity of Slaves

Much legal writing was devoted to the issue of the capacity of manumitted female slaves. Such discussions are important because of the analogies drawn between the legal capacity of slaves and that of minor females. If a woman was married while enslaved, and subsequently manumitted, does her right to rescind stem from her change in capacity (enslaved to free) or from the husband's change in suitability for her, i.e., whether he himself is a free man or a slave?

---

36 Ibn Abī Shayba, *Muṣannaf*, 9:58, ¶16260.

37 ʿAbd al-Razzāq, *Muṣannaf*, 6:158, ¶10519.

38 Ibid., ¶¶10517–8. ʿUmar, on the other hand, was willing to separate the pair, even if the marriage had been consummated (¶10525).

39 Ibid., 159, ¶10528. Another report, in contrast to Mālikī thought that allows poor women to forego having a guardian, has the reporter repeatedly devaluing (*uṣaghghir lahu min amrihā*) the woman in question in an effort to get al-Ḥasan al-Baṣrī to change the stipulation of a guardian. Al-Ḥasan does not flinch, referring the man to the judge (as a resort for the one who has no guardian) (¶10547).

40 Ibid., ¶10520; see also ¶10547 (relating how guardians would marry women according to the women's desires provided the desired spouse was "suitable").

In Ibn Abī Shayba's *Muṣannaf*, there are many conflicting reports on the subject. Still, the number of reports indicating that she can only have a right of rescission if married to a slave (i.e., invoking suitability) are fewer (four) while those asserting that she can have a right to rescind "even if married to the Commander of the Believers" (i.e., invoking capacity) are seven, with another opinion unsure with regard to the free husband, and one opinion predicating her ability to rescind upon a lack of consummation.[41] Meanwhile, the vast majority of opinions note that if a woman plans to rescind, the marriage should not have been consummated, with the declared loophole being that if the wife did not know that she would eventually have the right to rescind, it did not matter if her husband performed sex upon her "100 times," she would still be able to rescind.[42] "If he performs sex upon her, and she knew that she has the right to rescind, that [is the equivalent of] consent from her."[43] Such a concept calls into question female strategies for rejecting sexual relations; to what extent did jurists envision that a woman could refuse her husband's sexual advances? Given the lack of a concept of marital rape,[44] would sex performed without consent qualify to invalidate a woman's right to rescind, and how would she express (or prove) her lack of consent?

Sex, Maintenance, and Sexual Maturity

As we have seen, sexual maturity/availability was not always linked to puberty, and something as basic to marriage as sex often presented legal problems, particularly with regard to financial issues related to the sexual-financial exchange of the dower and the *nafaqa* (the man's duty to provide maintenance). In these early compendia, however, these problems do not always arise where we have come to expect them. No reports found in the *Sunan* of al-Awzāʿī reflect any ramifications of minor marriage for sexual issues pertaining to legal union.

The situations encountered in the two *Muṣannaf*s do not give any indication that the issue which caused so much difficulty for the consensus and *fiqh* writers came up at all. There are no reports indicating queries into the appropriate time to marry, or when a minor female is capable of tolerating sex, much less the maintenance responsibilities of the non-earning minor male. Thus this section will cover three issues bearing on minor marriages and minor sexual availability. It will end with some observations on sexual intercourse with

41 Ibn Abī Shayba, *Muṣannaf*, 9:171–173.

42 Ibid., 9:174–176.

43 Ibid., ¶16812.

44 See Azam, Hina, *Sexual Violation in Islamic Law: Substance, Evidence, and Procedure* (Cambridge: Cambridge University Press, 2015), esp. 16–18.

virgins and young girls provided by Ibn Abī Shayba from his chapter entitled, "What they said regarding marrying virgins."

The first issue lies in the fact that it is clear that there were marriages with pre-menstruant females. This does not necessarily emerge clearly from the anecdotes variously adduced to support the practice, but it is quite evident from the juristic opinions being offered on the subject. To this end, there was discussion of the proper time to divorce child brides, given strictures regarding time of divorce (typically after the end of a menstrual cycle) and how to sit for an *ʿidda* that cannot be measured by the menstrual cycle.

The second issue has to do with the payment of the dower. Maintenance itself is not an issue at this point. It may well have been that the concern of these compendia with gathering Prophetic reports and Companion opinions did not lead to an encompassing concern with such legal details. There are, however, sections pertaining to who pays the dower in cases where the groom is a minor. Two reports included by ʿAbd al-Razzāq indicate that a father has no financial responsibility for the dower (particularly in the case of the death of the minor son) unless there has been an express contractual stipulation to that effect.[45] In Ibn Abī Shayba's *Muṣannaf*, the reports[46] included are divided; one report alone contains two contradictory opinions.[47] Of significance, though, is the report that stipulates that if the son attains majority and divorces, half the dower is paid by his guardian, who presumably contracted the marriage.[48]

Finally, the third issue revolves around the sexual capabilities of minor males. The question arises, with regard to divorce, as to whether or not a young boy who can sustain an erection but who has not reached the stage of having nocturnal emissions can act as a *muḥallil*.[49] Two opinions deem this binding, while another disallows it.[50] This difference of opinion gives further insight

45 ʿAbd al-Razzāq, *Muṣannaf*, 6:133–134, ¶¶10412–10413.

46 Ibn Abī Shayba, *Muṣannaf*, 9:60, ¶¶16267–16270.

47 Ibid., ¶16269 relates that Shuʿba asked al-Ḥakam and Ḥammād regarding the man who contracts marriage for his minor son. Al-Ḥakam responded that the dower is the son's responsibility, while Ḥammād responded that it is the father's. Qatāda is added as relating that Ibn ʿUmar had said, "It is the responsibility of the one you have married off (*huwa ʿalā alladhī ankaḥtumūh*)."

48 Ibid., 9:60, ¶16267.

49 After a triple divorce, a woman must marry another and be divorced from a consummated marriage before she can be returned to her original husband. The *muḥallil* is the one who, by marrying, consummating the marriage, and willingly divorcing her, renders a woman licit (*ḥalāl*) for remarriage to her previous husband; when entered into with this intent, the marriage is considered a legal subterfuge.

50 ʿAbd al-Razzāq, *Muṣannaf*, 6:275, ¶¶11189–90 and ¶11191, respectively.

into the divided nature of what sex is according to the jurists. As we shall see, Saḥnūn opines that such a boy could not in fact function as a *muḥallil*, as Saḥnūn would have considered there to have been no effect on the female partner in such non-ejaculative sex.[51] Here, however, the third report of this group notes that if a woman commits adultery with a young boy (who is near pubescence and can sustain an erection) she is to be stoned.[52]

The reports which state that a young boy could perform the sexual functions of a *muḥallil*, and those which state that he should be responsible for his own dower, seem to confer upon the minor male comparatively more legal capacity than a female in a similar situation might otherwise be granted.

Rescission

As for the two *Muṣannafs*, there seems to be a clear tendency toward granting a right of rescission. Only the marriages contracted by fathers evoke doubt in the minds of the jurists. Shurayḥ, for example, was against the right of boys or girls married by fathers to exercise a right of rescission upon attaining maturity.[53]

Still, many of the rescission-affirming reports are buried amidst other subjects. The "Chapter on orphans" in the *Muṣannaf* of ʿAbd al-Razzāq includes multiple reports largely affirming the right to rescind for both male and female orphans as well as *children* generally. Significantly, there is a report from Ibn Shubrama:

> Two prepubescents can choose [whether or not to stay married] when they come of age (*al-ṣaghīrān bil-khiyār idhā adrakā*).[54]

For the orphan, the right to choose is generally affirmed, although, as with most of the issues in this study, there are differences of opinion. Of the reports found in Ibn Abī Shayba's *Muṣannaf*, two contain the dual,[55] referring to both sexes of orphan, while three others speak specifically of girls.[56] Only one suggests that the orphan girl has no right to rescind.[57]

---

51 See pp. 118–119 below.

52 See Motzki, *Origins*, 84.

53 Ibn Abī Shayba, *Muṣannaf*, 9:59, ¶16262. See also, 16263–16266.

54 ʿAbd al-Razzāq, *Muṣannaf*, 6:133, ¶10406.

55 Ibn Abī Shayba, *Muṣannaf*, 9:57 ¶¶16252, 16255.

56 Ibid., ¶¶16253, 16254, 16256.

57 Ibid., 9:58, ¶16257.

According to most reports, the minor male whose father contracted his marriage must defer to his father's decision, even after attaining majority. The following report is related from 'Aṭā':

> If a man contracts marriage for his minor son, the marriage stands, and he cannot divorce.[58]

It is surprising to encounter here the language of repudiation instead of the language of rescission. Most of the reports we have seen previously stipulate that a child cannot rescind against a father's contract. This obviation of the right to repudiation, so elemental among the rights of Muslim males, signifies to what extent fathers held authority (or sought to have it preserved) in the early period.

Repudiation

Unlike the fiqh manuals of later eras, the two *Muṣannaf*s address the issue of prepubescent divorce in some detail; in turn, the issue of repudiation itself reveals some of the most interesting contradictions with regard to prepubescents and marriage. This section will be divided into three parts. The first concerns "Repudiation and Compulsion," the second discusses "Repudiation and the Unconsummated Marriage," and the final section deals with repudiation and the legal capacity of the prepubescent male.

Repudiation is the area where cultural conceptions of obligations to the parent come even more sharply into relief. The father's role in repudiation (and, by extension, marriage) can be contextualized in early conceptions of both patriarchy and the concept of "being righteous [through treatment of] one's parents (*birr al-wālidayn*).[59]" Ibn Abī Shayba includes several anecdotes regarding children whose parent or parents have requested they divorce, some invoking that Qur'ānic vocabulary centered on *birr* (righteousness). "What shall I do with my wife?" asks one conflicted man of Ibn 'Abbās. He responded: "Do right by your parents (*abrir wālidayka*)."[60]

Only one opinion (that of al-Ḥasan) suggests that it would not be a matter of doing right by his mother for a son to repudiate the very woman the mother had commanded him to marry. Another anecdote records the famous conflict between 'Umar ibn al-Khaṭṭāb and his son 'Abd Allāh, noting that 'Umar hated his son's wife and insisted that he repudiate her. 'Abd Allāh, however, would

---

58 Ibid., 9:60, ¶16266.

59 See *al-Umm* 6:47.

60 Ibn Abī Shayba, *Muṣannaf*, 10:158–159.

not. The *Muṣannaf* of Ibn Abī Shayba records the Prophet as siding with ʿUmar, saying, "Obey your father and repudiate her."[61] This is quite possibly the very same Ibn ʿUmar whom Ibn al-Mundhir describes as having gone on to contract marriage for his prepubescent son. In that instance as well, the father's will over his son's was upheld.[62]

Whatever the case, parents were by all accounts intimately involved in matters related to their children's marriages. For this reason, it is all the more remarkable that there is so much early textual evidence for the rights of females to protest and be released from marriages contracted on their behalf by their fathers.

Repudiation and Compulsion

The *Muṣannafs* brim with anecdotes about jokes regarding marriage turning into actual marriages, as well as words of repudiation uttered carelessly becoming actual divorces. One chapter is entitled, "On the man who swears to repudiate his wife if his guest does not eat the last bite of food. … And a cat jumps on the table and consumes the last morsel." Such an oath to repudiation must stand, and the repudiation must be implemented. This is one kind of compulsion (*ikrāh*): a repudiation compelled by operation of law.

And yet, the *Sunan* of al-Awzāʿī and the *Muṣannafs* also include chapters full of opinions stating that the repudiation of an unwilling man (*ṭalāq al-mukrah*) does not stand,[63] and these far out-number those which state the opposite. In these sources we find the report that becomes prevalent, particularly in the later, non-Ḥanafī approaches to compulsion: "Three things that will not destroy people: mistakes, forgetfulness, and that for which they were compelled (*mā ukrihū ʿalayhi*)."[64] The point remains that this is yet another topic that presents a point of contention in the Islamic legal consciousness. A further question arises: Can a father who contracted marriage for a young girl request the marriage's termination? Ibn Abī Shayba notes that all of the early opinions

61 Ibid., 158. The *Muṣannaf* does not say whether ʿAbd Allāh indeed repudiated his wife, although al-Ṭabarī notes that at the time of ʿUmar's demise, he refused to recommend ʿAbd Allāh to succeed him saying to the one suggesting it, "Woe to you! How could I confer rule (*astakhlif*) upon a man who is unable even to repudiate his wife?!" See *Tārīkh al-Ṭabarī*, 4:228. Although one could feasibly assume a plurality of wives, ʿAbd Allāh may not actually have repudiated the wife whom the Prophet commanded him to repudiate.

62 *Al-Ishrāf*, 27.

63 See al-Awzāʿī, *Sunan*: ¶¶1107–1115; Ibn Abī Shayba, *Muṣannaf*, 9:569–575 and ʿAbd al-Razzāq, *Muṣannaf*, 6:314–318.

64 ʿAbd al-Razzāq, *Muṣannaf*, 6:317. See also the *Sunan*, ¶1107, with slightly different wording.

except al-Ḥasan al-Baṣrī's say no; yet there is still one report holding that a father can cause his daughter to be repudiated against her will (*wa lam tarḍa*).[65]

Repudiation and the Unconsummated Marriage

ʿAbd al-Razzāq's *Muṣannaf* includes entire chapters entitled, "Should a virgin be repudiated while she is menstruating?"[66] and "The chapter on repudiating virgins."[67] The notion, mentioned above in the section on rescission, that child marriages were not "true" marriages complicated the question of repudiation. The *ʿidda* waiting period is structured around the concept of the repudiated female being a menstruant; her menstrual cycle delineates the period of time in which her husband can change his mind about divorcing her.[68] What, then, of the girl who does not menstruate?

The two *Muṣannafs* both include reports concerning the repudiation of a pre-menstruant female. All the reports suggest that she waits three months, and if she begins menstruating during that time, she adds to this three menstrual cycles.[69]

As to the question of when the repudiation pronouncement(s) should take place (for the menstruant, this should technically be any time she is not menstruating), Ibn Abī Shayba includes reports that affirm a man's right to repudiation at any time (*matā mā shāʾ*), three out of four of these suggesting it was a practice to repudiate at the new moon if the female in question had no cycle.[70] As we will see with al-Shāfiʿī, there is no mention in his writings regarding "months" versus "cycles" (*qurūʾ*).[71] For al-Shāfiʿī, the lack of (presumably prophetic) "Sunna" on the subject simply rendered the non-menstruating female repudiated when her husband chose to so inform her.[72] So too will we see how al-Shāfiʿī equates the virgin with the non-virgin in matters of repudiation[73] by allowing—in theory at least—the repudiated prepubescent virgin authority over her next union.

This chapter has noted some of the practical issues that illuminate the legal challenges posed by prepubescent repudiation. It has also mentioned the

65 Ibn Abī Shayba, *Muṣannaf*, 10:165.

66 ʿAbd al-Razzāq, *Muṣannaf*, 6:246, ¶11018. The answer is, "There is no harm in it, for she has no *ʿidda*."

67 Ibid., 260. For a similar chapter in Ibn Abī Shayba, see 9:534–8.

68 Note that in *khulʿ*, woman-initiated repudiation, the waiting period is but one month.

69 Ibn Abī Shayba, *Muṣannaf*, 9:563, ¶¶18305–18307; ʿAbd al-Razzāq, *Muṣannaf*, 6:269, ¶11151.

70 Ibn Abī Shayba, *Muṣannaf*, ¶¶18308–18311. AR, 6:269, ¶11155–6.

71 The *Risāla*, however, addresses the ambiguity in the word *qurʾ*. See p. 137 n. 56 below.

72 *Al-Umm*, 6:462.

73 See pp. 136–139 below.

questions posed by the *ʿidda* waiting period for pre-menstruant females or virgins in unconsummated unions. There are corollary issues just as pressing, however, for the prepubescent male.

Repudiation and the Prepubescent Male

In this section we explore the issue of the young boy who finds himself in a marital situation not of his choosing and decides to exercise the male prerogative of unilateral repudiation. As with any legal undertaking of consequence, the power of repudiation requires legal capacity. As has already been established, the child, by definition, lacks legal capacity. What then of the married prepubescent male? Would his repudiation utterance be accorded the same weight as that of a pubescent male?

Both physical and mental criteria shape the jurists' reasoning with regard to this issue. One report has al-Ḥasan al-Baṣrī pointing out that no repudiation is binding until a boy has a nocturnal seminal emission.[74] The same report, however, includes Ibn al-Musayyib's[75] opinion that a boy who has understood the obligations of prayer and fasting is capable of uttering a binding repudiation.[76] Other reports expressly hold that his utterance of the repudiation formula is so weighty that the marriage itself should be concealed from him lest he destroy it with a casual word. Al-Ḍaḥḥāk[77] opines, for example, that every repudiation is binding unless the one uttering it is a raving lunatic,[78] and al-Ḥakam and Ḥammād[79] refuse any boy the right of repudiation.

> [It was the practice] that they would contract marriages for them as children and hide the marriage from them, out of fear that repudiation would slip off their tongues. Sufyān said, And if it did occur, they gave it little consideration.[80]

Of the reports we have included, this perhaps suggests that a cultural practice was coming to be viewed as a relic: *Kānū yuzawwijūnahum wa hum sighār*: "They would contract marriages for them when they were children."

74 Ibn Abī Shayba, *Muṣannaf*, ¶18238.
75 Saʿīd ibn al-Musayyib, d. 96/715, an early Medinan expert in *fiqh*.
76 Ibn Abī Shayba, *Muṣannaf*, this is repeated in report ¶18239.
77 Al-Ḍaḥḥāk b. Muzāḥim al-Hilālī, d. 105/723. See GAS 1:29.
78 Ibn Abī Shayba, *Muṣannaf* ¶18243: *Kullu ṭalāq jāʾiz illā ṭalāq al-mubarsam wa al-maʿtūh.*
79 Ḥammād b. Abī Sulaymān (d. 120/737).
80 The *isnād* for this report is Ibn Abī Shayba > Wakīʿ > Sufyān > Manṣūr > Ibrāhīm [al-Nakhaʿī].

The habitual past tense seems to be used almost nostalgically here, the "they" sounding very much as it does when one discusses a past generation. The tone perhaps even expresses a sense of wonderment. Three reports mention the need for hiding the marriage from children, affirming our assumption of a de facto separation between marriage and consummation or even cohabitation.

The final phrase of the report is, however, curious: *lam yarawh shay'an*. Several reports end with this or a similar phrase: *laysa bi-shay'in*. Inasmuch as it seems to mean that it does not merit consideration, the question remains, would the stated repudiation be binding or not? For the most part, it seems that the jurists are inclined to say no, it does not stand. And yet, two reports (¶18245–6) read as follows:

> I asked Ibrāhīm about the repudiation of a boy, and he said, "The women are many."
>
> Ibrāhīm said regarding the repudiation of a boy, "It means nothing (*laysa bi-shay'in*), and the women are many."

The concept of women being plentiful is one that might influence the meaning of "it means nothing" in a way that imbued the statement with the holistic meaning: it was no big deal; boys could repudiate and remarry easily. Still, that some jurists equated the ability to make an effective repudiation pronouncement with conscious participation in prayer and fasting is indication of an essential connection in their minds between marriage, mental maturity and legal capacity.

Suitability

In general, the early compendia project a world in which judges are authorized to contract marriage for a woman when her desire for a spouse is in conflict with her guardian. Still, the issue of suitability remains pertinent: a woman can marry over her guardian's objection, provided the suitability requirement is met. That means that the guardian is entitled to raise suitability as an objection to any such marriage.

> A man sought the hand of a non-virgin woman from the Banī Layth. Her father refused to marry her [to him], so she wrote to 'Uthmān. 'Uthmān wrote: "If he is a suitable match, tell her father to marry her [to him]. If he [still] refuses, then marry (m. pl.) her [to him yourselves]."[81]

81 Ibn Abī Shayba, *Muṣannaf*, 6:58, ¶16258.

Suitability is not here defined, nor is there a definition of the concept of "harm."[82] Discussions presuppose pre-existing rules or concepts for both harm and suitability. Later in the chapter on marriage, however, there are several reports having to do with suitability. Their primary concern is with preventing mixing between Arabs and *mawālī*, or non-Arab clients attached to tribes.[83] One also depicts ʿUmar forbidding marital unions between Arab males and slave women.[84] Only one report suggests that religion figures into the equation, but that same report still notes that *manṣib* (social status) is as important as religion.[85] Again, the significance for a discussion of woman's capacity lies in the paternalism of such statements as "I forbid the genitalia of noblewomen (*furūj dhawāt al-aḥsāb*) to anyone unsuitable."[86] Thus, ability to challenge a guardian's decision is linked in many ways to the doctrine of suitability; the choice of the woman is constrained by the concept of suitability.

Conclusion

This chapter has focused on some of the earliest texts in Muslim legal history. They are texts that, not having met the standards of formal hadith criticism with regard to their relaters, are often discounted in legal discourse, while other times relied upon for their unique insights into the development of Islamic law. By contrast, the reports are invaluable to modern scholarship for the light they shed on the earliest discussions of doctrine.

This chapter has focused on the proof texts adduced by early legal scholars on the topic of minor marriage. Al-Awzāʿī does not address the topic at all, not in any of its manifestations. Only ʿAbd al-Razzāq al-Sanʿānī included the report of ʿĀʾisha. Yet even therein, it is not used as a proof for the father's right to compel a child (as al-Shāfiʿī will use it), but by way of illustrating the existence of the practice of prepubescent marriage, alongside other anecdotal

82 Ibid., referred to in the following report ¶16259.

83 Ibn Abī Shayba, *Muṣannaf*, 9:497–498, ¶¶17996–18001. See also ʿAbd al-Razzāq, *Muṣannaf*, pp. 123–125, ¶¶10359–10371. ʿAbd al-Razzāq includes two distinctly classist reports and two reports from the Prophet encouraging racial and class mixing. Further, he adds an interesting twist to the ongoing discussion about mawālī versus Arabs. We recall that Salmān al-Fārisī is continuously adduced, all the way through Ibn Qudāma, as having said that mawālī and Arabs should not intermarry (nor should the former lead the latter in prayer). However, the *Muṣannaf* includes two reports, ¶¶10366 and 10370, stating that Salmān married two different Arab women. (It may be noteworthy that ʿAbd al-Razzāq was also a mawlā, of the Banū Ḥimyār; see *EI2*, "ʿAbd al-Razzāḳ").

84 Ibn Abī Shayba, *Muṣannaf*, 9:497, ¶17996.

85 Ibid., ¶18002.

86 ʿAbd al-Razzāq, *Muṣannaf*, 6:123, ¶10362.

proofs. The text does not even include the name of Abū Bakr as an agent in the proceedings.

With regard to the father's power to compel, the texts herein, more than in the following chapters, illustrate a conception of righteousness as obedience to a father's wish. There are a plethora of texts, many that contradict each other; the vast majority affirm the right of a daughter to reject a union contracted by her father, without imposing any limits or restrictions on age, while many others affirm the father's right over prepubescent sons and daughters. Some reports expand this last principle to mean that the newly-pubescent son who had been married in his minority by his father cannot divorce.

This chapter also assessed doctrines of legal capacity, noting the range of thought on whether mothers may contract marriages for their daughters as well as the emancipated slave woman's right to rescind her match.

Many key issues remained, at the end of the period under consideration in this chapter, unresolved in a way that could have been considered intellectually untidy. Ibn Abī Shayba (d. 235/849) died just sixty years prior to the death of the earliest consensus writer in this study, al-Marwazī (d. 294/906). As we will see in Part Two, the shift to consensus writing subjects many of the complex issues involved in prepubescent marriage, from consent, rescission, and repudiation, to maintenance, dower, sexual readiness, and suitability to a quest for a quick and less diverse range of answers. However, in the early formative era, the issues at hand still possess intense multivalence. One jurist whose work reflects this intensity is the Ḥanafī Muḥammad al-Shaybānī.

CHAPTER 3

Early Ḥanafī Thought

Al-Shaybānī (189/805):[1] Between Womens' Agency and Affirmation of Patriarchal Authority

The *fiqh* work attributed to the Ḥanafī jurist Muḥammad ibn al-Ḥasan al-Shaybānī, *al-Ḥujja ʿalā Ahl al-Madīna*, contains a valuable record of early Ḥanafī doctrine.[2] I give it the bulk of my focus on early Ḥanafīs due to the fact that it details the thought not only of Abū Ḥanīfa, his disciple Abū Yūsuf (d. 192/807),[3] and al-Shaybānī himself, but also of the Mālikī school at the time of al-Shaybānī's writing. Al-Shaybānī approaches the topic of prepubescent marriage through the Ḥanafī understanding of Q4:127.[4] Because this verse is deeply linked to

1 For biographical information on al-Shaybānī see *al-Ḥujja ʿalā ahl al-madīnah*, ed. Mahdī Ḥasan al-Kīlānī (Beirut: ʿĀlam al-Kutub, 2006), 1:8–10; Chaumont, E. "al-Shaybānī, Abū ʿAbd Allāh Muḥammad b. al-Ḥasan b. Farḳad." *EI2*. See also Calder, *Studies*, 39, and Muḥammad ibn Aḥmad al-Dhahabī, *Manāqib al-Imām Abī Ḥanīfa wa ṣāḥibayhi Abī Yūsuf wa Muḥammad ibn al-Ḥasan*, ed. Muḥammad Zāhid al-Kawtharī (Cairo: al-Maktabah al-Azhariyyah lil-Turāth, 1999).

2 Regarding issues of authenticity surrounding this work and others attributed to al-Shaybānī, see Calder, *Studies*, 39–66, and Schacht, *Origins*, 306–310, and *Introduction to Islamic Law*, 45. Both authors conclude that while al-Shaybānī had a major role in recording and elaborating on the thought of both Abū Ḥanīfa and Abū Yūsuf, it is impossible to say with accuracy, given the fluid nature of such concepts as "book" and "authorship" at al-Shaybānī's time (and indeed until much later) that he bears sole responsibility for this text [i.e., without additions/revisions from pupils or pupils of pupils who recorded and compiled the master's thought]. See also, Chaumont, "al-Shaybānī," *EI2*. It is important to note Behnam Sadeghi's crucial contribution to this discussion in his appendix to *The Logic of Law-Making in Islam* (Cambridge: Cambridge University Press, 2013), pp. 177–199. He determines that al-Shaybānī's works are rightly attributed to him through the redactions of two students attending his lectures.

3 See Schacht, J. "Abū Yūsuf Yaʿḳūb b. Ibrāhīm al-Anṣārī al-Kūfī." *EI2*. See also al-Dhahabī's *Manāqib*.

4 "And they ask thee to enlighten them about the laws concerning women. Say: 'God [Himself] enlightens you about the laws concerning them'—for [His will is shown] in what is being conveyed unto you through this divine writ about orphan women [in your charge] to whom—because you yourselves may be desirous of marrying them—you do not give that which has been ordained for them; and about helpless children; and about your duty to treat

 | DOI 10.1163/9789004344860_005

orphans and has engendered semantic debates over the meaning of orphanhood (i.e. can one be considered an orphan after pubescence?), the Ḥanafīs dwell on it as they seek guidance on the legal issue of how (not if) the minor can be married off. The primary concern is whether other than the father may contract marriage without a minor's permission. (By contrast, as we will see, Mālik and al-Shāfiʿī do not seem to mention orphans in their discussions of marriage, perhaps because neither grants that right to other than the father, while the orphan is, by definition, fatherless.)

After exploring the early Ḥanafī proof texts regarding prepubescent marriage, the discussion will turn to the Ḥanafī understanding of compulsion itself, finding that it is not an invalidating factor in three areas: divorce, manumission of slaves, and marriage. With regard to marriage, however, there exist modalities of termination of forced marriage which relate specifically to questions of capacity for children, the mentally deficient, slaves and for females generally (and virgins specifically).

Overall, the Ḥanafī position as elaborated by al-Shaybānī tends toward ceding to females capacity upon pubescence but allowing them none prior. Issues unresolved for al-Shaybānī include whether the position of slaves is analogous to that of females in their minority and the precise role of the marriage guardian, given a woman's right to contract her own marriage. More than anything, al-Shaybānī's writings can be viewed as an early stage in the evolution of doctrine concerning the role of the father in the developing Islamic legal system; although the right of rescission for children of both sexes is not allowed under any circumstances, the right of pubescent females, virgin and non-virgin, to overturn a father's marriage is affirmed.

The **Walī Mujbir** *and Proof Texts*

Al-Shaybānī has no doubt whatsoever about the permissibility of marrying off prepubescent males and females. An entire section of the "Chapter on Marriage" of his *Ḥujja* is devoted to that which is binding and nonbinding for children upon reaching pubescence.[5] Al-Shaybānī's positions therein include the idea that if a father[6] or a grandfather marries off a child, and then dies, the child has no right of rescission upon pubescence, and if any other guardian

---

orphans with equity. And whatever good you may do—behold, God has indeed full knowledge thereof."

5 *Bāb nikāḥ al-ṣaghīr wa al-ṣaghīra mā yajūz ʿalayhimā idhā adrakā. Al-Ḥujja*, 2:87–92.

6 There is an exception: the Christian father cannot contract marriage for his prepubescent Muslim daughter. See *al-Jāmiʿ al-ṣaghīr*, 140.

contracts the marriage, the right of rescission applies ("they can deem the marriage acceptable or refuse it").[7]

Because Ḥanafīs are alone in allowing other than the father to contract marriages for children, al-Shaybānī then produces what he considers Qur'anic evidence for this position, based on certain interpretations of Q4:127. Here, he guides the discussion into the issue of orphans, an issue that will figure prominently in the later arguments of al-Ṭaḥāwī (d. 321/933) and al-Jaṣṣāṣ (d. 370/981) when they give their attention to the marriage of prepubescents. The driving rationale for the Ḥanafīs is this: if only the father can contract marriage for children, how could it be that orphans, by definition fatherless, have their marriages contracted at all?

The later Ḥanafī positions on these topics originate with al-Shaybānī. From his writings we discover the opinion that there are no orphans after adulthood: he notes that Abū Ḥanīfa related a hadith to this effect, "No orphanhood after maturity."[8] Semantic debates over the word *yatīm* (orphan) determine whether marriage contracts are made before or after pubescence, and ultimately, whether the word orphan is by definition "one who is prepubescent." If so, then Q4:3 and Q4:127 are referring to marriages of prepubescents.[9]

> God Most High in His Book made binding the marriage of the orphan girl and the orphan boy who have not reached pubescence because there is no orphanhood after pubescence, nor is there an orphan girl who has a father.
>
> They said, "Whence comes this?"
>
> One responds, "Regarding the speech of God, {They ask you about the women. Say, God gives you a decision with regard to them and that which the Book tells you with regard to orphan women (*yatāmā al-nisā'*) whom you do not give their due} they have reported to us [that] the exegetes have explained that God's words, {you do not give (them)} [means] "you do not marry them."[10]

---

7 *Al-Ḥujja*, 2:87–88.

8 *Al-Ḥujja*, 2:90. *Lā yutm ba'd al-bulūgh*.

9 We cannot overstate the implications of these early discussions of Q4:3 for modern debates on polygyny.

10 One example of the exegesis in question can be found in Ṭabarī's quotation of 'Ā'isha's explanation of this verse. ['Ā'isha said,] "This refers to the orphan (*al-yatīma*) who is under the protection of a man (*'inda al-rajul*). Perhaps she is sharing [her money] with him [i.e., sharing the expenses of the household (*sharīkatuhu fī mālihi*)], and he is more deserving [of her partnership] than anyone else [due to his care of her]. So he is averse to marrying her, and prevents her [from marrying] for the sake of [keeping] her money

They reply, "This is exegesis and not revelation."

The response to them is, "God Most High has made other [statements] along with this and [given] clear evidence, for He said, {You do not give (them) their due by not marrying them.}.[11] Did He not then censure the desire not to marry them (*al-raghba ʿan nikāḥihinna*)?"

[available to him], and does not marry her to anyone else, lest anyone else share with him in her money" (*Tafsīr al-Ṭabarī, 7:531*).

The other explanations Ṭabarī includes are also useful. Among them: "If the orphan girl was ugly, they would not give her her inheritance, and they would prevent her from marrying until she died and they could inherit from her, so God sent down this verse."

Another category of explanation grounds the meaning in protests over the inheritance rights of women (which were to be found at the sūra's beginning). This was reported to have been said by Saʿīd ibn Jubayr: "Only mature males inherited. The prepubescent male (*al-rajul al-ṣaghīr*) and the woman (*al-marʾa*) did not inherit. When the inheritance [verses] were revealed in *Sūrat al-Nisāʾ*, this was difficult for people. They said, 'The prepubescent (boy) will inherit who does not work to earn money and has no responsibilities, and the woman who also does not do these things, and they will inherit as the man who works to earn money?!' So they begged for [an affirming] sign (*ḥadath*) to come from heaven. And they waited, and when they saw that no sign was coming, they said, 'Because this has happened [i.e., that no sign has come], then it is an obligation that can't be gotten around (*innahu la-wājibun mā min-hu budd*). Then they said, "Ask the Prophet!" So they asked him, and God revealed this ... concerning the verses at the sūra's beginning. ... And it was typical that if the woman was beautiful and had money, her guardian would desire her and marry her in order to take exclusive possession of her (*astaʾthara bihā*), and if she was not beautiful or wealthy, he would have sex with her and not marry her (*ankaḥahā wa lam yankiḥhā*)."

With regard to the meaning of *yatāmā al-nisāʾ*, Saʿīd ibn Jubayr's opinion is that this simply refers to the women discussed in the chapter's beginning, i.e., women whose parents have died and are technically orphaned and are now inheriting. (*Tafsīr al-Ṭabarī*, 7:532–3).

11 ʿAbd Allāh Yūsuf ʿAlī, for one, translates this as "... the orphaned women to whom ye give not the portions prescribed, and yet whom ye desire to marry ..." (p. 256). Al-Shaybānī has adopted an interpretation of this part of the verse which insists that the meaning is the opposite. This interpretation can also be found in Ṭabarī who includes, and himself champions, several opinions holding that "*wa targhabūna an tankiḥūhunna*" (and you want to marry them) actually means and "you do not want to marry them" (*wa targhabūna ʿan nikāḥihinna*). Ṭabarī is with those who believe the meaning of the verse was that the guardians of the orphans were preventing them from marrying in order to inherit from them. He does not, however, suggest that the orphans in question are other than pubescent women. (*Tafsīr al-Ṭabarī*, 6:532–544). No indication of this definition for r-gh-b could be found in Lane. It is telling, perhaps, that in al-Shaybānī's recounting of the report concerning ʿĀʾisha's contracting marriage for Ḥafṣa bint ʿAbd al-Rahmān, he notes that her father says. "It's not that I dislike [the marriage/Ibn al-Mundhir] ... (*mā*

They said, "Quite so!"

It is said to them, "Do not be averse to this [interpretation]. For how can He censure the desire not to marry she whom it is not permissible to marry?"

They respond, "Because the adult pubescent is called an orphan."

We reply, "If it is a case wherein the pubescent is called an orphan, it is only [a case of her being so called] by the name [which is typically applied to] the prepubescent. The basic meaning of the word orphan is for the prepubescent. Thus you have made one who is merely called orphan and is not actually an orphan the orphan about whom no one has doubts, [and in so doing] you have taken her beyond the semantic definition (*ḥadd*) of orphanhood."[12]

Al-Shaybānī wants the reader to come away from this verse knowing that a prepubescent orphan can be married by her guardian, either to himself or to another. The objectors aver that the passage is talking about adult females who have no fathers and are therefore called orphans. Al-Shaybānī claims that such an understanding, although seemingly clear from the text which refers to "women," overlooks the fact that the word orphan itself cannot refer to a woman but only to a minor female who has not reached pubescence. By the time this argument is taken up by al-Jaṣṣāṣ, the semantic debate is conducted with reference to the *ḥaqīqa/majāz* dichotomy.[13]

Ultimately, al-Shaybānī gives two reports,[14] neither going back to the Prophet, that affirm the right of rescission for the orphaned boy upon pubescence. One of these reports includes females as well:

---

lī raghbah)", which the editor interpolates via brackets as "*raghbah* [*ʿanhu*]," in order to bring it into line with modern understandings of *raghbah fī/raghbah ʿan*. In short, it is entirely possible that al-Shaybānī's understanding of the word (without the accompanying preposition *ʿan*) embraced both like and dislike, or perhaps even predominantly meant dislike, and with time this understanding fell into disuse. See *Ḥujja*, 2:71, fn. 7.

12 *Al-Ḥujja*, 2:89–90.

13 See p. 50, above.

14 Al-Shaybānī > ʿAbd Allāh ibn al-Mubārak > Maʿmar ibn Rāshid > Ibn Ṭāwus > Ṭāwus; al-Shaybānī > Ismāʿīl ibn ʿAyyāsh > Ibn Jurayj > ʿAṭāʾ.

> Ibn Jurayj heard from ʿAṭāʾ that he said, "If an orphan has a marriage contracted for him as a child, he may choose when he grows up (*idhā kabura*),[15] and also the orphan female."[16]

As discussed in Chapter One, the situation of orphans consistently merited the attentions of some scholars. Additionally, the *ayyim/bikr* hadith floats in and out of the sources with variations in its vocabulary. Sometimes it is rephrased such that its main focus is orphans.[17] There are chapters devoted to the topic of orphans in the *Muṣannafs*, with the majority of opinions therein indicating strongly that there is a right of rescission for both sexes upon pubescence.[18]

The issue of compulsion in al-Shaybānī's thought would be worthy of its own separate investigation. For the Ḥanafīs, there are certain areas of law in which compulsion is licit. These—marriage, freeing of slaves, and divorce—stem from the hadith which reads, "There are three things in which there is no joking (*hazluhunna jādd*), divorce, manumission of slaves, and marriage."[19] Because a man who divorces against his will has actually divorced, a woman who is married against her will is actually married.[20] Other situations, such as commerce, do not acknowledge a relationship between compulsion and being bound by words uttered.

Still, al-Shaybānī includes multiple anecdotes illustrating the illicit nature of forcing a virgin to marry.[21] One of these reads: "The Messenger of God separated a virgin woman (*imrāʾa bikr*) who had been married by her father against her will (*wa hiya kāriha*) from her husband." Another again uses the consultation vocabulary of the *ayyim/bikr* hadith: "Virgins are consulted with regard to themselves (*tustaʾmar al-abkār fī unfusihinna*), (both) those who have fathers and those who are without fathers."[22]

---

15 Again, the language of when capacity is attained is ambiguous. One report states "when he reaches maturity (*idhā balagha*)," and the other states, "when he grows up (*idhā kabura*)".

16 *Al-Ḥujja*, 2:92.

17 See, for example, Saḥnūn ibn Saʿd al-Tanūkhī, *al-Mudawwana al-Kubrā* (Beirut: Dār al-Ṣādir), 2:159.

18 See, for example, Ibn Abī Shayba, *Muṣannaf*, 9:57–58 and the Appendix.

19 See also, *al-Muwaṭṭaʾ*, 2:67: "There are three things in which there is no joking (*laysa fīhinna laʿib*), marriage, divorce, and slave-freeing," and ʿAbd al-Razzāq, ¶10281–10291.

20 *Al-Ḥujja*, 2:106–110.

21 See especially *Al-Ḥujja*, 2:83–85.

22 Ibid., 83.

He cites the story of Khansā' bint Khidām,[23] the preeminent text for affirming the choice of the non-virgin. She had gone to the Prophet protesting that her father had contracted her marriage against her will. There was, however, debate over her exact status; some versions show her to be of ambiguous status (perhaps *bikr*, perhaps *thayyib*; perhaps, as noted above, the husband was the one who was *thayyib*). One example reads as follows:

> *Ta'ayyamat Khansā' bint Khidām raḍiya Allāh 'an-humā fa-zawwajahā abū-hā fa-atat al-nabī ṣalā Allāh 'alayhi wa salam wa-qālat: inna abī zawwajanī wa-lam yasta'miranī wa qad malaktu amrī. Qāla fa-lā nikāḥ baynakumā fa-nkiḥī man shi'ti.*
>
> Khansā' bint Khidām (may God be content with them both) became widowed, so her father married her off. So she went to the Prophet (peace be upon him) and said, "My father contracted my marriage without consulting me, and I have attained legal capacity." He said, "Then there is no marriage between the two of you. Go marry whom you will."

The editor[24] of *al-Ḥujja* notes that in his source manuscripts, this anecdote begins with the word "*atat.*" He refutes the possibility of this word being appropriate, inserting instead *ta'ayyamat*, relying on sources like *Ṣaḥīḥ al-Bukhārī* and the fifteenth century *Fatḥ al-Bārī* for the correction. Although his correction makes sense (given the repetition of the word *atat* later in the text), the level of intensity he evidences in rejecting the initial *atat* is revealing: he refers to this alternative as a foul corruption (*taḥrīf fāḥish*). He seems to believe that any concession to the notion that the initial word might have been *atat*[25] (she came; i.e., an unspecified "sort" of woman, a female and not just a widow or divorcee) instead of *ta'ayyamat* (she was widowed) could open the door to a general notion of female consent rather than consent preserved only for the previously-married woman.[26] To be clear, it is apparent that al-Shaybānī

23 This name appears differently (Khidām, Khadhām, Ḥidām, etc) in almost every source (Kecia Ali in *Marriage and Slavery* has selected Khidhām as her reading, see p. 41). With Rif'at Fawzī, editor of *Kitāb al-Umm*, I have decided on Khidām and will use it consistently even where other editors have chosen other readings.

24 Al-Kīlānī, al-Sayyid Mahdī Ḥasan. 2:65, fn. 4.

25 See p. 65 n. 34.

26 The *Musannaf* of 'Abd al-Razzāq includes versions that use "*atat*" in this report. See 'Abd al-Razzāq, ¶10345–10346. One version includes instead of the word *āmat* (to become a widow), *anabat* (to reject and protest angrily).

himself thought that Khansāʾ was indeed previously married; he later includes discussion of her desire to marry her child's uncle. It is simply noted here what the editor recognizes as being at issue when considering the implications of the hadith: the wording itself could transcend context. For this reason he fights to delimit the vocabulary in order to argue for *his* understanding of the report's supra-meaning: only widows or previously-married women have the right to contest forced marriages.

With regard to capacity there are many differences between Ḥanafī thought and its counterparts. Here, I begin by noting the Ḥanafī position on women contracting marriage for other women and for themselves. Next I investigate al-Shaybānī's position on marriage of the mentally deficient, then the juristic comparisons between the relationship of slave to master and that of a woman to her guardian (a framework upon which al-Shāfiʿī relies in his thought). Finally, I note the Ḥanafī response to the Mālikī view that a woman's mental maturity is anchored in her sexual status.

Legal Capacity of Females

Al-Shaybānī in his discussion of this topic lays the groundwork for what we will see in a more mature form in the chapters of al-Ṭaḥāwī and al-Jaṣṣāṣ. In exploring the factors that have led to positions of paternal power being enforced and reinforced over female children, pubescent and prepubescent, it is helpful to view al-Shaybānī's positions for the sake of better understanding early thought on the subject. The Ḥanafīs allow women to contract their own marriages and even to contract marriages for other women. Still, there is—or at least there certainly emerges among later authors—a sort of structural ambiguity in regard to the position of the marriage guardian.

The first chapter of *al-Ḥujja*'s "Book of Marriage" bears the title, "The chapter on a woman marrying off her female slave or her male slave or entering into marriage contracts."[27] The role of a woman in the marriage process is debated in the following paragraph:

> Abū Ḥanīfa has said that "There is no harm (*lā baʾs*) in a woman contracting marriage (*tuzawwij*) for her slave woman or slave, and it is also fine for her to command the slave to marry (*an taʾmura ʿabdahā fa-yatazawwaju*) or to marry off her female slave. In the same way, there is no harm in a man commanding his slave to marry or to marry off his female slave."

27 *Bāb al-marʾa tuzawwij ammatahā aw ʿabdahā aw taʿqad ʿuqdat al-nikāḥ*. 2:64.

> The Medinans have said, "A woman may not marry off her female slave or her male slave, and if a woman wants to marry off her servant, she must designate (*istakhlafat*) a man to marry her, and the marriage then becomes binding."[28]

Al-Shaybānī notes that the Mālikī position invokes a report[29] which says, "Women have nothing to do with the marriage process" (*li-annahu jā'a anna al-nisā' laysa ilayhinna min al-nikāḥ shāy*[30]). The Ḥanafī response to this is that the act of delegating becomes part of the marriage process, in effect identical with the actions of the *walī* in conferring upon a marriage contract its legality. If, without her delegation of the man, the marriage contract fails, and by her delegation it is binding, then, "it is binding for her to be in charge (*jāza la-hā an taliya dhālik*)."[31] In other words, if the woman slave owner has the authority to delegate to someone, then she has that same power to act herself.

Al-Shaybānī presses on: It cannot be that women have no role in the marriage process, for marriage cannot take place without their consent. His stance here is not a little ambiguous. He has just noted that a woman can be a marriage guardian. Marriage guardians are "the ones who marry" (*al-awliyā' hum alladhīna yuzawwijūn*).[32] And yet their marriages are not licit, al-Shaybānī avers, without the consent of women. Without the consent there is no contract and thus no marriage. Thus there is indeed a portion of the contract that belongs only to women: they must be consulted (*lil-nisā' fī al-ʿuqda naṣīb lā budd min an yusta'marna*). This position allows him to introduce the hadith of Khansā' bint Khidām and various other hadith relevant to the issue of the impermissibility of forcing a woman in her majority to marry.[33]

Whereas al-Ṭaḥāwī will rely extensively on the notion that a woman must have the permission of her marriage guardian to marry, even though she can contract for herself, the picture drawn by al-Shaybānī is more ambiguous. It would seem that, for al-Shaybānī, a woman can contract her own marriage outright, with no role at all for the marriage guardian. And yet at certain points al-Shaybānī refers to the role of the *walī* as approving or disapproving and thus

28 *Al-Ḥujja*, 2:64.

29 *jā' anna*. This wording implies that there is a report, while not identifying any particular source for it.

30 *Al-Ḥujja*, 2:64.

31 Ibid.

32 Ibid.

33 He does not stipulate at this point that it is the fact of majority which prevents this. The issue only becomes clear in the later discussions of prepubescents.

allowing or disallowing the marriage to stand. As we will see in the following anecdotes, it remains unclear how much of a role al-Shaybānī allots to him (or her!) given the bride's legal capacity.

The first proof that al-Shaybānī offers is the anecdote involving Khansāʾ bint Khidām who complained to the Prophet of her marriage plight (and her father's compulsion of her).

> God's Messenger separated the two of them and ordered her to marry her son's uncle (*amarahā an tatazawwaja ʿamm ṣibyānihā*). Muḥammad [al-Shaybānī] said, thus [God's Messenger] gave her the right to contract her marriage (*jaʿala ilayhā ʿuqdat al-nikāḥ*).[34]

Another two versions of the hadith have the Prophet saying, "Marry whom you wish" (*fa-inkiḥī/fa-tazawwajī man shiʾti*).[35] This phrasing does not imply that the marriage must then be condoned by the father or by anyone else; as we will see, al-Shaybānī will not dismiss the need for the *walī* outright, although he seems only to directly address the *walī*'s importance in the chapter on a woman who contracts her own marriage with a non-suitable match and then moves to annul it.[36] The editor, al-Kīlānī, alludes to the power of vocabulary found in these hadiths. Just as these Prophetic reports instruct women to marry themselves (without alluding to guardians), the Qurʾānic verses are unambiguous in granting women the legal capacity to contract their own marriages. Al-Kīlānī's notes on this would seem to have been constructed (as al-Ṭaḥāwī's arguments almost certainly are) in at least partial response to the later Shafiʿī stance that Q2:281 refers to the rights of marriage guardians, a notion consistent with the hadith that provides "No marriage without a guardian."[37]

Then al-Shaybānī embarks upon the subject of ʿĀʾisha's role in the marriage of her niece, Ḥafṣa bint ʿAbd al-Raḥmān ibn Abī Bakr. His point against the Medinans is clearly that a woman can contract marriage for another woman:

---

34 *Al-Ḥujja*, 2:65.

35 Ibid., 67, 69.

36 See *Al-Ḥujja*, 2:295.

37 "How could [this be] when God Most High has linked marriage to them in His statement {Until she marries a husband other than him (*ḥattā tankiḥa zawjan ghayrahu*)}

It is to be noted that in there is a misprint in the 2006 edition which is clarified by the 1983 edition; the word *illā* was mistakenly inserted in the former.

> So here is ʿĀʾisha, may God be pleased with her, having married off al-Mundhir Ibn al-Zubayr to the daughter of ʿAbd al-Raḥmān. She saw that this was binding and proper (*jāʾizan mustaqīman*). Yet you have claimed that women have nothing to do with marriage. What then of slaves? If a master orders his slave to marry, it is not [then] possible for him to marry himself or for his marriage guardian to marry him [i.e. to someone other than the master's choice]. Why then is that nonbinding, when there is a hadith regarding it, and there are reports regarding a woman marrying herself and other than her from more than one of the Companions of God's Messenger and from ʿAlī and other than him.[38]

A distinction is made, but it appears to be rather a thin one: it appears that al-Shaybānī accuses the other side of being selective regarding historical precedent. Al-Kīlānī here attempts to clarify. He explains that ʿĀʾisha did in fact marry Ḥafṣa to ʿAbd al-Raḥmān ibn al-Mundhir, and the fact of this is not incongruent with the reports, "The marriage of any woman who marries without the permission of her guardian is void, void void!"[39] and "There is no marriage without a guardian."[40] With regard to the latter (which, al-Ṭaḥāwī will spend much time refuting),[41] al-Kīlānī is squarely in the camp of those who distinguish the guardian's permission from the expression of that permission.

> The report is proof that the permission of the guardian is necessary, not his expression (*ʿibāra*) [of the permission]. Marriage is carried out (*yanfudh*) whether the allowance (*al-ijāza*) and the permission precede or follow, whether the marriage took place with the expression (*ʿibāra*) of the guardian or the expression of the bride (lit. "the ward," *al-mawliya*).[42]

---

38 *Al-Ḥujja*, 2:72–73.

39 Hadith found in Tirmidhī, "The Chapter on 'No Marriage Without a Guardian,'" #1102, and Ibn Mājah, "Chapter on Marriage; The Chapter on a Woman's Marriage being Void," #1879.

40 Hadith found in Tirmidhī, "The Chapter on 'No Marriage Without a Guardian,'" #1101; *Musnad Aḥmad*, "The First of the Kufan *Musnad*," #19024, and *Sunan Abī Dāʾūd*, "The Chapter on Marriage; No Marriage Without a Marriage Guardian," #2085.

41 Spectorsky suggests, with Schacht, that this may have evolved from a report from ʿUmar into a Prophetic hadith, originating with al-Shāfiʿī and geared toward dismembering the Ḥanafī position. See Susan Spectorsky, *Chapters on Marriage and Divorce: Responses of Ibn Ḥanbal and Ibn Rāhwayh*, (Austin: University of Texas Press, 1993), fn. 31, p. 11.

42 *Al-Ḥujja*, 2:72, fn. 2. Al-Kīlānī insists on the importance of culture and tradition in such situations, noting the vile nature of a woman intruding on "the gatherings of men" to offer her permission for a contract.

At this point al-Shaybānī includes an example of a mother contracting a marriage for her young son. In the anecdote included, one al-Musayyib ibn Najaba has just become a father to a newborn baby girl (*jāriya*). He visits his female cousin[43] Farī'a bint Ḥabbān, and in an apparent effusion of joy, blurts out,

> Did you hear that a baby girl has been born to me? [Farī'a said,] "May God bless you!" He said, "I offer to marry her to your son (*fa innī ankaḥtuhā ibnaki*)!" She responded: "I have accepted (*qabiltu*)." When al-Musayyib had stayed for an hour or so, he said, "I wasn't serious; I was only joking." She replied, "You offered me marriage (*qad 'araḍta 'alayya al-nikāḥ*) and I accepted!" He said, "'Abd Allāh ibn Mas'ūd will decide this matter." 'Abd Allāh ibn Mas'ūd entered and, when they had told him the story, said, "Did you mention marriage, Musayyib?" He said, "Yes." He replied, "Seriousness and joking in marriage are as one, just like seriousness and joking are as one with regard to divorce." He allowed the expression of Farī'a, "I have accepted."[44]

This story illustrates both the ability of a mother to contract marriage (in this case, for a son), and that her testimony on such a matter does not require the presence of additional witnesses. No mention is made of consultation with or permission from any additional guardians, male or otherwise.

Further support for the capacity of women comes in an anecdote relating how a woman "married herself" (*ankaḥat nafsahā*). Her father entered into a legal dispute about it (or, alternatively, about *him*, i.e., the spouse, *khāṣamau*), and the matter was adjudicated by 'Alī ibn Abī Ṭālib who allowed the marriage (which had been consummated).[45] Another report shows 'Alī allowing a mother's contract for her daughter against the protests of the daughter's (male) guardians.[46] Another report has a judge allowing a marriage contracted by a daughter whose father had been absent and returned to find her married. The judge allowed this consummated marriage to stand.[47] Consummation in

43 The name is problematic; I have spent some time searching for her in the sources to no avail. *Al-Ḥujja* gives her name as first Qarī'a bint Ḥabbān and then Farī'a. The passage ends with designating her as "the wife of 'Abd Allāh", but this is apparently not the 'Abd Allāh who is named in the anecdote (Ibn Mas'ūd). Kecia Ali has chosen the name Quray'a and determined her to be the wife of 'Abd Allāh ibn Mas'ūd, *Marriage and Slavery*, 29.

44 *Al-Ḥujja* 2:74.

45 Ibid., 75.

46 Ibid., 76.

47 Ibid., 77.

such cases appears to carry great weight, and it could be that these last few instances of marriage might have been deemed more problematic (or at least revocable) if consummation had not yet taken place.

Al-Shaybānī ends the chapter on an ambiguous note:

> If it were to happen that a marriage guardian were absent, and a woman appointed as her guardian a man from among her people, and he contracted marriage for her, and then the marriage guardian came and protested that, and wanted to refute [the marriage], the Imām or the judge should ask about the groom. If he is deemed suitable (*kufu'*), [the Imam] should order the *walī* to deem [the marriage] licit. And if he refused to deem it licit, he would be considered out of line, and the Imam or judge would deem it licit. And only God knows.[48]

Again, this entire discussion takes place under the aegis of a chapter on "a woman marrying her slave (*'abd*) or contracting marriage." The legal reasoning progresses from a woman marrying her slave, in which her rights of *walā'* are affirmed, marrying herself (viz. Khansā'), to marrying off a relative (Ḥafṣa, far from being her servant, was the niece of 'Ā'isha), to mothers marrying off children of both sexes, to women contracting for themselves. Thus it would seem that there is a vital link of equivalence between the right of a woman to contract for others and the right of a woman to marry herself to whom she wishes. No mention occurs here of a differentiation between the marriage contract and the actual marriage, as will be discussed later by al-Ṭaḥāwī[49] and referenced by Ibn 'Abd al-Barr.[50]

And yet there is still some sense of the enshrined nature of authoritative assent to the marriage bond; it would be tempting to say, "patriarchal" assent, but al-Shaybānī has mentioned mothers in this role. The marriage must be "deemed licit" by *someone*. If the guardian is unwilling to do it, the imam can (and should), all things being equal. There is ambiguity: some reports do not

48 Ibid.

49 Al-Kīlānī goes out of his way to support al-Ṭaḥāwī's approach against the Shāfi'ī assertion (Bayhaqī in his *Sunan*) that 'Ā'isha said, "A woman cannot undertake a marriage contract," noting that the chain is weakened by al-Shāfi 'ī's reliance on an unknown transmitter and the *mursal* nature of a chain in which 'Abd al-Raḥmān ibn al-Qāsim's father is not mentioned (and all is passed down directly from 'Ā'isha to 'Abd al-Raḥmān himself). See *Al-Ḥujja*, n. 1 p. 72.

50 See Chapter 7 below.

mention this aspect; some reports do. Al-Shaybānī does not take it upon himself to offer a clear picture.

Legal Capacity of the Mentally Deficient[51]

Al-Shaybānī dedicates a chapter to what he terms, "the marriage of the one who is mentally deficient."[52] In his opinion, the mentally deficient (*al-safīh*) is on a par with the one who requires a guardian (*al-mawlā ʿalayh*) in regard to their ability to marry: neither needs the guardian to contract the marriage. This position is very different from that of the Mālikīs who declare for such persons an inability to marry without the permission/agency of their guardians. Such unions are sundered (in al-Shaybānī's understanding of Mālikī thought), and the woman in question receives nothing if there has not been consummation,

---

51 For further reading on mental impairment and its legal consequences, see the work of Vardit Rispler-Chaim, who translates *maʿtūh* as "mentally-deficient", which, along with *safīh* are degrees that differ from outright *junūn* (madness, in which the person in question has no legal capacity whatsoever) across the schools while sharing certain restrictions such as a need for guardianship; it is not evident that the early jurists distinguished between the two categories (*safīh* and *maʿtūh*). A later definition from Sarakhsī (d. 483/1090) classifies *majnūn* as *ʿadīm al-ʿaql* (lacking reason) and *maʿtūh* as *nāqiṣ al-ʿaql* (deficient in reason). See V. Rispler-Chaim, *Disability in Islamic Law* (Dordrecht, The Netherlands: Springer, 2007), 64–65. We here tend to equate the *safīh* with the *maʿtūh* because they appear closely related with regard to their legal treatment while both exist as a different category than *majnūn*. Likewise, the term *maghlūb ʿalā al-ʿaql* (also translated by us as mentally-deficient) in the *Umm* seems to be just short of actual insanity (*junūn*). This category also seems to resemble that of the "*safīha*" in Mālikī thought (see above). It could therefore be coarsely translated as "retarded" as well. "Disconnected from reality" would perhaps cover all necessary bases, but there seems to be a real implication of a troubled mind which could mend (to wit, al-Shāfiʿī's optimistic suggestion that marriage might be the cure). For more extensive reading see Dols, Michael, *The Madman in Medieval Islamic Society* (Oxford: Clarendon Press, 1992).

52 Kīlānī takes the definition light-minded (*khafīf al-ʿaql*) for *safīh*, based on "*Radd al-muḥtār ʿalā al-durr al-mukhtār*" of Ibn ʿĀbidīn (1258/1842); the book was the famed Ottoman-era (Ḥanafī) key to jurisprudential jargon, and the definition for *safīh* reads as follows: "a lightness (*khiffa*) [of intellect] that causes the person to do that which goes against the requirements of the intellect (*muqtaḍā al-ʿaql*)." Thus, says Kīlānī, the person's mind is not destroyed altogether (fn. 2, p. 253). For this early period it is likely well-rendered as "spendthrift"; however, we have chosen to translate this term as "mentally-deficient," in the same way we have translated al-Shāfiʿī's term, "*maghlūb ʿalā ʿaqlihi*", for it reflects a stratum of mental disability short of insanity, and because the two terms seem to represent, for the two different authors, the same notion. For Mālikīs invoking the term with regard to women, it is clear that mental deficiency is implied and the opportunity to be trustworthy with money would not yet have occurred.

and if there has, she should receive the very least amount a woman can receive (listed here as a dīnār) in compensation for his having 'touched' her.[53]

What is of significance for our purposes is whether or not the capacity of the mentally deficient is comparable in any way to that of the child. Abū Ḥanīfa is said to allow the pubescent *safīh* to enact divorce, marriage and manumission of slaves; the hadith about the joking and seriousness of such matters is repeatedly invoked.[54]

> Marriage, divorce and manumission of slaves are alike in their seriousness, and joking about them is [tantamount to] seriousness. All of these things are therefore binding for the mentally deficient and for the one who is under guardianship provided he is not retarded (*maʿtūh*) or a prepubescent (*ṣaghīran lam yablugh*). If he is retarded, or a child (*ṣabī*), then his divorce is not binding, nor is his marriage or manumission of slaves.[55]

The Mālikī interlocutor questions why the Ḥanafīs differentiate between the mentally deficient as opposed to the prepubescent boy and the retarded (*al-maʿtūh*), because all three are classed together in Mālikī thought due to the "weakness of mind [of the mentally deficient] and [his] inability to seek his own best interest."[56] But the issue of capacity is really a side issue; at stake is that the Mālikīs disallow marriage but allow divorce for the mentally deficient person. Because the Ḥanafīs group divorce with marriage and manumission of slaves, all must go hand in hand at all times. If a mentally deficient person can marry, he can divorce and free-slaves as well. If he cannot marry, as the Mālikīs contend, then he cannot do any of the three. (Al-Shāfiʿī's opinion is also that he requires a guardian; the mentally deficient can marry, or rather can be married by his father, but cannot divorce, as we shall see.[57])

In Ḥanafī thought, because the *safīh* can marry, divorce, and free slaves, he must not be in the same class as the child and the retarded. That the child and the retarded inhabit the same class of legally powerless persons leads us to ask if there are similar links between the child and slaves.

---

53 *Al-Ḥujja*, 2:253.

54 Ibid., 255 and also 254. The hadith is referred to four times in two paragraphs.

55 Ibid., 255–256.

56 Ibid., 256.

57 See pp. 132–133 below.

Legal Capacity of Slaves

Al-Shaybānī does not seem to emphasize, as will al-Shāfiʿī, a correlation between the legal capacity of slaves and masters, on the one hand, and women and guardians, on the other. Still, he juxtaposes remarks on marriage and slaves with remarks on women in back-to-back chapters of the *Ḥujja*. Abū Ḥanīfa disallowed the slave from marrying without his master's permission, and the Ḥanafīs took this view to mean that the couple in question should be separated, their marriage annulled.[58] Al-Shaybānī's remarks on this point are immediately followed by the section entitled, "the chapter on a woman marrying someone unsuitable (*ghayr kufuʾ*) without her guardian's permission."

> Said Muḥammad, "Abū Ḥanīfa informed us regarding the woman who marries someone who is not suitable without the permission of her guardian, and then the woman wants to reverse (*tanqaḍ*) that before her guardian arrives. This is not her right until the guardian arrives and either reverses or allows [the marriage]."[59]

The passage is intriguing. It is apparent that the woman has the authority to marry of her own accord someone "who is suitable." To reverse a marriage to someone who is not suitable, however, she requires permission. Suitability, again, is a term which is underdetermined (at best) for legal purposes.[60] Al-Shaybānī, for example, allows for compulsion in marriages between slaves and free persons, and includes an entire chapter on the subject. For al-Shaybānī, it is clear that slavery does not obviate suitability, even for a free woman.[61] His thoughts here are considerably different with regard to slaves than al-Shāfiʿī's.

58 *Al-Ḥujja*, 2:294–5. The editor here provides several reports to the effect that the slave in question would be considered an adulterer (fn. 2).

59 Ibid., 297.

60 Although in *Al-Ḥujja* al-Shaybānī does not explain who is suitable for whom, there is a passage in *al-Jāmiʿ al-ṣaghīr* which reads, with an isnād to Abū Ḥanīfa: "Quraysh are suitable for each other, and the Arabs are suitable for each other. Whoever has two Muslim parents is counted among the *mawālī* (clients), and they are suitable for them. Suitability is immaterial if he is unable to pay a dower or maintenance (*wa lā yakūn kufūan fī shayʾ in lam yajid mahran wa lā nafaqa*)" (140–141).

61 See also *al-Jāmiʿ al-ṣaghīr*, 140. See also, *Ikhtilāf Abī Ḥanīfa wa ibn Abī Laylā*, pp. 181–183. Ibn Abī Laylā averred that she had no right to rescission. Abū Yūsuf relates that part of Ibn Abī Laylā's argument hinged on the idea that Barīra's husband was a slave, while Abū Yūsuf cites ʿĀʾisha as saying he was free. Either way, Abū Ḥanīfa's response was that the slave woman (*amma*) owned neither herself nor her marriage, with the implication being that upon becoming free she should own both. (p. 183).

Al-Shāfiʿī allows a father to compel his prepubescent son or virgin daughter; however, the marriage must be with an equal, and slaves are explicitly disallowed.[62] Says al-Shaybānī:

> Abū Ḥanīfa said that "There is nothing wrong (*lā baʾs*) with a man marrying his slave woman to his son and his daughter to his slave if they (i.e., the free persons in such matches) consent to that [and] if they are mature. And if they are prepubescent, it is binding and they have no right to rescission upon maturity."[63]

Al-Shaybānī notes that the Medinans disallow this, but he demands to know the basis of their decision, and apparently believes it to be baseless.[64] Further, the son can marry a slave woman of a man other than his father; therefore, there is no reason why he cannot marry the slave woman of the father. "And if it is all right for a man to marry his daughter to another man's slave (with his master's permission), so it should be all right for him to marry his [own] slave to his daughter."[65]

Thus we see that, while al-Shaybānī may have been more accepting of marriages between slave and free, he still reports that Abū Ḥanīfa affirmed the power of the father, the powerlessness of the child vis-à-vis the father, and the powerlessness of the slave vis-à-vis his master. This view is apparently due to the fact that the slave (through emancipation), like the child (through pubescence), may go from being powerless to possessing full legal capacity.

Legal Capacity of Virgins

The Ḥanafīs believe it is possible for a woman to attain capacity while yet a virgin, a stance which differentiates them from the Mālikīs and, later, the Shāfiʿīs. Al-Shaybānī is dismissive of the Mālikī stance that an adult woman cannot have a mature mind. Financial matters are the principle sphere of conduct to which marriage is analogized.

> Abū Ḥanīfa has said in regard to the virgin who has reached pubescence (*qad balaghat mablagh al-nisāʾ*) and whose mind has matured (*ijtamaʿ la-hā ʿaqluhā*): "Whatever she does with regard to her assets is binding."

62 *Al-Umm*, 6:49.

63 *Al-Ḥujja*, 156–157.

64 Ibid.

65 Ibid., 157–158.

Al-Shaybānī notes the Mālikī position that the virgin is only allowed her own money when she has lived in her marital home and (thereby) shown evidence that she can cope with financial matters. He shows the Mālikī position as being that such a state can be presumed after one year.[66] Al-Shaybānī's response is caustic, and reveals his impressions of the dynamics of married life at the time:

> And how could you say this when a virgin could have been in her father's house for fifty years or more, mature of mind, attuned (*baṣīra*) to all that she should do and forego? Is not some authority allowed to one like this before marrying and being in a consummated marriage? Perhaps this virgin who marries is smarter than her father and more attuned to matters, and perhaps the father made no decision without her! So how could all that she did before entering her husband's house be rendered void? What if she entered her husband's house and stayed with him a year or two years and he does not have sex with her (*lā yaṣilu ilayhā*) and she remains a virgin. Does she gain authority [over her assets] (*a-yajūzu amruhā*)?
>
> If you reply, "It is permissible for her [to control her assets]," then on what basis is it permissible? Is it via the contracting of the marriage? There was marriage before consummation. Is it via her entry into his house? They replied, "The woman, if she enters her husband's house, she performs what she does [i.e. In the way of tending to hearth and home] between her and her husband out of love and familiarity (*al-mawadda wa al-ulfa*), and it is not permissible for her to do that until she has stayed in her [marital] house."
>
> The response to this is, "We have seen what you have said, and we have seen the way women are with their husbands if they have children and stay for a prolonged period of time. They exert more effort than those before them [i.e., those who are in the pre-child-rearing phases of marriage]. She who has not given birth from her husband lives in fear of his divorcing her. If she gives birth, she is assured, and at that point exerts more effort (*abdhal*) than the other [i.e., more than a childless woman]. This is a matter we have come to know with regard to [women]. If you consider these things to be baseless due to your description of [a woman's motivation being based on] "love and familiarity," and the situation here

66 *Al-Ḥujja*, 2:282. The actual wording in the *Muwaṭṭa'* does not mention a specific amount of time. "Mālik said, 'The virgin has no authorization over her assets (*laysa lil-bikr jawāz fī mālihā*) until she has entered her [marital] home and her condition (*ḥālihā*) is known'" (*Muwaṭṭa'*, 2:53).

> is what we have described to you, and this is what our women are known for, then it must be that the rule is different for our women than yours! This matter is all nonsense, and it is permissible for a woman to have authority [over her finances] if she becomes mentally mature (*idhā ʿaqalat*) and matures (*balaghat*) and is of sound opinion (*ijtamaʿa la-hā raʾī*).[67]

Al-Shaybānī here is dismissing the Mālikī stance outright, questioning its basis. Still, he does not necessarily empower jurists to take an alternative stance. For example, the attainment of mature judgment is not defined in any practicable way.[68] Further, the relevance of "virginity" as a classification is not evident to al-Shaybānī if a woman could acquire the experience necessary to run a household without sexual activity. Al-Shaybānī emphasizes the peculiarities of the Mālikī classification of virgin and non-virgin, and is willing to declare outright that not only is it possible for a woman to tend to her own finances, it is likewise possible that she could advise, and be deemed smarter than, her own father. This in itself is a direct challenge to Mālikī thought and the majority of even later Ḥanafī thought on the capacity of females.[69]

This same line of reasoning that we saw above in regard to the capacity of virgins appears in the chapter "on the man who wants to contract marriage for his virgin daughter, so she swears to free her slaves or donate all of her money." Al-Shaybānī is clear that the virgin cannot be married except with her consent, and he mentions and excoriates the Mālikī opinion with regard to the virgin's ability (or disability) to see to her own finances. He ends this chapter as follows: "Her freeing of slaves, her selling and buying, and her donations to charity are all allowed if she has reached pubescence and attained mature judgment [(ʿ*aqalat*)] and levelheadedness is detected in her [(*ūnisa minhā al-rushd*; referring to Q4:6)]. Women are in this regard exactly like the boy who has reached pubescence and in whom levelheadedness is detected."[70]

The relationship between financial power and marital capacity is further delineated in the following question posed by al-Shaybānī: "How could it be binding for a father to contract marriage for his mature virgin daughter? If he were to sell and buy [in her name] it would not be without her consent!"[71]

---

67 Ibid.

68 Recall the exegesis of al-Thaʿlabī offering practical methods for measuring "*rushd*" in both boys and girls. See pp. 46–47 in Chapter One, above.

69 See al-Marghinānī, *al-Hidāya*, 3:31.

70 *Al-Ḥujja*, 2:146.

71 Ibid., 2:79.

The Mālikī response to this is that the virgin may speak with regard to commerce; her silence in this case is not her permission; rather "her consent is only via speech."[72] Al-Shaybānī responds that it is "your scholar Mālik" who passed on to him the *ayyim/bikr* report. "So if the virgin was not [in fact] meant to be asked for her permission, it would not have been said that her silence is her permission." Permission still exists; it exists to be given or denied. That the permission can take the form of silence does not make it any less of a necessary element in the construction of a valid contract on her behalf.

Finally, in addition to what we have gleaned of his thought on the intertwined nature of financial authority and marital capacity, an observation must be made about al-Shaybānī's characterization of marriage in the example given above about the fearful new wife. Here we find that the "fear" experienced by a new wife before pregnancy affects how one evaluates the role of sex in marriage and the definition of marriage itself; al-Shaybānī seems to be depicting all marriages as temporary if no pregnancy results. As we will see with al-Shāfiʿī, "pleasure" is deemed to be the primary motivating factor in a man's marriage. With al-Shaybānī, although the issue of pleasure may be considered to have motivated the marriage, it is apparent that lack of children can spur divorce and cause concerns about "pleasure" to be cast aside. The wife, in this case, is depicted as eminently replaceable.

Sex, Maintenance, and Sexual Maturity

Al-Shaybānī explains Abū Ḥanīfa's positions concerning a pubescent female marrying a prepubescent male as follows: The former deserves maintenance because the withholding [of sexual activity] is from the groom and not from the bride. Alternatively, if a prepubescent girl who cannot tolerate sex is married by an adult male, she does not deserve maintenance until maturity (*ḥattā tablugh*) for the withholding [of sexual intercourse] is from her and not from him.[73]

Al-Shaybānī considers the Mālikī position to be absurd:

> How could the maintenance be voided[74] when the withholding is from his side? Have you considered the insane man who marries a woman and she consents to reside with him (*fa-raḍiyat bi-l-maqām maʿhu*), does she not receive maintenance although he does not perform sex upon her?

72 Ibid.

73 *Al-Ḥujja*, 2:279–280.

74 This is perhaps to what Saḥnūn was referring when he posited that the marrying pubescent female would have understood the prepubescent male's inabilities at the time of the contracting of the marriage, and therefore must still wait.

> Have you considered the man who agrees to a certain maintenance payment for his wife each month and then is imprisoned or flees from her or from his debts; is her maintenance then voided, although he is the one who caused that and made it happen or it happened to him? That does not void maintenance. If she is the one who is a little girl (*al-jāriya*), she does not receive maintenance, and also if she is prepubescent and has not reached the age of consummation. And so we were told by Abū Ḥanīfa from Ḥammād from Ibrāhīm[75] with regard to the man who marries a woman and does not cohabit with her (*wa lā yabnī bi-hā*):[76] if the withholding is from his side, he must pay maintenance.[77]

Of most interest is the semantic line that al-Shaybānī draws between the little girl (*al-jāriya*) and the prepubescent who has not reached the age of sexual intercourse (*al-ṣaghīra allatī lam tablugh al-jimāʿ*).[78] It is possible, because al-Shaybānī uses the term *jāriya* later in the *Ḥujja* to mean "newborn baby girl," to assume that he means the same here, or at least the very young girl.[79] Again, the ages in question are left undefined, as is the case throughout the *fiqh* on this subject.

What is important here is that the inability to engage in sexual intercourse clearly means that there is no maintenance due. Curiously, the lack of sexual intercourse is not a bar to the wife's inheritance; some jurists were willing to act on the assumption that the marriage would eventually have been consummated in order to allow the wife full inheritance, an assumption they were not willing to engage in in order to justify present maintenance for eventual sex. Abū Ḥanīfa held the opinion that upon the death of a husband who has not yet consummated the marriage and has not given his wife a dower, the wife merits

---

75 Ibrāhīm al-Nakhaʿī, d. *ca.* 96/717, major early Kufan scholar known for having transmitted from ʿAbd Allāh ibn Masʿūd, Anas ibn Malik and ʿĀʾisha . Lecomte, G. "al-Nakhaʿī, Ibrāhīm b. Yazīd, al-Kūfī, Abū ʿImrān." *EI2*.

76 The text includes the word *la-hā* before *bi-hā*, which strikes us as being possibly corrupt; no logical referent for *la-hā* emerges from context.

77 *Al-Ḥujja*, 2:282.

78 Ibid., 281–282.

79 Al-Shaybānī uses the above-discussed story of Qudāma ibn Maẓʿūn to argue that sick men and women may still marry. Al-Zubayr (ibn al-ʿAwwām) visited Qudāma ibn Maẓʿūn [in his sickness] and, while he was there, al-Zubayr was given the news of the birth of a baby girl (*bushshira al-Zubayr bi-jāriya*). Qudāma said, "Marry me to her!" Al-Zubayr replied, "And what would you do with a little girl (*jāriya ṣaghīra*) while you are in this condition?!" So he said, "If I survive, she is the daughter of al-Zubayr [i.e., a good catch], and if I die, she will be the most-beloved of my beneficiaries (*aḥabbu man warathanī*)." (*Al-Ḥujja*, 2:290).

both the dower and inheritance and has to undergo the waiting period.[80] This is very nearly in line with the Mālikī practice of stipulating a waiting period for unconsummated marriages and allowing the wife to inherit; the only difference lies in the Mālikī refusal to issue the dower.

Al-Shaybānī feels strongly that an unconsummated marriage is technically incomplete. "How can one reach inheritance without the [condition] of dower? How can she sit for a waiting period without having received her dower? There should be no inheritance or waiting period unless the dower [has been transferred to the woman] before that."[81]

The reports that al-Shaybānī adduces collectively support the idea that the bride in an unconsummated marriage that ends in the husband's death receives in full her stipulated dower (or that which women of her status receive).[82] We assume, although it is not stated directly, that the reason the Ḥanafīs take this position is the fact that this promised portion (due solely to the wife) should not technically be part of the larger pool of the husband's assets which are distributed among all of his heirs; the attainment of both dower and inheritance assures her a greater financial benefit upon his death.

How does this reasoning mesh with the above-discussed legal stipulations that maintenance is contingent upon sexual availability, and indeed that the dower itself is part of a larger legal regulation of such sexual availability in exchange for financial support? It is this connection which seems to be lacking in al-Shaybānī's arguments. It seems almost as if the payment of the dower is only to technically justify the inheritance. There can be no inheritance without the dower having first been paid. Therefore the dower *must* be paid before inheritance is distributed. The argument dissociates the underlying reason for the dower with the actual sexual act.

This section has noted contrasting legal approaches to the monies due (or not due) to a wife upon a husband's death where there has been no consummation and thus no payment of maintenance. Death prior to consummation and inability to provide sex due to underdevelopment are similar in that the female is not yet able to render herself sexually available due to circumstances beyond her control. But although al-Shaybānī is willing to assume, in order to allow a wife to inherit fully, that the marriage would eventually have been consummated had not the husband died, he does not seem willing to assume eventual consummation in order to justify maintenance payments for a sexually unavailable bride. In the latter case, the definition of marriage as sexual

80 *Al-Ḥujja*, 2:192.

81 Ibid.

82 Ibid., pp. 192–197.

union is used to prevent the wife from receiving maintenance. In the case of a husband's death before consummation, the technical aspect of dower being paid upon consummation is overridden by the concern of allowing the bride to be included in the pool of inheritors.[83]

Rescission

For reasons which apparently stem from disagreement with the Mālikī position, al-Shaybānī's focus on the question of *ʿidda* is limited to a discussion of the *ʿidda* following a death and not a repudiation. Al-Shaybānī gives far more attention to the issue of rescission.

As we have seen, the most remarkable feature of Ḥanafī thought on rescission is that there is no right of rescission upon pubescence for minors married by their fathers. Prepubescents married by anyone other than the father are typically allowed that right, although the *fiqh* literature seems to indicate that Abū Yūsuf would deny them the ability to rescind no matter who contracted the marriage for them.[84]

But there is a more complex tale to be told on this subject, and it is to be found in a section of the *Ḥujja* pertaining to the rights of slaves. With regard to capacity and rescission, we find in al-Shaybānī the story of Barīra, a slave woman who, after being freed and allowed to choose whether or not to remain with her husband, canceled the marriage herself. We will also encounter in al-Shāfiʿī's *Umm* the story of Barīra, coupled with many insistences that she was married to a slave. Here, though, al-Shaybanī understands this anecdote distinctly from al-Shāfiʿī and indeed from the Mālikīs. The Mālikīs hold that if Barīra's husband had been free she could not have exercised her right to rescind. Al-Shaybānī argues strenuously against this position.

> And how could that be [that she could not rescind] if she were married to a free man?
>
> They respond, "Because we have granted [her] the right to rescind [only] if she is married to a slave; as for the free man, she would have become free like him and become without any preferential status (*lā faḍl lahā*) over him and [therefore] without a right to rescission.
>
> The response to them is, "The right of rescission was not made mandatory for the freed slave woman on the basis you are assuming, but

83 Although al-Shaybānī does not expressly articulate this justification, the reasoning behind this may lie in the Ḥanafī acceptance of the Qudāma ibn Maẓʿūn report, referenced above, in which it was stipulated that the newborn daughter of Ibn al-Zubayr would, as his bride, have inherited from Qudāma upon his death.

84 See, for example, *al-Jāmiʿ al-ṣaghīr*, 138–139.

> rather the right to rescind became mandatory because she was married when the authority to marry her off belonged to someone else. Thus if she despised or consented to the marriage, this was of no regard because she was a slave woman, and someone other than her was forcing her [to marry]. Thus inasmuch as the authority belonged to someone other than her, namely her master (*al-mawlā*), and if she despised [the union], no regard was given to her protest and the marriage was deemed licit. Then she was freed, the authority became hers, and [it became] mandatory [to grant her] the right to rescind. It did not become mandatory due to the condition of the husband, [even if he had been][85] born free of a free man, in light of what came with regard to this in the reports that the husband of Barīra (whom God's Messenger gave the right to rescind) was a free man, the client of the family of Abū Aḥmad.[86]

This passage tells us a great deal. By arguing that Barīra's right to rescind emanates from her acquisition of capacity and not from the status of her husband, free or slave, al-Shaybānī effectively declares that compelled marriages are potentially provisional. It is also important to note that no mention is made of consummation as a bar to rescission. When we encounter this topic in al-Shāfiʿī's *Umm*, both of these issues will prove contentious. In particular, the implications for the prepubescent who, like the slave, was compelled when he or she did not possess capacity, do not escape al-Shāfiʿī. It is perhaps for this reason that al-Shāfiʿī, as we will see, argues so adamantly against an attainment of capacity as being the *ratio legis* for Barīra's choice, rather than a lack of *kafāʿa* resulting from her change of status which elevated her socially and thus rendered her husband "unsuitable."

Conclusion

Al-Shaybānī's explorations of marriage in the *Ḥujja* evidence a certain haphazard application of notions of capacity and an ambivalence toward the status of slaves and of women vis-à-vis their owners and guardians respectively. It would seem that the primary lacuna in al-Shaybānī's thought (which al-Shāfiʿī will later note and fight) is his willingness to allow a slave to rescind based on her lack of capacity at the time of marriage, but a concomitant unwillingness to allow such a right for a young woman under her father's control.

Of particular interest is the fact that one of the reports affirming the practice of prepubescent marriage is also a report affirming the legal capacity of

85 The brackets contain Kīlānī's editorial suggestion to render the sentence sensical (fn. 3, p. 313).

86 *Al-Ḥujja*, 2:310–316.

mothers to contract marriages, even for their sons. The role of women in the marriage contract has, in al-Shaybānī's jurisprudence, far-reaching implications for prepubescents of either sex, making his discussion one about the rights of children rather than solely about the rights of female children. We have not found any later jurists who allow mothers to contract for their prepubescent sons, indicating that this cultural practice fell out of use altogether. The ongoing question of this project is why there was no concomitant change in the habit of contracting marriage for the prepubescent daughter.[87]

Above all we can observe in these writings the profound disagreements between the early Ḥanafīs and Mālikīs. That they were deemed to have come together on the rights of a father to compel a prepubescent daughter to marry ignores the morass of issues upon which they disagreed, most importantly with regard to the capacity and ability of a female. In two places in *al-Ḥujja* we encounter al-Shaybānī arguing for a woman's right to control her own assets; he goes so far as to envision a woman whose acumen (and thus authority) with regard to assets could replace or surpass that of her father. In another, he insists that it is her authority over her assets which obviates her father's power to compel her marriage. He notes and protests against the Mālikī classification of women into virgins and non-virgins, replacing it with a notion of becoming mentally and emotionally mature. That such a state remains also poorly delineated, however, may well indicate the shortcomings of both systems of classification.

We see that al-Shaybānī is uncompromising in this regard on behalf of the pubescent virgin. The prepubescent, on the other hand, is denied agency and subject to compulsion. Compelled by the father, she has no resultant right to rescind. Compelled by other relatives, she may rescind. That right to rescind, however, would depend entirely on her knowledge of the complex workings of laws pertaining to minor marriage.

Such an obvious disadvantage, however, does not compare to the disadvantages for the female under Mālikī law. This chapter has seen al-Shaybānī challenging the Mālikī position that females should be classified based on their virginity or lack thereof. The next chapter will provide a platform for elaborations of that view.

---

87 See, for example, Judith Tucker, wherein women in Ottoman Turkey could still contract marriages for orphan daughters. "Questions of Consent: Contracting a Marriage in Ottoman Syria and Palestine," in *The Islamic Marriage Contract: Case Studies in Islamic Family Law*, eds. Frank Vogel and Asifa Quraishi (Cambridge: Harvard Univrsity Press, 2008), 125.

CHAPTER 4

Early Mālikī Thought

Mālik (179/795)[1] and Saḥnūn (240/854):[2] Legal Capacity through Sexual Experience

Mālikī thought as articulated by Mālik and his follower Saḥnūn reveals how compulsion was envisioned with regard to the mentally deficient and slaves and how it then extended to children. This chapter will also investigate the financial circumstances that empowered the father with regard to the lives of his children. Because of the brevity of Mālik's text on the topic of compulsion in minor marriages, and the lack of explanation offered therein, I touch upon its core materials, but rely in the main on the more expansive *Mudawwana* of Saḥnūn.

Issues of both class and virginity are inextricably tied to a woman's perceived lack of legal capacity. Generally speaking, a woman's rights over herself tended to decline relative to her increase in status, with a woman of unremarkable lineage being more capable of conferring capacity upon a random man to act as her guardian. Meanwhile, virginity was a state that conferred upon her "permanent mental deficiency,"[3] and only interaction with an unrelated male brought her into the domain of legal capacity. Curiously, the Mālikīs are hard-pressed to explain what constitutes the end of virginity, and this investigation has unearthed several intriguing legal conclusions in this respect.

Sex is deeply linked to financial issues within the Islamic marriage contract, namely the sexual exchange predicated upon the payment of dower so key to

---

1 For biographical information on Mālik ibn Anas see Schacht, J. "Mālik b. Anas." *EI2*. Note that Schacht is convinced that the majority of early sources on Mālik rely on Ibn Sa'd (d. 230/845). See also the introduction to *al-Muwaṭṭa'*, ed. Hānī al-Ḥāj (Cairo: al-Maktabah al-Tawfīqiyyah) 1:5–6. Additionally, see Sezgin, Fuat, GAS volume I: 457–484 for further primary sources on the subject.

2 For biographical information on Saḥnūn, see Ṭalbī, M, "Saḥnūn, Abū Saʿīd ʿAbd al-Salām b. Saʿīd b. Ḥabīb b. Ḥassān b. Hilāl b. Bakkār b. Rabīʿa al-Tanūkhī." *EI2*. See also, M. Talbi, *Biographies Aghlabides extraites des Madārik du Cadi ʿIyāḍ* (Tunis: 1968), 57–62, 86–136, and index. Additionally, consult ʿAzab, Muḥammad Zaynhum Muḥammad, "al-Imām Saḥnūn," (Cairo: Dār al-Fajr, 1992).

3 *ʿAlā al-sufh abadan*. This is the Mālikī ibn ʿAbd al-Barr's interpretation of Mālik's meaning when he denied the virgin "any right to her assets until she enters her own home and her status is known" (*al-Istidhkār*, 5:406–407).

 | DOI 10.1163/9789004344860_006

rendering the marital relationship valid. Mālikīs tried to reconcile this with the marriages of prepubescents whose ability to earn wages and control money were circumscribed by their status as children. Such discussions are complicated by the highly variable vocabulary attached to sexual encounters.

Overall, these texts revealed the increasingly tangled nature of issues surrounding compulsion and prepubescent marriage; in fact, the early Mālikī texts exposed new points of disjuncture at nearly every turn.

Proof Texts

Early Mālikī jurisprudential writings do not reference the story of ʿĀʾisha's marriage to the Prophet during discussions of prepubescent marriage. Rather, there is consistent reliance on both Medinan practice and the *ayyim/bikr* report related from Mālik:[4]

> *Al-ayyim aḥaqq bi-nafsihā min walīhā wa al-bikr tustaʾdhanu fī nafsihā wa-idhnuhā samāṭuhā.*
>
> The unmarried female [or, possibly, non-virgin] has more legal capacity with regard to herself than does her marriage guardian; the virgin's permission is requested with regard to herself, and her permission is her silence.[5]

The chapter on the subject of marriage and consent in the *Muwaṭṭaʾ* leads off with the above hadith, traced through Ibn ʿAbbās.[6] This is the only report that claims Prophetic origin in the whole sub-chapter entitled "Requesting Permission of the Virgin (*bikr*) and the Unmarried Female/Non-Virgin (*ayyim*) Regarding Themselves." The chapter also includes a report from ʿUmar ibn al-Khaṭṭāb[7] deeming it nonbinding for a woman to marry without the "permission

4 Both al-Shaybānī in Chapter 3, above, and al-Shāfiʿī in Chapter 5, below, accept this report from Mālik.

5 *Al-Muwaṭṭaʾ*, 2:53, *Muṣannaf* Ibn Abī Shayba, 9:46–7 ¶¶16217–8; *Muṣannaf* ʿAbd al-Razzāq, 6:114 ¶10320; *al-Umm*, 6:46; *al-Ishrāf*, 1:24.

6 The chain is Mālik > ʿAbd Allāh ibn al-Faḍl > Nāfiʿ ibn Jubayr ibn Muṭʿam > ʿAbd Allāh ibn ʿAbbās .

7 It is to be noted that al-Shāfiʿī is able to ground this idea as a Prophetic saying (*al-Umm*, 6:31–35) although the Mālikīs can only take it back to ʿUmar ibn al-Khaṭṭāb; al-Shāfiʿī insists as well on an interpretation of Q2:232 that renders its address to marriage guardians. Later, the title of al-Shāfiʿī's chapter "No Marriage without a Guardian" seems to have become a hadith itself, with the likes of the Shāfiʿī cum Ḥanafī al-Ṭaḥāwī spending the better part of a chapter disputing both it and al-Shāfiʿī's interpretation of 2:232, (*Maʿani al-athār*, 2:364–371).

of her marriage guardian, an authority figure (*dhū raʾy*) from her family, or the ruler." Finally we encounter the following:

> It had reached [Mālik] (*balaghahu*) that al-Qāsim ibn Muḥammad[8] and Sālim ibn ʿAbd Allāh[9] were marrying off their virgin daughters without consulting them (*wa-lā yastaʾmirānihinna*). Mālik said, 'And that it is the practice in our view (*ʿindinā*) with regard to virgins.[10]

It is not evident that he is considering in this context prepubescent females or older women, or whether he considers such an action to be contradictory to the content of the *ayyim/bikr* hadith just discussed in the sub-chapter. It is only apparent that Mālik is sure that sexual experience confers legal capacity. As is self-evident, this report is grounded in the practice of the Successor-era scholars adduced, but Mālik adds to it his affirmation of the practice, without offering any substantive elaboration. Further information is provided by the famed Mālikī Saḥnūn.

It is not unlikely that Saḥnūn would have affirmed the consensus-writing projects of a near-contemporary like al-Marwazī or the next generation of writers like Ibn al-Mundhir and al-Ṭaḥāwī; he was a relentless consolidator of proto-Sunni opinions, intent on eliminating innovation.[11] Nevertheless, in his writings on compulsion in the marriages of prepubescents in the *Mudawwana*,[12] consensus is not a term that appears even once. Contrast this with the writings of the eleventh-century Mālikī Ibn ʿAbd al-Barr, who uses the term Ijmāʿ no less than eight times in his exposition on this chapter of the *Muwaṭṭaʾ*.[13]

8 Al-Qāsim ibn Muḥammad ibn Abī Bakr, d. 108/726.

9 Sālim ibn ʿAbd Allāh ibn ʿUmar, known as the muftī of Medina, died in 106 or 108/724 or 726.

10 *Muwaṭṭa*', 2:53.

11 Talbi, M., "Saḥnūn", in: Encyclopaedia of Islam, Second Edition, Edited by: P. Bearman, Th. Bianquis, C.E. Bosworth, E. van Donzel, W.P. Heinrichs. Consulted online on 28 July 2016 http://proxy.library.upenn.edu:2146/10.1163/1573-3912_islam_SIM_6476, last accessed 7/28/16.

12 For insights into the textual history of the *Mudawwana*, see Calder, Norman, *Studies in Early Muslim Jurisprudence* (Oxford, Clarendon Press, 1993). The primary articulator of Mālik's thought in the *Mudawwana* is Ibn al-Qāsim. Thus Saḥnūn acts as both compiler of the opinions of Ibn al-Qāsim and interpolator of their import; often the line between the two roles is not altogether evident.

13 See Ibn ʿAbd al-Barr, *Kitāb al-Istidhkār*, 5:386–407.

The Walī Mujbir

The primary Prophetic reports which appear with relation to this subject are, first and foremost, the *ayyim/bikr* hadith, followed by various incarnations of reports which insist on the presence of a *walī*, roughly paralleling the structure provided in the *Muwaṭṭa'*. Saḥnūn's basis for allowing compulsion seems located entirely in practice. To wit:

> **The Chapter on a Father's Contracting a Marriage for his Daughter without her Consent:**
>
> "Do you think if [a potential bride] refuses men, man after man, that she can be compelled to marry (*a-tujbar 'alā al-nikāḥ*) or not?" [Ibn al-Qāsim] responded, "No one can be compelled to marry according to Mālik, and no one can compel anyone to marry according to Mālik, except the father with regard to his virgin daughter or his prepubescent son (*ibnuhu al-ṣaghīr*) or with regard to his female slave or his male slave or the guardian with regard to the male orphan in his charge." [He continued,] "When I was with Mālik, a man asked him: 'I have a niece who is a virgin and mentally deficient (*safīha*),[14] and I wanted to marry her to someone who would keep her chaste and care for her, and she refused.' Mālik said, 'She cannot be married without her consent.' The man repeated, 'She is mentally deficient.' Mālik replied, 'Even if she is mentally deficient, he cannot contract her marriage without her consent.'[15]

This passage is filled with points which allow us to reach certain conclusions about Mālikī *fiqh* generally and Saḥnūn's legal thought specifically. The first of these is the consideration of legal capacity with regard to marriage and the role of the father. A father can compel his virgin daughter; we can conclude based on this that virginity renders a female legally incapable, regardless of age.[16] A father can compel his prepubescent son; thus we can conclude that legal capacity for boys stems from pubescence.[17] It is significant that the Mālikīs'

14 For discussion of this choice of wording, see p. 91 n. 51.

15 *Mudawwana*, 2:155.

16 Mohammed Fadel refers to this as a "fundamental mistake of law in the Mālikī treatment of a guardian's powers over a female ward who has attained physical maturity ..." See "Guardian's Role in Marriage Contract," p. 11.

17 There is a later section entitled, "The Chapter on the Nocturnal Emission of a boy (*bāb fī iḥtilām al-ghulām*)." In it we find the question, "Is it your opinion that a father can prevent a boy who has had a nocturnal emission from going wherever he wants (*yadhhab ḥaythu*

views, or at least the Ḥanafī perception of them, are also framed with reference to financial obligations. Al-Shaybānī quotes the Mālikī position as being that fathers (and only fathers) can contract marriages for children because the father pays the maintenance for the son "until he grows up; and, if she is a woman (*in kānat imraʾa*), [he pays the maintenance for her] until she marries. And the son is bound to maintain his father if his father is in need. And no one is bound to maintain the two of them besides him [the father], and they are not bound to maintain anyone but him."[18]

It is the father's financial commitment to his children which places them in a state of *ilzām*, or being bound to defer to him. It is this state which obviates their later choice to endorse or repudiate the marriage in which they had no say. If other than the father has contracted the marriage, and the now-mature child chooses to refuse it, the resulting separation is deemed a single divorce.

Legal Capacity of Slaves and Orphans

As for slaves, regardless of virginity, pubescence, or gender, the master may compel their marriage. This is unless the term *ama* is considered applicable only to mature slave women (as opposed to the *jāriya*) and *ʿabd* applies only to mature males (as opposed to the *ghulām*). Further research is necessary on a far wider scale to attempt to delineate when these terms meant exactly what they meant. In any case, *ghulām* in the *Mudawwana* seems to mean "boy" generally and does not strictly have slave connotations. Here, *ṣabī* would also seem to mean young slave (rather than "young boy" or "child"). It is interesting to note that Saḥnūn makes a comparison between the master's power over the slave and that of the *waṣī* (executor). "If a young slave has been freed by a man who had married him off as a boy, does the marriage contracted by his master when he (the slave) was a young boy remain valid?" The response is that his liberation does not obviate the legitimacy of the marriage. For females, however, the same is not true. The analogy comes in that a *ghulām* (young boy) *can* be married off by an executor, while a young girl cannot be so married.[19]

Further discussion of slaves comes with the right of rescission allowed to a newly-freed woman who wishes to exit her union. Her right to rescind, as presented in the *Muwaṭṭa*ʾ in the form of a prophetic hadith,[20] is not predicated on having been married to a slave, although the interpretations included

---

*shā*ʾ)." Only a state of mental deficiency (*sufh*) can allow a father to consider preventing him. (*Mudawwana*, 2:155.).

18 *Al-Ḥujja*, 2:88.

19 *Mudawwana*, 2:173.

20 *Al-Muwaṭṭa*ʾ, Ch. 10, para 25, p. 74.

are explicit about this. Further, if he has "touched her," her right to rescind is obviated.[21]

The power to compel is also extended to a guardian in charge of an orphan (*yatīm*). Curiously, the orphan's gender is non-specific; the word *yatīm* could certainly include both males and females. However, the majority of the later debates revolve around the female orphan, and indeed the proof text adduced later in the *Mudawwana* itself mentions female orphans.[22] Because the latter text is specific with regard to the orphan girl's ability to protest any marriage, Saḥnūn can only be referring to a rule dictating that orphaned boys can be compelled into marriage.

In support of the orphaned girl's ability to refuse marriage, we turn to the final paragraph in the chapter on permission ("Regarding the Consent of the Virgin and the Non-Virgin"). After mentioning the hadith regarding the orphan girls, Saḥnūn relates the following from Ibn Wahb (d. 197/813):

> Scholars have informed me that ʿUmar ibn ʿAbd al-ʿAzīz and Ibn Shihāb said that the Messenger of God said, "Every orphan girl is to be consulted concerning herself [i.e. entering into marriage], and as long as she refuses, it is not valid for her, and as long as she remains silent and assents, it is valid for her, and that [silence] is her permission." (He continued,) And Mālik said the orphan girl requires a guardian until she reaches maturity (*ḥattā tablugh*) and she cannot be deprived of her right to rescission and capacity. It [the marriage] is not valid for her until she gives her permission based on the hadith that came from the Messenger of God regarding that.

The passage ends with an opinion from Wakīʿ (d. 197/812)[23] that originated from Shurayḥ (d. circa 80/700)[24] who insisted that "The orphan girl should be

---

21 Ibid., pp. 74–75.

22 "The orphan girl (*al-yatīma*) is consulted with regard to herself, and if she remains silent, this is her permission, and if she refuses, it is not considered licit for her." (*Mudawwana*, 2:159) There is no mention of the orphan in the *Muwaṭṭa*ʾ; it is possible that the Ḥanafī preoccupation with the orphan (see the chapter on Shaybānī, above) elicits later Mālikī discussions such as this one.

23 A scholar of legendary memory, said never to have been seen holding a book, Wakīʿ ibn al-Jarrāḥ was a well-known ascetic and *muḥaddith* who transmitted from al-Awzāʿī and Mālik. Khoury, R.G. "Wakīʿb. al-Djarrāḥ b. Malīḥal-Ruʾāsī, Abū Sufyān." *EI2*.

24 Shurayḥ ibn al-Ḥārith was a famed judge in the Umayyad period, possibly legendary; his traditions are sometimes deemed spurious, although given some credence by Sezgin

consulted regarding herself, and if she expresses anger or vexation (*maʿaḍat*) she is not to be married, and if she is silent, this is her permission."[25]

It seems to be Saḥnūn himself who adds the following observation:

> The evidence that the orphan girl [in question] can only be pubescent is that she is consulted with regard to herself. This is because the one who has not yet reached pubescence possesses no permission, so how could permission be requested of one who has no permission to give?[26]

This observation raises several questions. First, is Saḥnūn's assertion that the *prepubescent* orphan girl is marriageable yet need not be consulted? If that is the case, it would contradict several points from the above passage. Not least of those points is the Prophetic hadith that *all* orphan girls must be consulted. Another is that Saḥnūn has relayed Mālik's view that no orphan girl with a guardian can be married until she reaches maturity. Neither of the hadiths adduced gives any indication that there is an age to be considered with regard to the orphan girl; nor, for that matter, the status of her virginity. Thus our second question with regard to Saḥnūn's assertion: why does he differentiate between classes of orphan girls when no such differentiation was made in the exchange between Mālik and Ibn al-Qāsim? Both Ibn al-Mundhir and Ibn ʿAbd al-Barr will later echo these sentiments in their writings on this subject.

Legal Capacity of Virgins and Non-Virgins

We enter now into the marrow of Saḥnūn's discussion entitled, "With Regard to the Consent of the Virgin and the Non-Virgin."

First, it is argued that the silence of the virgin constitutes her consent, a point relayed by Mālik himself. Saḥnūn adds that many Mālikīs had indicated that the binding nature of the virgin's silence was predicated upon her knowledge of its implications.[27] He insists repeatedly that, based on this *ayyim/bikr* text it is impossible for the guardian of a *thayyib* to deem her silence as consent

and Motzki. Kohlberg, E. "Shurayḥ b. al-Ḥārith (or b. Shuraḥbīl) b. Ḳays, Abū Umayya al-Kindī." *EI2*.

25 *Mudawwana* 2:159.

26 Ibid.

27 Note that this is an important facet of Ibn al-Mundhir's thought on the subject; he seems to be the only one claiming consensus about this point, however. See Chapter 6 below, and *Mudawwana*, 2:157.

to an offer of marriage. The same silence is the indication of consent for the virgin.[28]

However, he is equally insistent that the father has the power to marry off a virgin daughter without her consent, a power he claims was exercised by the Prophet himself. Saḥnūn relies for proof upon Ibn Wahb:[29] "Ibn Wahb said, 'al-Sarī ibn Yaḥyā reported to me that al-Ḥaṣan al-Baṣrī told him that the Messenger of God married his two daughters to 'Uthmān ibn 'Affān and did not consult the two of them.'"[30] Ibn Wahb is a further source for an axiom related by Yaḥyā ibn Sa'īd:[31] "Only a father can compel marriage; he can contract marriage for his daughter if she is a virgin."[32] Such a pattern of reliance upon sources other than the Prophet for this practice is not peculiar. This is exactly the way that the *Muwaṭṭa'* itself is constructed. The primary propagators of the doctrine of forced marriage of virgins are al-Qāsim ibn Muḥammad and Sālim ibn 'Abd Allāh, as previously discussed.[33]

And yet, other opinions exist suggesting that virginity is not the only factor which grants a father the ability to compel. A father can compel his sexually-experienced daughter if he fears "scandal" with regard to her.[34] This point adds an entirely new dimension to the role of the father in Mālikī thought as expressed by Saḥnūn; the mechanisms to determine whether or not a non-virgin daughter has the potential to become embroiled in scandal are left undefined. Additionally, we note that Saḥnūn says the father does not need to consider the bridal gift for the daughter; as long as there is some "benefit" for her in the marriage, this is all that need be claimed.[35] Even so, Saḥnūn relates the story

---

28 *Mudawwana*, 2:157.

29 Cairene Mālikī scholar, died in 197/813. It is noteworthy given the above context that the "Book of Silence" among the only remaining papyrus fragments of his *Jāmi'*. For more information see *Le Djāmi' d'Ibn Wahb*, ed. J. David-Weill (BIFAO), Cairo 1939–48, i, XI, and J. David-Weill, *Manuscrit malékite d'Ibn Wahb*, in *Mélanges Maspéro*, Cairo 1940, iii, 177–83, and *EI2*.

30 Compare this with the reports included from the Two *Muṣannaf*s regarding the complex process of approval or disapproval of the Prophet's daughters regarding suitors. (Chapter 2, above.).

31 Died 157/774, Abū Mikhnaf Yaḥyā ibn Sa'īd is regarded as a weak traditionist. Gibb, H.A.R. "Abū Mikhnaf Lūṭ b. Yaḥyā b. Sa'īd b. Mikhnaf al-Azdī." *EI2*.

32 *Mudawwana*, 2:157.

33 *Muwaṭṭa'*, 2:53. The *Muwaṭṭa'*s final word on marrying a virgin without her permission is given as the opinion of the above two in addition to Sulaymān ibn Yasār (d. 107/726), a Medinan *faqīh*.

34 *Mudawwana*, 2:156.

35 Ibid., 155.

of a divorced woman who protests her husband's contracting of a marriage for their "desirable" daughter to a poor man. Mālik awarded the woman a right to an opinion (*"innī arā laki fī dhālika mutakallaman"*).[36] This point would seem to be of significance given the raw material of the *Muwaṭṭa'* (the report from 'Umar that someone, gender unspecified, "possessing an opinion" from the family of the woman must give permission).[37] The emergent point, nonetheless, is that the father can contract the marriage unless there is some harm (*ḍarar*) in it, in which case he is prevented from doing so.[38] This phrase is resonant of al-Shāfiʿī's position in the *Umm*, discussed below.[39]

Legal Capacity of Females

Mālikī law is unequivocal that women cannot marry themselves off, nor can they appoint other women to marry them.[40] Legal capacity is of two types: the capacity of a woman in appointing a man to carry out her marriage (rather than the ruler or an official marriage guardian) and that evidenced by the right of the virgin and non-virgin to be consulted by the father. As for the first, it is almost non-existent in Mālikī law, with one important exception. With regard to the latter, the non-virginity of the female is the only element which can prevent a father from forcing her marriage.

The impoverished woman is the only sort of woman allowed to appoint a man other than the usual marriage guardians.[41] Mālik envisions the recently-freed slave woman, a convert to Islam, or a poor village woman (*al-mar'a al-miskīna takūn fī al-qarya*), and suggests that these are the sort of woman who might need help from a man of good standing. But with regard to other "women of worth (*qadr*)," Mālik is clear: "As for the notable woman, or the

36 Ibid.

37 *Muwaṭṭa'*, 2:53.

38 *Mudawwanna*, 2:155.

39 See *al-Umm*, 6:49. He is concerned that unsuitable marriages cause a diminishment in the womans' status (*naqṣ*) and "harm for her" (*ḍarar ʿalayhā*).

40 No further space can be here given to the issue of 'Ā'isha contracting marriage for the daughter of 'Abd al-Raḥman ibn Mundhir (see Chapter 6 and the lengthy arguments of al-Ṭaḥāwī on this subject), but suffice it to say that Saḥnūn attempts to dispose of the issue as best he can, by noting that Mālik would have considered the contract voidable (*fāsid*). The report is still, at this time, well-known enough not to warrant even an *isnad*, and Saḥnūn admits, "We do not know the explanation [of this report]." *Mudawwana*, 2:177.

41 Al-Shaybānī suggests that there was a Mālikī position regarding the appointing of a man by a female slave-owner to contract marriage for her slave. The Ḥanafīs do not believe that the middle-man is necessary, noting that the woman here should be able to act as guardian. See the discussion of this in Ali, *Marriage and Slavery*, 44–45.

wealthy woman, it is not binding for anyone to marry her except for a marriage guardian or the ruler,"[42] (meaning, possibly, a judge). Class matters: as with issues such as modesty requirements, the poor woman has significantly more latitude than the "woman of worth."

Saḥnūn attempts to determine what causes a virgin to become a woman in possession of herself. The transition is partly related to "experiencing what women experience" (lit. "seeing/witnessing what women see/witness:" *mushāhadat mashāhid al-nisā'*). This phrase is left almost totally undefined, despite its importance in qualifying the categorization of women. What do women see? Perhaps it means anything from seeing a naked man to experiencing an orgasm or even simply menstruating. The only hadith I found that could bear on this subject of "seeing" is in Bukhārī's *Ṣaḥīḥ*. A woman asked if she must perform full lustration after a "wet dream" (*idhā aḥtalamat*), to which the response was, "Yes, if she sees fluid (*idhā ra'at al-mā'a*)."[43]

The question is posed to Saḥnūn:

> If a father has contracted marriage for his young daughter (*al-jāriya*), and her husband dies or divorces her after she has entered his household (*ba'd mā dakhala bi-hā*),[44] and the girl says, "He did not have sex with me," and the spouse claims that he did have sex with her, does the father contract her marriage for her with her status [vis-á-vis consent] as a virgin or not?[45]

> Saḥnūn responds: "I asked Mālik about a man who marries a woman who enters his household (*dakhala bi-hā*). He lives with her (*yuqīm ma'ahā*) then he separates from her before touching her (*yufāriquhā qabl an yamassahā*) and she returns to her father. Is she of the status of a virgin with regard to her second marriage or should her father not marry her off without her consent?"

At last we arrive at an opinion attributed to Mālik:

> Mālik said: "As for the one who stayed for a long time (*ṭālat iqāmatuhā*) with her husband and experienced what women experience, this one is not marriageable without her consent, even if her husband did not

42 *Mudawwana*, 2:170.

43 *Ṣaḥīḥ al-Bukhārī* (Liechtenstein: Thesaurus Islamicus Foundation, 2000), 1:60.

44 Note that this term, dakhala bi-hā, means for al-Shāfi'ī "to consummate."

45 *Mudawwana*, 2:156.

> penetrate her. But if it is something close (*al-shay' al-qarīb*)[46] then I am of the opinion that he [the father] can [still] contract her marriage [unilaterally]."
>
> Saḥnūn insists: "So the *Sunna*[47] is …?"
>
> Mālik responds: "The *Sunna* is length of stay."

Saḥnūn then attempts to address the original question on the basis of this anecdote.

> Thus your issue here is, If she insists that he did not perform sex upon her person, but that it was something close, [her father] can still contract her marriage because she is saying, 'I am a virgin.' She is validating that the action of the father is binding for her and she is not harmed by what her husband has said with regard to having had sex with her. But if she has stayed with him for a long time, then [the father] cannot contract her marriage except with her consent, whether she has claimed to have had sex or not."[48]

Thus there are two separate issues being defined. A brief cohabitation, in which a woman claims not to have actually experienced sex (even if she *did* experience physical intimacy), does not revoke her status as virgin even if her husband claims otherwise. As an evidentiary matter, her word is accepted as presumptively correct; Saḥnūn does not suggest that any sort of test be invoked, but instead supports the female's claim. The motive behind this reasoning may be that the change in her status places her squarely within the power of the father once again, or perhaps, as we will see below, because virginity does not seem to be defined by the presence or the absence of the hymen.

A long cohabitation, however, will not sustain a claim of virginity.

Nonetheless, if there is no actual intercourse, there is another opinion that she returns to her father and is still marriageable by him without consent as a virgin irrespective of the length of cohabitation.[49] At no time does the text offer any definition as to how long a "prolonged stay" might be.

---

46 I would suggest that this means, i.e. "something very close to actual sex in the form of physical intimacy."

47 The word *sunna* here clearly refers to the practice of the day, not the practice of the Prophet, since there is no identifiable report or practice of the Prophet cited here. Note that Ibn Ḥazm blasts this position as completely unfounded. See al-*Muḥallā*, 9:460.

48 *Mudawwana*, 2:156.

49 Ibid., 155.

Further issues related to virginity, lack thereof, and capacity have to do with the money due a woman upon divorce. Mālik addresses this in the *Muwaṭṭa'* as follows:

> If a man divorces his wife before having consummated the marriage and she is a virgin, then the father renounces his right to half the bridal gift. This is valid for the husband from her father for what he has given up (*fīmā waḍa'a 'anhu*).[50]

The proof text, according to Mālik, for this passage lies in Qur'ān 2:237.

> And if you divorce them before having touched them (*min qabli an tamassūhunna*) but after having agreed on a bridal gift (*wa qad faraḍtum lahunna farīḍah*), then [give them] half of what you agreed upon unless they relinquish (*illā an ya'fūna*), or the one in whose hands is the marriage contract relinquishes (*aw ya'fūwa alladhī fī yadihi 'uqdat al-nikāḥ*). And if you relinquish (*wa-an ta'fū*), this is nearer to [being in a state of] God consciousness.

This rather benign-sounding passage turns out to have been something of a battleground for competing views about the capacity of women in marriage and their capacity with regard to their money. This is not immediately obvious from the *Muwaṭṭa'*, but by the time of Ibn 'Abd al-Barr, he is able to list many different interpretations of this verse, most of which turn on identifying the pronoun referents. His explanation helps us determine the range of thought on the subject, whereas Mālik and Saḥnūn are actually silent about the possible interpretations of this verse.

Sex, Maintenance, and Sexual Maturity

The issues surrounding marriage and virginity become even more complex when we consider the case of the prepubescent boy. Because of the financial obligations attached to the masculine role in any marriage contract, it is important to examine these. Mālik's opinion was clear: any man who cannot pay the maintenance for his wife should be forcibly separated from her.[51] Bridal gifts and maintenance are firmly intertwined with the sexual act, which is in turn intertwined with the age at which said act is possible.

50 *Muwaṭṭa'*, 2:54.

51 *Mudawwana*, 2:253.

It is a given at this point that the father can compel his prepubescent son to marry in Mālikī law. Mālik does not talk about minority and majority when he discusses the ability of a father to force his virgin daughters; age does not enter the discussion, only sexual status (*ayyim* or *bikr*). He only refers to minority when addressing the case of the prepubescent male (*al-ṣaghīr*) who has had his marriage contracted for him and still has no money; it is Mālik's opinion that the father must pay the bridal gift.[52] "That marriage," Mālik notes, "is binding (*thābit*) for the son, if he is prepubescent and under his father's guardianship."[53] Payment of the bridal gift is generally perceived to be incumbent upon the groom by virtue of any private moment spent with the bride. To wit, the sub-chapters entitled "The lowering of the curtains" in the *Muwaṭṭa'* stipulate that the bridal gift is due in full whenever a curtain is "lowered" (or, presumably, a door shut) isolating the bridegroom and the bride.[54]

The issue of prepubescence generates questions that require answers. The *Muwaṭṭa'* does not directly address the minor's ability to tolerate or perform sexual intercourse. Saḥnūn does address this issue, however, by asking what changes a lack of sexual ability might bring. He first discusses the "age of sexual intercourse" and its relationship to maintenance (*nafaqa*).

> Mālik said, "[The bridegroom] is not responsible for paying maintenance and he is also not responsible for paying the dower until she reaches the age of having sexual intercourse." Mālik continued, "And so it is for the young boy if he marries a pubescent woman, and she invites him to consummate; there is no maintenance due her from him nor can she attain her bridal gift until the boy reaches the age of intercourse."[55]

Saḥnūn then seeks a more precise delineation of the relationship between maintenance and sexual ability or inability:

> I [Saḥnūn] asked, "When does a man start paying the maintenance for his wife, when he contracts the marriage or when he consummates (*yadkhulu*)?" [Ibn al-Qāsim] replied, "Mālik said, 'If they invite him to consummate, and he does not, he must pay maintenance." I said, "What if she is prepubescent, and the sexual act is not performed upon the like of her due to her youth, so they said to him, 'Enter upon your wife or

52 Those boys who have their own assets would have the bridal gift taken from same.

53 *Muwatta'*, 2:54.

54 Ibid., 2:55.

55 *Mudawwana*, 2:254.

> maintain her (*udkhul ʿalā ahlika aw unfuq ʿalayhā*).'" [Ibn al-Qāsim] said, "Mālik said, 'He does not have to pay maintenance, nor is he bound to pay the dower until she reaches the age of sexual intercourse.'"[56]

This age is undefined in these passages for girls; it is only much later in this section that that age for a boy is defined as being the age of "emission."[57] The situation is again proposed that a boy might be able to perform intercourse before having reached the age of emission, but the position of Mālik is reaffirmed: no monies are due the woman unless the intercourse in question is intercourse that culminates in male ejaculation.[58]

Although there is no corresponding age or criterion for the female as to when sex is possible, and thus when the maintenance would begin to be paid, the interlocutor presses on:

> What if she is a prepubescent female upon the like of whom sex is not performed, and the groom wants to cohabit (*yabnī bihā*), and the prepubescent females' guardians refuse him saying, we will not allow you to do so because you cannot have sex with her (*la taqdar ʿalā jimāʿihā*)?[59]

He then notes that Mālik spoke of a man who married under the condition, imposed by the guardians, that he not cohabit with his bride for a year. Saḥnūn notes possible reasons for such an arrangement, ranging from the bride being too young to the groom being a stranger (i.e. from outside the immediate area) who might want to journey with her, while her family wants to "enjoy" her (*yastamtaʿū bihā*). It is, we are told, their prerogative to make such a condition. It is thus clear that the guardians can prevent cohabitation until such a time as she is "mature" (*ḥattā tablugh*), again, an undefined state.[60] Another anecdote describes the situation in which a man marries and leaves (*tarakahā*) his bride, i.e., with her family) for ten years or more, during which time her family did not invite him to cohabit with her or pay her maintenance.[61] In any event, while Mālik here is said to have designated the age of intercourse for a male as

56 Ibid.

57 Ibid. *Lā yulzimuhu dafʿ al-naqd ḥattā yablughu ḥadd al-jimāʿ wa huwa al-iḥtilām.*

58 Ibid., 2:255.

59 *Mudawwana*, 2:255. It seems clear that *al-binā' bihā* could have levels of meaning in this instance; cohabitation rather than consummation, hence the family's insistence that the former is not allowed because of risk of the latter.

60 Ibid.

61 Ibid.

the age of nocturnal emission, it is clear from these passages that it is only the family's opinion which prevents a prepubescent female from being given to her husband at an early age. One final anecdote supports this:

> It is said that any man who marries a young girl does not have to pay any maintenance until she comes of age and can tolerate men (*tudrik wa tuṭīq al-rijāl*); and if she comes of age, he must pay her maintenance if her family desires (*in shāʾ ahluhā*) so that he might consummate with her (*ḥattā yabtanī bihā*).[62]

Idrāk here is clearly an age preceding *bulūgh*, but due to the difficulty of legally- determining such an age, the jurists have left the responsibility entirely in the hands of the family.

Having thus witnessed a set moment for boys to come of age with regard to sexual intercourse (identical with the onset of nocturnal emission) and an ill-defined, family-designated moment for girls, we must note some further ramifications of prepubescent marriage upon the matrix of marital obligations. These emerge from discussions of several arresting legal situations, not least of which being the following subheading:

> Regarding the wife of a boy (*al-ṣabī*) who does not [yet] beget children when she appears with child.[63]

The passage here describes a question that arose regarding a boy who is capable of having sex (*yaqwā ʿalā al-jimāʿ*) but "his peers do not beget" (*mithluhu lā yūlad lahu*).[64] If his wife has a child, should the child be ascribed to the boy? The answer is that if boys of his age are not capable of begetting children, and this is known (*wa ʿurifa dhālik*), then the child is not his responsibility (*lā yulzimuhu*).[65] There is no mention of the consequences for the wife herself. Although the wife is not addressed in this case, she is addressed in a case where she is widowed. What does one do with the pregnant widow of a boy capable of an erection but not ejaculation? This woman has the *ḥadd* for adultery, the death penalty, imposed on her.[66]

62 *Mudawwana*, 2:255.

63 Ibid. 2:444.

64 See also, Motzki, *Origins*, 84, in which he discusses ʿAbd al-Razzāq's inclusion of discussions of adultery punishments for a pubescent woman and a prepubescent boy.

65 *Mudawwana*, 2:444.

66 Ibid.

Finally, in situations wherein young married boys are capable of sex but not of impregnating, the woman does not have to go through a waiting period upon divorce, nor does she take anything of her bridal gift (*lā yakūn la-hā min al-ṣadāq shay'*). Almost as an afterthought, there is added that the woman does not have to perform the major ablution (*ghusl*) after intercourse with him, unless she has experienced orgasm.[67]

This passage raises many questions. One question stems from how determinations of body-type and sexual maturity could have been made. The *Mudawwana* has already suggested that the family of the girl bears the responsibility for such a determination. It is further likely that this task would have sometimes fallen to judges in cases of financial disputes over *nafaqa* and *ṣadāq*, wherein the disputing parties would have been parents providing for minors and expert witnesses were probably local female midwives or healers.[68] It is possible to postulate, given judicial reservations with regard to lone female witnesses, a conundrum for the pregnant widow of a prepubescent boy, who would presumably offer testimony in her own defense that the boy in question could indeed ejaculate.

Most importantly, there is the issue of the lack of waiting period and the inability of the woman to claim her bridal gift. If the sex that the young boy performs is not impregnative sex, then the passage seems to suggest that it is not actually sex. No ʿidda is necessary, no money changes hands, no *ghusl* need be performed. The question then arises, is sex itself defined as penetration of the female or ejaculation[69] of the male?[70] Left unresolved in this section is the

67 Ibid.

68 See Shaham, *Expert Witness*, 87–88.

69 I found no discussions of any status-changing implications for female orgasm.

70 Some early debate was recorded on the subject of what necessitates *ghusl*. Some early ideas revolved around the notion that *ghusl* is not stipulated for the sex act that does not culminate in male ejaculation. In Muslim, this debate is "resolved" by a putative comment of ʿĀ'isha's that any genital-genital contact necessitates *ghusl*. "Abū Mūsā said, a group of *Muhājirūn* and a group of *Anṣār* differed [over *ghusl*]. The Helpers said, '*Ghusl* is not necessary unless there is ejaculation or semen (*min al-dafq aw min al-mā'*).' And the Emigrants said, 'It is if he is intimate (*idhā khālaṭa*) then *ghusl* is necessary.' Abū Mūsā said, "I will solve this for you. So I [Abū Mūsā] stood and asked to enter ʿĀ'isha's house, and permission was given me. So I said to her, 'O Mother of the Believers ... What necessitates *ghusl*?' She responded, 'You're asking the expert!' (*ʿalā al-khabīr saqaṭta*). The Messenger of God said, "If a man positions himself between her four limbs, and the circumcision touches the circumcision, *ghusl* is necessary."'" *Ṣaḥīḥ Muslim*, 22:812 (*al-ḥayḍ*). Variations of this narrative appear in the *Muwaṭṭa'* itself, 2:31, chapter 18, "The Chapter on the Necessity of *Ghusl* if the Two Places of Circumcision Meet." The difference in vocabulary

sexual status of a virgin female who is penetrated (i.e. her hymen pierced) by a pre-ejaculative male. This is, perhaps, something that could be classified as "experiencing that which women experience." Whatever the case, such a situation could potentially cause ambiguity vis-à-vis her father's authority over her upon her return to his house. The delineation of the transition from virgin to non-virgin according to Mālikī *fiqh* merits further study due to its implications for legal capacity.

Assets are important. The *Muwaṭṭa'* contains Mālik's opinion on a virgin and her money. She is not given her assets until she has "entered her [husband's] house and her situation [*ḥālihā*, i.e. levelheadedness] is known.[71] Mālikī *fiqh* thus creates a framework by which interaction, consummative or otherwise, with the fully matured male spouse is the only means for a female to attain the shift in status that will allow her full legal capacity.

When the female in question has undisputedly remained a virgin, the father's role is preeminent. The match he contracts should be for the "benefit" of the bride (*'alā wajh al-naẓar la-hā*[72]). This can occur with or without the bridal gift she deserves, the *mahr al-mithl* or "bridal gift of her peers," which can only be determined by complex considerations based on socio-economic status of a given family and the cultural context of the particular society. Beyond this, the father is not allowed to bring 'harm' to his daughter; here again, however, we find that a key term ('harm') is not really defined. It is reasonable to assume that harm includes, among other things, entry into a financial situation which is beneath the bride. Financial concerns cannot be the only measure, however, for the mother in the above-cited anecdote was able to argue successfully for a voice in the deliberations regarding her daughter's marriage because the bride was described as "beautiful, desirable"—*mūsirah marghūb fīhā*. Nonetheless, worth here is evidently measurable by the amount of bridal gift (here *ṣadāq*) the bride can garner; in other words, it indicates present socio-economic status based upon personal (in this case, physical) characteristics.

The issue of virginity is particularly interesting. First, Saḥnūn asserts that the female who denies having penetrative sex with her husband is not required

here combines another hadith found in Muslim (22:813), asking what happens if a man "becomes lazy" (*yuksilu*) during sex (i.e., does not ejaculate). Although all of the reports in the *Muwaṭṭa'* do reference the "places of circumcision," this report in Muslim does not: "The Messenger of God said, 'I would do that [have sex without ejaculation] with this woman ['Ā'isha] and then we would perform *ghusl* together (*naghtasilu*)". (22:813).

71 See also *al-Muwaṭṭa'* 2:53.

72 *Mudawwana*, 2:155.

to offer proof.[73] Second, the female who marries and has intercourse with a pre-ejaculative boy is not deemed to have had sex (*waṭʾ*) at all, and she has no waiting period, receives no bridal gift, and does not even perform post-intercourse ablutions. Presumably, she returns to her father's house still a virgin in the eyes of the law.

Conclusion

In the *Muwaṭṭaʾ* there is no mention of prepubescents per se until the discussion of the financial responsibilities of young boys, while virginity, not age, holds major significance with regard to legal capacity for females. The *Mudawwana* depicts an increasingly complex interaction between the concepts of virginity and capacity and the modalities of prepubescent marriages. For Saḥnūn, sexual intercourse is defined not in terms of penetration but rather as ejaculation of the male; capacity seems linked wholly to interaction with the matured male spouse; and marriage contains many phases, with possibilities including a lengthy unconsummated "stay," an ambiguous time-frame that involves unspecified sexual "experiences." The precise financial obligations of the male, be he pre-pubescent or post-pubescent, vary widely, determined (or complicated) by the sexual status of his wife.

We do emerge with a sense of Saḥnūn's understanding of a certain semantic range with regard to certain technical terms. "*Al-dukhūl*" would seem to refer only to cohabitation, with *iṣābah, jimāʿ* and *waṭʾ* referring to actual intercourse.

---

73 In other words, her word is presumptively valid as an evidentiary matter, and he does not suggest that she be examined by a group of women, nor does he postulate what could happen if a second marriage and its concomitant wedding night result in a lack of proof as to her virginity. Simply, her word is acceptable and she is not "harmed" by her husband's counter-testimony. (Contrast this affirmation of her ability to give testimony versus that of the pregnant woman who claims the father is her young husband.).

For more on the "expert" female witness charged with establishing female virginity, see Ron Shaham, *The Expert Witness in Islamic Courts* (Chicago: Chicago University Press, 2010), 85–87.

Although there does not seem to be any corollary to Saḥnūn's discussion in the earliest Ḥanafī sources, perhaps due to the lack of bearing of virginity on capacity, there is an interesting note to this in Ḥanafi Ottoman practice. The three jurists Tucker investigated all condemned the cultural practice of "testing" the bride's virginity, particularly if it resulted in her return to her family. Khayr al-Dīn (al-Ramlī) made it clear that the existence or non-existence of the hymen had no bearing on the contracting and consummation of a valid union, nor was there any way to dissolve said union except through proper legal divorce. Affirming that a hymen could be broken or damaged in any number of ways, the mufti then affirms the legal validity of a woman's testimony as to her status of virgin or non-virgin (*House*, 68–69).

Non-penetrative physical intimacy is referred to idiomatically ("that which is close [to intercourse]" or "that which women experience"). The phrase "length of stay" seems to connote some level of non-penetrative physical intimacy. Because a sufficient "length of stay" obviates virginity a change of status occurs for the virgin, and a presumed accumulation of sexual experience causes legal capacity to be augmented. This enhanced capacity results from interaction with the husband, whatever the dimensions of that interaction might be. "Length of stay" is claimed as the "practice," although the length itself remains undefined; further, no proof text or Prophetic example is offered in support of this idea.

We have seen in the *Muwaṭṭa'* that Mālik himself never refers to a virgin as being of a particular age, nor does he define what exactly distinguishes the virgin from the non-virgin. Saḥnūn's attempts to organize Mālikī *fiqh* on marriage show that it is not so easy to define what makes a *thayyib* a *thayyib*. On the one hand, the ejaculation of the male appears to play a significant role in that transformative event; certainly it is his nocturnal emission, and only that, which legally propels the young boy out of the realm of his father's control.[74] But on the other hand, the amount of time a young wife spends in the home of the husband, whether or not intercourse of any kind has been performed upon her, is also a deciding factor.

Be that as it may, at no time is "long time" defined in any delimiting way. Virginity is of the utmost significance for rules regarding marriage in Mālikī *fiqh*; indeed it could be said to be a basic organizing principle. However, as is symptomatic of many early legal texts, we are offered no clear-cut definitions.

74 *Mudawwana*, 2:254–255.

CHAPTER 5

Al-Shāfiʿī

Al-Shāfiʿī (204/820): Bolstering a Weak Tradition

Al-Shāfiʿī's approach to minor marriage and compulsion differs in many ways from the jurists who preceded him chronologically. First and foremost there is his use of a proof text which was not relied upon by any of the earlier jurists. The report of ʿĀʾisha, like other reports of Hishām ibn ʿUrwa from the Kufan period of his old age, was not included by Mālik in the *Muwaṭṭaʾ*.[1] It had no place in Ḥanafī reasoning (through the time of al-Jaṣṣāṣ, d. 370/981), nor did it make its way into the other *fiqh* manuals of the pre- and early post-Shāfiʿī period. Of the other early scholars in this period, only ʿAbd al-Razzāq saw fit to include it in his *Muṣannaf*.

On the basis of this report, al-Shāfiʿī is able to reevaluate common understandings with regard to maturity and capacity. The age of fifteen is the age of maturity, unless pubescence arrives earlier; still, for a virgin, there is no point at which she is free of the father's authority. For the prepubescent virgin, this state of legal incapacity is intensified; however, it is thrown into doubt by al-Shāfiʿī's position that divorced prepubescent virgins are able to marry whom they wish.[2]

When considering whether or when the prepubescent female virgin can have the sexual act performed upon her, al-Shāfiʿī introduces further doctrinal complications. He includes opposing opinions on whether or not she need be maintained at all, stressing that sex is the cornerstone of marriage. He stresses this fact, although he must also admit that the prepubescent often cannot perform sexual functions. As with much of this study, it is worth considering whether or not the legal points that engendered these discussions stemmed from attempted normativity versus practical law. In any case, the complexities are left unresolved.

Finally, al-Shāfiʿī makes numerous comparisons between the state of dependence of a virgin (the prepubescent virgin in particular) and that of the slave or the mentally deficient. For all of these, the role of the father is directly analogous to the role of the slave owner. In al-Shāfiʿī's mind, such comparisons are

1 See n. 101 p. 43 above concerning Mālik's opinion on Hishām and also n. 134 p. 202 with regard to the unit tradition.

2 *Al-Umm*, 6:468.

 | DOI 10.1163/9789004344860_007

logical, given the fact that he also analogizes the role of the father to the role of the Prophet.

The Walī Mujbir *and Proof Texts*

Al-Shāfiʿī is nothing if not careful with his analogies and careful with his proof texts. It is important for the coming discussions to note how and when he uses reports. The use of the *ayyim/bikr* hadith is important for our understanding of how he conceptualizes consent, but far more important for his enduring influence is that he adds to it the report of ʿĀʾisha. Indeed he adduces that report in order to launch into his discussion of the power of the father to marry off his children.

It is related in the following way: "Sufyān [Ibn ʿUyayna[3]] informed me that Hishām ibn ʿUrwa related from his father that ʿĀʾisha said, 'The Prophet married me when I was a girl of six or seven, and consummated the marriage (*banā bī*) when I was a girl of nine.'"[4]

Al-Shāfiʿī rushes to reconcile this hadith with an established understanding of maturity as follows:

> Although it was the Prophet's practice (*lammā kāna min Sunnat rasūl Allāh*) to make jihād obligatory for boys of 15, and the Muslims adopted this [as the standard] for [applicability of] criminal punishments, and God ruled in this way for orphans, saying "*until they reach [the age of] marriage, then, if you observe in them mental maturity* (rushd) ...",[5] and only a fifteen-year-old boy or girl had a say with regard to himself or herself—unless he began having emissions or if a girl menstruated before that, and then they would have a say with regard to themselves—Abū Bakr's contracting of the marriage of ʿĀʾisha to God's Messenger when she was a girl of six, and his consummation of that marriage when she was a girl of nine, indicated that the father possesses greater legal capacity with regard to the virgin than she has for herself. And if it were the case that, were she to reach [the age of menstruation] as a virgin, she would

3 It is possible to assume that the Sufyān in question is Ibn ʿUyayna (d. 198/814). However, the hadith as it appears in al-Bukhārī is related by Sufyān al-Thawrī (d. 161/778), also through Hishām ibn ʿUrwa. The ambiguity is significant and provokes important questions of authenticity, as the likelihood of *both* Sufyāns reporting such an under-reported hadith is quite small. Sufyān ibn ʿUyayna was al-Shāfiʿī's teacher and an expert hadith relater with interest in exegetical traditions. See Kecia Ali, *Imam Shafiʿi*, 6 and 28–29.

4 *Al-Umm*, 6:45.

5 Qurʾān, 4:6.

> possess more legal capacity than he with regard to herself, it would indicate that it is *not* permissible for him [to override her wishes] until such a time as [even the prepubescent virgin] reaches maturity and gives her permission."[6]

In other words, even though it is possible to locate an age of maturity in the number fifteen and the idea of "attaining maturity of mind," as put forth by Sunnaic material and the Qur'ān, the marriage of 'Ā'isha made it clear that the father has power over the virgin. Moreover, people who believe that a pubescent virgin has more legal capacity than her father might also (mistakenly) believe that this rule suggests that prepubescent virgins might become pubescent virgins with capacity, and therefore the father should wait until she is old enough in order to then ask her. The way in which he goes on to harmonize the 'Ā'isha report with the *ayyim/bikr* hadith is crucial here. He uses the combination of the two to further affirm the power of the father.

After citing the 'Ā'isha report in the *Umm*, al-Shāfi'ī cites Mālik's report of the *ayyim/bikr* hadith exactly as it appears in the *Ḥujja* and the *Muwaṭṭa'*.[7] Al-Shāfi'ī then takes the position that only fathers can compel virgins as only masters can compel slaves.[8] Then he delves into his harmonization of the *ayyim/bikr* hadith with his position that virgins have no say when their fathers are contracting marriages.

> It would seem from the Sunnaic indicator that the Messenger of God—when he distinguished between the virgin and the non-virgin, and made the non-virgin to have more legal capacity than her marriage guardian, and made the virgin to have her permission requested with regard to herself—that the guardian he intended (and only God knows) is the father in particular. So he made the non-virgin[9] to have more legal capacity than him. And that indicated that the father's requesting permission of the virgin with regard to herself is optional, not an obligation (*ikhtiyār lā farḍ*) because if it were a matter of him not being able to marry her if she were to protest, she would be like the non-virgin [who can protest and not be married]. And [such an interpretation] would seem to suggest that the discourse on this subject renders *every* woman as having more

6 *Al-Umm*, 6:45–6.

7 See *Al-Ḥujja* 2: 79–80 and *al-Muwaṭṭa'* 2:53.

8 *Al-Umm*, 6:47.

9 Here he can only mean non-virgin, although the word used is *ayyim*, whereas earlier in the sentence he used *thayyib*.

> legal capacity with regard to herself than her marriage guardian, and that the permission of the non-virgin is speaking, and the permission of the virgin is silence.[10]

Here, he is saying that the guardians meant are fathers, and the act of requesting permission from a virgin is optional for the father.[11] Clearly, a female could not be endowed with the capability of protesting the marriage (and having her protest override her father's decision), because if that were the case she would be like the non-virgin. If the virgin is like the non-virgin, then every woman would have the right to consent to her own marriage.

That the father's seeking permission is merely optional is further affirmed by a surprising analogy. The father is compared to the Prophet himself with regard to the way the latter would perform consultation (*mushāwara*) of the community. It is as absurd, in al-Shāfiʿī's mind, to imagine the community actually refusing the Prophet or rejecting his advice as it is to imagine a virgin daughter rejecting her father's choice of husband. Still, asking her is of psychological benefit for her.[12] Al-Shāfiʿī states:

> If someone were to ask, "What proof is there that [the father] should be commanded to consult with the virgin, if she has no authority vis-à-vis her father who is commanded to consult her?"
>
> The response would be, "God Most High said to His Prophet, 'And Consult them in the matter,' (3:159), and [yet] God did not grant them any authority vis-à-vis the Prophet. Rather, He obligated them to obey him. The consultation [then] is for their psychological benefit (*li-istiṭābat anfusihim*) and that others may follow this practice who do not have the Prophet's same authority over the people. And the underlying reason is that goodness emerges from some of those who are consulting which would otherwise have escaped the consulted, and the like.[13]

Consultation, then, has no legal consequence and cannot seriously impede the marriage proceedings. It is but a ritual of "good manners" (*ajmal fī al-akhlāq*)

10 *Al-Umm*, 6:47; emphasis added.

11 See Kecia Ali's discussion in "Law, Consent, and Muslim Feminist Epistemologies," in *Jihad for Justice* (48HoursBooks, 2012), pp. 121–134.

12 *Al-Umm*, 6:47, *ʿalā istiṭābat nafsihā*.

13 Ibid., 6:48.

for the father that also serves to prevent a female from hating the marriage out of a sense of powerlessness.[14]

Al-Shāfiʿī next argues forcefully that a prepubescent can have her marriage contracted by her father "because she has no authority with regard to herself in that state" (*li-annahu lā amr lahā fī nafsihā fī ḥālihā tilka*).[15] As it is with the girl, so it is with the boy. Both are subject to the father's authority with regard to marriage, just as they are subject to his financial authority for their benefit.[16] A father can contract marriage for his virgin daughter if it is to someone who does not diminish her status. The same holds true for his prepubescent son. The father's orders are licit as long as the spouse in question is of equal or greater status.[17] Al-Shāfiʿī frames the locus of a father's power over his prepubescent children as being no different with regard to marriage than it is with regard to finances; in both spheres he is obligated to seek their benefit.[18] This is of interest us in particular because Ḥanafī discussions of legal capacity for females are analogized almost entirely from financial matters: they assert that a girl (like a boy) attains capacity upon reaching maturity, whereupon a father cannot assert his will.

In his chapter on legal interdictions on the mature, al-Shāfiʿī notes that the avowal of a prepubescent is as meaningless as his silence or his disavowal.[19] He then gives an exposition of verse 4:6, in which he notes the necessity of the presence of two elements in order for an orphan to attain his or her money. Both maturity and levelheadedness must inhere in the person in question. Moreover, if the person is not qualified to attain the money, the condition of legal interdiction must prevail, even if fully mature. Al-Shāfiʿī then takes the position that the word orphans (*yatāmā*) includes both males and females, just as the word "test them" (*abtalū*) is directed at both genders, for "God most high did not differentiate between men and women with regard to their assets."[20] This means that levelheadedness is attainable for a woman. "If a woman attains levelheadedness, and levelheadedness is as I described it for a man, then her guardian is ordered to give her her assets."[21] The indicators to which he is

14 Ibid., 6:47.
15 Ibid.
16 Ibid., 6:49.
17 *Al-Umm*, 6:49.
18 Ibid.
19 *Al-Umm*, 4:458.
20 Ibid., 4:459.
21 Ibid., 459–460.

referring are the ability to "give and take" in interactions with people, righteous behavior with regard to religion, and the ability to look out for one's own financial affairs.[22] Al-Shāfiʿī is emphatic that "there is no difference between her and [a man] in anything permissible for each with regard to assets"—whether she is a virgin or married or a non-virgin.[23] This, he asserts, is God's command and proven by the Sunna.

Thus one source of the power to compel is linked to the necessity of the father's or the guardian's role in managing finances. Another source of this power is the Qurʾānic idea of righteousness being linked to obedience to the parents.[24] Part of the essence of obedience to the father is perceived as following his will with regard to life decisions such as marriage and even divorce.

Al-Shāfiʿī notes this point in discussing the hadith of Khansāʾ bint Khidām . In his opinion, for the legally responsible non-virgin, the matter of doing right by one's parents is exclusive of matters of marriage:

> The Prophet voided the marriage of Khansāʾ bint Khidām when her father married her, and he did *not* say, "unless you desire to do right by your father through deeming valid his contract of marriage (*illā an tashāʾī an tabirrī abāki fa-tujīzī inkāḥahu*)."[25]

Thus, Khansāʾ's responsibility to obey her father was not posited as linked to her marriage choices.[26] Still, al-Shāfiʿī chose to highlight her status as a non-virgin. He did not, apparently, consider the virgin to be free from the obligation to submit to compulsion based on the idea that to obey the father is in keeping with the aforementioned Qurʾānic ideals of righteousness.

For al-Shāfiʿī, children are marriageable by fathers seeking their best interests; this is not unlike the positions of the earlier jurists. What is different is that he has found a *ratio legis* in a report that none of them saw fit to use—the report of ʿĀʾisha. This in turn leads us to interrogate al-Shāfiʿī's thought with regard to legal capacity generally and the legal capacity of females in particular. Issues of suitability, rescission and divorce all appear interwoven into these discussions of capacity. It is vital to our discussion to note two of the most important corollaries in al-Shāfiʿī's mind with regard to virginity and capacity.

---

22 Ibid., 459.

23 Ibid., 460.

24 See Qurʾān 19:14, 32; 17:23, 46:17.

25 *Al-Umm*, 6:46. Emphasis mine.

26 This was not always the case; some early opinions define obedience/righteousness as doing the parent or parents' will with regard to the marriage. See the Appendix, below.

The first of these is the link between being a virgin and being a slave. The second is the link between being a virgin and being out of one's mind.

Legal Capacity of Virgins and Slaves

There are many striking similarities between the relationship between the virgin, particularly the prepubescent, and the father and the slave woman and her master. Al-Shāfiʿī makes these similarities clear:

> It is the right of the virgin's father to contract her marriage whether she is young or old, without her consent. (It is preferable, in my opinion, to ask her consent if she is pubescent.) And that [prerogative also exists] for the master of the slave woman with regard to his slave woman. It is not, however for the master of the male slave with regard to his slave [i.e., the slave must be asked]. Nor does it exist for any of the marriage guardians beyond the father with regard to the virgin. It is also [permissible] for the father of the insane pubescent woman to marry her in the same way as he would marry a prepubescent virgin—whether [the insane woman] is a virgin or a non-virgin. And this is not for anyone other than the father except the ruler.[27]

Thus we see that the legal capacity of the virgin is exactly analogous to the legal capacity of the slave woman or the insane woman. However, the analogy is pushed even further when he arrives at the case of the right of rescission of a slave woman whose marriage is contracted for her when she is a slave and then she receives her freedom. As a free woman, is she still bound by the contract made during her enslavement? This section is critical for understanding the way that al-Shāfiʿī understands the lack of capacity of females.

Al-Shāfiʿī begins with a report related by ʿĀʾisha that a slave woman (Barīra) who received her freedom was given the right of rescission with regard to her husband.[28] Mālik is adduced for Ibn ʿUmar's statement that, "With regard to the woman who is married to a slave and then receives her freedom, she may exercise her right of rescission if he has not touched her, but if he touched her, she has no right of rescission."

This, al-Shāfiʿī points out, is a case of annulment and not repudiation. Repudiation, he insists, is for men. This point is also intriguing, given the selective way in which al-Shāfiʿī has approached the text. Everything on the subject of slavewomen attaining the right to rescission upon gaining their freedom

27 *Al-Umm*, 6:57.

28 Ibid., 314.

appears in *al-Umm* exactly as it appears in the *Muwaṭṭa*ʾ. This is so until al-Shāfiʿī comes to the following report, which appears thus in the *Umm*:

> Mālik reported from Ibn Shihāb from ʿUrwa ibn al-Zubayr that a client of Banī ʿAdī ibn Kaʿb called "Zabrāʾ" reported to him that she had been married to a slave when she was a slave; then she was freed. She said, 'Ḥafṣa the wife of the Prophet sent for her and invited her in, then said, "I heard something about you, and I want you to do something—your fate is in your hands (*inna amraki bi-yadiki*) if your husband has not touched you."' She said, 'So I separated from him triply' (*fāraqtuhu thalāthan*)."[29]

Perhaps it is not coincidental that al-Shāfiʿī has chosen not to include this report in full. Its incarnation in the *Muwaṭṭa*ʾ follows this exact model, until the last sentence. It reads,

> 'Your fate is in your hands if your husband has not touched you, but if he has touched you, then there is nothing you can do (*laysa laki min al-amri shay*ʾ).' So I replied, 'It is divorce, then divorce, then divorce!' So I separated from him triply.[30]

First, we encounter the obvious point that having had the sexual act performed upon her would have rendered Zabrāʾ unable to exit her marriage. The actual text of Barīra's report contains no information about consummation. Second, we see al-Shāfiʿī attempting to engage in what is tantamount to damage control: Concerning a freed woman's ability to effectively instigate a divorce, he insists that Zabrāʾ's situation was only annulment. For men, that which is annulled for them "is not counted against them, for, and God Most High knows best, [such a thing] is not of their speech or action."[31] Having made these assurances, al-Shāfiʿī goes on to note that such a right to rescind could only exist for Barīra or Zabrāʾ in the context of having been married to a slave. Had either been married to a free man, this could not possibly have occurred.[32]

29 *Al-Umm*, 6:317.

30 *Al-Muwaṭṭa*ʾ, 2:75.

31 *Al-Umm*, 6:316.

32 Here, al-Shāfiʿī is illustrating a strong difference of opinion between the Mālikīs (who allow the name of divorce to be given to a woman-initiated separation of this kind) and Ḥanafīs and Shāfiʿīs who do not use the term for female-initiated divorce or quasi-divorce. Al-Shaybānī is adamant in the *Ḥujja* about just this kind of issue, engaging the Mālikī position on the same terms as al-Shāfi ʿī, and noting that because the separation

There was, however, debate over the tradition regarding Barīra and her "choice." Some insisted that the tradition meant she could exercise that right with either a free man or a slave (and not only that this was the meaning—the tradition we encounter here and in the *Muwaṭṭa'* does not mention to whom she was married, while ancillary texts[33] are supplied, one stating that the husband was in fact a free man, another insisting he was a slave). Al-Shāfiʿī is convinced that the relaters of the tradition that she was married to a slave are more qualified than those who claim the opposite.[34] Among those claiming the opposite are the Ḥanafīs, as we have seen.

He explains further that the woman's freedom renders her husband no longer of equal status (*kufu'*) for her which is what makes it possible to annul the marriage. The opposite side, however, suggests that the reason she is allowed to rescind is that she was not "in possession of herself" (*ghayr mālika li-amrihā*) at the time of the contracting of the marriage. Here, we witness a fundamental debate between al-Shāfiʿī and his interlocutor, who is, perhaps, arguing a Ḥanafī position. It is an encounter of competing policy grounds for a rule (that based on the Prophetic hadith of Barīra) which is not accompanied by an explanation of its rationale. The competing rationales are a shift in legal capacity versus a shift in social status, and it is clear that al-Shāfiʿī has aligned himself with that which views the rule as being based solely on a shift in social status:

> I said to him, "Do you believe that the female child (*al-ṣabīya*) whose father contracts her marriage and who reaches puberty before the marriage is consummated—or after—should have the right to rescind the marriage when she reaches pubescence?"
>
> He said, "No."
>
> So, I said, "So, if you are claiming that [Barīra's] right to rescind was due to the contract having been [made] at the time in which she could not choose, and when the right of rescission became possible for her [she should have been able] to choose, you would be compelled to adopt this (*lazamaka hādha*) with regard to the minor female whose father marries her."

---

is invoked by the woman, she has no *ʿidda* waiting period and can remarry the very day on which the marriage is ended. (See *Al-Ḥujja*, 2:292–293; see also 2:310–319.) See also al-Shaybānī's arguments with regard to capacity for the newly-freed slavewoman in Chapter 3 above.

33 "They have said, 'We related from ʿĀ'isha that the husband of Barīra was free,'" (*al-Umm*, 6:316).

34 These he cites as ʿUrwa (ibn al-Zubayr) and al-Qāsim from ʿĀ'isha.

He asked, "And if I can differentiate between [the slave woman] and the minor female?"

I said, "Are they different?"

He said, "Yes."

I replied, "How do you analogize between her and the minor female when the minor female bequeaths and inherits and this woman cannot bequeath or inherit [even] through marriage? [Yet], you analogize the one to the other with regard to the right of rescission which differentiates them?"

He answered, "If indeed they are different in some matters, they come together in some."

I said, "Where is that?"

He said, "The prepubescent female was not, on the day she was married, of those who had a choice as to her youth."[35]

I replied, "And so it is with the female slave and her enslavement!"[36]

It is clear that al-Shāfiʿī will not accept any suggestion that the lack of power of the slave woman, which he posits as absolutely complementary to the situation of the daughter under her father's control, can be overridden by coming into a state of capacity at a later time. In order to cede that point—that the reason for rescission is her inability to contract at the time of the marriage—al-Shāfiʿī would have had to cede to any young girl whose father contracts marriage for her the right to rescind upon puberty. Further, he would have had to allow a pubescent virgin to rescind upon attainment of non-virgin status. By asserting that the *ratio legis* for a former slave woman's ability to rescind can only be related to the doctrine of suitability (*kafāʾa*), al-Shāfiʿī would negate that ability for prepubescent females or virgins under their fathers' control.[37]

---

35 *Lam takun mimman la-hā khiyār lil-ḥadātha.*

36 *Al-Umm*, 6:318.

37 It should be noted that, based on the undefined nature of the doctrine, it would be theoretically possible for almost any woman, and certainly a slave woman, to claim unsuitability even to a free man, should she so choose, either by pressing differences in lineage or claiming differences in levels of piety or socio-economic considerations. If a slave is theoretically a non-Muslim to begin with, one can often assume different ethnic backgrounds for various slaves, let alone for the population at large. The ideal, for some Arabs, of Qurashīs marrying only Qurashīs could not have weathered the passage of time and the expansion of a multi-cultural empire; and yet, as long as it was in place as a facet of Shāfiʿī's thought, very few marriages would have met the qualification of being from similarly-matched tribes of the same socio-economic level.

This stance is in keeping with his support for the caveat that suitability is what allows the father to compel his virgin daughter or prepubescent son.[38]

Legal Capacity of Virgins and the Mentally Deficient

Those with mental incapacities require guardianship under Islamic law. With regard to mentally deficient women, he uses the same vocabulary as that which is applicable to the virgin under guardianship, ceding power only to fathers and grandfathers. No one other than these can contract for her. She will never gain legal capacity and therefore the ability to give her consent by virtue, so the union must be beyond sundering. He can only justify the ruler's contracting a marriage for her because "marriage might be health and wealth, and perhaps it would be a cure."[39] Again, suitability of the groom renders her unable to rescind.

Al-Shāfiʿī's methods of dealing with mentally deficient males do not differ greatly from how he approaches the mentally deficient females. There is, however, one striking difference. The male in question might "become crazed and (then) regain awareness" (*kāna yujinn wa-yufīq*). If this is the case, the father must not contract marriage without the son's permission.[40] Such permission would have been asked for and granted during a period in which the son is attuned to reality. The mentally deficient male, however, like the female and the virgin, also "has no authority with regard to himself" (*lā amr lahu fī nafsihi*). It is this phrase which becomes so familiar as we traverse juridical history, and it becomes a stock phrase with regard to the prepubescent female.

The analogy breaks down, however, in regard to divorce. The mentally deficient can be married because he or she "has no authority" with regard to him- or herself. Yet for this same reason he or she cannot be divorced. Not only can he not be divorced (i.e. by a father or ruler), but his [statement of] divorce is of no worth. "If he divorces her, his divorce is not a divorce." There exists no mechanism by which he can refute his marriage because, "the Pen has been lifted from him."[41] It is of interest to note that Ibn Ḥazm will use precisely this reasoning (that the "Pen has been lifted") to support his position against "requesting permission" from prepubescents, in his efforts to show that the *ayyim/bikr* hadith does not apply to them. Al-Shāfiʿī makes no connection between the Pen hadith and the optional nature of permission requesting: requesting permission of a virgin is a purely symbolic exercise for a father, whose power over her resembles the power of the Prophet over the community of believers.

38 *Al-Umm*, 6:49.

39 *Al-Umm*, 6:53–54.

40 Ibid., 54.

41 Ibid., 55.

It is vital to note the extent to which al-Shāfiʿī was willing to go to affirm the power of the father. Despite the discomfort this will eventually cause later thinkers, Ibn Ḥazm in particular, al-Shāfiʿī equates the prepubescent boy with other categories of the helpless. For al-Shāfiʿī, the categories of person over whom the father has total power are four:

> (1) the mentally deficient, (2) the prepubescent daughter, and (3) the virgin woman (*al-marʾa al-bikr*). It is for fathers [alone] to contract marriage for (4) the prepubescent son, and he has no right of rescission if he reaches pubescence. And that [power] is not possessed by the ruler or the marriage guardian. If the ruler or guardian contracts [the young boy's] marriage, it is void, for we only allow the father this power over him because he can look to [his son's] best interest, in a way that [even the ruler] cannot. [The boy] has no right of rescission upon pubescence. As for the non-father, this [right] is not his. And if the boy is insane (*majnūn*) or an idiot (*makhbūl*), and his father contracts marriage for him, the marriage is void, for [such a boy] is not in need of marriage.[42]

There is nothing equivocal about al-Shāfiʿī's support for the power of the father to contract for his prepubescent son; it is authority that supercedes even that of the ruler. The father's authority is total. It is this aspect of al-Shāfʿī's arguments which seems least transmitted in the later sources.

Sex, Maintenance, and Sexual Maturity

Al-Shāfiʿī introduces several semantic issues in his vocabulary on early marriage. Through these issues we realize the extent to which marriage itself had many levels and phases. The easiest to recognize are the terms meant to refer to actual sexual intercourse. It is first worth noting that none of the terms al-Shāfiʿī uses are in consonance with the language of the report of ʿĀʾisha adduced so early in his discussions of marriage (*banā bī*). "*Aṣāba*" means with certainty "to penetrate/perform the sexual act upon" a woman,[43] as does "*dakhala bi-hā*."[44] But in the context of marriage, what of the terms "*dakhala ʿalā*" or, for the woman, "*khalat baynahu wa bayn nafsihā*"?

We get some sense of the meaning of these terms from the following passages:

---

42 *Al-Umm*, 6:54–55. Note that he has asserted both that mentally unstable males do not need marriage and that the mentally unstable female may be cured by it.

43 As in the tradition adduced on 6:33 of *al-Umm*, which differentiates between *nikāḥ* (contracting the marriage) and *iṣāba* (consummating the marriage).

44 See *al-Umm*, 6:232.

> There is no doubt that if a man's wife has reached the age in which women like her have the sexual act performed upon them, but he is [still] prevented from visiting her (*imtanaʿ min al-dukhūl ʿalayhā*), but she is not prevented from visiting him (*lam tamtanaʿ min al-dukhūl ʿalayhi*), or, having visited him once, not prevented after that from visiting [again], then he must maintain her as long as she is his wife, [whether she be] sick or healthy, [whether he be] present or absent from her.[45]
>
> If a man is contractually married to a woman upon the like of whom the sexual act can be performed, even if she is not pubescent, and she allows him to visit with her (*khalat baynahu wa-bayna al-dukhūl ʿalayhā*) or her family allows them to be together (if she is a virgin) (*khallā ahluhā baynahu wa-bayna dhālik in kānat bikran*), and she is not prevented from visiting him (*lam tamtaniʿ min al-dukhūl ʿalayhi*), he must pay her maintenance, just as it would be incumbent upon him if he had had sex with her (*idhā dakhala bi-hā*), *for the withholding is from his side.*"[46]

All of these various phases clearly denote parts of the marriage process. The purely contractual marriage allows visiting. Visiting eventually becomes unchaperoned. And finally, apparently at the groom's behest, the final phase of consummation occurs, presumably the point at which the sexual act occurs. Al-Shāfiʿī does not, as we encounter elsewhere,[47] address the possibility of there being a prolonged period during which a wife resides in the husband's home, cohabiting without having intercourse.

Sex is the primary goal of marriage in al-Shāfiʿī's thought. Maintenance of the wife is entirely predicated on her ability to give herself over to the man's pleasure.

> He maintains his wife whether she is rich or poor because she preserves herself for him that he might take pleasure in her (and other than that [*wa ghayr dhālik*]), and prohibits (*manʿuhā*) that [i.e. allowing pleasure to be taken in her] for other than him.[48]

This is why marriage to minor females presents such a peculiar challenge to al-Shāfiʿī's conceptualization of union. What does one do with the girl who is not

45 Ibid., 6:227.

46 Ibid., 232; emphasis mine.

47 See *al-Mudawwana*, 2:306–307 .

48 *Al-Umm*, 6:227.

yet ready for sex? By including two opposite opinions, al-Shāfiʿī is nothing if not ambiguous, and seems wholly aware of (but unwilling or unable to resolve) the ambiguities involved:

> If he marries a minor female upon the like of whom sex is not yet performed, and he is prepubescent or post-pubescent, then it has been said: "He does not have to maintain her, for he does not take pleasure in her, and *the main reason for him marrying is to take pleasure in her.*"[49] And this is the opinion of a number of the scholars of our time—that she receives no maintenance, because the withholding (of sexual activity) is from her side. But if someone were to say, he should maintain her because *he* has caused her to become [sexually] off-limits to others, this is a [reasonable] position.[50]

In other words, the very fact of marriage has changed the minor female's situation. True, she still does not provide intercourse and therefore does not warrant maintenance. But because she is now married and will therefore not be providing intercourse to anyone other than the groom when she does eventually provide it, this could be reason enough to merit maintenance. Although the marriage is, at this point, purely contractual and contains no physical element, the body of the bride has become a promissory note of sorts.

Marriage to a prepubescent male is no less of a conceptual challenge:

> And so it is if he is a prepubescent who marries a pubescent; he must pay her maintenance for the withholding [of the sexual element of the marriage] is from his side, and one like her would take pleasure in him.[51]

Still, al-Shāfiʿī includes another, contrasting opinion here as well:

> It has been said, 'If she knew him to be prepubescent but [nevertheless] married him then she is to receive no maintenance, for it is well-known that one like him cannot take pleasure in his wife.'[52]

---

49 Emphasis mine.

50 *Al-Umm*, 6:227.

51 Ibid., 228.

52 Ibid.

Al-Shāfiʿī at no point attempts to address the limbo implicit in either of these situations. Who maintains the young girl who is not yet ready for sex? Who earns the maintenance for the prepubescent male who might be found liable for paying it but is without the mental capacity to function in the adult world of commerce and earning? The assumption would be that the family of either child would continue financial support until the purely contractual marriage transitioned into the actual marriage. And yet the fact that debate occurred upon this topic indicates that it was an issue of some weight that posed conceptual challenges for the jurists.

A final note is to be found in a section on those for whom marriages are contracted. The passage admonishes fathers and rulers to choose carefully for those in their charge, refraining from marrying a prepubescent female to one who is a slave or who is not her equal, and refraining from marrying a prepubescent to a female who is insane or mentally deficient or a "woman with whom sex is intolerable." This passage interests us because the manuscript variant is, the "woman who does not tolerate sex" (*wa lā imrāʾa lā tuṭīq jimāʿan*).[53] The latter would imply that it is undesirable to be mated to a child not yet capable of tolerating penetration. The former would bring home the fact that sex is the primary reason for matrimony in the first place, and "bad sex" defeats the purpose. Either way, the words call into question the logic of marrying children who cannot perform this basic task.

Repudiation

Al-Shāfiʿī's thought on repudiation is interesting. In two different sections, al-Shāfiʿī contradicts his own thought on whether or not a woman upon whom no sex has been performed should sit for the *ʿidda* waiting period.[54]

The first position in question occurs in the chapter entitled "Various Sunnaic Repudiations (*tafrīʿ ṭalāq al-Sunna*) with regard to the one with whom the marriage was not consummated and the one who does not menstruate."

> If a man married a woman and then did not consummate the marriage, or if she is among those who menstruate or do not menstruate [i.e., has irregular periods with no definable regular cycle], there is no verifiable practice (*Sunna*) with regard to divorcing her, except that the repudiation

53 *Al-Umm*, 6:56 and fn. 10. The text reads, *wa-lā imraʾa lā yuṭāq jimāʿuhā* (or a woman with whom sex is intolerable).

54 This is keeping in mind, of course, the instability of early texts. The contradiction may well be due to the history of an oral collection of legal opinions transformed over time into a written work.

> occurs whenever he repudiates her, and he can repudiate her whenever he desires.[55]

Al-Shāfiʿī does not mention the choice of waiting for "months" as opposed to "cycles" (*qurūʾ*),[56] as was mentioned in the *Muṣannaf* of Ibn Abī Shayba.[57] "There is no Sunna" on the subject; therefore, for al-Shāfiʿī, there is no question. The non-menstruating female is simply repudiated when her husband tells her she is repudiated.[58]

Further, when it comes to repudiation, al-Shāfiʿī equates the virgin with the non-virgin. He includes in the *Umm* an anecdote about a man who had "repudiated his wife triply before having touched her."

> ʿAṭāʾ said, "I said, 'Repudiation of a virgin is but once.' But ʿAbd Allāh ibn ʿAmr [ibn al-ʿĀṣ] said, 'You are analogizing. One instance of repudiation makes her remarriageable, but a triple repudiation makes her unmarriageable until she marries another husband.'[59]

According to al-Shāfiʿī, it would seem that there is no triple repudiation for one for whom no consummation occurred, precisely because there is no waiting period in which reinstatement is possible, apparently because there is no possibility of pregnancy. "There is no waiting period for her."[60] Because there is no waiting period, *any* repudiation in this case is final, and she becomes illicit for him unless she remarries.

> He who repudiates his wife and has not consummated the marriage [even if he only intends the repudiation to be a first or second repudiation] cannot reinstate her as spouse, and she need not endure the waiting period and she can remarry whomever she wants among those who are licit for her. The virgin and the non-virgin are alike in this.[61]

---

55 *Al-Umm*, 6:56.

56 For al-Shāfiʿī's discussion of *qurūʾ* in the *Risāla*, see ed. Aḥmad Muḥammad Shākir (Cairo: Maktabat Dār Turāth, 1979), ¶¶1684–1699, pp. 562–567.

57 *Muṣannaf* of Ibn Abī Shayba, ¶¶18305–18311. Only one of the reports on this topic mentions the word *qurūʾ*; the rest are *ʿinda al-ihlāl* (at the new moon), or using the word *shuhūr*.

58 *Al-Umm*, 6:462.

59 Ibid., 6:468.

60 Ibid.

61 Ibid. It is of great interest as well that al-Shāfiʿī points out a logical flaw in the habit of pronouncing the triple repudiation (at least for the non-consummated marriage). "If a man says to a woman with whom he has not consummated marriage, "You are repudiated, you

This approach further engenders the question of whether a repudiated prepubescent virgin, according to this line of reasoning could attain the ability to select (and/or contract with) her next spouse? The basis for the virgin bride's legal capacity, sexual experience, must submit to redefinition. He is clear that she can marry whomever she wants after the irrevocable divorce from an unconsummated marriage,[62] and clear that the thayyib must give verbal consent to marriage.[63]

Repudiation in an unconsummated marriage is further complicated by the issue of maintenance. In the following passage, al-Shāfiʿī is discussing the maintenance of a woman in a marriage in which no vaginal penetration has occurred; the woman has occupied the ambiguous space of one who sees her contractual husband unchaperoned. Here, the ability to reinstate is linked fully to the payment of maintenance.

> If he repudiates [the woman upon whom he has not yet performed the sexual act but with whom he visits unchaperoned and therefore pays to maintain], he possesses the right to reinstate her and therefore he must pay to maintain her during the *ʿidda*, for it is possible that she will become licit for him at a later day, and no one else will take pleasure in her. And if two witnesses witness that he has reinstated her, then she is his wife. And if he does not do it [pay her maintenance], then he has lost the right to reinstate her. For he would not maintain her if he did not possess the right to reinstate her, for she would [then, by virtue of not being maintained by him] have more legal authority over herself than he does, and she would not be licit for him unless through a new marriage contract.[64]

Here, the repudiation is from an unconsummated marriage, but there is *ʿidda* and there is possibility of reinstatement. Do the previous passages on the repudiation of women in unconsummated marriages assume that these were women who were not maintained? It cannot be that the only difference

are repudiated, you are repudiated," she is subject only to the first of these, and the other two do not apply, on the basis that the first was a 'complete word' [i.e. legally complete], thus she becomes repudiated from her husband without any applicable waiting period, and repudiation does not occur upon a woman who is not [still actually] a wife" *al-Umm*, 6:469.

62 *Al-Umm*, 6:468.

63 *Al-Umm*, 6:47.

64 *Al-Umm*, 6:227.

between the two situations is a lack of paid maintenance, for grouped among these was the pregnant woman as well as the old woman or prepubescent female who does not menstruate. The inconsistency in stances might be due to a breakdown of comprehensive legal reasoning, or simply evidence that other voices entered into the construction of the *Umm*.

Still, it is clear from this final passage that not being maintained means the woman is, for all intents and purposes, beholden to no one. This is an essential point for understanding that the marriage contract creates a new framework for dependency for the woman beyond that of the original framework of dependency upon the father.

Conclusion

Al-Shāfiʿī's concern with substantive consent is real. Although he will not accord legal capacity to the virgin female, he also will not dismiss her out of hand, encouraging kind treatment and consideration of her psychological well-being. He further rejects altogether any match not made in her interest, although how exactly to define suitability remains amorphous. Because the previous raw material of the discussion of minor marriage was in the form of a hadith he finds problematic, al-Shāfiʿī resorts to two strategies. The first is to suggest that the necessity of asking a virgin's permission is more of a guideline than an actual command. The second is to provide a report which is clearer, in his mind, and more direct. He gives intense attention to what is a new addition to the juristic discourse on prepubescent marriage: the report of ʿĀʾisha. By using it, al-Shāfiʿī can reframe common understandings with regard to maturity and capacity.[65]

Similarities are drawn between the father's power and that of the master to a slave. Only a divorced prepubescent virgin can contract her own marriage, while he points out that an irrevocably divorced prepubescent virgin has the right to choose whom she marries.

---

65 Whether intentionally or not, however, he has created with the use of the text interesting ramifications. Witness Aḥmad ibn Ḥanbal's insistence that a nine year old girl must grant permission, and that orphan girls cannot be married at all prior to attaining age nine, a marker that is surely extrapolated from the ages put forward in the report of ʿĀʾisha. (*Chapters on Marriage*, 63–64) Aḥmad further avers that he believes husbands should not have intercourse with (orphan) wives below the age of nine. (144) Note that Isḥāq Ibn Rāhawayh adds that intercourse with a girl prior to menstruation is not lawful, although it is unclear whether he is only referring to the girl given in marriage by a guardian not her father, and this is possibly because she could still rescind the marriage upon pubescence. (144).

We have witnessed these jurists hard at work in the enterprise of decoding the divine lexicon for the issue of prepubescent marriage. Yet the legal assessments that emerge do not yet convey clarity with regard to what imbues capacity to the female. The texts in question do not communicate the semantic stability required for such a sensitive topic. Nonetheless, the jurists who will concern themselves with consensus rely upon these early articulations to shape their conclusions, as we shall see as we turn to Part Two.

PART 2

Consensus, Consensus Writing, Post-Formative Era Writing, and Whether Consensus Matters

CHAPTER 6

Consensus

The movement, in the tenth and eleventh centuries, to bring juristic polyphony into something resembling a monotone was not new. As early as the 2nd/8th century, we find Ibn al-Muqaffaʿ's (d. 139/756)[1] treatise on the necessity of consolidating, if not codifying, the sprawling, often-contradictory enterprise known as Islamic law. This treatise, largely ignored, was perhaps as much a product of his Sasanian cultural roots as it was part of a bureaucratic desire to streamline into clear, easily-referenced opinions the mass of competing voices and viewpoints typical of Islamic legal discourse.[2] The early ʿAbbāsid caliphs, although they had promised in their revolution to make religion central to their agenda, did not move to exercise state control over religion. The most famous attempt at this came a half century or so later, with only abbreviated success: the failure of Caliphal authority to determine theological doctrine in the Inquisition (*Miḥna*) of the first half of the 3rd/9th century eventually gave a victory to the scholars.

The scholars themselves were left to elaborate their own concept of religious authority in the absence of a Prophet or, as with the Shiʿīs after the ninth century, a divinely-inspired Imām. Consensus was "the central ideological component" of the process by which scholars asserted their authority.[3] It was only half a century after the *Miḥna* that we encounter the first of the consensus writers, al-Marwazī (294/906)[4] as he begins the work of teasing out whatever common ground was to be found from the cacophony of dissenting voices existing within Islamic legal scholarship. Given early conceptions of consensus, those who undertook to write on the subject had an important mission. On the one hand the project was to affirm the Prophet's Sunna, on the other it was to delineate the group that could appropriately be called the Sunnīs.[5]

Even so, the conscientious early consensus writers could not but include points of *khilāf* (legal disagreement) in their work. This fact alone must catch

---

1 It is probable though not certain that the Caliph in question is the ʿAbbāsid Caliph Manṣūr (r. 136–58/754–75).

2 Jonathan Berkey, *The Formation of Islam* (Cambridge: Cambridge University Press, 2003), 126.

3 Ibid., 128.

4 For more on al-Marwazī, Chapter 7, below.

5 Wael Hallaq, *Sharīʿa: Theory, Practice, Transformations* (Cambridge: Cambridge University Press, 2009), p. 98.

 | DOI 10.1163/9789004344860_008

and hold our attention. No early work of consensus could have ignored a dissenting voice, proving that "the insistence on getting God's law right led to the sanctioning and even encouragement of legal disagreement."[6] Thus although consensus was key to legitimating the jurisprudential enterprise, it was itself built to embrace ambiguity.

It is impossible to discuss the concept of consensus without considering certain late-antique ideals of unity and univocality. Two major trends characterized the religions of the late-antique world: their close association with states and empires and their universalist character and claims.[7] The very nature of monotheism would have fostered the tendency toward universalism. Islam's development was deeply linked to the transition away from polytheism, with monotheism stipulating a single approach to understanding the divine.[8]

This was undoubtedly part of al-Shāfiʿī's attempt to articulate a comprehensive legal theory that would hone down the mass of competing reports and opinions into a clear and reliable system. It was not, he averred, the practice of the community that should be honored but the divine word.[9] Community practice quite often could not even transcend borders, much less communicate divine intent. Only the Qur'ān and Sunna could do this. After all, the Medinans had one practice based on early forebears,[10] while the Ḥanafīs looked to the Kufans as models.[11]

In al-Shāfiʿī's view, texts alone housed the divine imperatives; moreover, the texts in question were in Arabic, the language of the Qur'ān. In an instance where the two primary sources, the Qur'ān and the Sunna that elaborated on it, failed to render up a rule, analogy and/or consensus could be brought to bear on a give issue. But these were analogies and consensus statements that were text-related. To be clear, al-Shāfiʿī, himself, was not the elaborator of the doctrine of consensus, although the *Risāla* is credited as the first work of Islamic legal theory. Rather, he saw consensus as a device for privileging one interpretation over another. He was interested in neither community consensus regarding a particular practice nor scholarly consensus generally.[12] His

6 Joseph Lowry, "Is There Something Postmodern about Uṣūl al-fiqh?" in Reinhart, A. Kevin and Robert Gleave, eds, *Islamic Law in Theory: Studies in Honor of Bernard Weiss* (Leiden: Brill, 2014), p. 288.

7 Berkey, *The Formation of Islam*, 6–7.

8 Ibid., 8.

9 El Shamsy, *Canonization*, 5.

10 Ibid., 38.

11 Ibid., 48.

12 Ali, *Scholar and Saint*, 73.

primary concern was finding precedent in prophetic Sunna. To that extent he was content to accept the isolated report (*khabar al-wāḥid*) which could only ever render probable knowledge, while the concurrent report alone engendered certainty. Consensus became a device by which the isolated reports he espoused could gain currency and strength.[13] Even if epistemologically less sound than a concurrent report, he still considered them preferable to an agreed-upon view generated by mere human reasoning (*raʾy*).[14] By reining in *raʾy* and limiting legislation to parameters dictated by God alone, al-Shāfiʿī was attempting to strengthen and consolidate the jurisprudential enterprise. The doctrine of consensus, as part of the roadmap of legal theory he offered, was eagerly accepted by tenth century jurists.

The evolution of the doctrine of consensus in Islamic law could well be symptomatic of the *Zeitgeist* which sought uniformity out of plurality, positing a united early community. The Islamic state, of course, played a central role in such efforts. Still, consensus itself often served to reinforce the relationship between religion and the state. Witness the refusal of the outspoken Syrian scholar Ibn Taymīya (d. 728/1328)[15] to renounce his position on the invalidity of the triple divorce utterance.[16] This came at a time when the scholarly establishment was closely allied with the Mamlūk state; the state was able to frame its desire for control in terms of a stated mission to preserve the religion. The furor caused by Ibn Taymīya's refusal to acknowledge a consensus on the validity of triple divorce utterances caused the state to declare his positions a danger to the religion of the people. For insisting that wives could not be irrevocably repudiated without a grace period in which a husband could reconsider his action, Ibn Taymīya was sent to prison.[17] "From the point of view

13 Brown explains further using the example of Ibn al-Farrā' (al-Qāḍī Abū Yaʿlā, d. 1066). In his work on Ḥanbalī legal theory, *al-'Udda fi uṣūl al-fiqh*, Ibn al-Farrā' explains that while isolated reports convey only probability (*ẓann*), when the *umma* reaches consensus on some piece of evidence such as a hadith the report then yields certain knowledge. See Brown, *Canonization of Bukhārī and Muslim*, 192.

14 Ali, *Scholar and Saint*, 73.

15 For more on Ibn Taymīya, see Abū Zahrā, Muhammad, *Ibn Taymīya* (Cairo: Dār al-Fikr al-ʿArabī, 1952).

16 For more on this topic see Baugh, C, "Ibn Taymīya's Feminism? Imprisonment and the Divorce *Fatwās*," in *Muslima Theology: New Voices of Muslim Women Theologians*, eds. Ednan Aslan and Marcia Hermansen, (Peter Lang, 2013).

17 For more on Ibn Taymīya's various trials and prison tenures, see Jackson, Sherman, "Ibn Taymīya on Trial in Damascus," *Journal of Semitic Studies* XXXIX/I Spring 1994, pp. 41–85, and Little, Donald, "The Historical and Historiographical Detention of Ibn Taymiyya," *International Journal of Middle East Studies*. Vol. 4, No. 3 (Jul., 1973), pp. 311–327.

of the head of state and his religious advisors, the propagation of certain theological beliefs jeopardized the salvation of individual Muslims and the stability of the state, so that the sultan [al-Malik al-Nāṣir, r. 693–741/1293–1341] as defender of the state took appropriate action."[18]

This was no less true for Ibn Taymīya's position on triple divorce.[19] He rejected the idea that there was a consensus allowing men to irrevocably divorce their wives all at once, insisting instead that the force behind the doctrine was a decision of ʿUmar ibn al-Khaṭṭāb.[20]

His refuters, primary among them the Shāfiʿī jurist Taqī al-Dīn al-Subkī (d. 744/1344),[21] relied upon consensus claims of scholars like (the Mālikī) Ibn ʿAbd al-Barr (d. 463/1070).[22] Al-Subkī, who eventually became Chief Shāfiʿī Qāḍī of Damascus, represented the consummate state-sponsored scholar. He used the 5th/11th century claims of consensus articulated by Ibn ʿAbd al-Barr as a tool against Ibn Taymīya's dissent. At the heart of the issue was Ibn Taymīya's rejection of Ijmāʿ. The function of Ijmāʿ at this time was to impose some semblance of legal uniformity on the communities beyond the urban centers. Where no judge was available, local scholars had to use the interpretive devices at their disposal, and a pre-established consensus made decision-making easier. The legal and social implications of a challenge to consensus, which was also a challenge to the stability of the state, were weighty.[23]

---

18 Little, "Detention," 321.

19 Ibid.

20 Taqī al-Dīn Ahmad Ibn Taymīya, *Majmūʿat Fatāwī Shaykh al-Islām Ibn Taymīya*, ed. ʿAbd al-Raḥmān ibn Qāsim al-ʿĀṣimī, 1977, 33:15–16. See also Rapoport, Yossef, "Ibn Taymiyya on Divorce Oaths," in *The Mamluks in Egyptian and Syrian Politics and Society*, ed. Winter Michael and Amalia Levanoni (Leiden: Brill, 2004), 204.

21 For more on al-Subkī, see his son Tāj al-Dīn's entry in the *Ṭabaqāt al-Shāfiʿīyah al-Kubrā* (ʿĪsā al-Ḥalabī Printers, 1964). Taqī al-Dīn's intellectual rivalry with Ibn Taymīya led him to write several treatises refuting the older scholar.

22 Ibn ʿAbd al-Barr, Abū ʿUmar Yūsuf ibn ʿAbd Allāh, *Kitāb al-Istidhkār* (Beirut: Dar al-Kutub al-ʿIlmiyyah, 2006), 6:3. "This is passed down from the majority of the righteous forebears, and the difference over it is isolated, [the sort that] only innovators would adopt, or the sort of person to whom no one would turn due to the isolated nature of his opinion from the majority, and using such an opinion is invalid due to it being a distortion of the Book and the Sunnah."

A useful biography of Ibn ʿAbd al-Barr can be found in the introduction to this edition of *al-Istidhkār*, a work which is widely relied upon as a manual of Mālikī fiqh (explaining the *Muwaṭṭaʾ* of Mālik (179/795), in addition to elaborating numerous claims of consensus.

23 Rapoport, "Ibn Taymiyya," 213.

Ibn Taymīya's willingness to contest the consensus claim revealed some deep flaws in the doctrine itself. Ibn al-Mundhir al-Nīsābūrī (d. 318/930),[24] for example, had earlier presented a far more nuanced discussion of triple divorce than did Ibn ʿAbd al-Barr, offering multiple dissenting opinions. Ibn Taymīya had himself provided numerous proof texts in the form of Qur'ānic verses and Sunnaic reports.[25] Despite the text-based evidence he brought to bear on the subject, Ibn Taymīya earned himself state persecution of the highest order.

This denunciation of Ibn Taymīya, however infamous, cannot itself fully reveal the complex interplay between the state and state-sponsored scholarly positions. The episode supports Berkey's claim regarding the symbiotic relationship between monotheistic states and religions, while also revealing that, at least in the Islamic world, the state could not bring scholars to heel without the active involvement of other scholars. Practically speaking, for Ibn Taymīya, this amounted to very little control indeed, for he continued to teach and issue juridical decisions until his death—in prison.

Ibn al-Mundhir, that most famous of early consensus writers, is discussed in greater detail. It is important to note that he was initially writing of consensus as something very different from the anonymous unanimity that other, later writers considered it to be.[26] The consensus to which Ibn al-Mundhir referred was that of those scholars with whom he had come in contact, and from whom he had verifiable information. Additionally—and of great importance—this consensus was never a simple convergence of scholarly opinion devoid of indicators. For Ibn al-Mundhir, consensus centers on proof texts and how they are understood and manipulated by the scholars. It is this approach to consensus that represents the "middle point" to which Hallaq refers when he discusses the evolution of consensus between Islam's first two centuries and the late fourth/tenth century. He charts the early period as one in which the consensus is largely Sunnaic, both determined by and "determinative of hadith" while still deeply tied to the consensus of the Companions.[27] The evolution culminates in fully developed legal theory in the fourth/tenth century that presented

---

24 See Ibn al-Mundhir al-Nīsābūrī, *Kitāb al-Ishrāf ʿalā madhāhib ahl al-ʿilm* (Beirut: Dār al-Fikr, 1993), 1:144–145, and its numerous differing opinions on the topic of triple divorce utterances, many of which are as concerned with intentionality as Ibn Taymīya's positions.

25 See *al-Fatāwā*, "Chapter on Sunnaic Divorce and Innovative Divorce," esp. 33:9, 13–16, and 21.

26 See, for example, Sayf al-Dīn al-Āmidī, *al-Iḥkām fī uṣūl al-aḥkām* (Beirut: Dār al-Kutub al-ʿIlmīyah, 1980), 1:281–282.

27 Hallaq, *Sharīʿa*, 48.

consensus as being scholarly agreement "that bestows on those rulings or opinions subject to it a conclusive, certain knowledge."[28]

It is this latter consensus that many Muslim scholars themselves have deemed unfeasible.[29] However, operating from the "middle point," consensus for Ibn al-Mundhir represents the "lowest common denominator" of the earliest juristic agreement. It also ignores the fact that consensus came to be used as a weapon in inter-madhhab polemical battles. Claiming consensus had the effect of silencing the other side.[30] Claims of consensus—when divorced from their accompanying qualifying arguments and from the careful disclaimer that those in agreement are "those whose opinions I have studied"—can belie the myriad realms of disagreement attached to a given subject. Finally, they can overshadow the original intent of many of the jurists' work: to elevate an uncertain proof text to the status of certainty enjoyed by the Qurʾan and the concurrent traditions.[31]

An observable change took place in the law: whereas the earliest jurists dealt with prepubescent marriage as equally relevant and applicable for both genders, the subject of early marriage for the male child became (and remains today) under-discussed. Initially, both boys and girls had marriages contracted for them at varying stages of their childhood. The practice of marrying off prepubescent boys began to dissipate[32] until it became (and remains), for all intents and purposes, obsolete; the issue persists, as we have discussed, for prepubescent girls.

Did the issue of compulsion in marriages of minor girls attain enduring relevance due to the claim of consensus that surrounds it? Multiple manuals upon which "modern" Muslim jurists rely state specifically that this doctrine is supported by consensus. Ibn Qudāma's *Mughnī*, for example, is among the standard works of substantive law upon which is based the legal system of the kingdom of Saudi Arabia.[33] *Kitāb al-Ijmāʿ*, despite being a truncated abridg-

28 Ibid., 98.

29 See in particular Mohamed Hashim Kamali, *Principles of Islamic Jurisprudence*, (Cambridge: The Islamic Texts Society, 2003), pp. 244–248. Kamali quotes ʿAbd Allāh ibn Aḥmad ibn Ḥanbal as attributing to his father: "It is no more than a lie for any man to claim the existence of ijmāʿ. Whoever claims ijmāʿ is telling a lie" (p. 246).

30 Abou el Fadl, Khaled, *Speaking in God's Name* (Oxford: Oneworld, 2005), 64–65.

31 See Zysow, *Economy of Certainty*, 114.

32 Motzki finds only 10 of the Ottoman-era *fatāwā* to concern minor boys, as opposed to 56 for girls (p. 137). Our research uncovered no figures for male prepubescent marriage in the modern period.

33 See Layish, Aharon, "Saudi Arabian Legal Reform as a Mechanism to Moderate Wahhābī Doctrine," p. 280, fn. 8a. in *Journal of the American Oriental Society*, vol. 107.2 (1987).

ment of the larger, more detailed works of Ibn al-Mundhir, received the following praise from ʿAbd Allāh ibn Zayd Āl Maḥmūd, former Chief of the Sharīʿa Courts and Religious Issues of the state of Qaṭar: "The *Book of Ijmāʿ* of Ibn al-Mundhir is the first book written of its genre, and the most trustworthy, and the most accomplished of scholars rely upon it, and do so for clarification of practical juristic rulings."[34]

On some level, abridgment itself must play a part in divesting the discussions of what is an extraordinarily complex topic of its nuances. Witness another work, *Kitāb al-Ifṣāḥ ʿan maʿānī al-ṣiḥāḥ* of the Vizier ʿAwn al-Dīn Abī Muzaffar Yaḥyā ibn Muḥammad ibn Hubayra (560/1164). This work is not included in the large compendium of books on consensus, *Kitāb al-Iqnāʿ fī masāʾil al-ijmāʿ* (discussed below). *Kitāb al-Ifṣāḥ* was, in fact, as its title suggests, a work explaining the hadith compendia of Bukhārī and Muslim, that included a chapter on what Ibn Hubayra understood to be matters of consensus (he includes, however, the many shades of graded dissent that any issue might provoke). Yet in 1993, just as occurred with the *K. al-Ijmāʿ* of Ibn al-Mundhir, Ibn Hubayra's book was transformed into a slim book of lists of consensus issues (also called *Kitāb al-Ijmāʿ*, or *al-Ijmāʿ ʿinda al-aʾimma al-arbaʿa*[35]) and lacking in any explanations

34 F.A. Aḥmad, ed, *Kitāb al-Ijmāʿ*, (Alexandria: Dār al-Daʿwah, 1982) p. 4. For the consensus ruling in the abridgment, see *K. Al-Ijmā'*, ʿAbd Allāh ʿUmar Bārūdī edition, (Beirut: Dār al-Janān, 1986) 76, ¶349. In addition to the Bārūdī edition, there are two other editions (also containing the ruling), one edited by Fuʾād ʿAbd al-Manʿam Aḥmad (Alexandria: Dār al-Daʿwah, 1982) and the other by Abū Ḥammād Ṣaghīr Aḥmad (Riyāḍ: Dār Ṭayyibah, 1982). For the ruling as it appears in the larger work, see *Kitāb al-Ishrāf*, page 1:26.

35 For the consensus claim concerning minor girls, see page 143 of Shata's abridgment. Note that the abridgment alludes to a contrasting opinion (of Ibn Ḥanbal) without including or citing it. The original cites Ibn Ḥanbal's opinion that the "nine-year-old girl cannot be married without her permission, be the guardian her father or anyone else." Then it goes on to relate that the minor virgin can be compelled to marry in everyone's opinion but this latter (which gives the early limit of nine years). See *Kitāb al-ifṣāḥ*, 2:90.

Note that the original is not free of textual problems, however. An editorial glitch has allowed the text to offer two contradictory statements with regard to the prepubescent female. The first says, "They have agreed that the father has the power to contract marriage for the minor virgin among his daughters." The second reads, "And they have disagreed over whether the father has the right to compel the minor girl (*al-bint al-ṣaghīra*) from among his daughters to marry." There is then a summary of the jurists' opinions, including that al-Shāfiʿī said "he could not marry her until she reaches maturity and gives her permission" (2:91). After a period of confusion, I realized that the only possible explanation is that the word "*bint*" shares the exact morphology of the word "*thayyib*" (non-virgin, or previously married). If the latter is substituted, the passage makes sense. This is in light of

by its modern abridger Dr. Muḥammad Muḥammad Shatā, a Cairene judge. It is not true to the original.[36]

Finally, the ruling on the compulsion of prepubescent females appears repeatedly in the compendium work *al-Iqnāʿ fī masāʾil al-ijmāʿ* by Ibn al-Qaṭṭān al-Fāsī (d. 628/1230). This work, containing between 4000–10,000[37] rulings upon which consensus is claimed, is portrayed as an essential manual for anyone concerned with any facet of the religion of Islam.[38]

And yet, despite the existence of a range of minor marriage rulings in so many consensus and legal works, the present study offers proof that the evidence is quite equivocal for the use of consensus to justify minor marriage. Modern legal manuals[39] assessing marriage practices in Muslim countries do

---

juristic classification of women according to virginity or lack thereof. Ibn Hubayra, *Kitāb al-Ifṣāḥ ʿan Maʿānī al-Ṣiḥāḥ* (Beirut: Dār al-Kutub al-ʿIlmīya, 1996).

Shatā, Ibn Hubayra's abridger, left out all mention of the legal status of the "minor non-virgin" (*Kitāb al-Ijmāʿ ʿinda aʾimmat al-sunna al-arbaʿa*, pp. 142–143).

36 See, for another example, *Bāb shurūṭ al-kafāʾa* in Shata's work (144–145) and contrast it with that of Ibn Hubayra's *al-Ifṣāḥ* (2:98–109).

37 *Kitāb al-Iqnāʿ*, 7. Referring to the work of Ibn al-Qaṭṭān, the editor says, "It is the most comprehensive work on issues of consensus. According to our calculations, it contains more than 4000 issues, and if we consider sub-topics (*law zidnāhā tafṣīlan*), the number nears 10,000." Compare this with the scant 767 topics of consensus claimed in Ibn al-Mundhir's *K. al-Ijmāʿ*.

38 Ḥammādah cites the knowledge of consensus issues as key for "anyone concerned with: exegesis of the Qurʾān … explanation of Prophetic example … deriving judicial rulings … and the spirit and intention of Sharīʿa" (*al-Iqnāʿ*, 7). For the consensus opinions on minor marriage, see 3:1153–1165.

39 See Pearl, David, *A Textbook on Muslim Law* (London: Croom Helm, Ltd, 1979), esp. pp. 43–45. For an overview of women's marital rights in Islamic countries, see *Women Living Under Muslim Laws: Women, Family, Laws and Customs in the Muslim World*, International Solidarity Network (New Delhi: Zubaan, 2006), with its focus on detailing legal codes while yet explaining the divide between law and culture. See especially the chapter on Child Marriage, 117–132.

For recent writings on child marriage in Muslim countries, see "Early Marriage, Age of Menarche, and Female Schooling Attainment in Bangladesh," Erica Field and Attila Ambrus, *The Journal of Political Economy*, Vol. 116, No. 5 (Oct., 2008) pp. 881–930. See also "Marriageable Age: Political Debates on Early Marriage in Twentieth-Century Indonesia," Susan Blackburn and Sharon Bessell, *Indonesia*, Vol. 64 (Apr. 1997) pp. 107–141. (Note in particular that this article points out the difference, lost on Dutch observers, between contractual marriage and consummated marriage, as well as the results of political debate on the subject, particularly when instigated by colonial powers.).

For more information on statistics on child marriage generally, see "Early Marriage Among Women in Developing Countries," Susheela Singh and Renee Samara, *International*

not evidence concern with the historical jurisprudence or the interplay of reasoning strategies and proof texts in the formative era of Islamic legal thought. Nor, I postulate, is sufficient attention given to post-formative era discussions that could well indicate an ongoing scholarly devotion to nuance that would have been entirely incompatible with the 7th/13th century consensus manual abridgement movement.

Ibn al-Qaṭṭān

In the 7th/13th century, an intrepid scholar and judge named Ibn al-Qaṭṭān al-Fāsī (d. 628/1230),[40] set out to make an encyclopedia of consensus, *al-Iqnāʿ fī masāʾil al-ijmāʿ*.[41] He was serving the Almohad state, and the state at that time was in a period of outright disintegration.[42] It is possible to postulate that, given the fact that divergent books of *furūʿ* were being burned, a work of consensus would serve the agenda of providing a clear set of guidelines for judges keen to provide clarity for their polities. Ibn al-Qaṭṭān compiled a massive work (the 2003 edition is in three volumes) in which he cited all the known instances of consensus, from a great field of works on the matter. Despite his efforts, contemporary 13th century writers like Ibn Qudāma and even al-Qurṭubī (d. 671/1272),[43] still relied nearly exclusively on Ibn al-Mundhir as a primary source when claiming consensus.[44] Ibn Qudāma, of course, was very

---

Family Planning Perspectives, Vol. 22, No. 4 (Dec., 1996), pp. 148–157+175, and International Women's Health Coalition, "Child Marriage," http://www.iwhc.org/storage/iwhc/documents/1-_child_marriage_new_links.pdf.
Last visited on 01/03/2011.

40 See the biography of Ibn al-Qaṭṭān in the recent Cairo edition (2004), ed. Ḥasan al-Ṣaʿīdī.

41 Ibn al-Qaṭṭān al-Fāsī, *al-Iqnāʿ fī masāʾil al-ijmāʿ* (Damascus: Dār al-Qalam, 2003).

42 See Mahmoud Makki, "The Political History of al-Andalus", in Jayyusi, ed., *The Legacy of Muslim Spain* (Leiden: Brill, 1994), 75–77.

43 It is worth noting that al-Qurṭubī cites Ibn al-Mundhir throughout his highly legalistic tafsīr, although, significantly, not with regard to the issue of prepubescent marriage (al-Qurṭubī argues from grammar against the marriage of children; i.e. that the order to marry "women" in Q4:3 is specific to adult women, see the *Tafsīr* [*Jāmiʿ al-Aḥkām*], 5:11. This argument is drawn from al-Ṭabarī; see pp. 47–48, above). One citation of Ibn al-Mundhir among many occurs on page 12 of volume 5, Abū Abd Allāh Muḥammad al-Qurṭubī, *Tafsīr al-Qurʾān* [*Jāmiʿ al-Aḥkām*] (Beirut: Dār al-Kutub, 2000).

44 The work is currently popular among modern Muslim scholars, who seem unconcerned with whether or not medieval scholars relied on it or found it useful.

distant from the Muslim west, but al-Qurṭubī was much more proximate to the source of this work.

Did Ibn al-Qaṭṭān's work matter? Was it used by judges in the Muslim west? Was it referred to by scholars? It is difficult to assess. For the purposes of this study, though, the work is a useful framework for understanding early presentations of consensus and a convenient way of exploring available Ijmāʿic opinions on the matter of prepubescent marriage. More than this, though, we find in its foreword a note on the importance of Ijmāʿ: getting back to the roots of the religion in order to shield Islam from the vicious attacks against it and the tendency of the community to stray from the proper path.[45]

The work is a compendium of legal matters, arranged as any *fiqh* book is arranged—chapters on Purity, Prayer, Fasting, Marriage, Divorce, Criminal Law, etc. For each chapter, there are sub-sections, and in each subsection, Ibn al-Qaṭṭān has undertaken to summarize consensus assertions of earlier scholars. A primary question in this chapter, then, is, how faithful was Ibn al-Qaṭṭān to the original texts he summarized? The underlying (and perhaps more compelling) question, however is: How does an assertion of consensus function when divested of its context (which undoubtedly included the original writer's presentation of proof texts and debates)?

Our test case, that of compulsion in minor marriage, is the topic which frames my inquiry into Ibn al-Qaṭṭān's methods and the original texts on which his summaries are based left behind. The summaries he includes are based primarily on the following works: *al-Ishrāf ʿalā madhāhib ahl al-ʿilm* of Ibn al-Mundhir, *Ikhtilāf al-ʿUlamāʾ* of al-Ṭaḥāwī (d. 321/933), *Ikhtilāf al-ʿUlamāʾ* of al-Marwazī (d. 294/906), and *al-Istidhkār li-madhāhib fuqahāʾ al-amṣār* of Ibn ʿAbd al-Barr (d. 463/1070). Note that all of the works in question except that of Ibn ʿAbd al-Barr are themselves summaries of larger works. Thus Ibn al-Qaṭṭān's efforts constitute a continuation of a trend of abridgment that began very early in Islamic legal history.

In presenting Ibn al-Qaṭṭān's work on the claimed consensus regarding a father's ability to compel his prepubescent daughter, I translate fully the excerpts he has chosen to include[46] and track them, where possible, in the originals.

45 Ibn al-Qaṭṭān, *Al-Iqnāʿ*, ed. Al-Ṣaʿīdī, p. 5.

46 It must be noted that two of the works referenced, *al-Nayyir* and *al-Nukat*, are not available. *Al-Nayyir* (no lengthier name is known) is a work by al-Qāḍī Abū al-ʿAbbās Aḥmad ibn Muḥammad ibn Ṣāliḥ al-Manṣūrī, d. c. 350/961. Ibn al-Nadīm, ibn al-Athīr, and al-Shīrāzī all reflect on the work of al-Manṣūrī, a major Ẓāhirī writer who, in addition to *al-Nayyir*, wrote other "mighty books," including *Kitāb al-Miṣbāḥ al-Kabīr* and *Kitāb al-Hādī*. He was considered by ibn al-Nadīm to be the best of the Ẓāhiris (min afāḍil al-Dāwudīyīn).

Then I give a brief introduction to each scholar in question, all of which paves the way for Chapter Six of this book in which each point of contention from the earlier scholarly debates that we encountered in Part One will be addressed by the consensus writers. How do their conversations differ from the early Ḥanafī, Mālikī, and Shāfiʿī scholars? I answer by delving into the underlying works themselves, where they are available, and abstracting from them the totality of the information offered on the topic in question.

I investigate also to what extent claims of consensus center[47] on evidential proof texts and to what extent the proof texts themselves are validated by consensus ("*al-Sunna al-mujtamaʿ ʿalayhā*"). Are invocations of consensus ever simply affirmations of the like-mindedness of the scholars of law?[48] More

---

Al-Manṣūrī learned hadith from al-Athram, and taught al-Ḥākim Abū ʿAbd Allāh. Ibn al-Qaṭṭān cites *al-Nayyir* extensively, a book which al-Shīrāzī designated as "famous and popular" in the fifth century. (See *al-Iqnā* 1:84). This book is, however, not extant to the best of our knowledge.

Likewise unavailable is *al-Nukat* (a.k.a. *Nukut al-ʿuyūn*) is an abridgment of the work by Ibn al-Qaṣṣār (d. 397/1007) *ʿUyūn al-adillah fī masāʾil al-khilāf bayna fuqahāʾ al-amṣār*. The editor of *al-Iqnāʿ* had access to the only manuscript of the pertinent section of this abridgment (extant in Qayrawān). All that has yet to be published of the original is the chapter on ritual purity (Riyadh: Jāmiʿat al-Imām Muḥammad ibn Saʿūd al-Islāmīyah, 2006) compiled from a manuscript of this chapter found in Madrid (*ʿUyūn al-adillah*, p. 53).

47 Lowry has called such claims "paraphrasing" but notes that they are in fact interpretations: "Since Shāfiʿī's appeals to *ijmāʿ* ... nearly all involve interpretations of revealed texts ... Shāfiʿī views *ijmāʿ* as offering a correct interpretation of a revealed text and in that sense instances of *ijmāʿ* are essentially paraphrases of propositions of law found in the revelatory sources and so dependent upon and constrained by those underlying sources." Lowry, Joseph E. *Early Islamic Legal Theory*, 327.

48 The editor of *al-Awsaṭ* provides a summary of viewpoints of early scholars on Ijmāʿ:

The scholars and lawyers have differed over the precise meaning of Ijmāʿ. Among them there are those who say that Ijmāʿ is when the overwhelming majority (*al-jumhūr*) agree to an opinion and if one of the scholars disagrees with them, then no attention is paid to that one, and the opinion of the majority is the real Ijmāʿ. And this is the opinion of Ibn Jarīr al-Ṭabarī.

And al-Ghazālī said, Ijmāʿ is when the community of Muḥammad in specific agrees about a religious issue (*amr min al-umūr al-dīnīya*). (*al-Mustaṣfā*, 1:173).

And al-Āmidī said, it is the agreement of the responsible believers of Muhammad's community in an era upon a ruling upon a certain occurrence (*ḥukm wāqiʿa min al-waqāʾiʿ*). (*al-Iḥkām*, 1:196).

And Ibn Ḥazm said, As for something related by a trustworthy relater from another that reaches back to the Messenger of God, there is that which there is consensus over opining to the effect of it (*mā ujmiʿ ʿalā al-qawl bih*), and that which there is difference

than anything, I am concerned with viewing and exploring the existence of Ijmāʿ as the "lowest common denominator" of agreement on the topic of compulsion in minor marriage, while delving into the discussions that lie beyond this denominator. The jurists usually present these issues as multivalent and complex; it is the intention of this chapter to suggest that divesting the claim of Ijmāʿ from the complex discussions surrounding it allows it far more power than the earliest writers would have granted it.

This section, then, presents the relevant entries from a consensus manual, listed in the order in which Ibn al-Qaṭṭān has included them, with his section titles underlined, the title of the work he cites, as he cites it (in some instances he uses only the author's name, as is the case with al-Marwazī), and the paragraph number[49] in *al-Iqnāʿ*. We have footnoted the quotations as they are located in the original works; where no match can be found, this is so noted.

Mention of the Marriages [contracted by] fathers (*inkāḥ al-ābāʾ*):[50]

Al-Ishrāf:
2124: "The contracts of fathers render permissible the forbidden genitalia."[51]

---

over it. This is the meaning of Ijmāʿ. There is no other meaning of Ijmāʿ in the religion at all. Whoever claims otherwise is alleging what he does not know … or understand, and claiming what he cannot know the truth of. (*al-Iḥkām*, 4:119).

[The editor charts a *hadith-fiqh* divide over the issue, then: *Ijmāʿ* over a hadith upon which a rule can be founded versus the *Ijmāʿ* of scholarly opinion. The latter, it is posed, is a stark impossibility.].

Ibn al-Mundhir, for his part, followed al-Ṭabarī in his methodology of stating an issue, and if there was disagreement or a singular unsupported opinion, he would consider it *Ijmāʿ* of the scholars, not taking into account one or two men. (*al-Awsaṭ*, 48).

49 The Cairo edition (Volume 2) numbers these beginning at 2134.

50 Ibn al-Qaṭṭān, *al-Iqnāʿ*, 3:1153–1167.

51 I did not actually find this phrase in Ibn al-Mundhir's *al-Ishrāf*; it is an assessment that could be deemed irresponsible given Ibn al-Mundhir's position that pubescent females are *not* subject to the father's marriage contracts. See Ibn al-Mundhir: Chapter 9 on Guardians Seeking the Orders of Non-Virgin Women and Requesting the Permission of Virgins, and Chapter 12 on Marriages Contracted by Fathers for their Virgin Prepubescent Daughters; *al-Ishrāf ʿalā madhāhib ahl al-ʿilm*, (Beirut: Dār al-Fikr, 1993) 1:24–26.

[*Ikhtilāf al-ʿulamāʾ* of] al-Marwazī:
2125: "There is consensus of the scholars that the father can marry off his pre-pubescent son and his daughter, and they have no right of rescission (*khiyār*) in the matter if later they reach maturity (*adrakā*)."[52]

2126: "I know no one who is of the opinion that a father can compel a non-virgin to marry except al-Ḥasan al-Baṣrī, who said: 'a father's marrying off of his daughter is binding, be she virgin or non-virgin, if he compelled her against her will (*akrahahā*) or did not compel her against her will.' I do not know anyone who follows him in that."[53]

Al-Nayyir
2127: "A marriage contract made for a man's daughter is binding, be she prepubescent or pubescent, compelled against her will or consenting, if it is for her benefit, and there is no dispute among scholars with regard to that."

Al-Nawādir[54] [*Ikhtilāf al-ʿUlamāʾ* of al-Ṭaḥāwī]
2128: "There is consensus that the father of a pre-pubescent may marry her off, although Ibn Shubrama dissented saying 'The marriage of a

52 Muḥammad ibn Naṣr al-Marwazī, *Ikhtilāf al-ʿUlamāʾ* (Beirut: ʿĀlam al-Kutub, 1986), 125. Note that al-Marwazī's work is characterized as an abridgment (*mukhtaṣar*) by al-Subkī, while Ibn al-Nadīm notes that there were "large" and a "small" versions of the work. See *al-Iqnāʿ*, 1:60.

53 Not a phrase that was found in the text.

54 *Nawādir al-Ijmāʿ* or *Nawādir al-fuqahāʾ*, it is an abridgment (by a 10th century author unknown but for his name, Muḥammad ibn al-Ḥasan al-Tamīmī al-Jawharī) of al-Ṭaḥāwī's *Ikhtilāf al-ʿUlamā*, and therefore we will rely upon the latter for purposes of analysis. To be clear, the work *Ikhtilāf al-ʿUlamāʾ* as we have it is also an abridgment, by al-Jaṣṣāṣ. However, this abridgment is much larger and contains far more detail than al-Jawharī's work. I feel it will provide for a more stable representation of al-Ṭaḥāwī's work, although an ideal further pursuit would be to make a full line-by-line comparison of the two works. Al-Jawharī was clearly concerned with accentuating the lone opinions of dissent from *Ijmāʿ* (*infirādāt*). Like the other Ijmāʿ works (*Kitāb al-Ijmāʿ* of ibn al-Mundhir and Ibn Hubayra), al-Jawharī's work takes the '*wa-jmaʿū anna* ...' form, divesting each 'point of consensus' from all accompanying debate and discussion. Al-Jaṣṣāṣ takes care to include multiple opinions and some idea of the reasoning behind them. I will use al-Jaṣṣāṣ' recension, then, while still referring to it as al-Ṭaḥāwī's *Ikhtilāf*. I will also have recourse to another of al-Ṭaḥāwī's works, *Maʿānī al-āthār*, in order to fill in any gaps.

pre-pubescent (girl) is nonbinding whatever the case (*lā yajūzu nikāḥ ṣaghīra ʿalā ḥālin*)."[55]

Mention of the Marriages [contracted by] Marriage guardians

Al-Nukat:
2132: "And Dawūd has said, If she is a virgin, she must have a guardian, and if she is a non-virgin, she has no need of a *walī*"—and Ibn al-Qaṭṭān interjects, "and this goes against the consensus; there is dispute regarding [the necessity of the marriage guardian in the case of] the pubescent, but with regard to the prepubescent virgin there is no dispute [regarding the necessity of having a *walī*]."

Mention of consultation (*istiʾmār*), requesting her permission (*istiʾdhān*), and the agreement of the woman (*riḍā al-marʾa*).

Al-Ishrāf:
2141: "It is established (*thubita*) that the Messenger of God said, 'The non-virgin is not to be married off unless she is consulted.'"[56]

2142: "Most scholars have reached the consensus that a father's marrying off of his non-virgin daughter without her agreement is nonbinding."[57]

Al-Istidhkār:
2143: "His [the Prophet's] saying that 'a virgin is not married off without the seeking of her permission' is a general statement (*ʿalā ʿumūmihi*) with regard to the prepubescent who has a father, by the proof of consensus upon her (*Lā tunkaḥu al-bikr ḥattā tustaʾdhanu hādhā ʿalā ʿumūmihi fī al-ṣaghīra dhāt al-ab bi-dalīl al-ijmāʿ ʿalayhā*)"[58]

---

55 Abū Jaʿfar Aḥmad ibn Muḥammad al-Ṭaḥāwī, *Ikhtilāf al-ʿUlamāʾ* (Beirut: Dār al-Bashāʾir al-Islāmīyah, 1995) 2:257; see also Muḥammad ibn al-Ḥasan al-Tamīmī al-Jawharī, *Nawādir al-fuqahāʾ*, (Damascus: Dār al-Qalam, 1993), 83.

56 *Al-Ishrāf*, 1:25. The actual report as recorded in the *Ishrāf* reads, "The non-virgin is not married until she is consulted, and the virgin is not married until her permission is sought." It is worth noting that Ibn al-Mundhir himself never halves this report; when talking about virgins, he includes the entirety which also refers to non-virgins, and vice versa.

57 *Al-Ishrāf*, 1:25.

58 *Al-Istidhkār*, 5:403; see Chapter Seven below for an extended discussion of this reference (to Ḥanafī arguments) and its place in Ibn ʿAbd al-Barr's discussion. The underlying text reads: *Lā tunkaḥu al-bikr ḥattā tustaʾdhanu hādhā ʿalā ʿumūmihi fī al-ṣaghīra dhāt al-ab*

2144: "And they have reached consensus that the father can marry off his prepubescent daughter and not seek her permission, and they have differed over whether he can compel his pubescent daughter or not.[59] And they have differed over anyone other than the father as marriage guardian; can such persons marry off the prepubescent or not?[60] And [they have differed] over the silence of the orphaned (i.e. fatherless) virgin: [does it suffice as] consent from her before her permission [is asked] or she is consulted on the subject?"[61]

Prepubescent boys:

Al-Nayyir:
2239: "They have reached consensus that the father if he contracts marriage for his prepubescent son for a non-extravagant bridal gift, it is for the son to pay, ʿand the bridal gift is incumbent upon the son and not the father, except for al-Ḥasan ibn Ṣāliḥ,[62] who made it incumbent upon the father, not the son."

Having included all the sections from Ibn al-Qaṭṭān's encyclopedia of consensus which are relevant to compulsion in minor marriages, I now turn to an exploration of the original texts he has cited. This discussion will focus on how the writers who came to be considered "sources" for consensus actually dealt with the topic, the proof texts they adduce, and the parameters within which consensus exists. Because he is cited first in *al-Iqnāʿ*, I will turn first to Ibn al-Mundhir, the most famous of the writers on the topic of consensus.

---

bi-dalīl al-ijmāʿ ʿalā maʿnā ḥadīth tazwīj al-nabī ṣalā Allāh ʿalayh wa-sallam ʿĀʾisha raḍī Allāh ʿanhā.

59 I did not find this phrase in *al-Istidhkār*.

60 *Al-Istidhkār*, 5:404.

61 I did not find this phrase in *al-Istidhkār*.

62 Ibn al-Qaṭṭān (and his editor) did nothing to clarify this identity. The closest match seems to be al-Ḥasan ibn Ṣaliḥ ibn Ḥayy al-Kūfī, a Zaydī scholar in 168/785 who is attributed with founding the Zaydī sect of the Ṣāliḥiyya. See Pellat, Ch. "al-Ḥasan b.Ṣāliḥ b.Ḥayy al-Kūfī, Abū ʿAbd Allāh." *EI2*.

The Consensus Writers

Ibn al-Mundhir: Last of the Independent Jurists?

As discussed, the Ḥanbalī Ibn Qudāma's manual of positive law is full of references to consensus as transmitted by Ibn al-Mundhir al-Nīsābūrī. A word should be said about how his scholarship has come down to us today.

Ibn al-Mundhir is most famous for his book *Kitāb al-Ijmāʿ*,[63] which, although a tiny abridgment, is relied upon until this day. The fact that medieval authors quoted from much, much longer works that are now lost is seldom if ever emphasized: Ibn al-Mundhir is less well known for the long chain of books from which *K. al-Ijmāʿ* was the eventual abridgment. The *K. al-Mabsūṭ*[64] was an enormous work on the disagreements of the scholars, which was abridged into the *K. al-Awsaṭ fī al-sunan wa-l-ijmāʿ wa-l-ikhtilāf*, a lengthy work which was then further summarized in the smaller work, *K. al-Ishrāf ʿalā madhāhib al-ʿulamāʾ*. This latter work must have been the basis for the comparatively miniscule work, *K. al-Ijmāʿ*, which "he summarized from his [other] books; and despite this, he was not faithful in it to the incidences of consensus that he related in the *Ishrāf* and the *Awsaṭ* and the others."[65]

Not to be confused with *al-Iqnāʿ fī masāʾil al-ijmāʿ* of Ibn al-Qaṭṭān, *al-Iqnāʿ* of Ibn al-Mundhir is another abbreviated work, although it affords many more details than *K. al-Ijmāʿ*. In the opinion of the editor of al-*Awsaṭ*, *al-Iqnāʿ* is an abridgment of *al-Awsaṭ* itself.[66] One hadith appears in each chapter, if there is a pertinent hadith, and they all match the hadith and content (*matn*) found in *al-Awsaṭ*.[67] Of it, the editor of Ibn al-Qaṭṭān's book states:

> It is a summary of the *aḥadīth* relating to rulings, and the jurisprudential decisions of Ibn al-Mundhir. He notes *aḥadīth* with their chains of transmission, and sometimes he mentions a hadith or part of a hadith without the chains in order to cite the location of a proof text to illustrate (a ruling's) establishment. Or, he will indicate sayings that the jurists

63 In addition to the above-mentioned Bārūdī edition, there are two other editions, one edited by Fuʾād ʿAbd al-Manʿam Aḥmad (Alexandria: Dār al-Daʿwah, 1982) and the other by Abū Ḥammād Ṣaghīr Aḥmad (Riyāḍ: Dār Ṭayyibah, 1982).

64 Information about the abridgment is based on the extensive research of Abū Ḥammād Ṣaghīr Aḥmad, editor of Ibn al-Mundhir's *al-Awsaṭ fī al-sunan wa-l-ijmāʿ wa-l-ikhtilāf*, (Riyāḍ: Dār Ṭayyibah, 1993), 1:31.

65 So says Fārūq Ḥammādah, the editor of *Al-Iqnāʿ fī masāʾil al-ijmāʿ* by Ibn al-Qaṭṭān al-Fāsī, (Damascus: Dār al-Qalam, 2003), 1:67.

66 It is also referenced in Sezguin, v. 1, pt. 3, 200–201.

67 *K. al-Awsaṭ*, 1:36.

> used that were not proven. It is a book that includes 244 hadith, some instances of Ijmāʿ, juristic opinions ... Al-Asnāwī described it in *al-Ṭabaqāt al-Shāfiʿīyyah* as being "extracted rulings (*aḥkām mujarradah*) like the *Muḥarrir* of al-Rāfiʿī in size and form."[68]

The chapter on marriage is quite short in comparison with *K. al-Ishrāf.* It contains only one sub-chapter pertaining to marriage and consent, entitled "Mention of the void status of a marriage (contracted) without a marriage guardian." The rest of the chapters relate to the encouragement to marry for those who can afford to do so, bride-gifts, marriage to relatives, breastfeeding, marrying slaves, equality between co-wives, and modalities of maintenance.

Within the above-referenced sub-chapter, Ibn al-Mundhir is quite brief. He cites no opinions of scholars, although he does give a detailed isnād for the hadith "There is no marriage without a marriage guardian."

> Marriage is not permitted without a marriage guardian, and the marriage guardians are the male members of the family (*al-ʿuṣba*). If there is no marriage guardian to be had, then the ruler is the guardian for those who have none. If a woman marries without the permission of her guardian or the ruler (if she has no guardian), then her marriage is void. If he has not performed sex upon her (*in lam yuṣibhā*), they are separated. If he has performed sex upon her then she is to receive the marriage gift of her peers, to make her genitalia licit for him (*bimā ustaḥall min farjihā*), and any child is ascribed to him, and she must submit to a waiting period, and he must marry her properly again (*wa lahu ʿan yankiḥuhā nikāḥan mustaʾnifan ṣaḥīḥan*).[69]

He quickly classifies those who cannot be *walī,* among them a woman for herself, and then says, "A man may marry (*yuzawwiju*) his virgin daughter who has not reached pubescence without her permission." Then he notes that the indicator relied upon in the marriage of prepubescent girls without their consent is the hadith of ʿĀʾisha. He continues that this applies only to fathers and grandfathers, not testators or the non-paternal marriage guardians. Not only this, but a man may "contract marriage for his prepubescent son. However, the pubescent virgin may not be married off without her consent due to the "*thābit*" (well-established hadith) from the Messenger that, "the virgin cannot

68 *K. al-Iqnāʿ*, 1:67.

69 Ibn al-Mundhir, *K. Al-Iqnāʿ*, ed. ʿAbd Allāh al-Jibrīn (Riyāḍ: Maktabat al-Rushd, 1987), 1:297.

be married until she gives her permission, and the non-virgin until she is consulted." His final comment with regard to females and consent is the sentence reading, "If a marriage guardian contracts marriage (*zawwaja*) for a woman (*al-mar'a*) without her consent, and then informs her and she permits it (*ajāzat*), the marriage is not valid until the contract is redone with her permission (*ḥattā tujaddid nikāḥan bi-idhnihā*)."[70]

This small paragraph, with a great deal more information than what is afforded us in *K. al-Ijmāʿ*, is still paltry, however, when compared to the depth of analysis on the subject of marriage and consent that Ibn al-Mundhir offers in *K. al-Ishrāf*—a book that is *also* an abridgment. Thus we see that it was only in the pages of the *Ishrāf* that we become familiar with the subtleties of the matters at hand.

Although Ibn Qudāma's editors continuously cite *K. al-Ijmāʿ* for the references to Ibn al-Mundhir, the differences in wording could not be ignored, and our research has shown conclusively that the source upon which Ibn Qudāma actually relied was the *Kitāb al-Awsaṭ fī al-Sunan wa-l-Ijmāʿ wa-l-Ikhtilāf*, of which only six volumes are today extant. At the reference for prepubescent marriage, as with every single incidence of consensus listed in *K. al-Ijmāʿ*, the text reads: "They have reached consensus (*ajmaʿū*)… ." The wording quoted above from *al-Mughnī* resembles more closely that used in *K. al-Ishrāf*: "The scholars of religion have reached consensus that a father's contracting marriage for his prepubescent virgin daughter is binding if he marries her to an equal;"[71] but the quotation is still not verbatim. The only possible conclusion is that this wording might have been found in *K. al-Awsaṭ*, for which the chapter on Marriage is not extant.[72] The wording differences are not trivial. Ibn Qudāma's quotation, here and elsewhere in the *Mughnī*, has Ibn al-Mundhir referring to instances of consensus as being those of "all with whom I have studied the religious sciences," or "the generality of the scholars of religion."

Although Ibn al-Qaṭṭān extracted minimal information from Ibn al-Mundhir's *Kitāb al-Ishrāf* (itself an abridgment of the latter's *Kitāb al-Awsaṭ*, as mentioned), Ibn al-Mundhir's book includes several chapters relating to the topic of prepubescent marriage. In these, he contextualizes his discussions within discussions of consent and marriage generally. He is keen, as well,

---

70 Ibid., 1:298.

71 Ibn al-Mundhir, *K. al-Ishrāf ʿalā madhāhib al-ʿulamāʾ* (Beirut: Dār al-Fikr, 1993), 1:26. Our edition of the Mughnī, published in 1996, would have post-dated the publishing of both *K. al-Ishrāf* and the Dār Ṭayyibah edition of *K. al-Awsaṭ* (both 1993).

72 Further, it is logical to assume that this was the source upon which Ibn Qudāma relied because of its extensive hadith content, which is not a feature of *K. al-Ishrāf*.

to attribute differences of opinion wherever they emerge—for example, and of particular note, his break with al-Shāfiʿī. There is much information to be gleaned from *Kitāb al-Ishrāf*'s presentation of these opinions; however, until the original chapter on marriage is discovered from the more detailed *Kitāb al-Awsaṭ*, or better yet that chapter which vanished with *Kitāb al-Mabsūṭ* (from which *al-Awsaṭ* is abridged), we will never know the actual contours of Ibn al-Mundhir's thought on the subject. He remains here, for the most part, very much a compiler of the opinions of others.

All of the writers presented in this chapter are included in Ibn al-Qaṭṭān's encyclopedia of consensus. Despite their inclusion (alongside many others throughout the four-volume work), none but Ibn al-Mundhir ever seems to have acquired significant legal authority: It is above all in the pages of *al-Mughnī* that we witness the development of the compiler of consensus becoming himself a source of consensus, for Ibn Qudāma's book is riddled with the words *qāla* or *ḥakā Ibn al-Mundhir*. As noted, the former Chief of the Sharīʿa Courts and Religious Issues of the nation of Qaṭar has claimed to rely upon the rulings of Ibn al-Mundhir as a legal resource.[73]

Assuming that the judge's words are true, reliance on *Kitāb al-Ijmāʿ* is reliance on rulings that cannot possibly give a true sense of the depth of conversation surrounding each issue. For the issue of prepubescent marriage in Islamic law, the simple consensus statement of Ibn al-Mundhir belies the multitude of sub-issues upon which consensus *cannot possibly* be claimed.

Al-Marwazī (d. 294/906):[74] *Bringing in Companions*

Al-Marwazī's chapter on marriage in *Kitāb Ikhtilāf al-Ulamā'* is relatively brief. By introducing Companions into the issue of the consensus (not an explicit strategy of Ibn al-Mundhir or the other writers included here, although it is a strategy of Ibn Qudāma in the *Mughnī*),[75] al-Marwazī attempts to bolster his claim of consensus by locating it in the righteous forebears of the religion. He is bringing their authority to bear on the subject in a way that emphasizes the rights of the father to contract marriages for children of *either* sex. Al-Marwazī

73 F.A. Aḥmad, ed, *Kitāb al-Ijmāʿ*, (Alexandria: Dār al-Daʿwah, 1982) p. 4, and see above, p. 149, for the judge's full quotation.

74 Muḥammad ibn Naṣr al-Marwazī was born in Baghdād and died in Samarqand, he was a leading hadith scholar in Khurasān, highly prolific as a writer of fiqh works. See *al-Iqnāʿ*, 1:58–62.

75 See *al-Mughnī*, 9:201. He does, however cite 'Ammār and Ibn Shubrama (who was not, in any case, a Companion, having died in 144/761, and whose opinions—as reported—seem to be constantly in flux).

does not, however, include his own opinion, as Ibn al-Mundhir did. His sole intent seems to be to compile the opinions of others; nonetheless there is a detectable bias for the jurisprudence of al-Shāfiʿī, as we will see.

Al-Marwazī's brevity is an outstanding characteristic. He folds his thoughts on female legal capacity and male suitability into his argument in support of the guardianship of compulsion. Likewise, his brief discussion of rescission comes closely on the heels of the treatment of who may compel marriage.

Al-Ṭaḥāwī (d. 321/933): A Shāfiʿī Boy Gone Bad

Ibn al-Qaṭṭān refers to *Nawādir al-Ijmāʿ* (or, *Nawādir al-fuqahāʾ*) of Muḥammad ibn al-Ḥasan al-Tamīmī al-Jawharī.[76] According to the editor of *al-Iqnāʿ*, *Nawādir al-Ijmāʿ* is an abridgment of al-Ṭaḥāwī's *Ikhtilāf al-ʿUlamāʾ*; therefore it makes considerably more sense to simply rely on the sections in the latter work that pertain to our subject, particularly considering that al-Ṭaḥāwī was a close contemporary of Ibn al-Mundhir and considered one of the first generation of writers on consensus.[77]

Like *Kitāb al-Ishrāf*, *Ikhtilāf al-ʿulamāʾ* is an abridgment,[78] and its language is brief and to the point. It seems clear that al-Ṭaḥāwī's "point" (or perhaps that of his abridger) is to list opinions, highlighting first and foremost the Ḥanafī position, which solidly supports prepubescent marriage. The only deviation from these summaries is his inclusion of the Qurʾānic proof text 4:3,[79] a text that has not been cited in any earlier work. The most interesting inclusion is that of Ibn Shubrama's position as being staunchly against the marriage of children. Thus the first section in an investigation of al-Ṭaḥāwī will exhibit his particular approach to consensus, which focuses on the Ḥanafī *madhhab* in particular.

Similarly to the previous works, al-Ṭaḥāwī's work also contextualizes the subject of prepubescent marriage within the larger subject of consent and marriage. As such, his concern with issues pertaining to the marriage guardian (a subject considered closed by the other schools) looms larger than that of other writers. Within his discussion of guardianship, we find his opinions on

---

76 Says the editor of *al-Iqnāʿ*, Fārūq Ḥammādah: "I have endeavored greatly to find out who he is and I was not successful." He does note, however, that Ibn Rushd quoted the author in *Bidāyat al-Mujtahid*, relying upon him as a source of consensus. *Al-Iqnāʿ*, 1:86.

77 Al-Ṭabarī, Ibn al-Mundhir, and al-Ṭaḥāwī were contemporaries who shared teachers and all wrote on disagreement and consensus in practical law (*furūʿ*).

78 It was abridged by al-Jaṣṣāṣ (d. 370/981).

79 Q4:3: "And if you have reason to fear that you might not act equitably towards orphans, then marry from among [other] women such as are lawful to you …" *wa-in khiftum a-lā tuqsiṭū fī al-yatāmā fa-nkiḥū mā ṭāba lakum min al-nisāʾ …*

women and capacity as well as on the capacity of children. Most significant in this regard are his comparisons between the capacity of children with that of the slave woman, an issue, as we have seen, that was of major concern to the pre-consensus jurists.

Finally, we will encounter briefly his thoughts on the subject of suitability. In regard to that issue, al-Ṭaḥāwī shows his affinity with the Shāfiʿī school by basing his position on this topic upon very similar logic.

The book is entitled "Disagreements of the Scholars," and al-Ṭaḥāwī does not use the vocabulary of consensus. Although the book looks quite similar to Ibn al-Mundhir's, and functions in the same way, there are still marked differences. It is not simply a semantic difference to note that al-Ṭaḥāwī does not begin sentences with the words, "And they agreed upon …" Rather, where there is no dissent, he says, "There is no disagreement regarding …" The only time in his chapter on marriage in the *Ikhtilāf* that I noted an occurrence of lack of dissent is in the small sub-chapter entitled, "Regarding the contract of a woman for herself." Here, the lack of disagreement (or tacit consensus) he is emphasizing is a Ḥanafī one, not a scholarly-wide one.[80] It could well be that his approach to consensus itself is considerably more pessimistic than that of his contemporary Ibn al-Mundhir.

We find in Ibn al-Qaṭṭān, however, the following:

> ¶2128: "There is consensus that the father of a prepubescent may contract marriage for her,[81] although Ibn Shubrama dissented saying 'The marriage of a prepubescent (girl) is nonbinding whatever the case (*lā yajūzu nikāḥ ṣaghīra ʿalā ḥālin*)."[82]

Meanwhile, what Ibn al-Qaṭṭān claims to quote, *Nawādir al-Ijmāʿ/al-fuqahāʾ*, reads like this:

> ¶5/71: They have reached consensus that contracting marriage for a prepubescent girl is binding (*ajmaʿū anna tazwīj al-ṣaghīra jāʾiz ʿalayhā*) except for ʿAbd Allāh ibn Shubrama, may God be pleased with him, for he said, "The marriage of a prepubescent (girl) is nonbinding whatever the case."[83]

---

80 For further discussion, see the end of this section.

81 This phrase does not exist in the *Ikhtilāf*. 3:1157, Ibn al-Qaṭṭān.

82 Abū Jaʿfar Aḥmad ibn Muḥammad al-Ṭaḥāwī, *Ikhtilāf al-ʿUlamāʾ* (Beirut: Dār al-Bashāʾir al-Islāmīyah, 1995) 2:257.

83 *Nawādir al-fuqahāʾ*, 83.

The difference is not minor. It is possible that the understanding of the rights of fathers over their daughters was so deeply entrenched that al-Jawharī might simply have been abbreviating. But according to this wording, al-Jawharī appears to have claimed consensus that anyone, not just the father, can contract marriage for the prepubescent girl (he does not mention boys). Ibn al-Qaṭṭān, then, has gone beyond the role of compiler to interpolater.

If al-Jaṣṣāṣ is to be believed, the actual wording from al-Ṭaḥāwī is as follows:

> Our companions have said: The guardians of children may contract their marriages, depending upon who is closest (as a blood relative), and they have no right to rescind if it is the contract of marriage made by a father or grandfather, and they have the right of rescission if they are married by other than these. This is the statement of Abū Ḥanīfa and Muḥammad. And Abū Yūsuf said, they have no right of rescission [no matter who has married them].[84]

Al-Ṭaḥāwī runs through the opinions of all of the scholars, including Ibn Shubrama, but never claims a consensus on the topic. Does this mean that he does not use the vocabulary of consensus at all? It is not evident from the terse passages that al-Jaṣṣāṣ has left for us in this abridgment. Al-Ṭaḥāwī's opinion on consensus is clear, however, in a passage of *Maʿānī al-Āthār*,[85] his detailed work on hadiths which are used as *ratio legum* in law. I include and contextualize it because it informs the discussion on prepubescent marriage.

Ibn ʿAbd al-Barr (463/1070): Rewriting Early Scripts

Ibn ʿAbd al-Barr is the first of our authors to engage in claiming consensus outright for what is in fact a Mālikī position—that fathers can contract marriages for virgins be they pubescent or prepubescent. Even though he does acknowledge other positions, the claim of consensus where there is in fact none (over the lot of the pubescent virgin) is a powerful foreshadowing of the future of Ijmāʿ generally, and typical of inter-madhhab polemical strategies. Ibn ʿAbd al-Barr's assessments about this subject include texts produced by jurists who are non-Mālikī; he best represents the long-term effects of al-Shāfiʿī's thought on the subject of the compelled marriage of prepubescents.

Like the writers before him, Ibn ʿAbd al-Barr's main conception of consensus seems to be that which serves to give weight to a particular legal meaning

84 Ibid.

85 Abū Jaʿfar ibn Muḥammad ibn Sallāma al-Ṭaḥāwī, *Maʿānī al-Āthār*, (Beirut: Dār al-Kutub al-ʿIlmīyah, 2006.).

derived from a hadith. In the case of prepubescent marriage, Ibn ʿAbd al-Barr discusses three main pertinent traditions, each of which has implications for the consent and capacity of females: the *ayyim/bikr* hadith, the "No marriage without a guardian" hadith, and the report of ʿĀʾisha.

Ibn ʿAbd al-Barr's analysis focuses mainly on the essential Mālikī text found in the *Muwaṭṭaʾ* on the subject, "The single woman/previously-married woman (*ayyim*) has more legal capacity ..." However, he structures the entirety of his interpretation on making it possible to retain what al-Shāfiʿī adduces in the *Umm* as a text of great importance: "There is no marriage without a marriage guardian" (*lā nikāḥ illā bi-walī*).[86] We have already discussed this text's importance for the likes of al-Marwazī and Ibn al-Mundhir and how it served to shape al-Ṭaḥāwī's arguments. What interests us here is that Ibn ʿAbd al-Barr has abandoned the Mālikī text—a report from ʿUmar that the marrying woman requires the permission of her guardian, a responsible member of her family, or the ruler.[87] Ibn ʿAbd al-Barr barely mentions this report, dealing with it in a cursory way even in the later chapter which is supposed to be devoted to it. We can only assume that the reasons behind this legal strategy relate to his attempt to anchor his proofs in Sunnaic reports that go all the way back to the Prophet. This, too, must be his reason for giving preference to the hadith of ʿĀʾisha over the only text that Mālik includes on the subject: an opinion from the Successors al-Qāsim ibn Muḥammad and Sālim ibn ʿAbd Allāh that it was their practice to contract marriages for their virgin daughters (*banātihimā al-abkār*), no age specified, even if against their will.[88]

In addition to his discussion of these three pertinent traditions, and unlike the three previous writers, he does make an Ijmāʿic claim for a general Muslim consensus with regard to the ability of fathers to contract marriages for their virgin daughters. This might have been, given the palette of legal strategies available to him, more expedient than to note that Mālik's opinion on this derives only from the practice of two Successors.

By looking to consensus to validate the derived meaning of hadiths, and invoking an Ijmāʿic claim emanating from "the Muslims" vis a vis the power of fathers over their virgin daughters, Ibn ʿAbd al-Barr creates a formidable case against the legal capacity of females, prepubescent or otherwise. Like the other consensus writers, his overwhelming concern with hadith and the way he uses consensus are built upon a Shāfiʿīan investment in unit traditions.

---

86 See *al-Umm*, section 9, 6:31–35.

87 *Al-Muwaṭṭaʾ*, 2:53.

88 Ibid.

Conclusion

This chapter has considered some of the legal-theoretical issues tied to the doctrine of consensus. Consolidating the vast body of juridical opinions emerging from so many different practices, proof texts, and legal approaches was posited as being in the interest of a strong and streamlined state. Reimagining a united and univocal early community allowed Muslim scholars to call believers into a fold of strength, while imposing legal uniformity would keep outlying areas from straying too far beyond community norms.

Still, whose consensus is being cited when consensus claims are made? It is this which is at issue. Abridging a citation of consensus often meant stripping it of words like, "the scholars with whom I have studied." Leaving only the words "*they* have reached consensus" could theoretically result in those using the citation to impose upon it the authoritative group of their choosing. Companions, scholars, early scholars, and indeed the entirety of the Muslim community all have, at some point or other, been characterized as having agreed about a particular point of law or a particular proof text's implications.

Thus it is useful, in turning to the next chapter, to consider the contexts of those writing on consensus, and to notice to what extent they still admitted of dissent. It is further useful to seek out the influence of al-Shāfiʿī in their writings. For whatever the theoretical underpinnings of consensus, and whatever the debates over the possibility or impossibility of establishing a consensus, the fact is that the methodologies used by the jurists in the next chapter, their proof texts and discussions, all develop an undeniably Shāfiʿīan air.

CHAPTER 7

Writing Consensus

This chapter will endeavor to present the consensus writing[1] of the 10th and 11th century writers whose opinions Ibn al-Qaṭṭān compiled. As an introduction, I will offer some observations regarding the influence of al-Shāfiʿī. The importance of his role in the transformation of Islamic law from a tradition-based discourse to "a community of interpretation" cannot be overstated.[2]

Early loyalty to the thought of al-Shāfiʿī was a noticeable feature in early writings on consensus,[3] whether such loyalty took the form of the use of arguments articulated in the *Umm* or simply the incorporation of al-Shāfiʿī's text-based legal methodologies.[4] Of the four earliest writers discussed in this chapter, three of them studied with al-Rabīʿ Ibn Sulaymān (d. 270/883), the great student of al-Shāfiʿī and prime articulator of his thought.[5] For two of our consensus writers, this fact evidences itself in their writings with undeniable clarity: El Shamsy has detailed the many incidences of direct quotations from al-Shāfiʿī in the writings of both Ibn al-Mundhir and al-Marwazī.[6] For al-Marwazī, El Shamsy has found extensive evidence of borrowings and quotations from the *Umm* and the *Risāla* in al-Marwazī's Sunna work, his book on prayer, and finally in the *Ikhtilāf al-ʿUlamāʾ*,[7] discussed here. The third writer,

1 It is important to note that the works under consideration were indeed consciously-written works instead of compilations of lecture notes, as the early juridical works under consideration would have been.

2 El Shamsy, *Canonization*, 6.

3 In *Ṭabaqāt al-Shāfiʿīya*, al-Subkī observes that Ibn al-Mundhir was "a *mujtahid* who followed no one" (*wa kāna mujtahidan lā yuqallidu aḥadan*). It is clear, however, that al-Subkī, as a Shafiʿī, took pride in claiming that the opinion of Ibn al-Mundhir corresponded with that of al-Shafiʿī: "for if they [the four Muhammads] depart from the opinion of the Greatest Imām on many issues, yet more often than not they have not departed, so know that and know that they are counted among the Shāfiʿīs." *Al-Ṭabaqāt*, 3:102, entry 117.

4 It is possible that some of the surge in obvious Shafiʿian influence has to do with entry into the "golden age" for the Shāfiʿis after Bakkār ibn Qutayba (in office 860–884) lifted the ban against his teaching. See El Shamsy, *Canonization*, 137–144.

5 El Shamsy, *Canonization*, 213–216.

6 In checking the indices of *al-Ishrāf*, for example, al-Shāfiʿī is invoked some 3471 times. I am grateful to El Shamsy, "From Tradition to Law: the Origins and Early Development of the Shāfiʿī School of Law in Ninth-Century Egypt," Harvard Dissertation, 2009, 246–7 for directing me.

7 Ibid.

 | DOI 10.1163/9789004344860_009

al-Ṭaḥāwī,[8] was the nephew of al-Muzanī, one of the most famous expounders of al-Shāfiʿī's legal theories; only later in life did al-Ṭaḥāwī switch camps and become a Ḥanafī. Both his *Ikhtilāf* book and his extensive tradition work, *Maʿānī al-Āthār*, bear the stamp of al-Shāfiʿī's thought,[9] especially a very un-Ḥanafī concern with locating legal precedent in traditions.[10] His use of al-Shāfiʿī's legal-theoretical arguments and traditionist methodologies is so extensive, in fact, that it can be considered "a significant milestone in the eventual convergence of the traditionalist and rationalist movements."[11]

The fourth writer, Ibn ʿAbd al-Barr, despite having cheered on Muḥammad ibn ʿAbd al-Ḥakam's refutation of al-Shāfiʿī,[12] quotes al-Shāfiʿī extensively, and engages unapologetically in the use of legal strategies that bear the stamp of al-Shāfiʿī. The effects of the latter's drive for use of traditionist methodologies in law is reflected in the work of major Mālikī scholars who post-dated him, and Ibn ʿAbd al-Barr, as we shall see, is no exception.[13]

Al-Shāfiʿī's thoughts on consensus link it almost invariably to the interpretation of "already relevant" texts from the Qur'ān or Sunna.[14] By making the report of ʿĀ'isha a cornerstone of his thinking on the subject,[15] he affected the discussion in ways he perhaps never would have anticipated, across all of the future schools of law. As noted this hadith was not used or relied upon in any of the early works of law prior to or contemporaneous with al-Shāfiʿī, with the exception of the *Muṣannaf* of ʿAbd al-Razzāq (d. 211/826); even then it was not used to obviate female consent or argue for a father's ability to compel.[16]

---

8 Al-Ṭaḥawī and Ibn al-Mundhir in fact had several teachers in common, including Muḥammad ibn ʿAbd al-Ḥakam (d. 268/881), who had been set to take the leadership of the Shāfiʿīs after the master's death (and subsequently left and wrote his famed, though not extant, refutation), and Bakkār ibn Qutayba (270/883), the "judge of Egypt and its [greatest] hadith scholar" (F. Aḥmad, 7).

9 We note particularly the similarity between his thinking and that recorded in the *Risāla* in reference to the use of evidence of correct interpretation (*dalāla*) in the face of any textual ambiguity (*iḥtimāl*). See Lowry, 67 and 328; *Risāla* ¶339, 397, 1320 and 1727; *Maʿānī al-āthār* of al-Ṭaḥāwī, 2:368.

10 It is a gross understatement to say that there are marked differences in approaches and proofs between al-Ṭaḥāwī's works cited here, and, for example, that of al-Shaybānī's *Ḥujja*.

11 El Shamsy, *Canonization*, 207.

12 Ibid., 209. Note that Ibn ʿAbd al-Ḥakam was something of a Shafiʿian fifth columnist and also, as noted above, the teacher of both al-Ṭaḥāwī and Ibn al-Mundhir.

13 Ibid., 208.

14 Lowry, *Early Islamic Legal Theory*, both p. 328 and Chapter 7 generally.

15 See *al-Umm*, 6:45.

16 In other words, this hadith is not used as a proof or referred to in the *Sunan* of al-Awzāʿī (158/774), the *Muṣannaf* of Ibn Abī Shayba, (235/849), the *Ḥujja* of al-Shaybānī (189/805), the *Muwaṭṭa'* of Mālik (179/795) or the *Mudawwana* of Saḥnūn (d. 240/854).

Eventually, however, even those initially most resistant to its incorporation, the Ḥanafīs, come to include it among their proofs.[17]

Weiss explains that al-Āmidī considered this to be the heart of consensus-making: the determination of the implications of a *ẓannī* ("inconclusive but otherwise productive of opinion") legal indicator. The conclusive indicator, accepted as clear and void of varying interpretations, would need no Ijmāʿ to replace it; it must remain as it is for every generation to consult and no Ijmāʿic statement can "convey the gist but not the actual words of the Sunna." This was the opinion of al-Shāfiʿī on the subject. "With the inconclusive indicator, on the other hand, there seems to be a meaningful role for the Ijmāʿ to play: it can accord absolute authority—authority that silences mujtahids and ends discussion—to what, solely by virtue of being based on the indicator, possesses no such authority."[18] The nonconcurrent, single report (*khabar wāḥid*), such as the report of ʿĀʾisha, would fall into such a category.

By claiming a consensus on the ability of a father to compel a female prepubescent, and pointing to the hadith of ʿĀʾisha as justification, late formative-era consensus writers were determining an otherwise indeterminate text through the engine of consensus.[19]

Ibn al-Mundhir

The Walī Mujbir and Proof Texts

Consensus for Ibn al-Mundhir centers almost exclusively around proof texts. The function of consensus is to locate the space in which jurists agree with regard to the total meaning of a verse or report. *Khilāf* is what occurs when the jurists begin hashing over the meanings of the component parts of a given verse or report which affect the legal application of the content. When he does assert an instance of consensus, then, Ibn al-Mundhir invariably links it to the legal meaning of a particular proof text. Nowhere is this more evident than

17 The hadith does not appear in the works of al-Ṭaḥāwī (d. 321/933) or even as late as al-Jaṣṣāṣ (d. 340/955). Even a text as late as al-Marghīnānī's (d. 593/1196) has him insisting that the Ḥanafī position is one that grounds the practice in an analogy with a father's charge over a child's finances, while acknowledging other schools' justifications for prepubescent marriage based on the text of the hadith ("In the opinion of Mālik ... the guardianship of the father is textually established.") Only his commentator (al-Laknāwī (d. 1304/ 1886) points to the hadith of ʿĀʾisha as being a source. (See *al-Hidāya, Sharḥ Bidāyat al-mubtadī* (Karachi: Maktabat al-Bushrā), 3:33.).

18 Weiss, *Search for God's Law*, 232–233.

19 Brown, *Canonization of Bukhārī and Muslim*, 192.

when he is discussing the legal status of the prepubescent female (*al-ṣaghīra*), and the meaning of the hadith of ʿĀʾisha for her.

In the chapter on marrying female children, he states immediately that it is "proven" (i.e. an established tradition) that Abū Bakr married (*zawwaja*) ʿĀʾisha to the Messenger of God when she was a girl of seven. The same basic statement that appears in *K. al-Ijmāʿ*[20] appears here: "The scholars have reached consensus that a father may marry off his child virgin daughter if he marries her to one who is equal in status."

As with most jurists, Ibn al-Mundhir cannot disassociate discussion of prepubescent marriage from discussion of marriage and consent generally. In *Kitāb al-Ishrāf*, he addresses marriage and consent in several chapters: The Chapter on Marriage Guardians Consulting Previously-Married Women and Seeking Permission from Virgins at the Time of Marriage, The Chapter on the Description of the Permission of the Previously-Married and the Virgin, The Chapter Mentioning the Invalidity of the Marriage (*nikāḥ*) of the Previously-Married who is Given in Marriage without her Permission, The Chapter on the *Nikāḥ* of the Father for his Prepubescent (*ṣaghīra*) Virgin Daughter, The Chapter on the *Nikāḥ* of a Father for his Infant Daughter (*ibnatuhu al-ṭifl*), and The Chapter on Testamentary Marriage.

Ibn al-Mundhir (here, unlike al-Shāfiʿī) sides with those who insist that the pubescent virgin, like the pubescent non-virgin, cannot be compelled to marry. His proof text is in a hadith of the following wording: "The virgin cannot be married until she is asked permission (*tustaʾdhan*), and the non-virgin (*al-thayyib*) [cannot be married] until she is consulted (*tustaʾmar*)."[21]

Because he was renowned as a relater of hadith, it is interesting to note that Ibn al-Mundhir's version exhibits a reversal in the order of the content of the hadith as we have seen it elsewhere (and as it appears in al-Bukhārī[22]): "The non-virgin is not married until she is consulted, and the virgin (is not married) until she is asked permission." This project remains concerned with the various incarnations of this hadith and interested in the changes it undergoes,

20 With the notable exception being that *K. al-Ijmāʿ* couches the agreement in terms of "*ajmaʿū*", and *K. Al-Ishrāf* has this written as "*ajmaʿ ahl al-ʿilm.*" Again, Ibn Qudāma's version is noted, as we can assume that this is a surviving quotation from the lost Chapter on Marriage from *K. Al-Awsaṭ*: "All of the scholars from whom we have taken knowledge have reached consensus that a father's contracting of marriage for his prepubescent virgin daughter is binding, if he marries her to an equal" (*al-Mughnī*, 9:201).

21 *Al-Ishrāf*, 24. *Lā tunkaḥ al-bikru ḥattā tustaʾdhan wa-lā al-thayyib ḥattā tustaʾmar.*

22 *Ṣaḥīḥ al-Bukhārī*, #6568, "*Kitāb al-ḥiyal.*"

recalling, for example, the vocabulary used in *al-Muwaṭṭā*ʾ is a juxtaposition of the word *ayyim* to the word *bikr*.[23]

The report used here by Ibn al-Mundhir continues in the following manner: "How is her permission (given), Oh Messenger of God?" He said, "Silence."

It is at this point that Ibn al-Mundhir interjects his opinion that this hadith indicates plainly that the virgin in question must be pubescent as children have no permission to give, their silence and their rage being equal.[24]

Despite the different word order, this hadith is an axis of consent. It applies, he tells us later, to all the marriage guardians, both fathers and others, except, again, in the case of the prepubescent virgin who possesses no say in her own affairs. It is, Ibn al-Mundhir tells us, a general statement (i.e. a rule of general applicability, *qawl ʿāmm*).

> And (for) all who contract a marriage (*kullu man ʿaqada nikāḥan*) in a fashion other than that determined by the practice of the Messenger (the marriage is) void, for he was the proof for all creation, and it is not for anyone to make an exception to the practice except by virtue of the practice itself.

It is the concept of "exception" that allows Ibn al-Mundhir to segue into a discussion of proof texts bolstering the father's ability to contract marriages for prepubescent females. The exception to it comes in the following form:

> When it was established[25] that Abū Bakr al-Ṣiddīq married ʿĀʾisha to the Messenger of God when she was a prepubescent (*wa hiya ṣaghīra*), she had no say with regard to herself (*lā amr lahā fī nafsihā*), (it showed that) the contract of a father for a prepubescent virgin, who (by definition) has no say with regard to herself, is binding. And that was an exception to the

23 See *Muwaṭṭaʾ*, 2:53, and *Umm*, 6:46. See Ibn ʿAbd al-Barr's discussion below for the significance of the wording. Ibn al-Mundhir does not list a source here for this hadith, but as mentioned *Ishrāf* is an abridgment of his longer work *al-Awsaṭ* and its defining characteristic is that all the referenced reports are divested of their *isnāds*. Sadly, *al-Awsaṭ's* chapter on Marriage is not extant, although it could plausibly be pieced together using Ibn Qudāma's *al-Mughnī*, as already mentioned; Ibn Qudāma includes the version of the hadith that uses both the "*ayyim*" wording and the ordering of females wherein the virgin comes second (*al-Mughnī*, 9:202).

24 *Al-Ishrāf*, 1:24.

25 Ibn al-Mundhir's method of referring to a hadith that is authentic is to use the term *thabata*, or *thabata ʿan rasūl allāh*.

> saying of the Messenger of God, "The virgin cannot be married until her permission is given."[26]
>
> And we have reported[27] from Ibn ʿAbbās that a father contracted marriage for a virgin against her wishes (*wa hiya kāriha*), so she went to the Prophet and he separated them.

Ibn al-Mundhir's analysis ignores the second report altogether. He posits the report of ʿĀʾisha as a prophetic exception to a Prophetically-articulated rule (but not, it should be noted, one of his *khaṣāʾiṣ*,[28] as some later jurists will argue). It is clear that Ibn al-Mundhir considers the second report above to have concerned the pubescent female, given its placement in his argument.

Al-Subkī[29] has mentioned that the outstanding feature of Ibn al-Mundhir's assessments of the consent debates was his inclusion of a caveat. His addition to the debate is found in this small chapter, wherein he mentions the necessity of the non-virgin's actual spoken consent ("Abū Thawr[30] has said that there exists no permission from a non-virgin *unless* through speech"[31]), and Ibn al-Mundhir notes the scholarly opinions with regard to the silence of the virgin.

> We say this as well, and the permission of the virgin is her silence if she knows before her permission is sought that her permission is her silence. If she knew that, she is bound by a silent response to having her permission sought.[32]

---

26 *Al-Ishrāf*, 1:24.

27 According to the editor of *al-Iqnāʿ*, the method by which Ibn al-Mundhir indicated a hadith possesses questionable authenticity is to say "ruwiyā" or "ruwwīnā" instead of "*thabata*" (*al-Iqnāʿ* 1:65). This hadith, or one very similar, is found in Abū Dāwūd and Ibn Mājah.

28 *Khaṣāʾis* refer to exceptions to certain laws applicable to other Muslims but not applicable to the Prophet himself. The most famous example is the permissibility of marrying more than four wives, while the rest of the Muslim male community is constrained to four (two for slaves).

29 "He [Ibn al-Mundhir] tied the existence of the virgin's permission with regard to marriage being her silence to her previous knowledge—before permission being asked of her—that her permission is her silence." See *Ṭabaqāt al-Shāfiʿīyah al-Kubrā*, 3:103–104; *al-Awsaṭ*, 1:92.

30 A Ḥanafī scholar turned Shafiʿī, Abū Thawr ibn Khālid studied with Sufyān ibn ʿUyayna (d. 196/811) and Wakīʿ ibn al-Jarrāḥ (197/812) in Baghdād, dying in 240/854. See GAS, 1:491.

31 *Al-Ishrāf*, 25.

32 Ibid.

It is important to note, however, that this point regarding the requisite knowledge of the meaning of silence was not included in either of Ibn al-Mundhir's other works with relevant chapters, the *K. al-Ijmāʿ* or the *Iqnāʿ*. We will see a paraphrase of Ibn al-Mundhir's passage on the meaning of silence in Ibn ʿAbd al-Barr's *al-Istidhkār*.[33] It is possible, if not probable, that the latter takes his information from the *Mudawwana* of Saḥnūn (d. 240/854).[34] It is not impossible, of course, that Ibn al-Mundhir himself found his precedent there.

By insisting that the virgin who is silent must fully understand the implications of her silence, Ibn al-Mundhir adds nuance to the discussions of consent. As for the non-virgin who expresses her lack of consent, she must be deferred to immediately. The text relied upon in this case is the hadith in which Khansāʾ bint Khidām protests to the Prophet her father's compulsion. The Prophet chastised her father and separated them, allowing her to marry whom she wished. Ibn al-Mundhir emphasizes her status as having been previously married[35] as he avers, along with the scholars he cites who echo this opinion, that the consent of the non-virgin is essential to the validity of her marriage.

What then of the prepubescent virgin daughter? Ibn al-Mundhir delves directly into his proof text for this point, that Abū Bakr contracted ʿĀʾisha's marriage when she was a girl of seven. He gives his assent to the Ijmāʿ on the subject put forward by the above-listed scholars (and it is the same statement given in *Kitāb al-Ijmāʿ*):

33 *Al-Istidhkār*, ¶23336: Ibn ʿAbd al-Barr is referring to the marriage procedures as applied to orphaned girls, who, because they do not have fathers cannot be compelled to marry.

34 Saḥnūn, *al-Mudawwana*, 2:157. The passage reads, "And he [Saḥnūn] said that [someone other than Ibn al-Qāsim al-ʿUtaqī] of Mālik's transmitters has said that this [her silence being her consent] is if she knows that her silence is her consent (*idhā kānat taʿlamu anna sukūtahā riḍā*)."

35 Multiple early reports regarding virgins who had their forced marriages annulled by the Prophet are included in the *Sunan* of al-Awzāʿī (¶1054, 1055–1059); reports stipulating the consent of virgins are found here (¶1047–1053), and in the *Muṣannaf* of ʿAbd al-Razzāq (¶10339–10340, 10344); report ¶10346 is an alternate version of Khansāʾs story, in which she is not mentioned as having been a thayyib although her desired spouse is designated as such. Other reports regarding consent of virgins are found in the *Muṣannaf* of Ibn Abī Shayba (¶16217–16220, 16222, 16228–16230). The editor of *al-Ḥujja ʿalā ahl al-Madīna* (Beirut: ʿĀlam al-Kutub, 1983) also notes reports of Khansāʾ herself being a virgin; these exist in al-Dāraquṭnī and al-Ṭabarānī (*al-Ḥujja*, 3:103–104). Her father's name appears variably as Khudhām, Khudām, Khidhām and Khidām.

> There is consensus among the scholars that a father's contract of marriage for his pre-pubescent virgin daughter is binding if he marries her to an equal (*kufuʾ*).[36]

Before addressing the issue of suitability, we must deal with an intriguing point found with the opinion of Ibn Ḥanbal which Ibn al-Mundhir relates. This point is illustrative of the range of thought at the heart of the debate over maturity and capacity. At what point does a female possess legal capacity? Here, apparently, the orphan girl is given the benefit of the doubt; in other words, the earliest possible date for marriage, that alleged to be ʿĀʾisha's, is listed as the age at which she is granted capacity.[37] However, this is granted to her because her father is, by definition, not living and therefore not in a position to contract her marriage for her. And yet, in Ibn al-Mundhir's summary of Ibn Ḥanbal's position, the orphaned girl is allowed to choose at seven. In other words, in this case, the hadith grants early capacity and empowerment to the prepubescent female, but only if she happens to be fatherless. The quotation reads: "Neither the guardian nor the judge may marry off the orphan girl until she reaches seven years; if she reaches seven years, and consents, then she has no right of rescission."[38]

Suitability

Ibn al-Mundhir's exposition on this topic engenders several questions. What, for Ibn al-Mundhir, is the definition of suitability (*kafāʾa*)? Because the framework for this investigation is rooted in the way in which Ibn Qudāma is arguing Ibn al-Mundhir's position, some attention to this topic is warranted here.

Ibn al-Mundhir begins his chapter on marriage with a small section on *kafāʾa*. He takes pains to include stories of mixed marriages between Arabs and clients (*mawālī*) not affiliated by birth with the tribes of the Arabian peninsula. He

---

36 *Al-Ishrāf,* 1:26.

37 Note how this differs from Ibn Qudāma's interpretation of Ibn Ḥanbal's opinion. See Chapter Eight, below.

38 The actual quotation from the *Chapters on Marriage and Divorce*, from the rescension of ʿAbd Allāh ibn Ḥanbal, reads: "If her father is alive, and she is under nine years of age, her father's giving her in marriage is valid and she has no option. But once she has reached nine years of age, neither her father no anyone else can give her in marriage without her permission. And [with regard to] the orphan who is not nine, if someone other than her father is to give her in marriage, I do not like him to so until she has reached nine years of age. Once she is nine, she must be consulted. Then when she gives her permission, she has no option." (98).

includes the narrative related by ʿĀʾisha that the famous Sālim, Abū Ḥudhayfa's *mawlā*/"adopted son"[39] was married to the daughter of al-Walīd ibn ʿUtba. Further, Ibn al-Mundhir includes the story of how Fāṭima bint Qays was told to marry Usāma (ibn Zayd, also a *mawlā*), and "found satisfaction with him."[40]

Ibn al-Mundhir continues:

> They are divided over *kafāʾa*, for a group has said that *kafāʾa* is with regard to religion, and Muslims (*ahl al-islām*) are well-suited to each other. This is the position of Mālik.[41] And Mālik was asked about the marriage of a client to an Arab, and he said, "There is nothing wrong with it. Haven't you seen that in the Book of God Most High [it is said]: {Oh people, We have created you from a male and a female}, the verse.[42]

Then he relates from ʿUmar ibn al-Khaṭṭāb a report that seems to affirm his support for disregarding background when it comes to marrying Muslims.[43] The final *ithr* Ibn al-Mundhir relates is from Ibn Masʿūd[44] who reportedly told

---

39 *Qālat anna Abā Ḥudhayfa tabannā Sāliman. ...*

40 According to tradition, Fāṭima's other suitors were Muʿāwiyah, whom the Prophet rejected because he was "poor", and Abu Jahm, whom the Prophet rejected because of his harsh treatment of women. He suggested Usāmah, and Fāṭima resisted; the Prophet repeated the suggestion, and Fāṭima acquiesced, whereupon we have her closing statement, "So I married him, and God made the match a good one (*jaʿala Allāhu fīhi khayran*), and I found satisfaction (*ightabaṭtu bihi*) with him." Related in Muslim, as well as al-Ṭaḥāwī's *Maʿānī* and others.

41 I did not find this in the *Muwaṭṭa*ʾ, which, unlike the *Umm*, has no chapter on "*al-akfā*ʾ".

42 Q49:13. "Oh, people, We have created you from a male and a female, and we have made you into nations and tribes in order that you may know one another; truly the noblest of you in the sight of God is the one who is most God-conscious."

43 *Mā baqiya min amr al-jāhiliyya ghayr annī lastu ubālī ayya al-muslimīn nakaḥtu wa ayyahum ankaḥtu.* It should be noted that the *Muṣannaf* of ʿAbd al-Razzāq includes this report (¶10359) in the following manner: *Mā fiyya shayʾun min amr al-jāhiliyya ghayr innī lastu ubālī ayya al-muslimīn ankaḥtu wa ayyahunna nakaḥtu.* However, it is followed by three reports (¶¶10360–10362) which exhibit ʿUmar's inclination toward constructing a rigidly-classed society. 6:123. See also *Muṣannaf* Ibn Abī Shayba, ¶17995 and see pp. 9:497–498 for similarly-minded comments on suitability requirements: six of eight reports prohibit the Arabs from intermarriage with non-Arabs.

44 Died 32/652 or 3. Close companion of the Prophet, a direct transmitter of the Qur'an from the Prophet; he was also the first to attempt to recite the Qur'ān in public in Mecca. For more information see Vadet, J.-C. "Ibn Masʿūd, ʿAbd Allāh b. Ghāfil b. Ḥabīb b. Hudhayl." *EI2*.

his sister, "I beg you by God, marry only a Muslim, be he a red Roman or a black Ethiopian."[45]

Next, Ibn al-Mundhir invokes the scholars who support unqualified mixing of ethnicities with other Muslims, among them ʿUmar ibn ʿAbd al-ʿAzīz,[46] Ḥammād ibn Abī Sulaymān,[47] ʿUbayd Allāh ibn ʿUmayr, Ibn Sīrīn[48] and Ibn ʿAwn. Then Ibn al-Mundhir claims that al-Buwayṭī[49] related from al-Shāfiʿī that "Suitability for a match is determined by religion," (*al-kufuʾ huwa fī al-dīn*).[50] It will be sufficient here to note that the opinion Ibn al-Mundhir advances as being al-Shāfiʿī's could well be closer to what is apparently Ibn al-Mundhir's own opinion: He adds the following report, which foreshadows many later legal discussions about the exact meaning of *kafāʾa:* "A woman is married based on four characteristics: Her money, her beauty, her lineage and her religion. Make the religion preeminent (among these) and you will be content (*fa-aẓfir fi-dhāt al-dīn taribat yadāk*)."

> And there is another opinion: and that is that the Arab woman cannot be married to a client. Al-Thawrī's position was that there should be separation if a client marries an Arab woman, and he was strict about this (*kāna yushaddid fīhi*). Aḥmad said the same: that they should be separated. And the Ḥanafīs said, "Quraysh are suitable for each other, and the (rest of the) Arabs are suitable for each other, and if a woman marries herself to someone who is unsuitable, it is up to her guardians (*al-awliyāʾ*) to separate them, and that can only be an act of a judge. None of the Arabs are suitable for Quraysh, and none of the clients are suitable for the Arabs.[51]

45 *Wa-law kāna aḥmaran rūmīyan aw aswadan ḥabashiyyan.*

46 ʿUmar ibn ʿAbd al-ʿAzīz, r. 98/717–101/720. Considered the most pious caliph after the four Rightly-Guided caliphs, his opinions were often considered to be legal precedent. For more information see ʿAli, Saliḥ Aḥmad, *ʿUmar ibn ʿAbd al-ʿAzīz, Khāmis al-khulafāʾ al-rāshidīn* (Beirut: Sharikat al-Maṭbūʿāt lil-Tawzīʿ wa-l-Nashr, 2000).

47 Ḥammād b. Abī Sulaymān (d. 120/737), major pupil of Ibrāhīm al-Nakhaʿī.

48 Abū Bakr Muḥammad Ibn Sīrīn (110/728), friend and companion of al-Ḥasan al-Baṣrī, known best for his dream interpretations.

49 Abū Yaʿḳūb Yusūf al-Buwayṭī (d. 231/846), al-Shāfiʿī's favorite disciple, who summarized his works.

50 The section on *kafāʾa* in the *Umm* does not mention religion at all, only money and esteem (*ḥasab*), noting that a woman settling for a man with little money is not necessarily a lessening of her esteem, or for that matter her lineage; he does warn, however, that once a woman has made that compromise, she cannot undo the marriage contract without becoming like "used goods" (*al-buyūʿ al-mustahlaka*). See *al-Umm*, 6:39–40.

51 *Al-Ishrāf*, 1:18.

It is logical to assume that Ibn al-Mundhir, hailing from Nishapur, might well have been sympathetic to those opinions which downplayed Arabism and instead centered on religion being the only necessary qualification for striking a suitable match.

It must be noted, however, that, just as there is no indication that had she dissented, ʿĀʾisha would have been compelled,[52] there is also no indicator that *kafāʾa* enters into the content of the adduced hadith. Certainly because no solid definition of *kafāʾa* is put forward, it is possible to conclude that Ibn al-Mundhir's claim does not rest on any actual indicator. Whatever the case, Ibn al-Mundhir does insist on *kafāʾa*. It is an insistence that, I believe, can only be attributed to the strong ties between the fiqh of Ibn al-Mundhir and that of al-Shāfiʿī. *Kafāʾa* is a crucial element of the consensus on marriage of prepubescent females: it is the one and only limitation on the father's power to compel, and the only way for the bride to mount a legal challenge to the match. Yet it is a difficult doctrine to delineate, given that *kafāʾa* itself remains, up until the time of Ibn Qudāma, if not beyond, legally underdetermined.

Rescission

Returning to Ibn al-Mundhir's chapters on marriage, we find another point of interest. This is his opinion with regard to two prepubescents being married by other than the father and then reaching puberty. "A group" allows the girl a right of rescission[53] upon puberty. No mention is made of the boy. Is Ibn al-Mundhir averring that girls are thus allowed more of a right to rescind than their male counterparts? Or is the assumption merely that the male upon reaching puberty has an unassailable right to rescind? The issue remains unresolved, and appears again in the paragraph on cousins, below.

---

52 In *Fatḥ al-bārī*, Ibn Ḥajar al-ʿAsqalānī includes in his discussion of the ʿĀʾisha hadith the following observation: "[Ibn al-Baṭṭāl] said: 'It is taken from the hadith that the father is permitted to contract marriage for the prepubescent virgin without her permission.' I say: This is as if he has taken that from the lack of its statement and not due to a clear indicator (*ka-annahu akhadha dhālik min ʿadam dhikrihi wa laysa li-wāḍiḥ al-dalālah*). Indeed, it is possible for this to have been before the appearance of the command to take the permission of the virgin, and this is the most apparent [conclusion], for this story occurred in Mecca before the Emigration." *K. al-Nikāḥ*, Chapter on the marriage of children to adults, *Fatḥ al-bārī bi-sharḥ ṣaḥīḥ al-bukhārī*, ed. Ṭaha ʿAbd al-Raʾūf Saʿd, (Cairo: Maktabat al-Kulliyāt al-Azharīyah, 1978) 19:149.

53 *Al-Ishrāf*, 26.

But what draws our attention most is a small paragraph not easily summarized.

> The Ḥanafīs have differed over the man who, as her marriage guardian, married (*zawwaja*) his brother's daughter to his [other] brother's son when they were both prepubescent. Then, they mature (*yakburān*), but the girl does not know of the marriage (*al-nikāḥ*). Al-Nuʿmān (Abū Ḥanīfa) has said, "They both have the right of rescission as long as she did not know of the marriage. And if she learns of it (*idhā ʿalimat*), then, if she is silent, this is her consent." Muḥammad and Abū Yūsuf[54] have said, "Neither of them has a right to rescind if they mature, and the marriage (*al-nikāḥ*) is licit."[55]

Again, the issue of the right of rescission of the male is left undefined. Certainly in sub-chapter 13, there will appear the fact that the young male may be married off by his father, in much the same way as the prepubescent female. But no mention is made of the other marriage guardians. Can we ascribe to misprints the statement that "they both have the right of rescission as long as *she* did not know of the marriage"? Is this a clear indication that the male's right to rescind remains either way?

Sex, Maintenance, and Sexual Maturity

Yet another legal consideration appears at this point. Ibn al-Mundhir does not always clearly define his technical terms. *Zawwaja* is used interchangeably with *nikāḥ*, creating confusion, or leaving the reader to, in essence, fill in the blanks. This paragraph clearly assumes that the marriage in question was a purely contractual marriage, with actual consummation postponed, presumably until (at least) the male's pubescence, if not well-beyond its initial stages (*al-kibar*). It can safely be assumed that marriages between two prepubescents can not be effectively consummated until male pubescence; however, is there anything to indicate that the consummation of a marriage of a prepubescent female to a pubescent male must be postponed?

54 Abū Yūsuf, Yaʿqūb ibn Ibrāhīm al-Anṣārī, died 182/798; disciple of Abū Ḥanīfa and Kūfan judge who served as the first chief justice (*qāḍī al-quḍāt*) under Hārūn al-Rashīd (r. 170/786–193/809). See Hallaq, Wael, *Origins and Evolution of Islamic Law* (Cambridge: Cambridge University Press, 2005).

55 *Al-Ishrāf*, 26. Usually this opinion is ascribed only to Abū Yūsuf (see al-Marwazī and Ibn ʿAbd al-Barr. Like the editor of the *Ḥujja*, Ibn Qudāma describes Abū Yūsuf as first having held the opinion that they could rescind, and then changing his mind.).

No such assumption can be safely based upon the hadith of ʿĀʾisha; there is no indication in any of the versions that the Prophet's consummation of the marriage (*bināʾuhu bihā*) was predicated upon her attaining puberty. The only information we are given is her age.

This issue brings us to a juristic concept, only barely addressed in the works of Ijmāʿ. At what point does a female become *muṭīqa lil-waṭʾ* (able to tolerate the sexual act upon her)?

Apparently, this was an issue that was underdetermined legally. Ibn al-Mundhir notes in Chapter 183, the Chapter on the Time for Consummating [an as-yet purely contractual relationship] with Women (*waqt al-dukhūl ʿalā al-nisāʾ*), that with regard to the report of ʿĀʾisha, there was dissent.

> It is established that the Messenger of God contracted marriage with ʿĀʾisha when she was a girl of seven, and consummated the marriage when she was girl of nine. The scholars have differed with regard to this issue. Aḥmad and Abū ʿUbayd supported a literal interpretation of this hadith (*kāna yaqūlān bi-ẓāhir hādha al-ḥadīth*), and this was [Abū Ḥanīfa's] opinion.[56]
>
> [Ibn al-Mundhir said:] Our opinion is other than this: If she reaches [nine years of age] and does not possess the body and strength [that would allow her to] tolerate a man, her family may keep her away from him (*li-ahlihā manʿuhā minhu*). And if she is not yet nine, and she possesses the body and strength that would tolerate a man, they should not keep her away from him.
>
> And al-Shāfiʿī said, "If the bride is husky (*jasīma*),[57] and others of her type (*mithluhā*) tolerate sexual intercourse, it means they should be allowed to be together (*khuliyya baynuhu wa baynuhā*). If she cannot tolerate that, then her family should prevent her until she can tolerate sex."[58]

Thus we see that there is nothing resembling precision in the determination of when a young female is "ready" for the sexual act to be performed upon her.

---

56 *Wa bihi qāla al-Nuʿmān*. If the "*bihi*" in this statement refers to the hadith itself and not the "manifest application" of it (i.e., for example, simply, "Abū Ḥanīfa agreed that marriages could be consummated at that age"), this is the first suggestion we have encountered that Abū Ḥanīfa was aware of this hadith. As we will see, the Ḥanafī position definitely allowed prepubescent marriage but it was never justified by this hadith.

57 Although semantically *jasīma* indicates large or fat, the idea is clearly to depict a girl with a bigger, more sexually-developed body.

58 *Al-Ishrāf*, 1:136.

Certainly there is nothing in the hadith, posited as the locus for this discussion, that suggests that ʿĀʾisha was "husky." In other words, Ibn al-Mundhir and al-Shāfiʿī, by acknowledging that operating under the manifest indicator of "nine years" could be harmful or should not be applied to smaller, weaker girls, have built a legal position that is bereft of a valid indicator. Without an obvious legal indicator, they are left only with perceptions of a girl's body type and assumptions about what other young girls of similar body type can withstand. Looking to "what girls of her [body] type can tolerate" is a peculiar reliance on analogy for the anti-analogy al-Shāfiʿī[59] (and Ibn al-Mundhir after him) to support.

We find other references to reliance upon analogy to body type buried among the several chapters in the section on *nafaqa* that deal with children in the marital context. These inform our discussion by noting a disparity between the contracting of the marriage and the time when sex begins to be performed. Ibn al-Mundhir's *al-Ishrāf* includes the following chapters, all of which are indicative of the difficulties jurists faced in wrestling with this issue. Titles include: "The chapter on when a man can be compelled to pay maintenance for his wife, and when he can perform the sexual act upon her," "The chapter on the maintenance of a prepubescent girl upon the like of whom the sexual act is not performed," "The chapter on the prepubescent boy for whom marriage of a mature woman is contracted."

Generally speaking, the jurists seem reluctant to deprive the prepubescent bride of her maintenance. Simultaneously, however, they cannot disassociate the sexual act from its relationship to maintenance, and therefore there seems to be a loss as to what to do with the girl who is not ready for sex but is yet living with a man as his wife. The opinions listed cover a wide range.[60] For the first chapter listed, we see that some scholars, including Mālik and al-Shāfiʿī, aver that "If the denial of sexual activity (*ḥabs*) is from his side, then he must maintain her; if it is from her side, then she has no right to maintenance." Al-Ḥasan al-Baṣrī concurs that sex is key to maintenance, saying: "There is no maintenance for a woman (*al-marʾa*) until her husband performs the sexual act upon her." Meanwhile, Ibn al-Mundhir's own opinion brings in the issue

59 It is possible to perceive much of the thrust of al-Shāfiʿī's legal-theoretical project as an effort to reign in the practice of analogical reasoning (*qiyās*), both that of the legal practitioners who based their analogies on traditional practice (the Mālikīs) that had lacked verifiable basis in direct Prophetic word, deed, or tacit approval, and those who relied on *raʾy* (opinion) and *istiḥsān* (juristic preference)—in this case, the Ḥanafīs. For al-Shāfiʿī, any analogy lacking in legal proof (*dalīl sharʿī*) was problematic. See Chaumont, E. "al-Shāfiʿī." *EI2*. For more information, see Lowry, *Early Islamic Legal Theory*, esp. 149–163.

60 *Al-Ishrāf*, 1:122.

of withholding of sex on the part of the female as being tantamount to disobedience. He says: "She has the right to be maintained unless she denies him herself; in this case her maintenance is obviated (*tazūl nafaqatuhā*) for as long as she is disobedient (*nāshiza*)."

Here is evidence of the juristic confusion over how to uphold the basic axiom of the marital contract: the sexual act necessitates that maintenance be paid. Denial of sexual availability obviates the right to maintenance, affirming that the scholars view the two as mutually dependent.

But another legal quandary logically ensues: If the prepubescent girl is not ready for sex, however readiness may be defined, on what basis is maintenance paid? Ibn al-Mundhir lists several opinions, including that "There is no maintenance for her until she is old enough (*tudrik*) or can tolerate men (*tuṭīq*)," and that if denial of sex "(*ḥabs*) is from the side of the woman, then the woman has no right to maintenance." Another, that of al-Thawrī, suggests he charge right in: "He must maintain her, and if she reaches (the age) where the sexual act is performed upon others of that age, then he can perform the sexual act upon her." Ibn al-Mundhir's opinion: she has had a category shift. She is now a wife. He expresses it thus: "The mature male who marries a prepubescent girl must maintain her due to the entry of this wife within the scope of those for whom maintenance is obligatory."

Still, Ibn al-Mundhir's position still does not explain how to deal with a prepubescent who does not provide sex. Her definition as being a wife (*zawja*) makes her the financial responsibility of her husband. However the definition of the wife as being the provider of sexual intercourse renders her position blurry at best.

The jurists encountered for the prepubescent bride a sort of limbo. The father has married her off to a man (a *kufu'*, as Ibn al-Mundhir claims is required), and is thus no longer constrained to maintain her. However, maintenance is not incumbent upon the husband until she is able to "tolerate" him sexually. What then could her legal status possibly be? It is only al-Thawrī who answers this question in a way that resolves the limbo.

There remains the issue of the prepubescent male who marries a mature woman, however.[61] Al-Shāfiʿī (in his Iraqi period, says Ibn al-Mundhir) argues he must still maintain her. Mālik says he is not obligated to do so, while an unattributed opinion is put forth that: "The prepubescent husband is obligated to pay maintenance, just as he is obligated to maintain out of his assets (*yufraḍu fī mālihi*) the maintenance of his parents and slaves."

61 Ibid., 1:123.

It is not unlikely that the final opinion here is that of Ibn al-Mundhir himself. This opinion acknowledges the maintenance of a bride might not differ so much from other maintenance obligations of a prepubescent. There is no reason to exclude the bride from this group, even if *he* is still below the age of financial responsibility.[62] Mālik's contrary opinion would perhaps require a re-evaluation of the basic tenets of marriage, unless prepubescents are regarded simply as an exception to a general rule. In this small section of *al-Ishrāf*, however, as is often the case, the jurists did not explore all the entailments of their pronouncements.

(*Kitāb al-Ishrāf*, *Kitāb al-Nikāḥ*, section 13) The father's contracting of marriage (*inkāḥ*) for his prepubescent son

This seems to be a clear case of corrupt text in our version of *al-Ishrāf*; the actual title of this small paragraph (sub-chapter 13) is entitled "A father's marrying off of his child/infant daughter (*inkāḥ ibnatihi al-ṭifl*)," but the content is focused on the prepubescent *boy*, as the proof-text refers to the son of Ibn ʿUmar. The first line reads, "All of the scholars from whom we have learned have agreed that it is permitted for the father to marry off his prepubescent daughter." The evidence he cites is that "Ibn ʿUmar contracted marriage (*zawwaja*) for his prepubescent son, and he and his son fought over this, taking the case to Zayd, who allowed it."[63]

It is possible to reconcile this paragraph with the rest of the chapter in one of three ways. First, Ibn al-Mundhir is adducing this text as a proof for marrying off prepubescent males. Second, he is retracting his opinion that prepubescent females can be married off based solely on the hadith of ʿĀʾisha. The third choice is that he is simply stating that Ibn Ḥanbal premised his belief that minor females could be married off based on *this* hadith as well.

My opinion is the first, with a supposition that the text is slightly corrupt. This position is supported by the entry on the previous page (sub-chapter 12) which deals exclusively with the marrying off of the prepubescent girl (and

62 Ibid.

63 *Al-Ishrāf*, 27. I did not find this story in any of the seven major hadith collections. It might be noted that Ibn al-Mundhir does not seem to know of the narrative in ʿAbd al-Razzāq that indicates that ʿUrwa ibn al-Zubayr contracted a marriage for his son to the daughter of Muṣaʿb (ibn al-Zubayr; ʿUrwa's niece) when they were five and six years old, *Muṣannaf*, nos. ¶¶'s10397 and 10398, 6:132. The first is related by al-Zuhrī, while the second is related by Hishām; both of them also relate ʿĀʾisha's hadith in the *Muṣannaf* (¶¶'s 10388 and 10390, respectively). The story of ʿUrwa does, however, appear in *al-Istidhkār*, 5:405.

relies on the ʿĀ'isha proof text). It is further supported due to the fact that the list of scholars opining varies slightly from the list of those supporting the marriage of the prepubescent female.[64]

Conclusion to Ibn al-Mundhir

Ibn al-Mundhir has detailed the range of opinions on consent. He has made a claim for consensus on the legality of a father's forcing his prepubescent daughter to marry someone of equal status. However, no definition of what equal status means is offered. And, as we have seen, no solid definition of "maturity"—or "youth"—is offered.

Thus, in essence, what are claimed as areas of agreement are the following: 1) the lack of capacity of children, and 2) the power of the father. Grounds for justification of both points can be located in the hadith of ʿĀ'isha which informs and influences the interpretation of the other main text (the *thayyib/bikr* text) discussed by Ibn al-Mundhir.

Throughout Ibn al-Mundhir's arguments, the influence of al-Shāfiʿī is present in both tone and in the proof texts used—even if he uses them in a fashion slightly different from al-Shāfiʿī himself. By disallowing the compulsion of pubescent virgins, virginity can no longer be the *ratio legis* for compulsion as it was for al-Shāfiʿī.[65] It must be replaced with a *ratio legis* of a lack of maturity (*bulūgh*), which, in the absence of any discussion proffered by Ibn al-Mundhir, we can only assume, for females, means the state of being previous to the onset of menses.

Still, Ibn al-Mundhir does not press his claim of consensus with regard to compulsion in prepubescent marriages without a relevant supporting text. Where he does claim consensus, it is with a clause: he repeats nearly verbatim the insistence of al-Shāfiʿī on *kafāʾa*, despite ibn al-Mundhir's clearly different conceptualization of the practice from that of al-Shāfiʿī.

Despite the slight anachronism, but in keeping with Ibn al-Qaṭṭān's model in *al-Iqnāʿ*, we turn now to the writing of al-Marwazī, for a different characterization of the scholarly consensus on these issues.

---

64 He lists al-Ḥasan al-Baṣrī, al-Zuhrī, Qatāda, Mālik, Sufyān al-Thawrī, al-Shāfiʿī, Aḥmad, Isḥāq and the Ḥanafīs. The list for the prepubescent virgin female reads: Mālik, al-Thawrī, al-Layth ibn Saʿd, al-Awzāʿī, ʿUbayd Allāh ibn al-Ḥasan [sic?], al-Shāfiʿī, Aḥmad, Isḥāq, Abī ʿUbayd, Abū Thawr and the Ḥanafīs (*al-Ishrāf*, 1:26–27).

65 See the *Umm*, 6:48 .

Al-Marwazī

The Walī Mujbir *and Proof Texts*

Similar to the writers who come later, al-Marwazī uses the presence or absence of virginity to categorize females who can be compelled to marry. The virgin, he tells us, can be compelled to marry according to some scholars (Mālik, al-Shāfiʿī, Aḥmad, Isḥāq, Ibn Abī Laylā). Al-Awzāʿī, Sufyān, the Ḥanafīs, Abū ʿUbayd and Abū Thawr agree that the virgin *cannot* be married without her consent, relying on the hadith (from, he notes, Abū Hurayra) that the "virgin cannot be married without her consent." It becomes clear only later in the chapter that al-Marwazī's understanding of "virgin" here includes only the pubescent virgin.

True to its title, the book is intent on outlining the areas of *ikhtilāf* among the scholars. In the entirety of the Chapter on Marriage, the only subject which is depicted as being characterized by consensus is that of the compelled marriage of prepubescents by the father. The illicit nature of the compelled marriage of the non-virgin is a topic upon which "there is no *ikhtilāf*". In both cases, though, the consensus (or tacit consensus) comes based upon a clear indicator: a hadith. In the case of the non-virgin, the inability to force is based on the hadith of Khansāʾ bint Khidām who, as a previously-married woman (*thayyib*), protested her father's compelled marriage of her and had it annulled by the Prophet.

In the case of the compelled marriage of prepubescents, the hadith relied upon is the hadith of ʿĀʾisha.

Says al-Marwazī:

> The scholars have reached consensus that the father's marriage of his prepubescent son or daughter is binding, and they (dual, Ar. *humā*) have no right of rescission upon reaching maturity. This is because the Prophet married ʿĀʾisha when she was a girl of six, and consummated the marriage when she was a girl of nine. Several of the Prophet's Companions deemed it valid, among them ʿUmar and ʿAlī and al-Zubayr and Qudāma ibn Maẓʿūn and ʿAmmār and Ibn Shubrama.[66]

66 *Ikhtilāf al-ʿUlamāʾ*, 126. Here we notice immediately that Ibn Shubrama, who al-Ṭaḥāwī will claim as the lone voice disallowing any sort of child marriage (2:257), and Ibn ʿAbd al-Barr will characterize as lending his opinion to the camp supporting her right to rescind upon pubescence (see below, 182), is clearly depicted as a supporter. We note that the Zubayr/Qudāma ibn Maẓʿūn story was also adduced by Ibn Qudāma (see Chapter 2).

It is immediately noted that there is a difference between Ibn al-Mundhir's claim and that of al-Marwazī. Where Ibn al-Mundhir claimed that the father can marry his prepubescent daughter without her consent provided it is to an equal, al-Marwazī (predating, we will recall, ibn al-Mundhir, while post-dating al-Shāfiʿī) does not refer to the suitability of the match at all. Instead, he adds the detail that those prepubescents (male and female) who have no say in their marriages cannot have them annulled upon pubescence.[67]

Again, as this sort of consensus marks the point of the "lowest common denominator of agreement", al-Marwazī begins listing the points of difference immediately thereafter. Sufyān and al-Shāfiʿī, Abū ʿUbayd and Abū Thawr all agreed that no one other than the father can marry prepubescents, and "if this is violated, their marriage is invalid."[68] Mālik, too, asserted both these points. For the prepubescent male, however, Mālik also holds that "other than the father" may contract the marriage.[69]

Al-Marwazī on Rescission and Sexual Maturity

This discussion segues into a discussion of the opinion held by some that "other than the father" may contract marriages for both boys and girls, with the caveat being that they (both) may rescind upon pubescence. The adherents to this notion are: al-Ḥasan, ʿAṭāʾ [ibn Abī Rabāḥ],[70] Abū Ḥanīfa, Ibn Ḥanbal and Isḥāq [ibn Rāhwayh].[71] According to al-Marwazī, this doctrine applies to mixed marriages of pubescents and prepubescents, no matter which sex is the elder.

---

67 Again, the wording here is most typical of the opinion of Abū Yūsuf, although he allows other guardians besides the father to contract such a marriage.

68 As we have seen, al-Shāfiʿī had gone on record allowing the grandfather to compel as well. As he bases his arguments for forced marriage on the hadith of ʿĀʾisha, we assume it to be a decision formed from analogy based on the power of the father (in this case Abū Bakr). See *al-Umm*, 6:48: "The grandfather is the father of the father; and his father and the father of his father [all] take the place of the father in marry the virgin and being marriage guardian for the non-virgin, as long as there is no one nearer to the father than him." Again, note Ibn Ḥajar's quarrel with al-Shāfiʿī's reasoning: *Fatḥ al-bārī bi-sharḥ ṣaḥīḥ al-Bukhārī*. Ed. Ṭaha ʿAbd al-Raʾūf Saʿd (Cairo: Maktabat al-Kulliyāt al-Azharīyah, 1978), 19:149.

69 I have not encountered this opinion of Mālik's in any other source.

70 Died 115/733, he was a famed Meccan scholar who is a major source of early traditions, and figures prominently in the *Muṣannaf* of ʿAbd al-Razzāq. See Motzki, Harald, *The Origins of Islamic Jurisprudence* (Leiden: Brill, 2002). See also GAS, 1:31.

71 Died 238/853, he related traditions to but was also a disciple of Ibn Ḥanbal and was a primary teacher of Ibn Qutayba (d. 276/889).

Among the Ḥanafīs, however, there is a group which suggested that any *walī* functions as the father functions (*nikāḥ al-awliyāʾ kulluhum bi-manzilat al-ab*). Any *walī* who contracts marriage for a young girl binds her with that marriage, and neither spouse has the right to rescission upon pubescence.[72]

Further exploring the dissent on the subject, al-Marwazī explains that those who do allow choice upon pubescence differed over inheritance. Some (Ṭāwus and Qatāda[73]) said the spouses do not inherit from each other; "Isḥāq ruled on the matter saying that the husband should not consummate the marriage as long as he has not reached pubescence and chosen the marriage."[74] In other words, it would seem that he linked inheritance to consummation, while assuming that prepubescent marriages were not consummated marriages until (at least) the mature male actively endorses the marriage.[75]

The section ends with al-Marwazī attributing to Abū Ḥanīfa the position that both inherit from the other, and that the male spouse may consummate even if the female is not yet pubescent.

Conclusion to al-Marwazī

These then are the points of difference arising beyond the common denominator of consensus over prepubescent marriage in the writings of al-Marwazī. Yet even the common denominator is not as solid as it would seem. Like Ibn al-Mundhir, al-Marwazī's argument for consensus is linked to the hadith of ʿĀʾisha. Unlike Ibn al-Mundhir, however, he does not predicate the father's power to compel on the finding of a suitable match; and also unlike him, he

72 The text here is slightly problematic in that there is little subject-verb agreement. It seems to be talking only about the minor female, yet then says that neither has a choice (*lā khiyār li-wāḥid min-humā*) if he reaches pubescence (*idhā adraka*). Unless the intent of the text is that choice becomes obviated for both once the male partner reaches pubescence (in which case consummation is then possible, no matter the age of the female), we might assume that it should read as I have interpreted it above. (p. 162).

73 Qatāda ibn Diʿāma ibn Qatāda al-Sadūsī, d. 117/735, he was a blind scholar of the successor generation, the student of al-Ḥasan al-Baṣrī and Ibn Sīrīn. See GAS, 1:31.

74 *Laysa lil-zawj an yadkhula bi-hā mā lam yablugh fa-yakhtār al-nikāḥ.*

75 Inheritance law (*farāʾiḍ*) is found in detail in the Qur'ān, and is one of the most complex branches of Islamic Law. Inheritance occurs either due to marriage or consanguinity. The general rule of spousal inheritance is based on the Qur'anic verses 4:7 and 4:11. "The husband is entitled to 1/4 when there are descendants and 1/2 in their absence, and the wife to 1/8 in the presence of descendants and 1/4 in their absence." (*Encyclopedia of Islamic Law*, adapted by Laleh Bakhtiar, (Chicago: ABC Publishing, 1996), p. 294.) See also Noel Coulson, *Succession in the Muslim Family* (Cambridge: Cambridge University Press, 1971).

does insist that no right of rescission exists for either prepubescent party upon pubescence.

Like Ibn al-Mundhir, al-Marwazī never defines maturity or childhood. But Ibn al-Mundhir deviates from al-Shafiʿī's opinion that virginity is itself the *ratio legis* for the father's power to compel (therefore, when exploring Ibn al-Mundhir's analysis, we are logically confronted with questions over when maturity begins and childhood ends). Al-Marwazī does not deviate on this point, holding that older virgins as well as younger ones can be equally compelled by the father; thus there is no need to address questions of maturity. We must note as well the amount of time al-Marwazī spends on the rules pertaining to the marriage of prepubescent boys, a trend that will decrease markedly among the authors on consensus with the passing of generations.[76]

Finally, we must observe that, although Ibn al-Qaṭṭān quoted al-Marwazī quite precisely with regard to the above determination of consensus, his second quotation, at *al-Iqnāʿ* ¶2126, reads: "I know no one who is of the opinion that a father can force a non-virgin to marry except al-Ḥasan al-Baṣrī, who said: 'a father's marrying off of his daughter is binding, be she virgin or non-virgin, whether he compelled against her will (*akrahahā*) or did not force her against her will.' I do not know anyone who follows him in that."[77] This passage does not actually exist in my edition; in fact, al-Ḥasan's opinion is not included at all; unless some other recension was used, it seems that Ibn al-Qaṭṭān has taken some liberty with the texts available to him.

It is in the writings of Ibn al-Mundhir's Shāfiʿī-cum-Ḥanafī contemporary al-Ṭaḥāwī that we see further development of these arguments.

Al-Ṭaḥāwī

Al-Ṭaḥāwī and the Walī Mujbir*: The Capacity of Females*

In the *Ikhtilāf*, al-Ṭaḥāwī spends a great deal of time (or perhaps al-Jaṣṣāṣ abridged substantially less from this section) on the rights of a woman to

---

76 Ibn al-Mundhir devotes some discussion to the subject of male prepubescent marriage. With later jurists, the discussions grow shorter and shorter, as the focus on prepubescent marriage (much like the reference in *Kitāb al-Umm*) becomes centered on females. This trend culminates in the work of Ibn Ḥazm (d. 456/1063) who, while affirming the right of the father over the prepubescent female, vehemently denies outright the permissibility of any marriage of a prepubescent boy. See Ibn Ḥazm, *al-Muḥallā*, (Beirut: Manshūrāt al-Maktab al-Tijārī lil-Ṭibāʿah), 9:462.

77 *Al-Iqnāʿ*, 3:1156.

contract her own marriage as well as, in a limited way, marriages for other women. He speaks at length of examples of ʿĀʾisha contracting marriages[78] and Umm Salama contracting her own marriage. The overall thrust of his argument was not altogether clear for us until we read the relevant passage in the *Maʿānī*. In that passage, we find a deeply detailed discussion of all of the objections put forth by al-Shāfiʿī to women contracting marriages for themselves or others, particularly the hadith "There is no marriage without a marriage guardian,"[79] and al-Shāfiʿī's interpretation of Q2:232.[80]

Al-Ṭaḥāwī spends considerable time criticizing the *isnāds* for the above hadith, in what is apparently an ongoing, heated debate over transmitters. But it is not enough for him to attempt to discredit the hadith simply on formal grounds. What is significant for our purposes is the argument that al-Ṭaḥāwī adduces in order to explain why a woman has the capacity to contract her own marriage. The "No marriage without a marriage guardian" hadith cannot be *ḥujja* in this instance because 1) it has many possible interpretations and 2) it can only be strictly applied to one possible meaning to the exclusion of others (i.e. that all women must have a *walī* in order to marry) "if there is an indicator which indicates that, either from the Book, the Sunna, or from Consensus."[81] In other words, this broad interpretation (which disregards exceptions) cannot be vested with such widespread power unless bolstered by further evidence.

This second point allows us to see the nature of consensus at this point in time. For al-Ṭaḥāwī, it has already become a source of law carrying legal weight which is for all intents and purposes equal with the Qur'an and the Sunna. The Sunnaic proof text which he uses to *disprove* this singular yet broader meaning (that all women must have a *walī* in order to marry) is the *ayyim/bikr* hadith.[82]

78 See also *al-Ḥujja*, 2:70–73.

79 Spectorsky points out that this was more likely to have been a legal maxim that evolved into a tradition. She cites Schacht, *Introduction*, 39–40. See Spectorsky, *Chapters on Marriage and Divorce*, fn. 31, p. 11. Compare also with *al-Muwaṭṭaʾ*: It reached Mālik from Saʿīd ibn al-Musayyib that he said, ʿUmar ibn al-Khaṭṭāb said, "The woman is not married without the permission of her guardian or someone of authority from her family or the ruler." 2:53.

80 See *al-Umm*, 6:31–35. Q2:232 reads: "And when you divorce women, and they have come to the end of their waiting-term, hinder them not (*lā taʿḍulūhunna*) from marrying (*an yankiḥna*) other men if they have agreed with each other (*idhā tarāḍū baynahum*) in a fair manner."

81 *Maʿānī al-Athār*, 2:368.

82 Ibid., 369. Recall that this hadith mentions that the *ayyim* has more legal capacity in the contracting of her own marriage than does her *walī* for her.

It cannot be overlooked that al-Ṭaḥāwī does not mention the hadith of ʿĀʾisha here or in the *Ikhtilāf*.

Returning to his first point against the "No marriage" hadith, we discover our first clues to understanding al-Ṭaḥāwī's thought on prepubescent marriage. He says that the "No marriage without a *walī*" hadith could have multiple interpretations. It is possible that it refers to three different sorts of *walī*: "the father for the prepubescent (*wālid al-ṣaghīra*), the master of the slave woman (*mawlā al-ama*), or the self of the mature freewoman (*bāligha ḥurra nafsuhā*)."[83] Clearly, the prepubescent is on a different plane from the pubescent/mature woman who can represent herself. With regard to legal capacity, the prepubescent has more in common at this point with a slave woman. Also at issue is the function and definition of the *walī*, a point which scholars have yet to agree on.[84]

But it is not enough for al-Ṭaḥāwī to focus on the "no marriage without a guardian" hadith itself. The Shāfiʿī argument for this doctrine rests additionally on the interpretation of Q2:232, wherein the group ordered not to prevent women from remarrying after divorce is said to be the marriage guardians.[85] Al-Ṭaḥāwī protests this point, and says that the interpretation is open, i.e. the address could be to other than the marriage guardians. Whereas the other side thinks that their interpretation of Q2:232 bolsters their argument, al-Ṭaḥāwī's argument that a free woman can marry herself is bolstered by both the hadith that the "non-married woman is more in possession of herself …" and the story of Umm Salama, who married herself to the Prophet without a *walī*.[86] This story, in turn, brings him to the point that we encountered in al-Shāshī's[87]

83 *Maʿānī al-Athār*, 2:368.

84 In other words, the early scholars are still bickering over the nature of the *walī*; the Ḥanafīs in particular give various gradations in the power of the *walī*, as they wrestle with whether or not his power is vested in him by the woman herself through her consent, or whether his permission is mandatory. The *ḥaqīqa/majāz* dichotomy is even invoked to explain that his power is merely metaphorical, but the literal act of consent rests with the woman. This point is fully articulated by later (post-Shaybānī) Ḥanafīs when they begin to differentiate between the permission and the contract. This issue is less problematic for early Mālikī and Shāfiʿī scholars who have a less-nuanced view because they do not evidence any belief in the woman's legal capacity without the *walī*.

85 See *al-Umm*, 6:31–32. Al-Shāfiʿī's point is that if marriage guardians are addressed, the necessary implication is that the guardians are the ones who have power over a woman's choice of spouse.

86 For the details of this story, see *Maʿānī*, 2:369–370.

87 See above, 51–53.

nearly-contemporaneous work of theory. It is here that al-Ṭaḥāwī states most explicitly his justification for prepubescent marriage, as we see clearly how the subject is intertwined with consent and marriage generally:

> We have seen that [with regard to] the woman, before maturity, her father's command upon her is binding with regard to her marriage contract and her assets (*fī buḍʿihā wa-mālihā*). Any contract in [both situations] is totally his, not hers, and his decision in [both situations] [would be] the same, without difference [for there is no difference between the two cases of control over assets or the marriage contract for these purposes]. And if she reaches maturity, then all have reached consensus (*kullun qad ajmaʿ*) that his control over her assets has ceased.
>
> If what had been his [authority] over her assets in her childhood has returned to her, then one has to investigate that (*al-naẓar fī dhālik*) as well in regard to her contract for marriage. It leaves the hand of her father upon her maturity.[88]

Al-Ṭaḥāwī uses both consensus and analogy to the female's financial situation here to arrive at his conclusion.

There are no further chapters in the *Maʿānī* which allude to the legal capacity of females or lack of same for children. In the *Ikhtilāf*, however, we encounter a summary chapter that explains again the Ḥanafī position on women contracting marriages. Here, it is couched in terms of internal consensus within the *madhhab*:

> There is no disagreement among our companions with regard to the permissibility of a woman contracting marriage for herself if her marriage guardian grants her permission.[89]

This formulation can only be considered an attempt to state the "lowest common denominator" of agreement. Such a general conclusion disregards outright early Ḥanafī texts like the *Ḥujja*, which is very clear about its proofs for the ability of a woman to contract her own marriage.[90] Because there is no mention of "No marriage without a marriage guardian," there is no need to divest the woman of full capacity. In other words, the differentiation between the permission (*idhn*) and the contract (*ʿaqd*) had not yet come into being at

88 *Maʿānī*, 2:370.

89 *Ikhtilāf*, 2:250.

90 See *al-Ḥujja*, 2:64–77.

Shaybānī's time. With al-Ṭaḥāwī, we see a reversal of sorts: he claims that the Ḥanafīs are united in allowing her to contract but only after she has asked permission. With this stance, the guardian still has a role, and the hadith, so key to the Shāfiʿī position, need not be challenged beyond the limits of its interpretation and applicability.

The position outlined for us in the *Maʿānī*, then, is the driving force behind al-Ṭaḥāwī's conclusions. He describes the Ḥanafī position with regard to the non-virgin prepubescent (*al-thayyib al-ṣaghīr*) as follows: "The marriage guardian for the non-virgin prepubescent may marry her off, just as he would if she were a virgin."[91] It is thus abundantly clear that al-Ṭaḥāwī is proffering a Ḥanafī position in which *bulūgh* (maturity/pubescence) rather than virginity is the legal criterion for determining the capacity of females.

The *Ikhtilāf* presents us with multiple opinions, generally supporting the idea that most scholars had by this time accepted: the prepubescent, male or female, is under the command of his or her father when it comes to marriage. Most of the discussion revolves around whether the marriages contracted by other than the father can stand, or whether the prepubescents can exercise the right of rescission once they reach maturity. The one voice in the entire discussion that disallows the marriage of prepubescents is Ibn Shubrama, as related by Bishr ibn al-Walīd from Abū Yūsuf.[92]

The passage on the marriage of prepubescents ends with al-Ṭaḥāwī adducing two proofs. The first is a report that ʿAlī ibn Abī Ṭālib and Ibn Masʿūd deemed marriages of prepubescents (male and female) binding when contracted by other than the father and grandfather from among the marriage guardians. The second is his claim that this was also the opinion of Ibn ʿAbbās and ʿĀʾisha with regard to the interpretation of the Q4:3.[93] The editor anachronistically

---

91 *Ikhtilāf*, 2:256.

92 *Ikhtilāf*, 2:257. This is not, as we have mentioned, the position of Ibn Shubrama as related by al-Marwazī, above, or Ibn ʿAbd al-Barr, below. See *al-Istidhkār*, ¶23330. Ibn ʿAbd al-Barr places Ibn Shubrama among those who allowed the prepubescent female to rescind upon pubescence, while affirming the right of any marriage guardian, paternal or non-paternal, to contract her marriage.

93 Throughout the tafsīr literature, opinions attributed to Ibn ʿAbbās and ʿĀʾisha with regard to Q4:3 have centered on orphans, but there is no specific mention of marrying prepubescents (*al-ṣighār*). The link in al-Ṭaḥāwī's mind is made clear by the explanation of al-Jaṣṣāṣ (see Chapter One, above) and centers on the word orphan (*yatīm*).

Because al-Ṭaḥāwī has included the statement of Umm Salama that she was a woman with orphans (*innī imrāʾa dhāt aytām*), he concludes based on this that ʿUmar at the time was prepubescent (*wa huwa yawmʾidhin ṭiflun ghayr bāligh*). Al-Ṭaḥāwī's (very Ḥanafī) focus is on allowing her to contract her own marriage; thus, because she assigned a child

points out a corroborating text in *Aḥkām al-Qurʾān* of al-Jaṣṣāṣ, and indeed the entirety of al-Jaṣṣāṣ's chapter on marrying prepubescents would seem to hinge on the exegesis of verse Q4:3.[94] Much of al-Jaṣṣāṣ's argument is built on the arguments of al-Ṭaḥāwī, and al-Shaybānī before him; none of these relies on the hadith of ʿĀʾisha.

Suitability

Al-Ṭaḥāwī notes that the Ḥanafī position is one that requires suitability for any given match.[95] This position is attributed also to Sufyān al-Thawrī and al-Ḥasan ibn Ḥayy. The Mālikī position he relates as follows:

> Ibn al-Qāsim[96] related from Mālik that: If a father refuses to marry his daughter to a man who is not an equal match in social status and nobility (*al-ḥasab wa al-sharaf*), but he is an equal match in religion, then it is for the ruler to marry her [to him] without regarding the opinion of the father and the marriage guardian, if she is content with him and he is her match in religion.[97]

Al-Ṭaḥāwī assesses al-Shāfiʿī's position succinctly, using very nearly the same vocabulary as is found in the matching section in the *Umm*. In that section, al-Shāfiʿī explains that settling for one who is less in lineage or social status represents a diminishment of status for the woman and her guardians.[98] Al-Ṭaḥāwī acknowledges this, stating—as indeed al-Shāfiʿī does—that settling in this fashion is not, however, forbidden.

---

to marry her to the Prophet, "it was as if she had contracted her own marriage" (*ka-annahā ʿaqadat al-zawāj ʿalā nafsihā*). (*Maʿānī al-Āthār*, 2:368).

94 *Ikhtilāf al-ʿUlamāʾ*, 258–259, *al-Ḥujja*, 2:87–92, and Al-Jaṣṣāṣ, *Aḥkām*, 2:51–55.

95 *Ikhtilāf al-ʿUlamāʾ*, 2:252.

96 The most famous of Mālik's pupils, he died in 191/806. His responsa to Asad ibn al-Furāt (d. 213/828) and then to Saḥnūn form the basis of the *Mudawwana*, a major work of Mālikī jurisprudence quoted extensively in Chapter Four, above. See Schacht, J. "Ibn al-Ḳāsim, Abu ʿAbd Allāh ʿAbd al-Raḥmān b. al-Ḳāsim b. Ḳh̲ālid b. D̲junāda al-ʿUtaḳi." *EI2*.

97 Al-Ṭaḥāwī, 2:252; cf. the assessment of Ibn al-Mundhir of Mālik's position on page 175 above. The two positions are essentially the same, although Ibn al-Mundhir has Mālik quoting the Qurʾān (49:13); it is probable that both Ibn al-Mundhir and al-Ṭaḥāwī gleaned their information about the Mālikī position from the *Mudawwana*, for Saḥnūn has Mālik citing this verse and including the issue of recourse to the governor. (See *al-Mudawwana*, 2:163.).

98 *Al-Umm*, 6:39–40.

Then he includes a hadith that reads, "Oh people of the tribe of Bayāḍah, marry the children of Abū Hind, and marry (your children) to his." Al-Ṭaḥāwī insists that in this report there is no indicator that there should *not* be consideration paid to suitability (*laysa fīhi dalāla ʿalā suqūṭ iʿtibār al-kafāʾa*). He then adds the observation of Salmān al-Fārisī regarding the preeminence of the Arabs; al-Ṭaḥāwī adds no further discussion.[99] Like other scholars before and after him, he does not leave the reader with a solid sense of what the scholars concurred upon, if anything, with regard to *kafāʾa*.

Conclusion to al-Ṭaḥāwī

Al-Ṭaḥāwī has given us insights into a particular moment in the development of the discussion of prepubescent marriage. We have seen how the Ḥanafī focus at this time is defined by its defensive posture against arguments favored by al-Shāfiʿī. We have seen how this Ḥanafī scholar has delved deeply into hadith criticism in order to debate the other side. Ultimately he has argued the point that there is no support for al-Shāfiʿī's interpretation of the hadith "No marriage without a guardian" in the face of the *ayyim/bikr* hadith. Ibn al-Qaṭṭān's encyclopedic compilation misleads in this case. Stopping short of claiming consensus on the matter of prepubescent marriage, the only claim of "non-disagreement" that al-Ṭaḥāwī makes is with regard to an inter-Ḥanafī position on marriage guardians.

If nothing else, we must mark Ibn al-Qaṭṭān's inclusion—and the unknown al-Tamīmī's before him—of that one, small footnote in the long history of the issue of prepubescent marriage. Ibn Shubrama, whose positions the scholars toss back and forth among themselves, caused Abū Yūsuf,[100] who would not have agreed with him by any means, to relate a position condemning the marriages contracted by parents for their minor children as illegal.

It is this admission of dissent to the overwhelming agreement—even if it was agreement to an extremely low common denominator—that we take away from al-Ṭaḥāwī.

---

99 He does not here opine on or include the alleged quotation of Abū Ḥanīfa that "Persians are not suitable for Arabs and Arabs are not suitable for Qurashis, and Qurashis are suitable for each other." (See *al-Mughnī,* 9:195, and above, in the section on Ibn al-Mundhir of this chapter.).

100 I have been unable to find this reference in Abū Yūsuf's extant works.

Ibn ʿAbd al-Barr

The Walī Mujbir: The Capacity of Females

Of the many lexically-fraught passages in this study, Ibn ʿAbd al-Barr's approach to the *ayyim/bikr* hadith shows how very seriously he takes his jurist's mandate vis-à-vis language.

> When God's Messenger said that the *ayyim* has more legal capacity than her guardian, he indicated that the marriage guardian has rights, but she has more of a right than he does. He also indicated that the right of the marriage guardian over the virgin is superior to this, for the marriage guardian cannot contract marriage for the previously-married woman without her permission, whereas he can contract marriage for the virgin without her permission. It is preferable (*wa yustaḥabb lahu*) that he request her permission and consult her.[101]

He approaches the hadith as having very different possible interpretations: The first is that the word *ayyim* is to be interpreted as equivalent in meaning to the word *thayyib*. Thus the *thayyib*, the previously-married woman who is by definition no longer a virgin, and the virgin are placed in apposition, with no mention of age. He even adduces a saying that inserts the word *thayyib* instead of *ayyim*,[102] and other non-Prophetic versions of the same wording (i.e., using *thayyib* instead of *ayyim*) which Ibn ʿAbd al-Barr says that he has included as a non-prophetic report in his book *al-Tamhīd*.[103] Nonetheless, Ibn ʿAbd al-Barr suggests that whoever quotes this hadith with the wording "the *thayyib* is more in possession of her self" is inserting his own understanding into the wording (*qad jāʾ bihi ʿalā al-maʿnā ʿindahu*).[104]

Whatever the case, he then takes up the debate over the language of the hadith. "Some of them say that the *ayyim* is the one who has been made spouseless by the death of her husband or his divorce, and she is (equivalent to) the *thayyib*."[105]

He adduces poetry ("[After the battle of al-Qadisiyya] the women of Saʿd have no widows (*ayāmā*) among them!") and the hadith of Ḥafṣa who was

101 *Al-Istidhkār*, 5:388.

102 "Related through Ibn ʿUyayna from Ziyād ibn Saʿd."

103 *Al-Istidhkār*, 5:386. The book to which he refers is *al-Tamhīd li-mā fī al-Muwaṭṭaʾ min al-maʿānī wa-l-asānīd* (Lahore: Al-Maktabah al-Quddūsīyah, 1983).

104 Ibid., 387.

105 Ibid.

widowed (*ta'ayyamat*) upon the death of Khunays ibn Ḥudhāfah al-Sahmī. Further, he notes the word's application to ʿUthmān in support of the grammarian's usage: "the lack of a spouse after having had one." The Arabs, on the other hand, "if they perhaps use *ayyim* for whomever has no spouse at all, this is merely a (vernacular) generalization (*ittisāʿ*)."[106]

Those who understand it to be a reference to the *thayyib*[107] understand it to be so because of the addition of the information regarding the *bikr*. Because the reference to the virgin follows the reference to the *ayyim*, this is sufficient linguistic proof that the two are in apposition. Further, the understanding of this group is intertwined with the hadith that "there is no marriage but through a *walī*." If the *bikr* is not bound by her virginity to the decision of the *walī*, then the hadith has no meaning. In other words, if *all* single women (*ayāmā*) possess legal capacity in marriage, then there is contradiction in the hadith. If only non-virgin (i.e. previously married) single women have self-possession, the *walī* still has a *raison d'etre* in the virgin, be she pubescent or prepubescent. This point is extremely important, however.

The alternative meaning for the word *ayyim* is "every woman who has no spouse, be she virgin (*bikr*) or non-virgin (*thayyib*)."[108] He adduces three separate verses of poetry and a hadith supporting the view that it is simply the state of being spouseless, as well as the opinion of Ismāʿīl ibn Isḥāq[109] who further insists that her state of physical maturity (*bāligh* or not) is not relevant. The final indicator lies in the Qurʾānic text 24:32, {*wa-nkiḥū al-ayāmā minkum*}.

Ibn ʿAbd al-Barr believes that the hadith must keep its original wording—*ayyim* cannot be replaced with *thayyib*: All single women have more legal capacity with regard to their marriage contracts than does their *walī*.[110] But key to his thinking about this subject is that he excludes the father from the status of being a "common *walī*." Rather, the father holds the position of being a sort of über-walī, a "*walī muṭlaq*": "The father is not included among the generality of marriage guardians, because his status is so exalted that he should not be

---

106 Ibid.

107 Ibn ʿAbd al-Barr names them as: al-Shāfiʿī, his companions, Aḥmad ibn Ḥanbal, and Isḥāq ibn Rāhawayh.

108 Ibid., 5:390.

109 This is most likely the Mālikī Judge of Baghdād, referred to as "Shaykh al-Islām" by al-Dhahabī. He had a recension of the Muwaṭṭaʾ, and a refutation of al-Shaybānī that spanned "over 200 volumes." He died in 282/895. See *Siyar*, 13:339.

110 *Al-Istidhkār*, 5:390.

included with marriage guardians who do not resemble him and do not share the powers specific to him."[111]

Ibn ʿAbd al-Barr informs us that there are two lessons to be drawn from the hadith. The first is that all single women have more legal capacity than the *walī*, unless the *walī* is the father who is excluded from the generality of marriage guardians.[112] And the second meaning is teaching how to ask the permission of the virgin; her silence is her permission because she is shy to respond with her tongue.[113] Permission of the virgin, however, is in his thinking a non-essential technicality, as will be further discussed below.

> Proof of this is in the fact that the father can contract marriage for the prepubescent if she reaches maturity, and this is binding according to the consensus of the Muslims. She must defer to this, and she has no right of rescission with regard to herself if she reaches maturity.[114]

Ibn ʿAbd al-Barr does not stop at suggesting this consensus; he uses the term once again in stating there is a consensus that the *walī* in question in the *ayyim/bikr* hadith is the *walī* of agnatic kinship (*min al-nasab wa-l-ʿaṣaba*).[115] Yet, we have already witnessed other schools, such as the Ḥanafīs, investing mothers with the power of guardianship.[116]

Continuing, Ibn ʿAbd al-Barr considers the source of the father's power to compel his daughter:

> His contract of marriage for his prepubescent daughter is only binding due to the fact that she is among the general class of single women. If she had more legal capacity it would not be permissible for him to contract her marriage until such a time as she reached maturity and could be asked.[117]

---

111 Ibid. Although this is the practice of the other schools (except the Ḥanafīs who allow any guardian to contract marriage for the female), this is our first encounter of the father as *walī muṭlaq*.

112 Ibid.

113 Ibid.

114 Ibid., 390–391.

115 Ibid., 393.

116 See p. 41 and 41n97.

117 *Al-Istidhkār*, 5:391. The complementary passage in the *Umm* reads: "And if it were the case that, were she to reach [the age of menstruation] as a virgin, she would possess more legal capacity than he does with regard to herself, it would indicate that it is not permissible for

True to Mālikī doctrine, and mirroring the stance of al-Shāfiʿī, in Ibn ʿAbd al-Barr's thought the limitations on the father's rule over his daughter only end with the end of her virginity. Ibn ʿAbd al-Barr insists that the significance of the hadith regarding the *thayyib* who was married off by her father and allowed to end her marriage by the Prophet is due to her state of having been a non-virgin when the father contracted the marriage for her.[118]

Further, it is of consequence that Ibn ʿAbd al-Barr here makes several claims of Ijmāʿ. We are particularly interested in the one he adduces with regard to the right of a father to compel his pubescent virgin daughter. As we have seen, all of the earlier writers have informed us that there is a difference of opinion on this subject. Thus, this can only be considered an attempt at bolstering the Mālikī opinion by making the claim of an overwhelming consensus on the subject—and note that it is a Muslim-wide claim, not a claim attributed merely to the consensus of the scholars).[119] It is significant that Ibn ʿAbd al-Barr would choose to rely on consensus itself as an indicator without offering any supporting evidence.

His stance may well be illustrative of the symbiotic relationship between Ijmāʿ and hadith: For his argument to stand, the only possible interpretation of the *ayyim/bikr* hadith can be the one Ibn ʿAbd al-Barr has chosen (the virgin is

---

him [to override her wishes] until such a time as [even the prepubescent virgin] reaches maturity and gives her permission" (6:45–46).

118 A reference to the hadith of Khansāʾ bint Khidām. When discussing the inability of a woman to contract her own marriage (i.e. without a *walī*), he brings all three reports into harmonization in the following way:

"There is no evidence in his statement that the *ayyim* has more right to herself than her guardian for those who believe that a woman can marry herself. This is because of his statement "there is no marriage without a guardian, and any woman who marries without a guardian, her marriage is void." In this he did not specify the virgin or the non-virgin. In both of these hadith there is what proves that the non-virgin has more of a right to herself than the virgin, and that the *walī* has a right that does not equal his right over the virgin. For the father can contract marriage for the virgin without her permission, and he cannot contract marriage for the non-virgin except with her permission. And the evidence for the fact that he meant "permission" without meaning the actual "contract" (*al-idhn dūn al-ʿaqd*) is that the Messenger of God annulled the marriage of Khansāʾ, and she was a non-virgin, and her father married her without her permission" (5:398).

Note here Ibn ʿAbd al-Barr's own interpolation of *thayyib* instead of *ayyim*.

119 It is not impossible, however, that this term comes in the same vein as al-Shāfiʿī's references to Ijmāʿ as something "Muslims" produce (causing Schacht to attribute to him a certain egalitarian conception of Ijmāʿ), even though his intention was clearly to reference the intellectual efforts of scholars. See Lowry, 346, and Chapter Seven of *Early Islamic Legal Theory.*

in apposition to the non-virgin, who has her own set of rules vis a vis her marriage guardian), because of the 'Ijmāʿ' about the nature of the capacity of virgins generally (their fathers can force them, be they pubescent or prepubescent).

In his analysis of the last section of Mālik's chapter on marriage, Ibn ʿAbd al-Barr returns to the subject of virgins. In the *Muwaṭṭa'*, authority for the father's power to compel his virgin daughters to marry derives from statements of al-Qāsim ibn Muḥammad and Sālim ibn ʿAbd Allāh and are not related to any Prophetic hadith or Ṣaḥābic *ithr.* Mālik validates their opinion, however, by saying, "And this is the way we deal with the marriage of virgins (*wa kadhālika al-amr ʿindanā fī nikāḥ al-abkār*)."[120] In other words, Mālik invokes the practice of Medina, in order to validate the practice relayed to him.[121] Rather than locate the opinion with these Successors, Ibn ʿAbd al-Barr elects to be vague: "It is well-known that whosever can marry off the prepubescent virgin, being as she is of those whose permission is not (even) taken into consideration (*wa hiyā mimman lā yuʿadd idhnuhā idhnan*), can marry off the pubescent without her permission if she is a virgin, although the scholars prefer that they (virgins) be consulted (*yustaḥibbūna mushāwaratahunna*)."[122]

This discussion of consultation is taken directly, and almost verbatim, from *K. al-Umm*: Following in al-Shāfiʿī's footsteps, Ibn ʿAbd al-Barr compares the *mushāwara* of women and the *mushāwara* of the Prophet: it is inconceivable that anyone would go against the opinion of the Prophet. Nonetheless, he was ordered[123] to consult his community. In the same way, females should be consulted out of respect for their psychological state, with no serious consideration given to the idea that they might be allowed to disagree. Simply, it makes them feel better (*li-taṭayyub anfusihinna*).[124]

---

120 *Al-Muwaṭṭa'*, 2:53.

121 Later jurisprudential theory works, particularly of the Shāfiʿī school, will condemn this approach of Mālik as an appeal to a Medinan Ijmāʿ (see particularly al-Shāfiʿ when he refutes the Medinan "consensus" that was preferred over isolated reports, See *Jimāʿ al-ʿilm*, ed. Rifaʿt Fawzī ʿAbd al-Muṭṭalib in volume 9 of *Kitāb al-Umm* (Manṣūrah: Dār al-Wafā' lil-Ṭibāʿah wa-l-nashr wa-l-tawzīʿ, 2000), and the translation by Aisha Musa, found in p. 130). Despite the claims of the polemicists, it is not at all clear that it was Mālik's intention to enshrine a Medinan consensus more than to avoid reliance on weak information, but most probably to promote Medina as the site of authoritative practice in Islam.

122 *Al-Istidhkār*, 5:406.

123 Q3:159: *wa shāwirhum fī al-amr*. See *al-Umm*, 6:47–8.

124 *Al-Istidhkār*, 5:389. See *al-Umm*, 6:47–8. The expression al-Shāfiʿī uses is also: *Istiṭābat nafsihā*. Note that Ibn Qudāma also refers to this approach in the *Mughnī*; all of the hadith which seem to indicate the necessity of female's consent are, for him, merely suggestions for good manners on the part of the father. See *al-Mughnī*, 9:208.

If this, then, is the approach to dealing with the daughters, yet how does Ibn ʿAbd al-Barr approach the topic of the father's power over his sons? As we have seen, the earlier consensus writers have discussed the right of the father to compel his minor child, son or daughter. Witness what Ibn ʿAbd al-Barr presents as Ḥanafī stances:

> Abū Ḥanīfa and Muḥammad ibn al-Ḥasan have said: "The guardian's contract of marriage for the minor female, whether [the guardian] is her father or not, is binding. However, she has the right to rescind when she reaches majority."
>
> This is the position of al-Ḥasan, ʿAṭāʾ and Ṭāwus, ʿUmar ibn ʿAbd al-ʿAzīz, Qatāda, Ibn Shubrama, and al-Awzāʿī.
>
> And Abū Yūsuf has said: "The minor female who attains majority has no right to rescind, whether her father or another guardian has married her off."
>
> All of these say: "Whosoever can be married off in her majority, can be married off as a minor." [The editor adds: And God knows best.][125]

We know from the consensus writers, and in particular the Ḥanafī al-Ṭaḥāwī who specifically cited Ibn Shubrama as presenting an anti-prepubescent marriage stance, that the opinions of these scholars are not so easily presented, and certainly not as supportive of compelling pubescent virgins. But what is of real interest here is the way that Ibn ʿAbd al-Barr has taken Ḥanafī opinion and divested it of the male-comprehensive dual address. It is as though he is rewriting the Ḥanafī opinions to focus them on the female. Although al-Shaybānī's views have already been discussed at length in Chapter Three, it is worth including the relevant passages here:

> Muḥammad said, "Abū Ḥanīfa said, "If the minor female and the minor male are married off by their father (or the paternal grandfather if the father is dead), the marriage is binding, and neither has the right to rescind upon pubescence (*lā khiyār la-humā idhā balaghā*). If they [dual] die, they [dual] inherit. If their guardian (*walīyuhumā*) marries the minor male and the minor female, and he is other than the father or the grandfather … then the marriage is binding, if they [dual] die, they [dual] inherit. And they [both] have the right to rescind upon pubescence; if they [dual] so desire, they can deem valid the marriage, and if they [dual] so desire they [dual] can reject it."[126]

125 *Al-Istidhkār*, 5:405.

126 *Al-Ḥujja*, 2:87–88.

We see, then, to what extent Ibn ʿAbd al-Barr has rewritten or reinvented earlier thought on minor marriage, effectively eliminating the dual gender. Despite himself, however, he is forced to include a sole Mālikī opinion that refers to both sexes: There is only one small reference to the marriage of prepubescent boys which he includes, without analysis, that poses a possible contradiction. It is the opinion of Abū Qurra who says: "I asked Mālik about [the Prophetic report] 'the virgin should have her permission sought with regard to herself': does this apply to fathers? He responded, 'No, he did not mean fathers here. He meant other than fathers.' He [Abū Qurra] said, "The marriage contract of a father is binding upon his young children, male or female, and they have no right to rescind before maturity."[127] This, along with a brief allusion to ʿUrwa Ibn al-Zubayr's contract of marriage for his minor son,[128] are the only references to males throughout Ibn ʿAbd al-Barr's analysis of this subject; the subject of the right of rescission post-maturity is not addressed.

Ibn ʿAbd al-Barr and Proof Texts

Ibn ʿAbd al-Barr is unequivocal with regard to his position that the law allows fathers to marry off their prepubescent daughters, and indeed their virgin daughters generally. However he will not disavow any of the now-relevant hadith, and so he must work to reconcile the content of the *ayyim/bikr* hadith with the hadith of ʿĀʾisha.

His first reference to the report of ʿĀʾisha comes alongside a reference to consensus:

> The scholars have reached consensus upon (*ajmaʿū ʿalā anna*) a father's ability to contract marriage for his prepubescent daughter without consulting her, and (*wa ʿalā anna*) that God's Messenger, peace and blessings be upon him, married ʿĀʾisha the daughter of Abū Bakr when she was prepubescent, a girl of six or seven. Her father married him to her.[129]

This dual invocation of consensus serves to explain the legal import of the hadith while affirming its veracity. Not far from this mention of consensus, however, is one that would in some ways challenge it:

127 *Al-Istidhkār*, 5:401.

128 See *al-Istidhkār*, 5:405.

129 Ibid., 400–401.

> They have advanced as an argument his saying, peace be upon him, "The virgin is not married until she gives her permission." And they said, this applies unrestrictedly to every virgin, except for the minor female who has a father, based on the evidence of the *consensus upon the meaning* of the hadith of the marriage of the Prophet to ʿĀʾisha."[130]

This second consensus reference comes quite deep in Ibn ʿAbd al-Barr's analysis of Ḥanafī positions. As we will recall, the statement that the ayyim/bikr hadith is general (*ʿāmm*) with regard to virgins, while the ʿĀʾisha hadith is specific (*khāṣṣ*) to the case of the prepubescent virgin is precisely the justification used by Ibn al-Mundhir in his assessment of the relationship between the two statements. The only difference is that his vocabulary centers on the concept of the "exception" (*mustathnā*): "[The marriage of Aisha] was an exception to the statement of the Prophet, 'The virgin is not married until her permission is sought.'"[131]

In Mālikī thought, the use of the *ʿāmm/khāṣṣ* dichotomy to differentiate between the virgin and the prepubescent virgin flies in the face of their position that any virgin can be married off by her father. As Ibn ʿAbd al-Barr explains:

> Mālik, al-Shāfiʿī, and Ibn Abī Laylā have said: If a woman is a virgin, it is the right of her father to compel her to marry, as long as there is no evident harm in it, whether she is minor or major (*ṣaghīra* or *kabīra*). And this is the position of Aḥmad, Isḥāq and a large group.
>
> Their argument for this is that just as it is permissible for him to contract marriage for a prepubescent, it is permissible for him to contract marriage for the pubescent if she is a virgin, because the *ratio legis* is virginity. For the father is not like all other marriage guardians, due to his ability to make decisions with regard to her money,[132] and the way he looks out for her (*wa naẓarihi la-hā*), and the fact that his motives cannot be questioned with regard to her (*annahu ghayr muttaham ʿalayhā*). If it were not licit for him to contract the pubescent virgin's marriage except by her permission, it would be not permissible for him to contract marriage for the prepubescent.

---

130 Ibid., 403. This is the passage that Ibn al-Qaṭṭān cites incorrectly in the *Iqnāʿ*, see above p. 156–157.

131 *Al-Ishrāf*, 1:24. Lowry addresses the issue of the "exception" being similar to the *ʿāmm/khāṣṣ* dichotomy in *Early Islamic Legal Theory*, ch. 2, esp. 69–87.

132 See also, *al-Umm*, 6:49.

> Just as persons other than the father cannot contract marriage for a mature virgin without her permission, it is not for other persons to contract marriage for a prepubescent female; if her father needed her permission to marry her, then he would not marry her until she became one of those who have permission to give, via pubescence.
>
> Thus, when they reached consensus upon a father's ability to contract marriage for the prepubescent, she being without permission to give, it is also correct for her, based upon this, that he contract marriage for her without her permission for as long as she remains a virgin. [This is] because the difference between the virgin and the non-virgin has been elaborated in the [*ayyim-thayyib/bikr-*] hadith.[133]

Thus Ibn ʿAbd al-Barr would extend the concept of the consensus for the minor virgin, claiming that it should rightly apply, based on this interpretation of the *ayyim/bikr* hadith, to the major virgin as well. Such a stance forces him to be hostile to the following isolated report (or, unit tradition, Ar. *khabar al-wāḥid*), the meaning of which would obviate the legal implications derived from ʿĀʾisha's report that fathers can compel their daughters, and that no right of rescission exists when they become mature agents.[134] Ibn ʿAbd al-Barr is criticizing the Ḥanafī position of capacity for pubescent females, even virgins, which rests on the evidence of a hadith related by Ibn ʿAbbās:

> A young virgin (*jāriya bikr*) came to the Prophet, peace be upon him, and recounted to him that her father had married her against her will. So the Prophet allowed her to rescind, peace and blessings be upon him.[135]

Whereas Ibn al-Mundhir skimmed over this report with no assessment, Ibn ʿAbd al-Barr is swift in dismissing it outright. His reason? "Only Jarīr ibn Ḥāzim narrated it (*infarada bihi*) … none of Ayyūb's other companions related it, to the best of my knowledge."[136]

---

133 *Al-Istidhkār*, 5:401.

134 This is assuming the text's veracity, which is in fact an assumption of the veracity of the then-reputedly-senile Hishām ibn ʿUrwa (see *Tahdhīb al-tahdhīb*, 275–276); see also n. 52 p. 177 above, regarding Ibn Ḥajar's acknowledgment that the hadith does not contain within it a valid indicator for compulsion.

135 *Al-Istidhkār*, 5:404.

136 Ibid. Note that this is the same report that Ibn Qudāma has included and discarded as mursal (al-*Mughnī*, 9:202) and Ibn al-Mundhir's *al-Ishrāf*, 1:24. See also p. 122, above. This report also occurs in *Sunan Abī Dāʾūd* #2096, and *Sunan Ibn Mājah*, #1875. See also the Appendix, for the *Muṣannaf* of ʿAbd al-Razzāq, ¶10339, *Sunan al-Awzāʿī*, ¶1054–59.

Conclusion to Ibn ʿAbd al-Barr

Through semantic analysis of the *ayyim/bikr* hadith, we have seen Ibn ʿAbd al-Barr affirm and reaffirm the right of the father to unilaterally contract marriage for virgins, both prepubescent and pubescent. The key to his thought in this has been to declare the father to be not simply the *walī mujbir* but indeed the *walī muṭlaq*, the guardian with absolute power. We have further witnessed the way in which he has omitted discussing the minor male when it comes to minor marriage or marriage under compulsion, going so far as to rewrite early sources in order to eliminate mention of the male.

When Ibn ʿAbd al-Barr speaks of a consensus existing upon the meaning of the report of ʿĀʾisha, two things are clear: One, there is no quibbling over the fact that this was a unit tradition; and two, any other conclusions that might have once existed had, in his mind, been purged from the scholarly discussion. Herein lies a key point with regard to the intersection of Ijmaʿ and hadith, found here in a way that is not so clearly articulated in later sources. This is a telling illustration of what al-Shāfiʿī understood to be the function of Ijmāʿ with regard to non-*mutawātir* Sunnaic materials, or materials from which the extraction of a ruling is not necessarily self-evident: The consensus can serve to establish a sense of certainty where before there was none, to invest meaning that is not otherwise obvious, and above all give weight to a tradition that is otherwise shaky.[137]

Ibn ʿAbd al-Barr accepts the conclusions about what the report of ʿĀʾisha means for prepubescents, as exemplified by early consensus writers like Ibn al-Mundhir and al-Marwazī (although, as we have seen in his analysis, unlike these two, Ibn ʿAbd al-Barr does not refer to *boys* at all). The only protest against al-Shāfiʿī's conclusions with regard to this report is expressed in a single sentence: "There is no role for the grandfather in that (*lā maʿnā lil-jadd fī dhālik*)."[138]

In Ibn ʿAbd al-Barr's writing we find no consideration of the power now vested in a unit tradition that had no place in the *Muwaṭṭaʾ*. Mālik's major concern was whether any tradition conflicted with Medinan practice, and it was well-known that he did not rely upon the unit tradition as a source.[139] Perhaps it is

137 As noted in Lowry, *Early Islamic Legal Theory*, 326–330 and Zysow, *The Economy of Certainty*, 200.

138 *Al-Istidhkār*, 5:405.

139 See See also Schacht, *Origins*, where he preferred the practice of the Medinese to traditions related from the Prophet (pp. 64–65). Note also the discussion on page 67 wherein he observes blurred lines between Medinese 'practice' and actual custom, and 68 where he notes the "the 'practice' of the Medinese merge[s] into the common opinion of the recognized scholars, which becomes the final criterion of the 'living tradition' of the school."

indicative of the transformation of the doctrine of Ijmāʿ that it could, by the time of Ibn ʿAbd al-Barr, give such weight to such a tradition.

Conclusion

This chapter has given us insights into the way that writers from the tenth and eleventh centuries approached consensus on the matter of compulsion in minor marriage. It has highlighted the "lowest common denominator" of agreement that consensus seemed to represent for the jurists: the multiple, multi-faceted debates attached to the issue of minor marriage ultimately gave way to short sentences highlighting surface agreement. This seems representative of a larger trend of abridgment, of which Ibn al-Mundhir's *Kitāb al-Ijmāʿ* is one major example. Complex works of law were honed into shorter, thinner works that belied the legal field's rich polyvalence. Perhaps such abridgment was in service to political crises that demanded a strong and united corps of jurists to keep the populace anchored in religion and law, as is possible to postulate for Ibn al-Qaṭṭān's manual.

Beneath the thin sentences of consensus statements are illustrated some of the areas of fundamental disagreement on the issue of prepubescent marriage: principle among these is the underlying *ratio legis* for a father's ability to compel the marriage (Virginity? Prepubescence?). The group that supports classification of women by virginity (the Shāfiʿī al-Marwazī, the Mālikī Ibn ʿAbd al-Barr) also supports a stronger role for the father: a daughter's attaining legal capacity upon pubescence would mean a diminishing of paternal power. Discarding the possibility of her gaining "authority with regard to herself" upon pubescence is only possible by linking her legal capacity or lack thereof to her virginity (a term which reveals itself in legal discourse as quite difficult to define). The assumption is that the female will cease being a virgin only when transferred to another man's control, in which case paternal power is irrelevant, while patriarchal power is still affirmed.

Other areas of disagreement are to be found in the condition of suitability (*kafāʾa*), the very condition upon which some of the writers like Ibn al-Mundhir (and, later, Ibn Qudāma) make the consensus claim. A further lack of definition surrounds the age at which a girl is able to tolerate sexual activity. Even more problems arise when attempting to decide whether or not the prepubescent male is liable for maintenance payments; or whether two parties to an unconsummated marriage may inherit from each other. Finally, there is a glaring difference of opinion over whether or not prepubescents for whom marriages have been contracted may rescind these contracts upon pubescence (a state which is also, for all intents and purposes, still undefined).

This chapter gives credence to the notion of the "Ijmāʿic Shāfiianism" of even the non-Shāfiʿīs like Ibn ʿAbd al-Barr. The major conclusions of these writers show a narrowing of proof texts and their interpretations, with a distinct inclination toward elevation and enshrinement of one method of arriving at a legal opinion on the topic, that of al-Shāfiʿī. Of greatest interest are the continuous, if unspoken, assumptions underlying all of these decisions with regard to the lack of opinion ceded to children generally and the female prepubescent specifically, as well as the firm affirmation of the power of the father. This is not altogether foreign, for prepubescents lack capacity in legal systems throughout the world even today. What is most different is that the father's role is compared quite blatantly to the role of the prophet, as constructed by al-Shāfiʿī and repeated by Ibn ʿAbd al-Barr.

By claiming a consensus on the ability of a father to compel a female child, and pointing to the report of ʿĀ'isha as justification, early writers such as al-Marwazī and Ibn al-Mundhir were determining an otherwise indeterminate text through the engine of consensus. As noted, to even assume its veracity, given all of the sources in which it does not appear, is to take a huge legal step. It is intriguing legal logic—based on the text as presented—to assume that had ʿĀ'isha protested she would have been compelled, or to analogize the father's role to the grandfather, or to suggest that the Prophet's suitability could be analogized down to the suitability of a non-Prophet, i.e. to invoke the doctrine of *kafāʿa* from a situation involving the Prophet. And yet all of these were al-Shāfiī's conclusions based on this report, and all of these eventually came to be inserted into the consensus discussions. If at first the non-Shāfiʿīs held out against inserting the report of ʿĀ'isha into this discussion, they later gave way, and other proof texts such as the *ayyim/bikr* hadith would eventually be cast aside. By the time of the Ḥanbalī Ibn Qudāma, the only text given any real emphasis is the ʿĀ'isha report.

In addition to noting legal strategies, we have observed how the earliest writers, al-Marwazī and Ibn al-Mundhir, allotted space and ink to the subject of compelled marriage of male prepubescents, al-Ṭaḥāwī rather less, and Ibn ʿAbd al-Barr actually rewrites earlier opinions to eliminate the male element.

Thus the classical period's consensus writers have left their mark, to be investigated in abridged and unabridged form as the seeker desires. Were their efforts enough to transform the discourse in a substantive way? The next chapter's investigation of post-formative era scholarship may provide an answer.

CHAPTER 8

Post-formative Scholars

Consensus manuals did not depict the topic of minor marriage with all of its nuance and applicability to both genders, or the reservations of the jurists regarding its many interrelated topics. However, many discussions of depth could still be found in books of positive law. These discussions show independence of thought and creative approaches that were not necessarily in keeping with the opinions of the early formative era founding scholars or the late formative era's consensus writers.

It would be possible to linger interminably in explorations of the scholarship pertinent to minor marriage. However, in considering the effects and import of consensus, this final chapter looks mainly to Ḥanbalī scholars, principally Ibn Qudāma, of the thirteenth and fourteenth centuries, with some reference to Ottoman practices thereafter. How did jurists like Ibn Qudāma, Ibn Taymīya (728/1328), and Ibn al-Qayyim (751/1350) approach minor marriage? If claiming consensus, whose consensus claims were valid for them and why? If affirming consent, how do they do so? How did Ottoman-era scholars consider this issue and its many ramifications? The writings of these scholars can give us some indication, however small, as to whether the consensus discussions had any notable effect on later juristic thought, and if the tendency of abridgement necessary for the consensus "lists" might have resulted in truncated discussions of these complex issues. I have chosen to focus on these luminaries of Ḥanbalī law because because of the role of Ḥanbalī thought in Saudi Arabia, where concerns over the marriage age debate remain a pressing issue. Many modern fatwas take their shape from scholars such as these. We have seen how Ibn Qudāma relies heavily on Ibn al-Mundhir and his conception of consensus; yet he was coterminous with Ibn al-Qaṭṭān. Was it too early for Ibn al-Qaṭṭān's work to influence him? What of later Ḥanbalīs? It is therefore chronologically expedient to consider Ibn Taymīya and Ibn Qayyim al-Jawzīya, particularly where they differ from Ibn Qudāma.

Likewise, the wealth of court records and writings of the Ottoman era should provide useful insights into how positive law was affected or not by consensus discussions. Modern legal historians have provided a great service in their thorough coverage of Ottoman developments: Amira Sonbol's research covers a period ranging from the sixteenth through the nineteenth

 | DOI 10.1163/9789004344860_010

centuries;[1] Judith Tucker's work focuses on the seventeenth and eigheenth centuries, while the work of M. Yazbak covers nineteenth century Palestine.

Above all, this chapter will delineate the major enduring legal challenges presented by minor marriage for jurists who had to reconcile what they accepted as basic legal tenets of marriage and divorce with a minor's lack of sexual maturity and legal capacity.

Post-formative Ḥanbalī thought

The Walī Mujbir

It seems clear from the outset that Ibn Qudāma believes strongly that a father can compel his virgin daughter to marry against her will. Her maturity does not obviate the father's power over his daughter. Early in his opinion, he says that it is only the change in sexual classification from virgin to non-virgin that affects the status of her legal capacity. He does not elaborate on this point here, but only later when he investigates the common proof texts on female legal capacity and consent in marriage. Note, however, that later in his discussion of the basis of power to compel, he will bring three different opinions before stating that only God knows.

He cites two relevant, closely-related hadith. The first is related through Abū Hurayra which states that the Prophet said:

> "The *ayyim* is not married until she is consulted, and the virgin (*bikr*) is not married until her permission is requested."[2] They asked, "How is [the virgin's] permission expressed?" He replied, "That she remain silent."

1 While a thorough treatment of the modern manifestations of these discussions throughout the Muslim world is imperative, it lies beyond the scope of the current project. For further reading see also *Īḍāḥ al-bayān fī nikāḥ al-ṣibyān*, ʿAbd Allāh Ḥumayyid al-Sālimī, (Beirut: al-Dār al-ʿArabiyah lil-ʿUlūm, 2006); *Muslim Family Laws* (Lahore: Legal Research Center: 1982); Saad, Reem and Nicholas Hopkins, eds, *Upper Egypt: Identity and Change* (Cairo: American University in Cairo Press, 2004). See also Shaham, "Custom." See also An-Na'im, Abdullahi, *Islamic Family Law in a Changing World: A Global Resource Book* (Zed Books, 2002).

2 It is probable, in this context, that Ibn Qudāma, with Ibn ʿAbd al-Barr, understood it to mean previously-married and not "single." Recall that in many sources the wording indicates orphans.

The second hadith, which Ibn Qudāma declares similar to the first, reads:

> The *ayyim* has more authority over herself than her marriage guardian, and the virgin's permission is requested, and her permission is her silence.

These two texts, in their various versions, have been of great importance to discussions of a father's power to compel highlighted throughout this study. How does Ibn Qudāma reconcile the second report in particular with his notions about the *walī mujbir?* Ibn Qudāma says,

> When [the Prophet] divided women into two categories, and established the right of one [category] of them, this indicated the lack of (that) right (*dall ʿalā nafyīhi*) for the other, this being the virgin. [For her,] the guardian is in more possession of authority than she is. And the hadith [also] indicates that consulting and requesting permission is [only] commendable (*mustaḥabb*) not obligatory (*wājib*), just as Ibn ʿUmar related, saying that the Messenger of God said, "Consult women with regard to their daughters."[3]

Here, Ibn Qudāma links consulting mothers and consulting intended brides. Although neither proof text contains language to that effect, Ibn Qudāma makes the claim that these commands are commendable instead of obligatory. Opinions of early scholars, notable among them al-Shāfiʿī,[4] could have charted such a course, but Ibn Qudāma adduces no such opinions here to support this position.

Ibn Qudāma reads the reports in question in a way that interprets the word "*ayyim*" to mean "previously-married." He finds the precedent for classification of women according to their virginity in the thought of Mālik and al-Shāfiʿī.[5]

It is significant, however, that between discussing the first report and the variant related through Ibn ʿAbbās, Ibn Qudāma takes time to attend to one report that has remained salient for the topic of the legal capacity of women with regard to their marriages.

---

3 *Āmirū al-nisāʾ fī banātihinna.* This hadith occurs in ʿAbd al-Razzāq's *Muṣannaf* ¶10319 and ¶10348 (see Appendix) and Abū Dāʾūd, #2095.

4 See the discussions of al-Shāfiʿī and Ibn ʿAbd al-Barr that have almost certainly provided the basis for Ibn Qudāma's idea that the hadith is referring to "recommended" consultations. See on this also Ali, "Just Say Yes," 125–127.

5 *Al-Mughnī*, 9:201.

> Ibn ʿAbbās related that a young virgin (*jāriya bikr*) came to the Prophet and mentioned that her father had married her off against her will. So the Prophet gave her a choice, because she possessed legal capacity (*jāʾizat al-taṣarruf*) with regard to her assets. Thus he invalidated her compulsion, as [he would have done] with the previously-married woman and the man.[6]

Ibn Qudāma explains that this hadith is *mursal* (the chain of transmission does not reach the Prophet directly). It is not entirely clear why Ibn Qudāma dismisses it outright.[7] Ibn Qudāma then adduces another hadith in which a virgin complained of an unwanted marriage,[8] implying that the circumstances of that marriage warranted termination while the precise circumstances in the Ibn ʿAbbās report remained unclear.

That which is crystal clear is Ibn Qudāma's lack of tolerance for any infringement on the right of the father to compel his daughters, provided they are virgins. His discussion of the prepubescent non-virgin's status vis à vis her father, however, shows that the issue is quite unresolved. The reason it is still unresolved by the thirteenth century is that there is simply no resolution about what imbues legal capacity. On the one hand, Ibn Qudāma says that she cannot be compelled because she is a non-virgin and the basis for compulsion is the status of being a virgin.[9] On the other, he says that it may be that she can be compelled because she is still prepubescent. He brings up the final point that perhaps the state of being nine means that her consent is necessary. After all of this he can only concede that *God knows*.

---

6 Ibid., 202.

7 Ibn al-Mundhir also holds the opinion that it is not a strong hadith, also without any elaboration; perhaps Ibn Qudāma is basing his opinion on Ibn al-Mundhir's position. The hadith as related would have borne up under Ḥanafī and Mālikī standards of acceptance of the *mursal* ("relied upon if the narrator is trustworthy"); al-Shāfiʿī would have accepted such reports provided they did not contradict other, accepted hadith. For more on the *mursal*, see Kamali, Mohammad, *Principles of Islamic Jurisprudence*, 108–109. A similar text can be found in the *Ḥujja* of al-Shaybānī, 84–85, although the term used is a "virgin woman" instead of *jāriya*.

8 The hadith of "the woman whose father married her off to raise his own status" can be found in multiple collections, including #1874 in *Sunan ibn Mājah*, #3269 in *Sunan al-Nasāʾī*, and see also the Appendix. Here, the Prophet gave the young woman the right to rescind her marriage, but she claimed not to be unhappy, only concerned to know whether or not daughters had rights when it came to marriage.

9 On the necessity of her explicit consent, see Paul Powers, *Intent in Islamic Law: Motive and Meaning in Medieval Sunni Fiqh* (Leiden: Brill, Studies in Islamic Law and Society, 2006), 126–127.

Unlike Ibn Qudāma, the Ḥanbalī Ibn Qayyim al-Jawzīya (d. 1382) decries the use of "guardianship of compulsion" (*walāyat al-ijbār*). Ibn al-Qayyim opines:

> The father of a mature, mentally-sound virgin cannot have authority over the slightest bit of her assets unless she consents. He cannot compel her to mete out even a small amount of it without her consent, so how could he marry her, and cause her to mete out her very self without her consent, to the one *he* wants. In such a case, she is of those who are compelled, and [the groom] is the most hated of things for her, and despite this, he marries her to him forcibly and makes her his hostage?[10]

In *Zād al-maʿād*, whence the above quotation is taken, Ibn al-Qayyim, after having elaborated a strong argument against forcing the physically mature female, summarizes the various schools of thought on the issue of compulsion in marriage:

> The scholars have differed over the key factor that makes compulsion licit (*manāṭ al-ijbār*); there are six different opinions:
>
> > The first is that [the *walī*[11]] can compel [due to the existence of] virginity, and it is the opinion of al-Shāfiʿī, Mālik, and one of [the opinions] related from Aḥmad.[12]
> >
> > The second is that he can compel due to prepubescence (*al-ṣighar*), and this is the opinion of Abū Ḥanīfa and the second [of the opinions] related from Aḥmad.
> >
> > The third is that he can compel when both are present, and this is the third of [the opinions] related from Aḥmad.
> >
> > The fourth is that he can compel based on whichever of the reasons applies (*yujbir bi-ayyihimā wujida*), and this is the fourth [of the opinions] related from Aḥmad.
> >
> > The fifth is that he can compel by having given life (*bil-īlād*) [i.e., as the father], thus the mature non-virgin is [also] compelled. The Judge Ismāʿīl related this from al-Ḥasan al-Baṣrī. [The Judge] said, "This is against the consensus." [The Judge also] said, "There is

---

10 See Abū Zahrā, *Lectures on the Marriage Contract and its Implications*, 157. Abū Zahrā actually misquotes Ibn al-Qayyim, whose wording reads: "… So how is it permissible for him to enslave her (*fa-kayf yajūz an yuriqqahā*)?" (*Zād al-maʿād*, 859).

11 It would seem that Ibn al-Qayyim is referring almost exclusively to fathers.

12 See also Spectorsky, *Chapters*, pp. 9–11. Aḥmad is, of course, Aḥmad ibn Ḥanbal.

something to this from the point of view of the jurisprudence (*wa lahu wajh ḥasan min al-fiqh*)." And I wish I knew what that black and iniquitous point of view might be! (*fa-yā layta sh'irī mā hādhā al-wajh al-aswad al-muẓlim!*)

And the sixth is that he can compel whoever is among his dependents.

The preferable [stance] among all these schools of thought is surely apparent.[13]

Like Ibn al-Qayyim, Ibn Taymīya does not share Ibn Qudāma's support of the *walī mujbir*. Still, he explains that the verification of a woman's consent is not necessary and, in the four schools, requires no witnessing. "If the guardian says, 'She gave me her permission,' the marriage contract is deemed valid. The witnessing is for the [proceedings] between the guardian and the husband."[14] Thus although he agrees in principle that a woman cannot be compelled to marry without her consent, there are essentially no mechanisms in place for proving that she has or has not consented.

It is clear that the difference in stances on the issue of *walāyat al-ijbār* lies in different thoughts on the capacity of women. Ibn Taymīya bases the female's capacity in this matter not on a lack of virginity but, as did the Ḥanafīs, on her status as a mature female.[15] Ibn Taymīya expounds in no uncertain terms on what he considers the pernicious nature of forced marriage and the ways in which it obviates the basic premises of marriage:

> With regard to contracting marriage for her against her will: This is against the fundamentals [of the religion] and against reason (*mukhālif lil-uṣūl wa-l-'uqūl*). God did not intend for her guardian to compel her to sell or buy (property) except with her permission, or [force her] to eat, drink, or wear that which she does not desire. So how could [her guardian] compel her to have intercourse and live with someone she despises sleeping and living with? God has created between spouses affection and loving compassion (*mawadda wa-raḥma*). If [the marriage] can only occur despite her hatred of it and desire to flee from it, what affection and loving compassion can there be therein?[16]

13 Ibn al-Qayyim, *Zād al-Ma'ād fī Hadī Khayr al-'Abbād* (Beirut: Dār ibn Ḥazm, 1999), 860.

14 Ibn Taymīya, *Fatāwā*, 32:56.

15 Ibid., 32:25.

16 Ibid.

Despite such strong stances in favor of female consent, neither Ibn Taymīya nor his student Ibn al-Qayyim suggests that a prepubescent, by virtue of being legally capable in the future, should not be married off. Ibn Taymīya is clear that it is possible to compel a female minor to marry;[17] Ibn al-Qayyim appears more hesitant to give all-out validation to the concept. He notes the Prophetic hadith that an orphan girl must be asked her permission before a contract of marriage is made for her; then he notes the Ḥanafī position that there are no orphans after the age of puberty. The two together "prove that it is possible to marry an orphan before pubescence." This is, Ibn al-Qayyim notes, a position traced back to ʿĀʾisha; he then notes her exegesis of 4:127 and the necessity of paying an orphan bride her dower.[18] Neither Ibn Taymīya nor Ibn al-Qayyim adduces the report of ʿĀʾisha marrying as a child as evidence for their positions; both rely consistently on the *ayyim/bikr* hadith.

Sex, Maintenance, and Sexual Maturity

One gets a sense of the Mamlūk-era debates on the sexual nature of unions involving prepubescents from Ibn Qudāma. As we have seen, he uses Q65:4 to support the marriage of females who have yet to menstruate. In other words, Ibn Qudāma's position, like that of many other jurists,[19] is that God would not be stipulating an *ʿidda* for a child unless sex had actually occurred; this is justification enough for him to espouse marriages for prepubescent females that move beyond the merely "contractual," on-paper phase.

This idea is supported by his later chapters on maintenance (*nafaqa*). Here the main topic is the relationship between maintenance and the performing of the sexual act upon young girls. Ibn Qudāma is explicit that the husband does not have to pay to maintain a minor girl who does not make herself sexually available. The vocabulary used is by now familiar: "He need not pay maintenance for his bride if the sexual act is not performed upon [women] like her" (*lā yūṭaʾ mithluhā*).[20] Still, "maintenance is in return for pleasure" (*al-nafaqa fī muqābilat al-istimtāʿ*) says Ibn Qudāma. In Ibn Qudāma's opinion *istimtāʿ* is not necessarily vaginal intercourse. Later, he makes the point that if a woman is very small (*naḍwat al-khalq*), and her husband very large (*jasīm*), and she

17 Ibn Taymīya, *Fatāwā*, 32:39 .

18 Ibn al-Qayyim, *Zād al-maʿād*, 860 .

19 See also al-Jaṣṣāṣ, *Aḥkām al-Qurʾān*, 3:456–457; *Tafsīr al-Ṭabarī*, 23:54. See also my section on exegesis in the Introduction, above.

20 Ibn Qudāma, *Al-Mughnī*, 9:621.

fears intimacy (*al-ifḍāʾ*)[21] due to his hugeness (*ʿaẓm khalqihi*), then she can prevent him from having sex with her (*la-hā manʿuhu min jimāʿhā*) and he may take pleasure in her in other (non-vaginal-intercourse) ways (*fī mā dūn al-farj*). Importantly, he must pay the maintenance.[22]

This point is particularly pertinent for child marriage due to the opinion that Ibn Qudāma includes of Ibn Ḥanbal, that if a husband requests his minor spouse, and she has reached the age of nine, she must be given to him. "[Her family] cannot keep her from him after the age of nine."[23] Ibn Qudāma explains that this opinion is based upon the report of ʿĀʾisha.[24] He then cites al-Qāḍī Abū Yaʿlā[25] who makes some effort to lessen the impact of Ibn Ḥanbal's stance by saying, "In my opinion, [his saying nine years] is not to delineate [a specific age] (*laysa ʿalā ṭarīq al-taḥdīd*) but he mentioned this because, generally, pleasure can be had from the nine year old" (*ibnat tisaʿ yatamakkan min al-istimtāʿ bi-hā*).[26]

Although it is unclear whether Ibn Qudāma is still quoting Abū Yaʿlā, the next passage is interesting:

> If she cannot viably have the sexual act performed upon her (*matā kānat lā tuṣlaḥ lil-waṭʾ*) her family should not surrender her to him, even if he claims that he will care for her, raise her, and he has servants for her. Because he does not [yet] possess the right to take pleasure from her and she is unlawful for him (*laysat la-hu bi-maḥall*), and he cannot trust the evil of his self (*sharr nafsihi*) such that he might fall upon her and have sex with her or kill her (*yafuḍḍuhā aw yaqtuluhā*).[27]

Further, the state of being prepubescent (*al-ṣighar*) is equivalent to the state of being sick (*al-maraḍ*); it is a temporary impediment to intercourse. Within his discussion of both sick and prepubescent brides, Ibn Qudāma makes an appeal to culture with respect to when a bride should be delivered or surrendered

21 Although, according to Lane (1:2414 http://www.tyndalearchive.com/tabs/lane/, last accessed, 7/31/16), this could mean skin-to-skin contact it could also mean causing a fistula, which is probably the more accurate translation.

22 Ibid., 624.

23 Ibid., 623.

24 Ibid.

25 Abū Yaʿlā Muḥammad ibn al-Ḥusāyn al-Baghdādī (d. 458/1065), Ḥanbalī judge and scholar.

26 *Al-Mughnī*, 9:623.

27 Ibid. Again, the meaning may be to do injury to her, as in creating a fistula.

and thus when marriage should be consummated (*al-taslīm fī al-ʿaqd yajib ʿalā ḥasab al-ʿurf*).

It is intriguing to observe the way that he has made a case for the highly variable role of culture. He notes that it is culturally rare for a woman to give herself over to a man when she is ill; above, he noted that a minor female's family must assess her for signs of sexual viability. Although it is clear that Ibn Qudāma believes that prepubescent marriage is viable marriage, he also believes there is a time when the sexual immaturity of the prepubescent female renders her "unlawful" to her spouse. He quotes the view of Abū Yaʿlā again, who points out that "girls are different" (*annahunna yakhtalifna*), and "the possibility of sex with a prepubescent female depends on her condition and what she can tolerate."[28] It is to be noted that this discussion is very distant, both in tone and in physical presence, from the initial approval of the compulsion of prepubescent females issued near the beginning of Ibn Qudāma's very long chapter on marriage.

Ibn Qudāma's thoughts on *ʿidda* and *nafaqa* with regard to prepubescent females contrast with those of his later Ḥanbalī colleague Ibn al-Qayyim. Ibn al-Qayyim couches his discussion of verse Q65:4 in a larger framework of the discussion of the *ʿidda* generally. He is concerned with the "wisdom" behind the verses and rulings; as such he is keen to explain that the waiting period for divorce and death is not designed simply to make sure that there is a lack of pregnancy. This is one of the reasons, he says, but not the only reason. Other reasons include: understanding the full significance of the marriage contract (*taʿẓīm khaṭr hādhā al-ʿaqd*); lengthening the time period in which a divorcing husband may return his wife (*taṭwīl zaman al-rajʿa*)—such that he might regret his action; and the allowance for the rights of the wife to be secure, with regard to her residence and maintenance (i.e. to prevent her from being unfairly and hastily ejected from her home).

The waiting period is not simply for making sure there is no pregnancy (*istibrāʾ al-raḥm*), because this could be achieved by one menstrual cycle; nor is it simply three months on account of an arbitrary rule of religious devotion (*al-taʿabbud al-maḥḍ*).[29] For it is incumbent upon "the prepubescent female, the old woman, the rational and the insane woman, the Muslim and the non-Muslim woman. It is not lacking in Divine intention."[30]

---

28 Ibid., 622.

29 In Islamic law, there are those rules which are subject to rational analysis (*muʿallala*) and those which are followed out of "faith-based servitude" (*taʿabbudiyya*).

30 *Iʿlām al-Muwaqqiʿīn* (Beirut: al-Maktabah al-ʿAṣrīyah, 2003) 2:55.

He explores the wisdom behind the waiting period of, among others, the widow, the absolutely divorced, the woman who seeks to initiate divorce (*al-mukhtaliʿa*), and finally the menopausal woman and the minor female.

> If it is said [with regard to the previous points] that these have made sense, then how can [the waiting period] be made sensical with regard to the menopausal woman and the prepubescent female who is not of the age at which the sexual act could be performed upon her (*al-ṣaghīra allatī lā yūṭaʾ mithluhā*)[31]

If there is more to the *ratio legis* for the waiting period than ruling out pregnancy, then it is not necessary to assume that the prepubescent females in question are having the sex act performed upon them, and the ensuing definition of marriage (*nikāḥ*) of prepubescents must expand. In other words, in Ibn al-Qayyim's opinion, Ibn Qudāma's assumptions (that the female's obligation for *ʿidda* is linked to having had intercourse performed upon her) fail on two fronts: first because the widow, whether or not her marriage has been consummated, must undergo *ʿidda*; second because the *ratio legis*, for Ibn al-Qayyim, is much more complex than simply determining whether the woman is pregnant, which could be done by waiting only one period.

Ibn al-Qayyim clearly assumes that the prepubescent in question is one who has not had sex performed upon her. Ibn al-Qayyim still anchors the age for sex in the individualized framework of what the girl's body type can tolerate. Yet he clearly advocates for a multi-phase conception of marriage in cases involving prepubescent girls. This is in keeping with his general lack of support for child marriage in his other writings.[32] In light of Ibn Qudāma's stance, however, Ibn al-Qayyim's position comes as a surprise.

Rescission

Ibn Qudāma does not ignore *khiyār al-bulūgh* altogether; he refers to it later in his chapter on marriage. He cites early opinions that when someone other than the father has contracted the marriage, the prepubescent female may opt to rescind upon attainment of majority. Closely following this is his first reference to minor males, as he cites the position that Abū Ḥanīfa disallowed rescission

---

31 Ibid.

32 See in particular *Zād al-maʿād*. He echoes the Ḥanafī position (espoused by Ibn Taymīya) that an orphan can be married before puberty, but falls short of mentioning any other category of child (as Ibn Taymīya does). See *Zād*, p. 883 and *Fatāwā*, 32:43–50 (on orphans) and p. 39 on minor virgin females.

for marriages arranged "for two children" by other than the father.[33] This is followed by an opinion transmitted by ʿAbd Allāh ibn Aḥmad ibn Ḥanbal that "is like the opinion of Abū Ḥanīfa," that Q4:3, in referring to orphans, means that other than the father can marry off prepubescents. It would seem Ibn Qudāma, perhaps reluctantly, acknowledges the existence of a right to rescind, but, like (most) Ḥanafīs, this is only against non-paternal contracts.

Suitability

Ibn Qudāma includes two of Aḥmad ibn Ḥanbal's[34] rather different opinions related on the subject. The first relates that Ibn Ḥanbal and Sufyān al-Thawrī[35] were both averse to Arab/non-Arab unions. Ibn Qudāma includes reports that allege the preeminence of Arabs, such as one wherein Salmān al-Fārisi[36] refuses to lead prayer, saying that leading Arabs in prayer or marrying Arab women is simply not done.[37]

The second opinion is that *kafāʾa* "is not a condition of marriage." Interestingly, Ibn Qudāma adds here, "This is the opinion of most of the scholars of religion."[38] Here, he includes a long list of scholars, among them Mālik, and gives as a proof text for all of these the verse Q49:13, which, he suggests, emphasizes piety rather than social station.[39] Ibn Qudāma's point is that *kafāʾa*

33 According to al-Shaybānī's editor al-Kīlānī, this is the opinion of Abū Yūsuf only, after he had originally supported a right to rescission. See *al-Ḥujja*, 2:88, fn1. Indeed, it would appear to be contradictory in the text of *al-Mughnī*, as it plainly contradicts the previous sentence wherein Ibn Qudāma cites Abū Ḥanīfa as allowing the minor female to rescind non-paternal contracts. *Al-Mughnī*, 9:204.

34 Aḥmad ibn Ḥanbal, (241/855). For more information see Muḥammad Abū Zahrā, *Ibn Ḥanbal* (Cairo: 1965) and Michael Cook, *Commanding Right and Forbidding Wrong in Islamic Thought*, Cambridge, UK; (New York: Cambridge University Press, 2000).

35 Sufyān b. Saʿīd b. Masrūq Abū ʿAbd Allāh al-Kūfī (161/778). Major early Kufan scholar who had the particularly un-Iraqi habit of intense preoccupation with hadith. An early school of law, now extinct, bore his name. Raddatz, H.P. "Sufyān al-Thawrī." *EI2*.

36 Salmān al-Fārisī, d.c. 36/656–7. For more information see L. Massignon, "Salmān Pāk et les prémices spirituelles de l'Islam iranien," *Publications de la Soc. des Études iraniennes* no. 7, Paris 1934, repr. in Opera minora, Damascus 1957, i, 443–83.

37 Found in *Sunan al-Bayhaqī*, vol. 7/134 cited in *al-Mughnī*, fn. 69, p. 190.

38 Here, he includes the same list of scholars as Ibn al-Mundhir in a similar discussion (see Chapter Seven), although Ibn Qudāma includes Ḥanafīs in the list, which Ibn al-Mundhir did not.

39 "Oh People! Truly we created you from a male and a female, and we made you nations and tribes that you may come to know one another; truly the best of you in the sight of God is the one who is most God-conscious, and truly God is all-knowing, all-informed."

cannot be posited as essential to the match, unlike the necessity of a bridegroom being free of debilitating physical or mental defects (*ʿuyūb*).

Continuing, Ibn Qudāma explains Ibn Ḥanbal's understanding of the conditions of being suitable (*kufuʾ*): "religion and status (*manṣib*)."[40] "And by status he means esteem (*al-ḥasab*) and this is lineage (*al-nasab*)," Ibn Qudāma tells us. Yet religion is really the most consistently important aspect for Ibn Ḥanbal.[41]

This is not the case at all for Ibn Qudāma. Sheer volume would indicate that Ibn Qudāma cares very deeply about lineage. His discussion of suitability delves deeply into conceptions of Quraysh as preeminent among the Arab tribes due to the exalted status of the Prophet, its most famous member, and he relates multiple reports alluding to this. He mentions the child of adultery, who, although Ibn Ḥanbal claimed he is marriageable and should marry, "brings shame to the bride and her guardian, which transfers to her children; he is not suitable for an Arab woman, and there is no difference of opinion upon this, because he is lower in status than a client (*adnā ḥālan min al-mawlā*)."[42]

Ibn Qudāma also includes a list of three other areas in which *kafāʾa* is required: freedom, trade, and wealth (*yasār*). For each, however, he gives conflicting reports: The Prophet informed Fāṭima bint Qays that she should not marry Muʿāwiya due to his poverty; and yet "poverty is an honor in the religion" due to a hadith in which the Prophet prayed that he live and die poor.[43]

A hundred years later, Ibn al-Qayyim (himself of humble origin), is also quite unequivocal on this subject. He does not bother to include the conflicting hadiths; rather, every hadith he adduces is blatantly against the idea of any social stratification of any sort playing into the suitability equation. Further, he adduces historical examples to the effect that the Prophet himself encouraged inter-tribal, inter-racial, and inter-class mixing through marriage.[44]

> [The Prophet's] rulings refer basically and completely to a consideration of religion in [the doctrine of] suitability. A Muslim woman should not marry a non-believer, a chaste woman should not marry a profligate. The Qurʾān and the Sunna took nothing beyond this into consideration. [The Qurʾān] made it illicit that the Muslim woman marry a filthy adulterer and gave no consideration to lineage or trade, wealth or freedom. It made

40 Ibn Qudāma, *al-Mughnī*, 9:193.

41 Spectorsky, *Chapters on Marriage and Divorce*, 14.

42 For more information on the subject of clients (*mawālī*) see Wensinck, A.J.and Crone, P. "*Mawlā*." EI2.

43 *Al-Mughnī*, 9:189–199.

44 *Zād*, 883.

> it licit for the slave to marry the noble, wealthy free woman if he is chaste and Muslim. It made it licit for non-Qurayshites to marry Qurayshites and non-Hashimites to marry Hashimites, and for the poor to marry the rich.[45]

He clearly feels obliged, however, to note what have come to him as early variances in opinions on the subject. Mālik, he says, considered religion to be the only factor in suitability, although in another version of his opinion, Mālik is said to have called for matches based on religion, freedom, and lack of physical disabilities. Abū Ḥanīfa invoked lineage and religion. Ibn Ḥanbal, in one opinion, chose religion and lineage, while in another he listed five elements: religion, lineage, freedom, trade and finances. As for al-Shāfiʿī, he is to have added to these the lack of repellent flaws (*al-ʿuyūb al-munaffira*).[46]

Thus we see that the positions of the early jurists are portrayed in a way that is consistently obscure in post-formative texts. The lack of resolution regarding all of the issues linked to minor marriage remains. Difference of opinion remains pervasive. It is worth asking how these discussions take shape in the Ottoman context.

Ottoman Developments

The Walī Mujbir

Because the Ottoman legal system was officially Ḥanafī, broad powers were conferred on the father and paternal grandfather, with significantly curbed rights for other members of the family. Here, the power to compel lapsed only with the attainment of puberty, because there was no classification of females by virginity or lack thereof. Instead, females were classified, strictly speaking, as prepubescent or not, and considered to have no consent to give prior to pubescence.

The father or grandfather's rights were total. Even the suitability of the match was irrelevant, unless an extreme case warranted judicial intervention.[47] On the contrary, anyone else acting as guardian was obliged to respect the suitability requirements. Further, those matches arranged by non-paternal guardians were subject to refusal and annulment, even if consummated.[48]

45 Ibid., 883.
46 Ibid., 883–884.
47 Tucker, *House*, 46.
48 Ibid., 48.

As alluded to above on the subject of judicial intervention, not all fathers operated out of a desire to secure their children's future. The ability to arrange a match unencumbered by societal restraints such as "suitability", caused some fathers to use their blanket power of compulsion in a way that was not always in the best interests of the child.

Motzki, and after him, Yazbak, basing themselves on the *fatāwā* literature, detail some motivations. Class and financial factors seemed to play a significant role, as the fathers of minors would be the recipients of the dower, theoretically to be held in trust until the minor's maturity.[49] It was customary with the minor bride, particularly in rural areas and among the urban poor, for the father to keep the *mahr*, "either to pay off a debt or to arrange a son's marriage."[50] Some marriages were arranged simply in the hopes of relieving the father of the burden of maintaining his minor child or ward, while others had the express goal of strengthening kinship or social ties to particular families.[51]

Thus the Ḥanafī model does not prevent and may even have encouraged minor marriage. Indeed, in his study of Ottoman era child marriage, Harald Motzki provides numerical proof for incidences of minor marriage based on the *fatāwā* (juristic opinions) at his disposal. Nearly forty percent deal expressly with prepubescent marriage. While Motzki hesitates to extrapolate based on the figures of his sample to make assumptions about the practice in seventeenth-century Palestine generally, he feels comfortable asserting that it was "not uncommon."[52]

Sex, Maintenance, and Sexual Maturity

The sexual pleasure to be had in marriage was almost-exclusively that of the man,[53] a fact expressed in the judicial understanding of the marital exchange: in exchange for her obedience, largely translated in this Ottoman Ḥanafī context as sexual compliance,[54] the wife receives maintenance (*nafaqa*).

49 Harald Motzki, "Child Marriage in Seventeenth-Century Palestine," in *Islamic Legal Interpretation, Muftis and their Practices*, ed. Masud et al., (Harvard: Harvard University Press, 1996), 138.

50 Yazbak, M, "Minor Marriages and Khiyār al-Bulūgh, *Islamic Law and Society*, vol. 9 #3 (2002), p. 400. See also Khayr al-Dīn al-Ramlī, *al-Fatāwī al-Khayriyya*, vol. 1, 27, for this jurist's warnings regarding the illegality of such practices. See also Motzki, 138.

51 Motzki, "Child Marriage," 138–139.

52 Ibid., 137.

53 Tucker, *House*, 151, and pp. 148–178 generally.

54 Ibid., 63.

This financial aspect of the relationship devolves solely upon the male; failing to adequately provide food, clothing and housing could result in jail.[55] This is why the marrying prepubescent male raised such quandaries. Most were non-earning, leaving the jurists at a loss. Certain issues which were not obvious to the earliest jurists, such as who maintains the bride who does not yet provide sex, appear to have been worked out by Ottoman times. Although most remained home until pubescence,[56] payment of dower could result in cohabitation and consummation with a prepubescent. In the event she did remain at home until pubescence there was a Ḥanafī position that no support was due her unless the husband was able to derive some level of "enjoyment" from her. A contrasting Shāfiʿī position expected him to pay all support prior to consummation.[57]

Still, a serious issue presented by prepubescent marriage was how to determine sexual readiness. This could be done either by the family of the minor in question or by the muftis themselves. Motzki describes situations in which the father or guardian would decide the issue, or even the bridegroom himself, if there was preconsummative cohabitation. The fatwas he studied include one in which a nine year old girl has her marriage consummated, one of twelve cases in which the bride was delivered to her husband before having experienced her first menstrual period.[58]

Ottoman muftis did not assess female readiness for sexual intercourse in light of a girl's desire or active capabilities, but rather they asked whether or not she could "tolerate intercourse." Often, the entire assessment would be based on weight and body curvature. If a prepubescent girl ran away from her husband out of fear and sought refuge in her father's house, she had to be returned to her husband if she looked to be "ready for intercourse."[59]

In the event, unconsummated contractual marriage poses less of a logical challenge to the doctrine of the "pubescent's right of post-facto refusal" than its alternative.

Rescission

Yazbak explores how some girls in Ottoman times used the *khiyār al-bulūgh* to their full advantage. However, due to the complexity of the process, he

55 Ibid., 42, and the *Fatāwā* of Khayr al-Dīn al-Ramli, 1:21–22.

56 See Shaham, *Expert Witness*, 87.

57 Amira El Azhary Sonbol, "Adults and Minors in Ottoman Shari'a Courts," p. 242, in *Women, The Family, and Divorce Laws in Islamic History*, ed. Sonbol (Syracuse: Syracuse University Press, 1996).

58 Motzki, 137–138. See also Shaham, *Expert Witness*, 87–88.

59 Tucker, *House*, 155.

theorizes that the girls who did so were beneficiaries of coaching from family members keen on the union's end.[60] Unlike modern systems disallowing rescission after consummation, Tucker has found that for Ottoman-era jurists, consummation or lack thereof was not a factor; the only factor to be considered was the now-mature female's refusal of the marriage.[61] Thus it is clear that definite transformations occurred in the judicial practice.

As mentioned, consent was often perceived as necessary for a valid marriage contract involving any female in her majority. Yet for Ottoman-era Ḥanafīs, case law indicates that it was possible to sidestep the concessions to the pubescent female's legal capacity by simply marrying her deliberately early.[62] One fascinating aspect of Ottoman-era rescission issues is the way in which the woman in question used her right to invoke rescission to her advantage. Even retroactively claiming maturity enabled the right to rescind.[63] In other words, maturity is the undisputed key to whether the marriage contracted for her was valid or invalid.

Suitability

In later pre-modern texts, *kafāʾa* is a clearly delineated concept highly pertinent to a potential marriage. Ottoman-era Ḥanafī texts affirm fully the right of a woman to marry herself to a "suitable" man. The Ḥanafī jurists in Tucker's study seem to have a fairly set idea of what constitutes *kafāʾa*. For the muftis queried about licit and illicit unions, *kafāʾa* was "the legal concept of the suitability of the match in terms of lineage, legal status, social class, and moral standards."[64] For these jurists there were set notions about what was a compatible match, notions that matched only on some levels with the notions found in the formative period in Islamic law. For example, Tucker notes that the Ḥanafī muftīs consistently held that "A *sharīfa* (a member of the relatively high-status group of descendants of the Prophet) should marry only within her lineage; a woman of free origins should not be permitted to marry a slave …; a girl from "people of learning and religious piety" should not be married to an

60 See Yazbak, "Minor Marriages," especially pp. 405–406 in which is recounted the story of Jamīla who is significantly versed in the intricacies of this legal strategy (i.e., noticing her first menstrual blood and announcing its onset immediately and publicly, while simultaneously announcing her "self-choice" before witnesses) to annul an unwanted marriage contracted for her by her uncle to her cousin.

61 Tucker, Judith E, *Contracting a Marriage In Ottoman Syria and Palestine*, 125. See also p. 18 fn. 52.

62 Ibid.

63 Ibid., 126–127.

64 Tucker, *House*, 41.

"illiterate profligate" and a girl of good background should not be married to a man who is sinful, poor, or employed in a vile profession."[65]

Kafāʾa's pre-modern reality was that suitability considerations were given great importance. The issue of trade (*ṣināʿa*) took on particular importance in the Ottoman era. Ibn ʿĀbidīn (d. 1258/1842) detailed the extent to which trade was considered, and even documented evolving thought with regard to the relative merits of various professions.[66] Of further interest are his attempts to create degrees of suitability in order systematize situations in which a match exists with regard to one of the elements but not to others. A learned Arab spice merchant would be higher in status than his non-Arab counterpart, while an ignorant merchant is the inferior of a learned barber.

The ongoing changes with regard to perceptions of professions gives credence to Ziadeh's observations about the lack of set "estates" in Islamic societies. Noting the relationship between legal/social stratification and social classes as "estates"[67] recognized by law, Ziadeh points out that "the doctrine of *kafāʾa* is not sufficiently strong or widespread to constitute estates."[68]

It is entirely possible that the jurists felt compelled to produce the contradictory texts, being aware that the social strictures in place in any given society would be effective enough in keeping the doctrine in place. Perhaps they were confident that knowledge of the sayings in question would nourish reformers like the Ḥanbalī Ibn al-Qayyim enough to allow the societal taboos to be broken when a particular situation demanded.

Kafāʾa is the one major limit on *ijbār*. And yet, beyond the notion of social equality, which is variously defined, we have yet to encounter a clear definition of suitability. Nonetheless, the language of the consensus claim at issue in this project is predicated quite specifically upon *kafāʾa*. It is not an issue that acquired resolution at any point in Islamic legal history.

65 Ibid.

66 Ziadeh, Farhat, "Equality in the Muslim Law of Marriage," The American Journal of Comparative Law. Vol. 6, No. 4 (Autumn, 1957), pp. 503–517, p. 513.

67 The "estates" to which she refers are medieval western Christendom's rigid class and social structures that divided society between clergy, aristocracy, and commoners.

68 Ziadeh, 503.

Conclusion

This chapter has discussed some post-formative era understandings of minor marriage and compulsion; the outstanding feature of these discussions is their lack of univocality. It looked in greater depth at the thought of the oft-cited Ibn Qudāma. On legal capacity for females, he found it to be tied to their virginity rather than majority or minority, a position that allows wide power of compulsion for the father as guardian. This position is not shared universally even by Ḥanbalīs such as Ibn Taymīya and his student Ibn al-Qayyim. Ibn Qudāma's ultimately admits, later in the chapter, that he cannot be sure as to the basis for the doctrine of compulsion. He also includes his school's position that a nine-year-old girl may be competent to issue consent by virtue simply of being nine. These points have been underemphasized, at best, in the internet fatwas that claim him as a source.

Regarding sexual maturity, Ibn Qudāma has expressed his position that the Qur'ānic stipulation of *ʿidda* for "those who have not yet menstruated" means that prepubescent females can be married and divorced without consideration of their wishes. His implication here is unmistakably that it is licit to perform the sexual act upon them before pubescence. Although a later Ḥanbalī like Ibn al-Qayyim would seem to disagree with this understanding of *ʿidda*, and indeed seems reluctant to offer support for minor marriages generally, practice seems to indicate that prepubescents indeed entered into consummated unions. Consistently, Ottoman concerns showed a prioritization of male sexual satisfaction. In contrast, the bulk of the attention with regard to female sexuality has been with regard to "what a girl can tolerate."

Next, the chapter also explored later presentations of suitability, as the father who would compel may do so by putting a prepubescent female in a suitable match. No firmly delineated concept of *kafāʾa* emerges from these discussions. The early jurists are invoked in support of differing opinions; multiple contradictory traditions are used to support extremes of either social stratification or social equality. Meanwhile, Ottoman fathers exercising their right to compel paid it little heed, and judges did not feel obliged to insist upon it. Although the doctrine itself is proven to be legally underdetermined and difficult to define, and although it is not a substantive part of most modern legal systems that claim Islamic bases, it has in the past and continues to be a tool by which guardians can sunder unions and compelled females should be able to protest them.

It would have been crucial in the Ottoman era for some support network to help a young girl negotiate the legal system and prove her attainment of majority and rejection of an unwanted union. Meanwhile, those married off by fathers or grandfathers could not enjoy this right, a fact that induced some fathers to marry off their daughters before pubescence.

This chapter has presented some “post-consensus writing” modalities of approaching the topics pertinent to this study. If so much is left unresolved, what weight does a consensus statement regarding the licit nature of the forced marriage of a child possess? From the proof texts to the issues of the *walī mujbir*, the doctrine of suitability, rescission rights and sexual readiness, the tangled topics key to the legality of minor marriage have posed problems for jurists throughout Islamic legal history.

Conclusion: Does Consensus Matter?

The conclusion to this study asks the question: So what?

In order to formulate this answer, it is useful to leap backward in time for a moment. One jurist was not among those investigated in the chapter on consensus writing, but his insights, born of a visceral quest for jurisprudential rigor, might help shape understanding of the topic at hand. Ibn Ḥazm (d. 465/1072) has his own book of consensus, *Marātib al-ijmāʿ*. Known as the champion of the literalist Ẓāhirī movement, his work engendered a lengthy refutation by Ibn Taymīya. Ibn Taymīya himself had many interesting ideas on consensus, most emanating from Ibn Ḥanbal's distaste for the notion, and others shaped by his conflict with the state over the role of consensus in silencing scholarly endeavors, as discussed in Chapter Six, above.

Investigating Ibn Ḥazm's ideas in the conclusion to this work is useful for two main reasons. First, we see the way that he too is influenced by al-Shāfiʿī's legal-theoretical methodologies and his specific contribution to the debates on minor marriage and compulsion. And second, we see how he approaches the issue himself, and how he insists that this is not consensus but instead clearly a matter of Sunna. Ibn Ḥazm claims that "a group" has declared marrying off the male prepubescent to be licit. Their justification for this is but a poor analogy against the ʿĀʾisha report. It is this very "group" that has figured prominently throughout the bulk of this study.

The refutation of Ibn Ḥazm's thought and the reservations regarding the doctrine of consensus voiced by Ibn Taymīya are also useful. It is worthwhile to consider the extent to which early and pre-modern scholars worried about this juristic tool. Thus it is this point that closes this study. It is, after all, the abject lack of modern worry about consensus that is most troublesome: who were its articulators, who were its dissenters, what proof texts were used and what semantic range is involved? What does acceptance of consensus mean if these questions cannot be adequately answered?

The Thought of Ibn Ḥazm

Ibn Ḥazm threw down a gauntlet of sorts when, in the eleventh century, he claimed that no marriages for prepubescent males could be validly contracted. He posited that any such marriage for boys is but a weak analogy to the marriage rules as derived from the report of ʿĀʾisha. As we have seen, early jurists and early social history as reflected in the legal manuals show that marriage

 | DOI 10.1163/9789004344860_011

of the prepubescent male was common and licit. It is of interest that al-Shāfiʿī was unambiguous about the permissibility of contracting marriages for prepubescent males. Without al-Shāfiʿī's reliance on the report of ʿĀʾisha, it is perhaps unlikely that Ibn Ḥazm would have come to rely on it at all.

Like Ibn ʿAbd al-Barr, Ibn Ḥazm exhibits what may be an eleventh-century trend toward disavowing compelled marriages for minor males. Ibn Ḥazm rails against the notion of forcing a boy to marry, suggesting it is only through analogy with the female (as depicted in ʿĀʾisha's report) that anyone could imagine a boy having his marriage contracted for him. Although Ibn Ḥazm seems to have been the first to articulate this idea so forcefully, by the time of Ibn Qudāma in the 13th century, marriage of prepubescent boys is mentioned only briefly in the *Mughnī*; in the following century, the Shāfiʿī Ibn ʿAbd al-Raḥmān (d. c. 780/1378)[1] ignores the topic of prepubescent males altogether.

Ibn Ḥazm does not make a claim of Ijmāʿ with regard to prepubescent marriage and the guardian's ability to compel minor females to marry against their will. No such claim is included among his collected instances of consensus in the *Marātib al-Ijmāʿ*.[2] Rather, he is clear in the *Muḥallā* that he believes the licit nature of compelling a prepubescent female to marry is an issue which is based directly upon Sunnaic evidence.

> The evidence (*al-ḥujja*) for the permissibility of a father contracting marriage for his prepubescent virgin daughter is the marrying of Abū Bakr of his daughter ʿĀʾisha to the Prophet when she was a girl of six years old. And this is a well-known matter for which we are not required to provide chains of transmission.[3]

In discussing this issue on a previous page of the *Marātib* (without mentioning the above Sunnaic evidence), he notes that there is "disagreement" over the law with regard to minor marriages. He quotes Ibn Shubrama (d. 144/761) as saying something altogether different from what we have so far encountered: "It is not permissible for the father to contract marriage for his prepubescent daughter until such a time as she reaches pubescence and gives permission."[4] Ibn Ḥazm continues that Ibn Shubrama "was of the opinion that the situation with ʿĀʾisha was of the special prerogatives of the Prophet, like the case of

1 See Muḥammad Ibn ʿAbd al-Raḥmān, *Raḥmat al-umma fī ikhtilāf al-aʾimma* (Beirut: Muʾassassat al-Risāla, 1994) p. 390.

2 Ibn Ḥazm, *Marātib al-Ijmāʿ* (Beirut: Dār al-Ifāq al-Jadīda, 1978).

3 *Al-Muḥallā*, 9:460.

4 *Marātib al-Ijmāʿ*, 459.

the woman who granted herself to him (*al-mawhūba*) and marriage to more than four."[5] Because no writings of Ibn Shubrama are extant, we cannot divine whether or not this is Ibn Ḥazm's own assumption as to why Ibn Shubrama disallowed prepubescent marriage. As we have seen, the statement of Ibn Shubrama's adduced by al-Ṭaḥāwī addresses both genders (*al-ṣighār*);[6] here, however, it is claimed that Ibn Shubrama was only concerned with girls.[7]

When it comes to his discussion of the 'Ā'isha hadith as a proof text, Ibn Ḥazm takes care to refute this position of Ibn Shubrama's. He says,

> Whosoever claims that [marriage to a prepubescent] was a specific prerogative (*khuṣūṣ*) [of the Prophet] is not aware of God Great and Powerful [who has said]: {You have in the Messenger of God a beautiful example for whosoever seeks God and the Last Day}.[8] Thus we have to follow the Messenger in his example unless a text comes along to render it specific only to him.[9]

As with other writers, Ibn Ḥazm discounts the possibility of the applicability of the *ayyim/bikr* (or, for him, *thayyib/bikr*) hadith to the prepubescent girl because of the inability of the prepubescent to grant permission. Unlike previous writers, however, he does not consider that inability to be based on a mere cultural assumption. He is the first to adduce a hadith in support of his opinion:

> Requesting of permission (*al-isti'dhān*) takes place only with the physically mature, reasonable person (*al-bāligh al-'āqil*) due to the established report (*al-ithr al-thābit*) from the Prophet, "The Pen has been lifted from three," and he mentioned among them the child until he matures.[10]
>
> For this reason, the *thayyib/bikr* distinction does not apply to prepubescent females, and the application of the hadith is only for the sexually experienced female (prepubescent or pubescent) and the pubescent virgin.[11]

5 Ibid.

6 See al-Ṭaḥāwī's *Ikhtilāf*, 2:257.

7 This revision of the original reference to both genders in such a discussion would seem to be symptomatic of a 5th/11th century trend. See above in the discussion on Ibn 'Abd al-Barr.

8 Qur'ān, 33:21.

9 *Al-Muḥallā*, 9:462.

10 *Sunan Abī Dā'ūd*, #4402; *Sunan Ibn Mājah*, #2042; *Musnad Aḥmad Ibn Ḥanbal*, #1366.

11 *Al-Muḥallā*, 9:460.

Next, Ibn Ḥazm delves into the topic of the prepubescent male. Because Ibn Ḥazm is convinced that the only legal justification for prepubescent marriage stems from the report of ʿĀʾisha, and because he states in the previous paragraph that "all analogy is corrupt (*al-qiyās kulluhu fāsid*)," it is no surprise to find that Ibn Ḥazm comes down strongly against the right of anyone to contract marriage for a prepubescent male.[12] He says,

> It is not permissible for the father or anyone to contract marriage for a prepubescent male (*al-dhakar al-ṣaghīr*) until he matures and if it is done, it is annulled permanently. A group has allowed this, and they have no evidence except analogizing [the prepubescent male] with the prepubescent female.
>
> Analogy is all error (*bāṭil*) and if it were true (*wa law kāna al-qiyās ḥaqqan*) they would have subjected this analogy to another like it. For they have reached consensus to the effect that neither the father nor anyone has power over the pubescent male with regard to his marriage. In that regard, he is different from the female with regard to whom the father and others do have power, either by [requesting her] permission, or by contracting the marriage, or by tending to [the requirements of] equal status [of the mate]. Thus it is that the rules regarding the two are different before pubescence.[13]

Early jurists did not differentiate between the sexes with regard to the right of the father or, in some cases, other relatives to contract their marriages. Yet Ibn Ḥazm builds on the methodologies of al-Shāfiʿī and his use of the ʿĀʾisha anecdote as the primary proof supporting early marriage to eject the male from the category of marriageable prepubescents. Further, he claims consensus (that the prepubescent male cannot be married off) where it is unsupported by early evidence. He, like many jurists in Islamic legal history, has engaged in the practice of using a consensus claim to render authoritative a particular interpretation of the law.

Ibn Ḥazm and Ibn Taymīya

In considering whether consensus ultimately "matters" at all, it is useful to see how Ibn Taymīya elaborates specific ideas about the modalities of Ijmāʿ as he takes Ibn Ḥazm to task in his short treatise, *Naqd Marātib al-Ijmāʿ* (a critique of Ibn Ḥazm's book). Ibn Taymīya's complaints are many, but a few specifics

12 Ibid.

13 Ibid.

highlight the ongoing debates about this subject, while yet evidencing Ibn Taymīya's familiarity with the history of differences pertaining to religious law.

Ibn Taymīya's arguments against Ibn Ḥazm are multi-layered and subtle. His first objection is to the idea of rendering Ijmāʿ synonymous with the concept of the widely-related or concurrent report (*mutawātir*). Ibn Ḥazm describes Ijmāʿ as being:

> What it is certain that none of the scholars of Islam disagrees about. We know this in the way in which we know undisputed history without doubt, such as that the Muslims went out of the Ḥijāz into Yemen and conquered Iraq and Khurasān and Egypt and Syria, and that the Umayyads ruled for an age, then the Abbasids came to power, or that Ṣiffīn and al-Ḥarrah occurred, and all that which is known with certainty and of necessity (*bi-yaqīn wa ḍarūra*).

To which Ibn Taymīya responds,

> I say: He has made a condition of Ijmāʿ that which many of the theologians and jurists (*ahl al-kalām wa al-fiqh*) have made ... that is, [making Ijmāʿ a matter of] the knowledge of a disproof of dissent (*al-ʿilm bi nafī al-khilāf*), and that knowledge of Ijmāʿ is widespread (*tawāturan*). He has placed the knowledge of Ijmāʿ among the types of necessary knowledge, like the knowledge of the science of widespread reports for most. It is well known that many of the incidences of Ijmāʿ that he has related are nowhere near this description ... So how could it be, when among them there is well-known dissent, and among them there is what he himself denies consensus in, and (even) chooses a position of dissent where none had existed![14]

He takes issue with Ibn Ḥazm's conclusions on some forty alleged incidences of Ijmāʿ. He notes, however, that although for the most part the incidences of consensus listed by Ibn Ḥazm are sound, there are more than these forty which merit opposition. More than anything, his quarrel with Ibn Ḥazm is his claim of comprehensive knowledge about issues for which there is none to be had (*daʿwā al-iḥāṭa bi-mā lā yumkin al-iḥāṭa bi-hi*).[15]

For example, Ibn Taymīya points to Ibn Ḥazm's claim that women cannot lead men in prayer. By consensus, Ibn Ḥazm claims, the prayer of men who

14 *Naqd marātib al-ijmāʿ*, 205–206.

15 Ibid., 220.

know they are being led in prayer by a woman is corrupt. Ibn Taymīya responds that this is not a case of Ijmāʿ. His reply is as follows: "I say: Unlettered men can be led by learned women in the night prayers of Ramadan (*fī qiyām Ramaḍān*), as is found to be binding by a *mashhūr* tradition related by Ibn Ḥanbal. And, [the learned woman can lead unlettered men] in all of the voluntary prayers, according to two reports."[16]

Most importantly perhaps, for our purposes, and as against modern interpretations of his position, he refutes Ibn Ḥazm's claim that there is Ijmāʿ with regard to dissent ("whosoever goes against a certain consensus after knowing it to be consensus is an unbeliever"). Responds Ibn Taymīya, simply and succinctly, "In that there is well-known debate among the scholars."[17]

The above is evidence of a certain level of premodern discomfort with Ijmāʿ. This may be unsurprising from the theoretical standpoint of a Ḥanbalī, given Ibn Ḥanbal's hesitations over the doctrine. Then again, given that Ibn Taymīya was, as we saw in Chapter Six, imprisoned for having broken with consensus, his might be a voice worth hearing.

Conclusion

Does consensus matter? In Saudi Arabia, the refusal to set a minimum marriage age is couched in arguments that appeal to consensus. There is consensus that a father can marry off his prepubescent virgin daughter even against her will. This book has attempted to interrogate this consensus. It has done what a typical prepubescent Muslim female without access to early Arabic legal manuals cannot do: it has asked each individual jurist (considered part of the unassailable "They" in "They have come to consensus") to explain himself. The claim of consensus might matter indeed if this unassailable "they" serves to affirm or even inspire her father's decision to give her in marriage without her consent. Further, it surely matters on some level as a rhetorical device geared at silencing dissent: progress remains elusive in setting a marriage age in Saudi Arabia consistent with internationally-established norms that would ensure the psychological and physical health of every bride.

Modern jurists often engage in asserting an over-arching importance for "consensus;" it is possible to assert that their understanding of consensus differs radically from the concept of consensus that earlier jurists invoked. The preceding pages have explored contradictory texts used in contradictory

16 *Naqd Marātib al-Ijmāʿ*, 207–208.

17 Ibid., 217.

manners. In such contradiction, we may find what Muslim jurists would refer to as "mercy":[18] legal maneuverability borne out of differences of opinion.

Who then consulted books of consensus, and to what end? We have seen a modern judge from the Gulf claiming that such a resource is essential, and perhaps this is our best clue to where such a manual would have found a home: the beleaguered *muftī* or shaykh on the front lines of the legal enterprise, perhaps in much the same peripheral position as that described by Rapoport when considering al-Subkī's ire over ibn Taymīya's anti-consensus stance. But surely the contemplative *mujtahid* would have spurned such truncated and often incorrect representations of legal debate as those represented by Ibn al-Qaṭṭān. To his credit, Ibn al-Qaṭṭān had sought to meet a need by compiling points of consensus into an accessible source; it was at heart an attempt to embody in text an amorphous and ill-defined concept, one that Muslim jurists have struggled with throughout the centuries:

> Although Muslim legal theorists' discussions of *ijmāʿ* focus heavily on the mechanics and meaning of agreement, the delineation of conditions of actual consensus seem largely if not entirely aspirational, even when they discuss the Companions, the Successors, the inhabitants of early Islamic Medina (or other important metropoles), the four orthodox *khulafāʾ*, or the Prophet's family, all plausible sites of actual consensus. This fact suggests that the idea of unanimous agreement serves a mostly symbolic or theological (or ideological) function.[19]

As noted, much of the power of consensus has to do with delineating the proper Muslim identity.[20] It is possible to detect within the various approaches to child marriage discussed in this study the jurists' attempts to determine a position for the Muslim father in society. It is further possible to imagine that preserving such a position is considered by some to be even more crucial in an age where human rights discourses have chipped away at the authoritarian powers not only of states over their subjects but also those of husbands over their wives and fathers over their daughters.

---

18 "The differences among my community are a mercy" (*ikhtilāf ummatī raḥma*) is deemed to be a weak or falsified hadith (*lā aṣl lahu*). See Muḥammad Nāṣir al-Dīn al-Albānī, *Silsilat al-aḥādīth al-ḍaʿīfa* (N.P, N.D.), p. 11. Despite this, it has remained a near-ubiquitous juristic maxim, with the Shāfiʿī Ibn ʿAbd al-Raḥmān even publishing a book by the title.

19 Lowry, "Something Postmodern," p. 288.

20 See Berkey, *Formation*, 147. See also Hallaq, *Sharīʿa*, 98.

Once consensus on the power of the father to compel his prepubescent daughter to marry was articulated, and the consensus itself became intertwined with al-Shāfiʿī's interpretation of the implications of ʿĀ'isha's report, further discussion within the context of the consensus manual became extraneous. No homage was paid in that genre to the diversity of material in earlier sources relating to prepubescent marriage and females and consent.

Even so, the late formative-era books documenting instances of supposed consensus, such as those of al-Marwazī, Ibn al-Mundhir, and al-Ṭaḥāwī, typically included juristic opinions on marriages of children of both sexes. Some consensus writers, such as al-Ṭaḥāwī and Ibn Ḥazm after him, acknowledged Ibn Shubrama's forceful opinion opposing child marriage. That same opinion is undermined by Ibn Shubrama's appearance in the opposite camp in the writings of scholars like al-Marwazī and Ibn ʿAbd al-Barr. Whether one's definition of consensus is "all the scholars with whom I have studied" (like Ibn al-Mundhir) or an unassailable unanimity (like later scholars of legal theory), the idea of a strong opposing opinion could theoretically give one pause. In practical terms, it is thus noteworthy that Ibn Shubrama's voice has traveled relentlessly through the literature, to enter today's discourse—on the internet sites of web *muftīs*, in the lectures of modern judges, and even here in the pages of this study. That Ibn Ḥazm denied outright that child marriage was an issue of consensus is only as weighty an opinion as the respect one accords Ibn Ḥazm's thought. Still, the fact that he claims consensus that marriage of prepubescent males is altogether illicit should give one pause. He is able to discard the earlier deluge of opinions relating to boys with ease. No less troublesome is Ibn ʿAbd al-Barr's claimed consensus on the power of the father over his virgin daughter. Was a consensus claim simply a matter of asserting one's position with the most bravado?

In order to reconcile the action of Abū Bakr vis à vis ʿĀ'isha, those jurists who still accorded weight to the virgin's permission were obliged to work hard to explain that any mention of a requirement of the virgin's consent could only have meant consent for the pubescent virgin. Prepubescents, after all, were subject to the perception that, in terms of legal capacity, they possessed no consent to give, although only Ibn Ḥazm offers any evidence in support of this idea.[21]

Like Ibn Ḥazm, Ibn ʿAbd al-Barr shows a marked reluctance to discuss prepubescent marriage as applicable to boys; in citing early sources he ignores the dual- gendered tenses of the original texts. Was this indicative of a nascent juristic discomfort with dealing similarly with the prepubescent male and

21 See Ibn al-Mundhir, *al-Ishrāf*, 1:24; and *al-Muḥallā* 9:460.

the prepubescent female? One of the books of consensus omitted from Ibn al-Qaṭṭān's compendium supports this idea: in Ibn al-Hubayra's (d. 560/1164) work we find mention only of a consensus concerning a father's power over his prepubescent daughter; there is no mention of the boy at all throughout the entire chapter.[22] Ibn Qudāma, as noted, does mention the male, citing Ibn al-Mundhir as stating that all scholars allow the prepubescent boy to be married by his father. Still, male prepubescent marriage is only addressed as a portion of a chapter the focus of which is on whether or not the insane male can have his marriage contracted for him by his father.[23] By the time of the Shāfiʿī Ibn ʿAbd al-Raḥmān (d. c. 780/1398), there is no mention of compulsion in regard to boys whatsoever, or even a concept of "*tazwīj al-ṣaghīr*", although he gives attention to the marriage of virgins without their consent.[24]

Ibn Qudāma, as discussed, relies heavily on Ibn al-Mundhir's consensus claims throughout *al-Mughnī*, and on the topic of prepubescent marriage specifically. The claims of consensus on the matter of compelled marriage of prepubescents mask underlying dissent over everything from the age of maturity, to the proper age of consummation, to the modality of attaining legal capacity for both males and females. Most importantly, they mask the earlier legal doctrine that gave the prepubescent girl the power to consent or withhold consent, as recorded in the earliest compendia.

Lingering tendencies in some Muslim countries to contract marriages for prepubescent girls against their will can be understood as a refusal to accord capacity to the female child. That the male child is not dealt with in this way could well be the result of an evolution in juristic thinking about males and capacity. Ibn Ḥazm, in *al-Muḥallā*, articulated quite firmly his belief that an individual male's future legal capacity carried enough weight to prevent him from being compelled to enter into marriage contracts.[25] It is difficult to say if such thinking was *de rigeur* in the 5th/11th century or if it is just coincidental that Ibn Ḥazm's contemporary Ibn ʿAbd al-Barr, concerned as he was with consensus and disagreement, eschewed the topic of compulsory prepubescent male marriages.[26] A modern consensus manual, *Kitāb al-fiqh ʿalā al-madhāhib*

22 See "*Kitāb al-Nikāḥ*", vol. 2, pp. 88–98, of *Kitāb al-ifṣāḥ*, Ibn Hubayra.

23 *Al-Mughnī*, 9:220.

24 Ibn ʿAbd al-Raḥmān, *Raḥmat al-umma*, p. 390.

25 Ibn Ḥazm,*al-Muḥallā*, 9:460.

26 Other writers of the eleventh and twelfth centuries were not so sure. The Shāfiʿī Abū Isḥāq al-Shīrāzī (d. 476/1083), in *al-Tanbīh fil-fiqh al-Shāfiʿī, Kitāb al-Nikāḥ*, p. 226, notes that it is commendable for the prepubescent male who has reason and religion to be married. The Ḥanbalī Qāḍī Abū Yaʿlā (d. 458/1066) insists that a boy's marriage, like that of the orphan

al-arbaʿa, notes that a *walī mujbir* can compel both the prepubescent female and the prepubescent male, just as he can compel the male and female in their majority who have become insane; but there is no depth to the ensuing discussion and the copious notes are entirely devoted to the issue of prepubescent females.[27]

We have seen that although there was a notable absence of discussion of compulsion in marriages of prepubescent males in the later consensus manuals, the discussions continued in books of positive law, in some cases taking on a certain nuance. In practice, as late as the Ottoman era, Motzki's work shows a small percentage of marriages to be those of young boys; it is only in the modern era that no statistics show the phenomenon is still practiced. And so we are left with the age-old question: did an evolution in juristic thought make itself felt on the level of social practice? Or did juristic thought possess no true normative value, simply responding and reshaping itself as social practice changed?

It is possible to sympathize with Muslim jurists who, faced with the concept of prepubescent marriage, would have been forced to work incredibly hard to harmonize it with basic juridical precepts such as the role of the husband to provide financial maintenance for his wife and the importance of the sexual availability of both spouses. As discussed, concepts of capacity in divorce, maintenance of a bride when one has yet to earn an income, and lack of sexual ability would all have posed challenges to the logic of accepted legal doctrine. Classification of women by virginity or lack thereof pushes jurists to engage, as we have seen, in some very tortured logic. The Ḥanafīs have emerged from this relatively unscathed by locating maturity in age and pubescence for the female, and making possible, by analogizing the girl to the boy, a more egalitarian system—at least in this respect.

Viewed through the prism of antique and late-antique conceptions of paternal power, much of Islamic law concerning the rights of the father can be read as an effort to curb the power of the father rather than to augment it. This engenders the question of when a father's power over his children ceases.

---

female, is reversible upon pubescence. A hundred years later, the Ḥanafī al-Marghinānī (d. 593/1196) insisted that contracts made by guardians are binding on both males and females. *Al-Hidāya*, 3:31–32.

27 See especially vol. 4 p. 32 in the note on Ḥanbalī fiqh (un-numbered) in which the editor explains that the *walī mujbir* is concerned with the compulsion of one who has no legal capacity, "and this is the prepubescent [masc.], whether or not she is a virgin" (*wa huwa al-ṣaghīr, bikran kānat aw thayyiban …*" Note the gender shift. ʿAbd al-Raḥmān al-Jazīrī (d. 1941), Ed, Muḥammad Bakr Ismāʿīl, *Al-fiqh ʿalā al-madhāhib al-arbaʿa* (Dār al-Manār, 1999).

If the standard for attaining legal capacity is reaching one's majority, how precisely is majority attained, and what is the role of mental maturity (*rushd*)? The jurists appeared aware that a nocturnal emission was not enough to qualify a boy to dispose of his assets. Majority was a tricky state to measure, and appeared even more difficult in the case of women. Jurists, exegetes and theorists explored these issues in great depth. On the practical side, it is not completely unreasonable to postulate a concerned father thinking twice before entrusting property to an unseasoned, uneducated girl simply by virtue of the onset of her menses.

Thus when the state of being "*thayyib*" is considered as imbuing capacity, it indeed may not mean simply "non-virgin," but instead refer literally to "one who has been married." A girl's transfer into the home of her husband would often have meant that she gained first-hand experience of asset-management (from the standpoint of running her household—the job her mother would have had in her previous home) and also that another man, presumably with some experience (unless he is also a minor!) in dealing with financial affairs, would have been able to offer guidance for her financial decisions (and thus presumably share blame for any losses she incurred). With regard to the choice of a spouse, the issues become all the more complex, and it becomes quite impossible to assess what would have empowered a previously fully-dependent female to make a competent, informed choice with regard to a spouse.

As with Jewish law, however, the issue of what to do with the prepubescent non-virgin challenged this classification scheme that identified marriage with non-virginity. It is possible to imagine most of those Muslim jurists who easily classified women according to the presence or absence of virginity squirming uncomfortably at the challenge presented by the prepubescent non-virgin, who, though technically a child, is still understood as having the "real-world" experience gained from the exit from her "father's house." She is, as Abū Yaʿlā explained, "free."[28]

Only the opinion attributed to al-Ḥasan al-Baṣrī has remained consistently uncluttered throughout jurisprudential history: "A father may compel any of his daughters to marry, old or young."[29]

But this, we are told, is "against the consensus."[30]

What, then, is consensus? In the case of minor marriage this study has shed light on the fact that a claimed consensus on the topic masks intense and wide-ranging interpretive diversity. This project contends that other such claims of

---

28 Ibn al-Farrāʾ, *al-Masāʾil al-Fiqhīya min Kitāb al-Riwayatayn wa al-Wajhayn*, (Riyāḍ: Maktabat al-Maʿārif, 1985), 2:82.

29 The *Muṣannaf* of Ibn Abī Shayba, ¶16263; *al-Iqnāʿ* of Ibn al-Qaṭṭān, ¶2126; see also Ibn al-Qayyim, *Zād al-maʿād*, 860.

30 Ibn al-Qayyim, *Zād al-maʿād*, 860.

consensus may well be as entwined in doctrinal wrangling and *madhhab* divergences. The lack of consensus regarding the theoretical basis for consensus has been dealt with at length in modern scholarship. If consensus "guaranteed not only the infallibility of those *fiqh* rulings subject to juristic agreement but also the entire structure of law,"[31] then the lack of any true incidence of practical consensus (i.e. one existing in the realm of practical life—*muʿāmalāt*—as opposed to spiritual life--*ʿibādāt*) could in essence undermine the legal system's underpinnings. Consensus existed to "establish unity in the law and disallow diversity."[32] But the diversity inherent in the enterprise of Islamic law has persevered.

Indeed that very diversity has proven indigestible for those outside the scholarly realm and incompatible with modern cries for codification and unification. As such, with the march of time, most of Islamic law has been consigned to the realm of theory. The colonial era's visceral uprooting of native intellectual heritage, particularly the educational pathways necessary to acquire the status of legal expert, left most majority Muslim countries with only the palest ghosts of their original systems of jurisprudence. Meanwhile, the necessities of modern codification have obliterated the concept of what Schacht termed "jurists' law," making Ibn al-Muqaffaʿ's early appeal for systematic consolidation look quite mild in comparison.

Ibn al-Qaṭṭān's motivations for compiling his manual, we are told, were linked to the social upheaval of late-era Almohad Spain. It is interesting to compare, then, the motivations of those bringing his work to light today. The publisher of the most recent edition of Ibn al-Qaṭṭān's consensus manual explains that the worldwide Islamic community is under siege. It is in "true crisis," with "enemy arrows aimed at it from every side." This attack seeks to harm the umma's "roots and beliefs" (*uṣūlihā wa muʿtaqidātihā*). It is for this reason that the consensus manual is so important. Only strict attention to heritage and curing "corruption" (*taḥrīf*) will preserve the community. There is a need for such a book, we are told, because it "closes the door in the face" of anyone trying to change the religion by erecting the "foremost wall of repulsion": the "agreed upon sources."[33]

This statement, interestingly, mentions as crucial to the umma's health both the "sources that the Muslims agreed upon" and what "the leaders and scholars

31 Hallaq, *Sharīʿa*, 98.

32 Weiss, *Spirit of Islamic Law*, 126.

33 *Al-Iqnāʿ*, 6.

of the religion agree upon."[34] In other words, the publisher's definition of consensus is just as opaque as any other definition put forth in this study.

Consider the conditions for the role of implementing a consensus in modern systems as outlined by Kamali. His approach can only be termed anathema to many basic precepts of Islamic law, if the enterprise is defined by scholarly independence from political rule and the preservation of regional and *madhhab* differences. And yet, in many ways it crystallizes the original symbiosis between state and religion that has often sparked the call for identifying and advertising points of consensus.

> … *Ijmāʿ* could be feasible if it were to be facilitated by the ruling authorities. The government in every Muslim country could, for example, specify certain conditions for attainment to the rank of *mujtahid*, and make this contingent upon obtaining a recognized certificate. This would enable every government to identify the *mujtahidūn* and to verify their views when the occasion so required. When the views of all the *mujtahidūn* throughout the Islamic lands concur upon a ruling concerning an issue, this becomes *ijmāʿ*, and the ruling so arrived at becomes a binding *ḥukm* of the Sharīʿah upon all the Muslims of the world.[35]

This study has forcefully argued that such a simplistic notion of the inner workings of consensus is misguided at best. Modern political realities dictate that such a plan could also be dangerous, given its assumptions about the benevolence of state power. Not least problematic in the above statement is the assumption that consensus could exist at all.

Postscript

As a tool for investigating consensus claims, this study has focused on discussions of minor marriage in early Islamic legal texts. However, it is my wish to call attention to minor marriage within its broader context throughout history and, currently, throughout the globe. It is my hope that this research might contribute to legal and cultural efforts toward reform in those systems that claim an Islamic identity, even as the global culture continues to combat forced marriage for all persons, major or minor, male or female.

---

34 Ibid., 7.

35 Kamali, *Principles of Islamic Jurisprudence*, 246.

APPENDIX

Excerpts from the Early Compendia

***Sunan al-Awzāʿī* (*d. 158/774*)**

On consulting the non-virgin and the virgin:

¶1047: *Isḥāq ibn Manṣūr related that Muḥammad ibn Yūsuf reported that al-Awzāʿī related from Yaḥyā ibn Abī Kuthayyir from Abū Salama from Abū Hurayra who said:*

> The Messenger of God said, "The non-virgin is not married until her authority is sought, and the virgin is not married until her permission is sought, and her permission is silence."

¶1048: *Muhammad ibn Makhlad related that ʿAbd Allāh ibn Muhammad ibn Zayd al-Ḥanafī related that ʿAbdān related that ʿAbd Allāh ibn al-Mubārak related that al-Awzāʿī related that Yaḥyā ibn Abī Kuthayyir related to him that Abū Salama related to him saying, Abū Hurayra related to me*, saying the same thing.

¶1049–1053: *All possess the same content, all through al-Awzāʿī, through Yaḥyā ibn Abī Kuthayyir through Abū Salama ibn ʿAbd al-Raḥman through Abū Hurayra from the Prophet.*

On when the marriages of fathers for their virgin [daughters] are annulled:

¶1054: *Abū Ṭāhir al-Faqīh and Ibn Abī ʿAmr both said that Abū al-ʿAbbās Muḥammad ibn Yaʿqūb related that Muḥammad ibn Isḥāq al-Ṣaghghānī related that al-Ḥakam ibn Mūsā informed that Shuʿayb ibn Isḥāq related from Al-Awzāʿī from ʿAṭāʾ from Jābir ibn ʿAbd Allāh that:*

> A man married off his virgin daughter without her consent, so she came to the Prophet and he separated them.

¶1055: *Muḥammad ibn Ṣāʿid related that al-Ḥasan ibn Muḥammad al-Zaʿfarānī and Aḥmad ibn Manṣūr and al-ʿAbbās ibn Muḥammad and Abū Ibrāhīm al-Zuhrī all related; and ibn Makhlad and al-ʿAbbās ibn Muḥammad al-Dūrī and Aḥmad ibn Ṣāliḥ al-Ṣūfī and others all said: that al-Ḥakam ibn Mūsā related that Shuʿayb ibn Isḥāq related from Al-Awzāʿī from ʿAṭāʾ from Jābir ibn ʿAbd Allāh that:*

> A man married off his virgin daughter without seeking her permission, so she came to the Prophet and he annulled their marriage (in the words of Abū Bakr). Ibn Ṣāʿid said that she was a virgin whose permission had not been sought, and she came to the Prophet and he separated them.

¶¶1056–1059: of near-identical content.

On a difference of opinion arising between the previously-married woman and her marriage guardian:
¶1060: *Muḥammad ibn Makhlad related that Abū Aḥmad ʿAlī al-Qūhistānī related that Isḥāq ibn Rāhawayh related that ʿĪsā ibn Yūnus related from al-Awzāʿī from Ibrāhīm Ibn Murrah from al-Zuhrī from Abū Salama from Abū Hurayra that:*

> The Messenger of God said, "The virgin is not married without seeking her permission, and the previously-married woman has a measure of authority (*naṣībun min amrihā*) as long as she does not assert that she is unwilling. If she claims displeasure, and her guardians claim [that she gave her] consent, it is referred to the ruler."
>
> Isḥāq ibn Rāhawayh said, "I asked ʿĪsā if the last part of the hadith had come from the Prophet? He replied, 'This is how the hadith was related (*hakadhā al-ḥadīth*), so I don't know.'"

On there being no marriage contract without a guardian, and a woman cannot give a woman in marriage
¶1061: *Abū ʿAbd Allāh al-Ḥāfiẓ wa Abū ʿAbd Allāh Isḥāq ibn Muḥammad ibn Yūsuf al-Sūsī wa Abū Bakr Aḥmad ibn al-Ḥasan al-Qāḍī wa Abū Saʿīd ibn Abī ʿAmr wa Abū Ṣādiq ibn Abī al-Fawāris [all said], Abū al-ʿAbbās Muḥammad ibn Yaʿqūb related to us that Baḥr ibn Naṣr related that Bishr ibn Bakr informed al-Awzāʿī from Ibn Sīrīn from Abū Hurayra, may God be pleased with him:*

> A woman may not give a woman in marriage, and a woman cannot give herself in marriage, for the adulteress is the one who gives herself in marriage.

The divorce of a compelled (man) does not take place
¶1107: *Muḥammad ibn al-Muṣaffā al-Ḥimṣī related to us that al-Walīd ibn Muslim related to us that al-Awzāʿī related to us from ʿAṭāʾ from Ibn ʿAbbās from*

> The Prophet [who] said, "Truly God does not hold my community responsible for mistakes, forgetfulness, or that which they did under compulsion."[1]

1 *Inna Allāha waḍaʿa ʿan ummatī al-khaṭaʾ wa-l-nasyān wa-mā ustakrihū ʿalayh.* Also occurring in Ibn Mājah, ḥadith #2045.

¶1108–1112: of identical content

¶1113: *Abū Bakr related to us Wakīʿ related to us, from al-Awzāʿī from a man, from ʿUmar ibn al-Khaṭṭāb that*

> [ʿUmar] gave no consideration to a compelled divorce (*lam yarahu shayʾan*).

¶1114–1115: Opinions of Ibn ʿAbbās and ʿAṭāʾ to the same effect.

ʿAbd al-Razzāq al-Ṣanʿānī (d. 211/826)

Chapter on the authority of women being sought with regard to their marriages

¶10315: *ʿAbd al-Razzāq from Maʿmar from Yaḥyā ibn Abī Kuthayyir from al-Muhājir ibn ʿIkrama who said,*

> The Messenger of God, peace be upon him, would consult his daughters when contracting their marriages. He said, He would sit by the room (*khidr*)[2] of the one getting engaged, and say, 'Fulān is mentioning Fulāna.' If [his daughter] moved the curtain, he would not marry her, and if she remained silent, he would marry her.

¶10316-¶10317: another isnād and a slight variant of the same hadith.

¶10318: *ʿAbd al-Razzāq from al-Thawrī from ʿAbd al-Karīm al-Jazarī from Ibn al-Musayyib who said,*

> The Messenger of God, peace be upon him, said, "Consult virgins with regard to themselves, for they are shy. If they are silent, this is their consent."

¶10319: *ʿAbd al-Razzāq from Maʿmar from ʿAbd al-Karīm al-Jazarī from Ibn al-Musayyib who said,*

> The Messenger of God, peace be upon him, said, "Consult women (*āmirū al-nisāʾ*) with regard to themselves."[3]

¶10320: *ʿAbd al-Razzāq from al-Thawrī from ʿAbd Allāh ibn al-Faḍl from Nāfiʿ from Jubayr ibn Muṭʿam from Ibn ʿAbbās who said,*

---

2 The *khidr* is an area of the house separated by a curtain.

3 This could also be read as, "Appoint them as commanders over themselves." See Lane, a-m-r, subset 4.

> The Messenger of God, peace be upon him, said, "The non-married woman (*al-ayyim*) has more authority with regard to herself (*aḥaqq bi-nafsihā*) than does her marriage guardian, and the virgin should be consulted."

¶10321: (variant chain:) *'Abd al-Razzāq from Mālik that 'Abd Allāh ibn al-Faḍl related to him from Nāfi' from Ibn 'Abbās* "the same thing."

¶10322: *'Abd al-Razzāq from Ibn Jurayj who said, "'Uthmān ibn Abī Sulaymān that a man related to him from 'Abd Allāh ibn al-Faḍl from Nāfi' ibn Jubayr who said,*

> The Messenger of God, peace be upon him, said, "The previously-married woman (*al-thayyib*) controls her own affairs (*mālikah li-amrihā*) and the virgin is to be consulted with regard to herself, and her silence is her assent."

¶10323: *'Abd al-Razzāq from Ibn Jurayj who said, "I heard Ibn Abī Malīka say, Dhakwān the client of 'Ā'isha said, '[I heard 'Ā'isha] say,*

> I asked God's Messenger about a young girl (*al-jāriya*) whose family contracts her marriage, should she be consulted or no?" So God's Messenger replied to her, "Yes, she should be consulted." 'Ā'isha said, "So I said, 'And what if she were shy, [and as a result] she would be silent (*fa-innahā tastaḥyī fa-taskut*).'" So the Messenger of God said, "Then that is her permission, if she is silent."

¶10324: *'Abd al-Razzāq from Ma'mār from Yaḥyā ibn Abī Kuthayyir from Abī Salama ibn 'Abd al-Raḥmān from Abī Hurayra that*

> God's Messenger said, "The previously-married woman should be consulted, and the virgin should be asked her permission." They said, "And how does she give her permission, O God's Prophet?" He replied, "She is silent."

¶10325: *'Abd al-Razzāq from Ibn Jurayj who said,*

> I asked 'Aṭā', "Are women consulted with regard to themselves, both the previously-married and the virgin (*al-thayyib wa-l-bikr*)?" He said, "Yes." I said, "And [even] the father consults her (*wa-l-ab yasta'mir*)?" He said, "Yes."

¶10326: *'Abd al-Razzāq from Ibn Jurayj who said, "Ibn Ṭāwus reported to me from his father who said, 'I heard him say,*

"Women are consulted with regard to themselves." And Ibn Ṭāwus, "Except [...] in this, men are dealt with identically to girls (*al-rijāl fī dhālik bi-manzilat al-banāt*), they should not be compelled; fie! (*lā yukrahū wa ashadd ba'san*)"[4]

¶10327: *ʿAbd al-Razzāq from Ibn Jurayj from ʿAṭā' al-Khurasānī that*

Zaynab the daughter of the Prophet was married in the Jāhiliyya, and ʿAlī and ʿUthmān married [after the coming of] Islām.

The Prophet would go to the *khidr* of the candidate for engagement among his daughters and say, "Fulān is here to request marriage of Fulāna." If she poked the curtain with her hand, then this meant she declined, so he would not contract her marriage. If she did not poke the curtain with her hand, he would contract her marriage."

¶10328: Ibn Jurayj said, "It was reported to me from ʿIkrima the client of Ibn ʿAbbās something similar to this ḥadīth."

¶10329: *ʿAbd al-Razzāq from Maʿmar from Ḥabīb from Nāfiʿ who said,*

Ibn ʿUmar would consult his daughters regarding their marriages.

¶10330: *ʿAbd al-Razzāq from al-Thawrī from ʿĀṣim from al-Shaʿbī who said,*

The father must ask the virgin and the non-virgin.

¶10331: *ʿAbd al-Razzāq from al-Thawrī from Manṣūr from Ibrāhīm who said,*

As for the virgin, her father does not consult her, and as for the non-virgin, if she is dependent on him, he does not consult her, and if she is not dependent on him, he consults her.

¶10332: *ʿAbd al-Razzāq from Ibn Jurayj from ʿAṭā' who said,*

The father's contract of marriage for a virgin is binding, but not upon a non-virgin.

4 The text is missing after "except."

On Consulting the Orphan with Regard to Herself

¶10333: *ʿAbd al-Razzāq from Maʿmar from al-Zuhrī from Ibn al-Musayyib who said,*

> The Messenger of God said, "The orphan is consulted with regard to herself, and her silence is her assent."

¶10334: *ʿAbd al-Razzāq from Maʿmar from Ayyūb from Ibn Sīrīn who said,*

> "The orphan is consulted, and her silence is her consent."

¶10335: *ʿAbd al-Razzāq from al-Thawrī from Muḥammad ibn ʿAmr ibn ʿAlqama from Abī Salama from Abī Hurayra that*

> The Prophet said, "The orphan is consulted with regard to herself and if she is silent, this is her consent."

¶10336: *ʿAbd al-Razzāq from al-Thawrī from Manṣūr from Ibrāhīm who said,*

> "ʿUmar wrote that the orphan should be consulted with regard to herself, and if she is silent, this is her consent." He said, "Al-Shaʿbī said, if she is silent, or cries, or laughs, this is her consent. And if she refuses, [the contract] is not binding for her."

¶10337: *ʿAbd al-Razzāq from Maʿmar from Ṣāliḥ ibn Kaysān from Nāfiʿ ibn Jubayr ibn Muṭʿam from Ibn ʿAbbās, that*

> The Messenger of God said, "The marriage guardian has no authority over the previously-married woman, and the orphan is to be consulted, and her silence is her assent."

On issues of marriage compulsion that render it non-binding

¶10338: *ʿAbd al-Razzāq from Maʿmar from al-Ḥasan and al-Zuhrī who both said,*

> A father's authority is binding upon his virgin daughter with regard to marriage contracts if he is not mentally-deficient (*idhā lam yakun safīhan*).

¶10339: *ʿAbd al-Razzāq from Maʿmar from Yaḥyā ibn Abī Kuthayyir from Muhājir ibn ʿIkrima that*

> A father contracted marriage for a virgin against her will, so he went with her to the Prophet who returned to her her own authority (*fa-radd ilayhā amrahā*).

¶10340: *ʿAbd al-Razzāq from Jaʿfar ibn Sulaymān who said, Kahmas ibn al-Ḥasan related to me that ʿAbd Allāh ibn Barīda related to him saying,*

> A virgin woman came to the Prophet and said, "Oh, Messenger of God, my father married me to a nephew of his in order to raise his status through me, and he did not consult me, so do I have authority with regard to myself?" The Prophet said, "Yes." So she said, "I didn't want to undo anything my father had done, but I wanted women to know whether or not they had authority over themselves."[5]

¶10341: *ʿAbd al-Razzāq from Isrāʾīl from Abū Salama ibn ʿAbd al-Raḥmān who said,*

> "A [widow] wanted to marry the uncle of her child, [but] her father married her to another, and he did not have her best interests in mind (*lam yaʾlu ʿan khayr*). So she came to the Prophet and related that to him saying, "I wanted to marry the paternal uncle of my child so I could be with my child, for I hated being unmarried (*wa karahtu al-ʿuzba*). [My father] married me to another, not intending good. The Prophet sent for her father and said, "You married her against her will?" He said, "Yes." [The Prophet] said, "Go away (masc. sing.), there is no marriage contract for you (masc. sing.); go (fem. sing.) and marry whom you will (*fa-tazawwajī man shiʾti*)."

¶10342: *ʿAbd al-Razzāq reported to us from Ibn Jurayj who said, Abū al-Zubayr reported to me from a righteous man from the people of Medina from Abū Salama ibn ʿAbd al-Raḥmān who said,*

> There was a woman of the Anṣār married to a man of the Anṣār, but then her husband had been killed on the day of Uḥud. She had a child from him. [Both] the paternal uncle of her child and another man requested her hand in marriage from her father, and her father contracted her marriage to the man, leaving the uncle of her child. She went to the Prophet and said, "My father married me to a man I do not want, and he refused [to marry me to] the uncle of my child. My son will be taken from me."[6]

---

5 *Wa lākin aḥbabtu an yaʿlamū al-nisāʾ a-la-hunna fī anfusihinna amrun am lā.*
The edition from al-Maktab al-Islamī contains only the masculine singular verb (¶10302). Ed. Ḥabīb al-Aʿẓamī (Beirut: al-Maktab al-Islāmī, 1983), 6:146.

6 This is the only recorded version which explicitly mentions the custody implications for the widow who remarries, or that these implications were influencing or were a priority in her decision.

So the Prophet summoned her father and said, "Did you marry Fulān to Fulāna?" He said, "Yes." The Prophet responded, "Go away (masc. sing.), you have contracted no marriage. Go (fem. sing.) and marry the uncle of your child."

¶10343: *ʿAbd al-Razzāq from Maʿmar from Yaḥyā ibn Abī Kuthayyir from Abū Salamah and Ayyūb from ʿIkrima that*

A father contracted marriage for a previously married woman, so she went to the Prophet and said, "My father contracted marriage for me against my will." So the Prophet gave her authority over the affair" (*fa-jaʿala al-nabī al-amr ilayhā*).

¶10344: *ʿAbd al-Razzāq from Ibn Jurayj who said, Ayyūb informed me from ʿIkrima and from Yaḥyā ibn Abī Kuthayyir that*

"A father contracted marriage for both" (*ankaḥahumā*[7]) a previously-married woman and a virgin. So she went to the Prophet and said, "My father contracted my marriage." So [the Prophet] annulled her marriage.

¶10345: *ʿAbd al-Razzāq from al-Thawrī from Abū al-Ḥuwayrith from Nāfiʿ ibn al-Jubayr who said,*

Al-Khansāʾ bint Khidām became widowed (*āmat*)[8] so her father married her against her will, so she came (*atat*)[9] to the Prophet and said, "My father has married me against my will, and he did not take my feelings into consideration, and I have authority over myself (*wa qad malaktu amrī*). He said, "Then you are

7 The editor notes that the original and one of the rescensions contains this dual pronoun, here and in the final word of the passage, contrasting with the singular verbs used as the woman addresses the Prophet. The editor suggests that the "and" should perhaps have been an "or" with the pronoun being a mistake, the correct version being "her" instead of "both of them", rendering the meaning, "A father married a *thayyib* or a *bikr* and she went to the Prophet and he annulled her marriage." See footnotes 1–3, p. 119 (vol. 6).

8 The editor has taken this from al-Bayhaqī in conjunction with the *ʿAyn* recension, while the "Original" says *anabat*. *Anabat* is a possible alternative, however, because *anabahu* means to blame, reprove, or chide angrily or "with utmost severity or harshness; or he repulsed him, meaning a person who asked something of him, in the most abominable manner" (Lane, entry a-n-b).

9 Note that this is the same verb used in the version rejected by al-Shaybānī's editor in the *Ḥujja*.

not married. Go marry whom you will." So he annulled her marriage and she married Abū Lubāba al-Anṣārī.

¶10346: *'Abd al-Razzāq from Ibn Jurayj who said, 'Aṭā' the Khurasānī reported to me from Ibn 'Abbās that*

Khidām the father of Wadī'a married his daughter to a man, so she came (*atat*) to the Prophet and complained to him that she was married against her will. The Prophet removed her from her husband and said, "Do not compel them" (*lā tukrihūhunna*). So she married after that Abū Lubāba al-Anṣārī, who had been previously married (*wa kāna thayyiban*). [Ibn Jurayj] said, It has been reported to me that Khansā' bint Khidām was from the people of Qubā'.

¶10347: *'Abd al-Razzāq from Ma'mar from Sa'īd ibn 'Abd al-Raḥmān al-Jaḥshī from Abū Bakr ibn Muḥammad that*

A man of the Anṣār called Anīs ibn Qatāda married Khansā' bint Khidām and was killed on the day of Uḥud. So her father contracted her marriage to another man. She came (*jā'at*) to the Prophet and said, "My father has contracted my marriage to a man and my child's paternal uncle is dearer to me than him. So the Prophet put the matter in her hands (*ja'ala al-amra ilayhā*).

¶10348: *'Abd al-Razzāq from Ibn Jurayj who said, Ismā'īl ibn Umayya who reported from more than one person from Madīnah,*

Na'īm ibn 'Abd Allāh had a daughter. 'Abd Allāh ibn 'Umar asked for her hand in marriage and named a large bridal gift for her. Na'īm married her to an orphan in his care from the Banī 'Adī ibn Ka'b who had no money. So her mother went to the Prophet and explained that to him. She said, "'Abd Allāh was mentioning my daughter [and he had named] a large price [for her],[10] and her father married her to an orphan who has no money, and he left 'Abd Allāh who had named a large bridal gift for her!" So the Prophet summoned [Na'īm] and recounted this to him. And he said, "Yes, I married her to my orphan, for he is the most deserving of the orphans I have raised and ushered into [adulthood] (*aḥaqq man rafa'tu yutumahu wa-waṣaltuhu*)." Then [Na'īm] said, "She can have of my money

10 There is a corruption in the text here, which the editor suggests should fixed in this way. Because this thought is repeated in the next line, it may well be that this portion is meant to read that the groom in question is one who has many assets.

that which ʿAbd Allāh offered her." So the Prophet said, "Consult women with regard to their daughters" (*āmirū al-nisāʾ fī banātihinna*).

¶10349: *ʿAbd al-Razzāq from al-Thawrī from Ismāʿīl ibn Umayya who said, a trustworthy person (or one who cannot be criticized) reported to me from Ibn ʿUmar that:*

He sought engagement from the daughter of a relative. The mother of the woman desired Ibn ʿUmar [to be her daughter's groom] while her father desired an orphan in his care. He said, "So the father married her to that orphan. The Prophet came along and I recounted that to him. He said, 'Consult women with regard to their daughters.'"

¶10350: *ʿAbd al-Razzāq from Maʿmar who said,*

I was informed that the orphan girl is not compelled by her brother to marry, even if he is level-headed (*rashīd*).

¶10351: *ʿAbd al-Razzāq from Ibn Jurayj who said,*

I said to ʿAṭāʾ, "Is it binding for a man to contract marriage for his daughter against her will when she is a virgin?" He said, "Yes." I said, "What about a previously-married woman, against *her* will?" He said, "No. A previously-married woman possesses authority over herself. It is not binding [to contract her marriage against her will]." He continued, "And I prefer that if the father of the virgin chooses a man, and she chooses another, even if the one her father chooses is of higher status and [can pay] a higher bridal gift, if there is no problem in the one she chooses, and she is not allowed to realize her love (*lam tulḥiq hawāhā*), I worry that she might still desire him (*akhshā an yakūn fī nafsihā min-hu*). But if her father overrules her, he has a right to do so."

¶10352: *ʿAbd al-Razzāq from Ibn Jurayj from ʿAṭāʾ who said,*

We heard (*samiʿnā*) that an orphan girl possesses full authority over herself, and it is not permissible for her brother to contract her marriage without her permission.

¶10353: *ʿAbd al-Razzāq from Ibn Jurayj who said, Ibn Ṭāwus reported to me from his father who said regarding the previously-married woman,*

"Do not compel anyone to marry against her will (*lā tukrih ʿalā al-nikāḥ man takrah*)." I said, "She has fallen in love (*hawiyat hawā*) and her father has fallen in love (*wa-hawiya abūhā hawā*)." He said, "He [the Prophet?][11] would have liked (*kāna yuḥibbu*) for her to realize her love (*tulḥaq bi-hawā-hā*)."

¶10354: *ʿAbd al-Razzāq from Maʿmar and others from Yaḥyā ibn Saʿīd from al-Qāsim ibn Muḥammad that*

A woman from the Banī ʿAmr ibn ʿAwf was married by her father against her will. So she came to the Prophet and he annulled her marriage unless she were to give her permission. She had been previously-married.

¶10355: *ʿAbd al-Razzāq from Ibn Jurayj and Maʿmar from Ayyūb ibn Abī Tamīma from Ibn Sīrīn who said,*

A Medinan woman became single (*āmat*). ʿUmar found her marriage guardian and said, "Mention me to her." So when [the guardian] had been slow [in answering him], ʿUmar went to her in the presence of her guardian. He said, "I don't know if this one has mentioned anything to you." She said, "Yes, and I have no need of you or of what he mentioned, but order him that he might marry me to Fulān." The guardian responded, "No, by God, I will not do it." So ʿUmar replied, "Why?" The guardian said, "Because you mentioned her and Fulān mentioned her, and Fulān mentioned her, and I do not know if there is a noble man left in Medina who hasn't mentioned her, and she has refused all except Fulān."

So ʿUmar said, "I warn you that it is very serious (*innī aʿzamu ʿalayk*), if you do not marry her to him unless you know of some major flaw in his religion."

¶10356: *ʿAbd al-Razzāq from Maʿmar from Ayyūb from Ibn Sīrīn*: the same thing.

¶10357: *ʿAbd al-Razzāq from from Maʿmar from Ibrāhīm ibn Maysara who said,*

A young man became engaged to a woman who had fallen in love [with him]. Then, [her family] refused to marry her to him. I asked Ṭāwus [about it] and he said, "The Messenger of God said, I have not seen better for those who are in love [than to get married], and he ordered me to marry [them]."[12]

---

11 The pronoun here is ambiguous; the editor does not indicate by the "pbuh" that the speaker is the Prophet. Still, it would seem to make sense.

12 This text appears in Bayhaqī, Ibn Mājah (deemed authentic by al-Albānī). The *Muṣannaf* text is missing "than to get married" (*mithl al-nikāḥ*), which the editor supplied from Bayhaqī, *al-Sunan al-kubrā*, 7/78. Because the wording (*lam yara lil-mutaḥābīn mithl al-nikāḥ*) seemed to have at least two possible meanings, we sought an explanation, and found it to be explained by al-Manāwī in *Fayḍ al-qadīr* as: "If a man looks upon a strange

¶10358: *ʿAbd al-Razzāq from Ibn Jurayj who said, ʿAmr informed me from ʿIkrima that he said,*

> The Messenger of God said, "Do not force upon women that which they hate" (*lā tuḥḥamilū al-nisāʾ ʿalā mā yakrahūn*).[13]

On the marriage of two children

¶10388: *ʿAbd al-Razzāq from Maʿmar from al-Zuhrī from ʿUrwa who said:*

> The Prophet married ʿĀʾisha when she was a girl of seven, and she was given to him (*uhdiyat ilayh*) when she was a girl of nine, and her toys were with her. He died when she was eighteen.

¶10389: *ʿAbd al-Razzāq from Maʿmar from Hishām ibn ʿUrwa from his father*: the same thing.

¶10390: *ʿAbd al-Razzāq from Maʿmar from Ayyūb and others from ʿIkrima that*

> ʿAlī ibn Abī Ṭālib married his daughter as a little girl who still played with little girls (*jāriya talʿab maʿa al-jawārī*) to ʿUmar ibn al-Khaṭṭāb.

¶10391: *ʿAbd al-Razzāq from Ibn ʿUyayna from ʿAmr ibn Dīnār from Abū Jaʿfar who said,*

> ʿUmar ibn al-Khaṭṭāb asked ʿAlī for his daughter's hand in marriage. He [ʿAlī] replied: 'She is still little.' So it was said to ʿUmar, 'He means by that to prevent you!'" [Abū Jaʿfar] continued, "So he spoke to him. So ʿAlī said, 'I will send her to you, and if you are satisfied with her, she is your wife.'" Abū Jaʿfar said, "So, he sent her to him." He said, "So ʿUmar went to her, and bared her leg (*kashafa ʿan sāqihā*), and she said, 'Back off (*arsil*)! If it weren't that you were the Commander of the Believers, I would have slit your throat (*la-ṣakaktu ʿunuqaka*).'"

¶10392: *ʿAbd al-Razzāq from Ibn Jurayj who said, I heard al-Aʿmash say,*

---

woman and she colonizes his heart (*akhadhat bi-majāmiʿ qalbihi*), then marrying her will engender even more love; this is what al-Ṭayyibī has expressed. More eloquent than this is what some of the greats have said, the significance of which is that the greatest medicine for longing (*al-ʿishq*) is marriage."

13 The version from al-Maktab al-Islāmī reads "*yakrahna*." ¶10320, 6:152.

"'Umar ibn al-Khaṭṭāb sought to marry (*khaṭaba*) the daughter of 'Alī. [Upon 'Alī's protest,] He said, 'You only seek to prevent her.' ['Alī] said, 'I will send her to you, and if you are satisfied [with her] she is your wife, and I will marry [her to] you.' So he adorned her and sent her to him. He said, 'I am satisfied.' Then he touched her leg, so she said, 'By God, if you were not the Commander of the Believers, I would have cut out your eye (*la-ṣakaktu 'aynaka*).'"

¶10393: *'Abd al-Razzāq from Ma'mar from Ayyūb from 'Ikrima who said,*

'Umar ibn al-Khaṭṭāb married Umm Kulthūm bint 'Alī ibn Abī Ṭālib when she was a young girl (*jāriya*) who [still] played with young girls. So he went to his friends, who congratulated him, and he said, "I did not marry for entertainment, but I heard the Messenger of God say, 'Every line and lineage is cut off on the Day of Judgment except for my line and lineage.' So I desired that there be line and lineage between myself and the Messenger of God."

'Abd al-Razzāq added: "Umm Kulthūm is [the daughter] of Fāṭima the daughter of God's Messenger. 'Umar consummated the marriage with her and she bore him a son called Zayd. It reached me that 'Abd al-Malik ibn Marwān poisoned the both of them [Zayd and his mother] and they died. 'Abd Allāh ibn 'Umar prayed [their funeral prayer]. [The murder occurred] because it was said to 'Abd al-Malik that this was the son of 'Alī and the son of 'Umar. He feared for his caliphate, so he poisoned them both."

¶10394: *'Abd al-Razzāq from Ma'mar from al-Ḥasan and al-Zuhrī and Qatāda. They said,*

"If fathers marry off young children, the marriage is valid."

¶10395: *'Abd al-Razzāq from al-Thawrī from Jābir from al-Shu'bī who said,*

Only a father can compel marriage.

¶10396: *'Abd al-Razzāq from Ma'mar from Ibn Ṭāwus from his father who said,*

If a father contracts marriage for two children, they may choose [to rescind] upon maturity (*idhā kabarā*).

¶10397: *'Abd al-Razzāq from Ma'mar from al-Zuhrī that*

'Urwa ibn al-Zubayr married his son as a child to the daughter of Muṣ'ab, who was also a child.

¶10398: *ʿAbd al-Razzāq from al-Thawrī from Hishām ibn ʿUrwa who said,*

> "My father married his son as a child. The boy was five and the girl was six.[14] [The boy] died and she inherited from him four thousand dīnārs, or something like that."

Ibn Abī Shayba (d. 235/849)

Chapter on the man who contracts marriage for his daughter: those who say consult her

¶16217: *ʿAbd Allāh ibn Idrīs related to us from Ibn Jurayj from Ibn Abī Malīka from Abū ʿAmr the client of ʿĀʾisha that ʿĀʾisha said:*

> "The Messenger of God said: 'Women are to be consulted with regard to their marriages (*tustaʾmar al-nisāʾ fī abḍāʿihinna*).'" She continued, "I said, 'Oh, Messenger of God, they are shy!' He replied, 'The unmarried woman is more in possession of herself (*al-ayyim aḥaqq bi-nafsihā*), and the virgin should be consulted (*al-bikr tustaʾmar*) and her silence is her assent.'"

¶16218: *Ibn Idrīs related from Muhammad ibn Isḥāq from Mālik ibn Anas from ʿAbd Allāh ibn al-Faḍl from Nāfiʿ ibn Jubayr that ʿIbn ʿAbbās said:*

> "The Messenger of God said, 'The unmarried woman is more in possession of herself than her guardian, and the virgin is to be consulted, and her silence is her assent.'"

¶16219: *Ḥafs related to us from Ibn Jurayj who said:*

> "The Messenger of God, if a suitor came to propose to one of his daughters, would sit next to her curtain (*khidrihā*) and say, "Fulān is proposing to Fulāna," and if she was silent, he would contract the marriage, and if she poked with her hand—and Ḥafṣ signaled with his index finger, poking in the thigh—he would not marry her."

¶16220: *Jarīr related to us from Layth from al-Ḥakam who said:*

> ʿAlī said, "A man cannot marry his daughter until he consults her."

¶16221: *Fuḍayl ibn ʿIyāḍ related from Manṣūr from*

---

14 There is confusion in the text: it gives the ages and their accompanying pronouns in the male gender (*hādhā ibn khams wa hādhā ibn sitt*), with the editor suggesting that one should be read in the feminine.

Ibrāhīm [al-Nakhaʿī] who said, "If a woman is still among her father's dependents, he does not have to consult her, and if she is not his dependent, he must consult if he wants to contract marriage for her."

¶16222: *ʿAbda ibn Sulaymān related to us from ʿĀṣim from al-Shaʿbī who said:*

A man must consult his daughter with regard to marriage, whether she is a virgin or a non-virgin.

¶16223: *Ibn ʿUlayya related from Yūnus from al-Ḥasan that he would say:*

The marriage [contract enacted by] a father is valid for his daughter, whether she is a virgin or a non-virgin, whether she likes it or not.

¶16224: *Abū Khālid related to us from Ibn Jurayj from Ibn Ṭāwūs from his father who said,*

A man cannot compel his non-virgin daughter to marry if she dislikes it.

¶16225: *Abū Khālid related to us from Mālik ibn Anas who said al-Qāsim and Sālim were saying:*

If a virgin's father contracts a marriage for the virgin, then she is bound by it even if she despises it.

¶16226: *Abū Khālid related to us from Ibn Jurayj from ʿAṭāʾ who said,*

If the father of the virgin prefers a man, and she prefers another, he should follow her desire if there is no problem with [the man], even if the one he prefers for her is providing a better marriage gift. I fear that it would cause her psychological difficulty (*akhshā an yaqaʿ fī nafsihā*). And if her father does compel her, it is within his rights (*wa-in akrahā fa-huwa aḥaqq*).

¶16227: *Sharīk related to us from Jābir from ʿĀmir who said:*

Only fathers can compel marriage.

¶16228: *ʿAffān related to us that Ḥammād ibn Salama related from Ayyūb from ʿIkrima that*

If ʿUthmān ibn ʿAffān wanted to contract marriage for one of his daughters, he would sit next to her curtain (*khidrihā*) and say, "Fulān is proposing to you."

¶16229: *ʿAmr ibn Muḥammad related to us from Ibrāhīm ibn Nāfiʿ from Ibn Ṭāwus from his father* [*Ṭāwus*] *who said:*

The virgin is consulted, even if she is still a dependent of her parents (*wa in kānat bayna abawayhā*).

¶16230: *Khālid ibn Idrīs related to us from Kahmas from Ibn Barīda who said:*

A young girl (*fatā*) came to ʿĀʾisha and said, 'My father married me to his nephew in order to raise his status through me (*li-yarfaʿa bī khasīsatahu*), even though I did not want it (*wa innī karihtu dhālik*).' So ʿĀʾisha said to her, 'Wait until God's Messenger comes. And when God's Messenger came, he sent for her father, and he allowed her to decide for herself (*jaʿala al-amra ilayhā*).' And she said, 'If it's up to me, I would permit what my father did, but I wanted to know, do women have any authority in this matter?' (*hal lil-nisāʾ min al-amr shayʾ*?)

Concerning the orphan girl and those who said that she be consulted with regard to herself.

¶16231: *Sufyān ibn ʿUyayna related to us from al-Zuhrī from Saʿīd who was told by the Prophet:*

The orphan girl is consulted with regard to herself, and her silence is her assent.

¶16232: *Abū Muʿāwiya related to us from Muḥammad ibn ʿAmr from Abī Salama from Abū Hurayra who said:*

The Messenger of God said, "The orphan girl's orders are sought with regard to herself, and if she accepts (*in qabilat*), this is her permission, and if she refuses, nothing can bind her (*lā jawāz ʿalayhā*)."

¶16233: *Sallām related to us from Abū Isḥāq from Abū Burda who said:*

The Messenger of God said, "Any orphan girl for whom a proposal of marriage is made, is not to be married until her orders are sought with regard to herself, and if she assents, she may be married, and her assent is her silence, and if she rejects, then she is not married."

¶16234: *Jarīr related to us from Manṣūr from Ibrāhīm who said:*

ʿUmar said, "The orphan girl's orders with regard to herself are sought, and her consent is [evidenced] if she is silent."

¶16235: *Fuḍayl ibn ʿIyāḍ related to us from Manṣūr from Ibrāhīm from ʿUmar*: the same thing.

¶16236: *ʿAbda ibn Sulaymān related to us from Mujālid from al-Shaʿbī from ʿAlī and ʿUmar and Shurayḥ who said:*

> The orphan girl's orders are sought with regard to herself, and her consent is silence.

¶16237: *Hushaym related to us from Mujāhid from al-Shaʿbī from ʿAlī that he would say:*

> When marriage is proposed to the orphan girl, if she remains silent, this is her consent, and if she dislikes it, she is not married.

¶16238: *Hushaym related to us from Ashʿath from Ibn Sīrīn from Shurayḥ who said:*

> If she is silent, she has consented and given herself, and if she dislikes [it] and is upset (*wa-in karihat wa-maʿidat*) she is not married.

¶16239: *Hushaym and Jarīr both related to us from Mughīra from Ibrāhīm with regard to the orphan girl if she marries; he said:*

> If she is silent or cries, it is her consent, and if she dislikes it, she is not married. (Jarīr did not say 'if she dislikes it'.)

¶16240: *Ibn Mahdī related to us from Sufyān from Khālid ibn Dīnār from al-Shaʿbī who said:*

> I heard him say with regard to the orphan girl: "If she is wed and laughs or cries or is silent, this is her consent."

¶16241: *Yaḥyā ibn Ādam related to us saying: Yūnus ibn Isḥāq related to us saying Abū Burda related to us saying Abū Mūsā said:*

> The Messenger of God said, "The orphan girl's orders are sought with regard to herself, and if she is silent, she has given her permission, and if she refuses, she is not married."

The chapter on the man who contracts marriage for his prepubescent son: who allows it

¶16261: *Ismāʿīl ibn ʿAyyāsh related to us from ʿAbd Allāh ibn Dīnār from someone who related from al-Ḥasan that:*

The Messenger of God said: "If a man marries off his son and he dislikes it, it is not marriage, and if he marries him off and he is prepubescent, it is binding."

¶16262: *Muṭarraf related to us from al-Ḥakam from Shurayḥ who said:*

If a man marries off his son or daughter, both have no choice [to rescind] when they mature (*idhā shabbā*).

¶16263: *ʿAbd Allāh ibn al-Mubārak related to us from Maʿmar from al-Zuhrī and al-Ḥasan and Qatāda who said:*

If fathers marry off their children, the marriage is valid.

¶16264: *Hushaym related to us from Yūnus from al-Ḥasan who said:*

If a man contracts marriage for his minor son, that marriage is legally binding (*tazwījuhu jāʾiz ʿalayh*), and the son must pay the marriage gift.

¶16265: *Sharīk related to us from Jābir from ʿĀmir who said,*

Only fathers can compel marriage.

¶16266: *ʿUbayd Allāh ibn Mūsā related to us from al-Ḥasan from Layth from ʿAṭāʾ who said:*

If a father contracts marriage for his prepubescent son, his marriage of him is legally binding, and he is not allowed to divorce (*lā ṭalāq lahu*).

Bibliography

Ibn ʿAbbās, ʿAbd Allāh, *Tanwīr al-Miqbās min tafsīr Ibn ʿAbbās.* Beirut: Dār al-Kutub al-ʿIlmīyah, 1992.

Ibn ʿAbd al-Barr, Abū ʿUmar Yūsuf ibn ʿAbd Allāh, *Kitāb al-Istidhkār*. Beirut: Dar al-Kutub al-ʿIlmiyyah, 2006.

Ibn ʿAbd al-Raḥmān, Abū ʿAbd Allāh Muḥammad, *Raḥmat al-ummah fī ikhtilāf al-aʾimmah*. Beirut: Muʾassasat al-Risāla, 1994.

Ibn Abī Shayba, Abū Bakr, ʿAbd Allāh ibn Muḥammad ibn Ibrāhīm, *Muṣannaf* ed. Muḥammad ʿAwwāmah. Beirut: Dār Qurṭubah, 2006.

Abou el Fadl, Khaled, *Speaking in God's Name.* Oxford: Oneworld, 2005.

Abū Yūsuf Yaʿqūb, *al-Radd ʿalā siyar al-Awzāʿī.* ed. Abū al-Wafā al-Afghānī Cairo: Raḍwān Muḥammad Raḍwān, ND.

Abū Yūsuf Yaʿqūb, *Ikhtilāf Abī Ḥanīfa wa ibn Abī Laylā.* Edited by Abū al-Wafā al-Afghānī. Cairo: Raḍwān Muḥammad Raḍwān, 1357/1938.

Ali, Kecia, *Imam Shafii, Scholar and Saint.* Oxford: Oneworld, 2011.

Ali, Kecia, *Marriage and Slavery in Early Islam*. Cambridge, Mass: Harvard University Press, 2010.

Ali, Kecia, *"Marriage in Classical Islamic Jurisprudence"* in *The Islamic Marriage Contract: Case Studies in Islamic Family Law*, edited by Asifa Quraishi and Frank Vogel. Cambridge: Harvard University Press, 2008.

Ali, Kecia, *Sexual Ethics in Islam.* Oxford: OneWorld, 2008.

Ali, Kecia, "Just Say Yes: Law, Consent, and Feminist Epistemologies," in *Jihad for Justice*, edited by Kecia Ali, Laury Silvers, and Juliane Hammer. USA: 48Hrs Books, 2012.

al-Āmidī, Sayf al-Dīn, *Al-Iḥkām fī uṣūl al-aḥkām*. Beirut: Dār al-Kutub al-ʿIlmīyah, 1980.

Ibn al-ʿArabī, *Aḥkām al-Qurʾān li-Ibn al-ʿArabī*. Beirut: Dār al-Kutub al-ʿIlmīyah, 2006.

Arjava, Antti, "Roman Family Law after Barbarian Settlements," in Mathisen, ed, *Law, Society and Authority in Late Antiquity*. Oxford: Oxford University Press, 2001.

Asad, Muhammad, *The Message of the Qurʾān*. Gibraltar: Dār al-Andalus, 1984.

al-ʿAsqalānī, Ibn Ḥajar, *Fatḥ al-bārī.* N.P., 1978.

al-ʿAsqalānī, Ibn Ḥajar, *Tahdhīb al-tahdhīb*. Beirut: Dār Ṣādir, 1968.

Azam, Hina, *Sexual Violation in Islamic Law: Substance, Evidence, and Procedure.* Cambridge: Cambridge University Press, 2015.

Bakhtiar, Laleh, ed. *Encyclopedia of Islamic Law*. Chicago: ABC Publishing, 1996.

Berkey, Jonathan, *The Formation of Islam.* Cambridge: Cambridge University Press, 2003.

Biale, Rachel, *Women in Jewish Law: An Exploration of Women's Issues in Halakhic Sources* New York: Schocken Books, 1984.

al-Dhahabī, Muḥammad ibn Aḥmad, *Mīzān al-iʿtidāl*. N.P., 1963.

al-Dhahabī, Muḥammad ibn Aḥmad, *Siyar aʿlām al-nubalāʾ*, ed. Shuʿayb al-Arnaʾūṭī. Beirut: Mu'assassat al-Risāla, 1981.

al-Dhahabī, Muḥammad ibn Aḥmad, *Tadhkirat al-Ḥuffāẓ*. Hyderabad: Majlis Dā'irah al-Maʿārif al-Niẓāmīya, 1915.

El Shamsy, Ahmed, *The Canonization of Islamic Law: A Social and Intellectual History.* New York: Cambridge University Press, 2013.

Fadel, Mohammad, "Reinterpreting the Guardian's Role in the Islamic Contract of Marriage: The Case of the Mālikī School," *The Journal of Islamic Law*, 3:1, Spring/ Summer, 1998.

al-Fāsī, Ibn al-Qaṭṭān, *Al-Iqnāʿ fī masāʾil al-ijmāʿ*, ed. Fārūq Ḥammādah. Damascus: Dār al-Qalam, 2003.
Other Edition: Edited by Ḥasan ibn Fawzī al-Ṣaʿīdī. Cairo: al-Fārūq, 2004.

Fisher, Greg, ed. *Arabs and Empires before the Sixth Century*. Oxford: Oxford University Press, 2015.

Gaiman, Aharon, "Marriage and Divorce Customs in Yemen and Eretz Israel," in *Nashim: A Journal of Jewish Women's Studies and Gender Issues*, No. 11, Yemenite Jewish Women (Spring, 5766/2006).

Giladi, Avner, "Ṣaghīr." *Encyclopaedia of Islam, Second Edition*. Eds. P. Bearman et al. Brill, 2010. Brill Online.

Hallaq, Wael, "On the Authoritativeness of Sunni Consensus," *International Journal of Middle East Studies*, Vol. 18, No. 4, (Nov. 1986), Cambridge University Press, pp. 427–454.

Hallaq, Wael, *Origins and Evolution of Islamic Law*, Cambridge: Cambridge University Press, 2005.

Hallaq, Wael, *Sharīʿā: Theory, Practice, Transformations*, Cambridge: Cambridge University Press, 2009.

Ibn Ḥazm, ʿAlī ibn Aḥmad, *Marātib al-Ijmāʿ*. Beirut: Dār al-Ifāq al-Jadīdah, 1978.

Ibn Ḥazm, ʿAlī ibn Aḥmad, *al-Muḥallā*. No publisher, N.D.

Hopkins, M.K., "The Age of Roman Girls at Marriage in *Population Studies*, Vol. 18, no. 3 (Mar. 1965).

Jackson, Sherman, "Ibn Taymīya on Trial in Damascus," *Journal of Semitic Studies* XXXIX/1 Spring 1994, pp. 41–85

al-Jaṣṣāṣ, Abū Bakr Aḥmad ibn ʿAlī, *Kitāb Aḥkām al-Qurʾān*. Beirut: Dār al-Kitāb al-ʿArabī, 1970.

Jayyusi, Salma Khadra and Manueal Marin, eds. *The Legacy of Muslim Spain*. Leiden: Brill, 1992.

Ibn Kathīr, Ismāʿīl ibn ʿUmar, *al-Bidāyah wa-l-nihāyah*. Beirut: Bayt al-Afkār al-Dawliyah, 2004.

Kamali, Mohammad Hashim, *Principles of Islamic Jurisprudence*, Cambridge: The Islamic Texts Society, 2003.

Laiou, Angeliki, "Sex, Consent, and Coercion in Byzantium," in Angeliki Laiou, ed., *Consent and Coercion to Sex and Marriage in Ancient and Medieval Societies.* Washington, D.C.: Dumbarton Oaks, 1993.

Lamdan, Ruth, "Child Marriage in Jewish Society in the Eastern Mediterranean during the Sixteenth Century," in *Mediterranean Historical Review* 11 (1996).

Layish, Aharon, "Saudi Arabian Legal Reform as a Mechanism to Moderate Wahhābī Doctrine," in *Journal of the American Oriental Society*, vol. 107.2 (1987).

Little, Donald, "The Historical and Historiographical Detention of Ibn Taymiyya," *International Journal of Middle East Studies*. Vol. 4, No. 3 (Jul., 1973).

Lowenstein, Steven M. "Ashkenazic Jewry and the European Marriage Pattern: A Preliminary Survey of Jewish Marriage Age," *Jewish History*, Vol. 8, No. 1/2. The Robert Cohen Memorial Volume (1994).

Lowry, Joseph E., *Early Islamic Legal Theory*. Leiden: Brill, 2007.

Lowry, Joseph E., "Is There Something Postmodern about Uṣūl al-fiqh?" in Reinhart, A. Kevin and Robert Gleave, eds, *Islamic Law in Theory: Studies in Honor of Bernard Weiss* (Leiden: Brill, 2014), pp. 285–315.

Lowry, Joseph E., *Sayf al-Dīn al-Āmidī's Doctrine of Ijmāʿ: A Translation and Critical Introduction*, University of Pennsylvania, Master's Thesis, 1991.

Makdisi, George, *The Rise of Humanism*. Edinburgh: Edinburgh University Press, 1990.

Mālik ibn Anas, *al-Muwaṭṭaʾ*, Cairo: al-Maktabah al-Tawfīqīyah, N.D.

Ibn Manẓūr, *Lisān al-ʿArab*. Beirut: Dār Ṣādir, 1955.

al-Marghinānī, Burhān al-Dīn ʿAlī ibn Abī Bakr, *al-Hidāyah*, vol. 3, Karachi: Al-Bushra Publishers, ND.

al-Marwazī, Muḥammad ibn Naṣr, *Ikhtilāf al-ʿUlamāʾ*. Beirut: ʿĀlam al-Kutub, 1986.

Motzki, Harald, "Child Marriage in Seventeenth-Century Palestine," in *Islamic Legal Interpretation, Muftis and their Practices*, ed. Masud et al. Harvard: Harvard University Press, 1996.

al-Nīsābūrī, Muḥammad Ibn al-Mundhir, *Kitāb al-Ijmāʿ*, ed. ʿAbd Allāh ʿUmar Bārūdī, (Beirut: Dār al-Janān, 1986).

Other Editions:

Kitāb al-Ijmāʿ, ed, Fu'ād ʿAbd al-Manʿam Aḥmad. Alexandria: Dār al-Da'wah, 1982.

Kitāb al-Ijmāʿ, ed. Abū Ḥammād Ṣaghīr Aḥmad. Riyāḍ: Dār Ṭayyibah, 1982.

Kitāb al-Awsaṭ fī al-sunan wa-l-ijmāʿ wa-l-ikhtilāf, ed. Abū Ḥammād Ṣaghīr Aḥmad. Riyāḍ: Dār Ṭaybah, 1993.

Kitāb al-Ishrāf ʿalā madhāhib al-ʿulamāʾ. Beirut: Dār al-Fikr, 1993.

Ibn Qayyim al-Jawzīya, *Iʿlām al-Muwaqqiʿīn*. Beirut: al-Maktabah al-ʿAṣrīyah, 2003.

Ibn Qayyim al-Jawzīya, *Zād al-Maʿād fī Hadī Khayr al-ʿAbbād*. Beirut: Dār ibn Ḥazm, 1999.

Powers, Paul. *Intent in Islamic Law: Motive and Meaning in Medieval Sunni Fiqh*. Leiden: Brill, Studies in Islamic Law and Society, 2006.

Powers, Paul, "Finding God and Humanity in Language: Islamic Legal Assessments as the Meeting Point of the Divine and Human," in *Islamic Law in Theory*. Brill: Leiden, 2014.

Rapoport, Yossef, "Ibn Taymiyya on Divorce Oaths," in *The Mamluks in Egyptian and Syrian Politics and Society*, ed. Winter Michael and Amalia Levanoni. Leiden: Brill, 2004.

Richard P. Saller in "The Social Dynamics of Consent to Marriage and Sexual Relations" in *Consent and Coercion to Sex and Marriage in Ancient and Medieval Societies*, ed. Angeliki Laiou. Washington D.C.: Dumbarton Oaks, 1993.

al-Ṣanʿānī, ʿAbd al-Razzāq ʿAbd al-Razzāq ibn Hammām ibn Nāfiʿ, *Muṣannaf*. Beirut: Dār al-Kutub al-ʿilmiyyah, 2000.

Satlow, Michael. *Jewish Marriage in Antiquity*. Princeton: Princeton University Press, 2001.

Satlow, Michael, *Tasting the Dish: Rabbinic Rhetorics of Sexuality*. Atlanta: Scholars Press, 1995.

Schereschewsky, Ben-Zion, and Elon, Menachem. "Child Marriage," in Encyclopedia Judaica, Ed. Michael Berenbaum and Fred Skolnik. Vol. 4. 2nd ed. Detroit: Macmillian Reference USA, 2007.

al-Shāfiʿī, Muḥammad ibn Idrīs, *Kitāb al-Umm*, ed. Dr. Rifʿat Fawzī ʿAbd al-Muṭṭalib. Al-Manṣūrah: Dār al-Wafāʾ, 2008.

Shaham, Ron, "Custom, Islamic Law, and Statutory Legislation: Marriage Registration and Minimum Age of Marriage in the Egyptian Sharīʿah Courts," in *Islamic Law and Society*, Vol 2, no. 3, *Marriage, Divorce and Succession in the Muslim Family* (1995).

Shaham, Ron, *The Expert Witness in Islamic Courts*. Chicago: Chicago University Press, 2010.

Shaki, Mansour, "Children iii. Legal Rights of Children in the Sasanian Period," *Encyclopaedia Iranica*, Online Edition, 20 July 2005.

al-Shāshī, Niẓām al-Dīn, *Uṣūl al-Shāshī*, ed. Muḥammad Akram al-Nadwī. Dār al-Gharb al-Islāmī, 2000.

al-Shaybānī, Muḥammad ibn al-Ḥasan, *Kitāb al-Ḥujja ʿalā ahl al-Madīna*, ed. Mahdī Ḥasan al-Kīlānī. Beirut: ʿĀlam al-Kutub, 2006.

Spectorsky, Susan, *Chapters on Marriage and Divorce: Responses of Ibn Ḥanbal and Ibn Rāhwayh*. Austin: University of Texas Press, 1993.

Stone, Suzanne, "Jewish Marriage and Divorce Law," in Quraishi, Asifa and Vogel, Frank, eds, *The Islamic Marriage Contract: Case Studies in Islamic Family Law.*Cambridge: Harvard University Press, 2008.

al-Subkī, Tāj al-Dīn, *Ṭabaqāt al-Shāfiʿīyah*. ʿĪsā al-Ḥalabī Printers, 1964.

al-Ṭabarī, Muḥammad ibn Jarīr, *Jāmiʿ al-bayān ʿan taʾwīl āyy al-Qurʾān*, ed. ʿAbd Allāh al-Turkī. Gīza: Dār Hijr, 2001.

al-Ṭabarī, Muḥammad ibn Jarīr, *Tarīkh al-Ṭabarī: Tarīkh al-rusul wa-l-mulūk*. Beirut: Maktabat Khayyāṭ, 1965.

al-Ṭaḥāwī, Aḥmad ibn Muḥammad ibn Sallāmah, *Sharḥ maʿānī al-athār*, ed. Ibrāhīm Shams al-Dīn. Beirut: Dār al-Kutub al-ʿIlmīyah, 2006.

al-Ṭaḥāwī, Aḥmad ibn Muḥammad ibn Sallāmah, *Mukhtaṣar Ikhtilāf al-ʿUlamāʾ, ikhtiṣār*: Aḥmad ibn ʿAlī al-Jaṣṣāṣ, ed. ʿAbd Allāh Naẓīr Aḥmad. Beirut: Dār al-Bashāʾir al-Islāmīyah, 1995.

al-Tanūkhī, Saḥnūn ibn Saʿd. *al-Mudawwana al-Kubrā*. Beirut: Dār al-Ṣādir, N.D.

Ibn Taymīya, Taqī al-Dīn Ahmad, *Majmūʿat Fatāwī Shaykh al-Islām Ibn Taymīya*, ed. ʿAbd al-Raḥmān ibn Qāsim al-ʿĀṣimī, 1977

al-Thaʿlabī, Aḥmad ibn Muḥammad, *Al-Kashf wa-l-bayān*, ed. Muḥammad ibn ʿAshūr. Beirut: Dār al-Turāth al-ʿArabī, 2002.

Tucker, Judith, E., "Questions of Consent: Contracting a Marriage in Ottoman Syria and Palestine," in *The Islamic Marriage Contract*. Harvard: Harvard University Press, 2008.

Tucker, Judith, E., *In the House of the Law: Gender and Islamic Law in Ottoman Syria and Palestine*. Berkeley: University of California Press, 1998.

al-Ṭūsī, Muḥammad ibn al-Ḥasan, *Kitāb al-Khilāf*. N.P. 1956?

Weiss, Bernard, *The Search for God's Law: Islamic Jurisprudence in the Writings of Sayf al-Dīn al-Āmidī*. Salt Lake City: University of Utah Press, 1992.

Weiss, Bernard, *The Spirit of Islamic Law*, Athens: The University of Georgia Press, 2006.

Wegner, Judith Romney Wegner. *Chattel or Person: The Status of Women in the Mishnah* New York: Oxford University Press, 1988.

Westrup, C.W., *Family Property and Patria Potestas*. London: Oxford University Press, 1936.

Yazbak, M, "Minor Marriages and Khiyār al-Bulūgh, *Islamic Law and Society*, vol. 9 #3 (2002), pp. 386–409

al-Zamakhsharī, Maḥmūd ibn ʿUmar, *Al-Kashshāf ʿan ḥaqāʾiq al-tanzīl wa-ʿuyūn al-aqāwīl*. Dār al-Fikr, N.D.

Ziadeh, Farhat, "Equality in the Muslim Law of Marriage," *American Journal of Comparative Law* vol. 5 (4), 1968.

Zysow, Aron, *The Economy of Certainty:An Introduction to the Typology of Islamic Legal Theory*. Atlanta: Lockwood Press, 2013.

Zysow, Aron, *Women Living Under Muslim Laws: Women, Family, Laws and Customs in the Muslim World*. International Solidarity Network, New Delhi: Zubaan, 2006.

Electronic Resources

Encyclopedia of Islam: http://proxy.library.upenn.edu:2403/subscriber/uid=1721/title_home?title_id=islam_islam&authstatuscode=202

Encyclopedia Iranica: www.iranicaonline.org/articles/zoroastrianism-i-historical-review

Encyclopedia of Hadith: http://hadith.al-islam.com/Loader.aspx?pageid=261

Index

ʿAbd Allāh ibn Aḥmad ibn Ḥanbal 148n29, 216
ʿAbd Allāh ibn ʿUmar ibn al-Khaṭṭāb 39n82, 40n91
ʿAbd Allāh ibn al-Mubārak 41, 63n20, 82n14
ʿAbd Allāh ibn Zayd Āl Maḥmūd 149, 161
Abd al Rahmān ibn al Mundhir 88
ʿAbd al-Razzāq al-Ṣanʿānī 17, 39, 59, 59n2, 59n4, 60–62, 64–65, 69–70, 73, 76–77
Abū Bakr al-Ṣiddīq 43n101, 77, 170, 171, 173, 200, 226, 232
Abū Ḥanīfa 45, 46n113, 78n2, 80, 85, 92–94, 98, 164, 179n56, 186, 193, 199, 210, 215, 216, 218
Abū Hudhayfa 175
Abū Lubāba 65, 66
Abū al-Qāsim al-Khiraqī 7
Abū Yūsuf 54, 54n38, 60, 78, 78n2–3, 93n61, 100, 164, 178n54–55, 185n67, 193, 199, 216n33
Abū Yaʿlā ibn al-Farrāʾ (al-Qāḍī Abū Yaʿlā) 145n13, 213n25, 214, 234n26, 235
Abou el Fadl, Khaled 6n26, 8n34, 148n30, 150n34, 158n63–64
Agrippina 27
Aḥmad, Abū Ḥammād Ṣaghīr 8n37
Aḥmad ibn Ḥanbal 9, 88n41, 148n29, 174, 182, 185, 216, 216n34, 217
ʿĀʾisha (bint Abī Bakr) 7, 7n32, 9, 11, 12, 39n85, 42, 43n101, 44, 50, 61–62, 76, 80n10, 87–88, 90n49, 93n61, 104, 118n70, 123–124, 127, 128, 133, 138, 139n65, 159, 165, 168, 169, 169n17, 170, 172, 174, 175, 177, 177n52, 179–180, 182–183, 184, 188–189, 191, 200, 201–203, 205, 212, 213, 225–228, 232
ʿAlī ibn Abī Ṭālib 9, 38, 67, 89, 192
Ali, Kecia 3n13, 6n25 9n43, 11n49, 41n93, 42n97, 52n133, 81n23, 81n43, 123n3, 125n11
Ali, Nujood 43n101
Al-Awzāʿī 11n50, 17, 54, 59, 59n1, 60–64, 66, 68, 72, 76, 108n23, 168n16, 173n35, 183n64, 184, 199
Augustus 27, 28
ayyim/bikr hadith 11n50, 61, 64n26, 83, 97, 104–105, 109, 123–124, 132, 165, 170–171, 188, 193, 194, 196, 197, 199, 201–205, 212
see also *thayyib/bikr* 11n50, 61, 63, 65, 183, 202, 227

Barīra 67, 93n61, 100–101, 128–130, 130n33
bāligh 53, 54, 191n93, 195, 227
bāligha 12, 49, 56, 189
Biale, Rachel 26n6, 26n8–9, 32n43, 34n57, 37n71, 37n73
bikr 8, 8n32, 8n38, 10, 12, 26, 56, 56n146, 61, 64n26, 83, 84, 95n66, 104, 115, 133–134, 171, 195, 202, 207, 209, 234n27
bulūgh 11, 33n48, 37, 45, 46n113, 47, 47n117, 48, 51, 52, 53, 80n8, 117, 183, 191, 215, 219n50, 220
Al-Bukhārī 11, 11n48, 33n48, 42n100, 84, 112n43, 123n3, 170, 170n22, 177n52, 185n68
Brown, Jonathan 11n48, 145n13, 169n19

Calder, Norman 15n59, 78n1–2, 105n12
Chad 3
Code of Hammurabi 33
Consensus 5, 5n23, 6–8, 10, 11–13, 15–19, 19n71, 20, 20n75, 21, 38, 44, 51, 52, 60, 68, 77, 105, 109n27, 140–141, 143–149, 149n34–35, 150, 150n37–38, 151–153, 153n48, 154–155, 155n54, 156–159, 161–162, 162n76–77, 163–170, 170n20, 171, 173–175, 177, 179, 181, 183–191, 193, 195–198, 198n121, 199–206, 210, 222, 224–226, 228–237, 246
Consent 1, 3, 4n17, 6n25, 9–10, 15, 15n63, 26, 28, 30, 32, 51, 52n133, 56, 56n147–148, 58, 60, 63–64, 66, 77, 84, 86, 94, 96–97, 101, 104, 106, 108, 110, 112, 113, 125, 128, 132, 138, 139, 155, 157, 159, 160, 162, 165, 168, 170, 172, 173, 173n35–35, 174, 178, 183, 185, 189n84, 190, 198n124, 206, 207, 209n9, 210, 211, 212, 213, 218, 221, 223, 230, 232, 233
Convention on the Elimination of all Forms of Discrimination against Women 1
Cooperson, M. 11n49

Al-Dhahabī 12–13n52, 20n75, 78n1, 78n3, 195n109
divorce 3n11, 5n19, 6, 7n28, 9, 9n42, 10, 11, 14n58, 16, 26n3, 26n7, 29n28, 32, 33, 41, 41n96, 60, 62, 63n17, 69, 69n49, 71, 72, 77, 79, 83, 83n19, 84, 88n41, 88, 92, 97, 107, 111, 112, 114, 118, 120, 122, 127, 129, 129n32, 132, 138, 139, 145, 145n16, 146, 146n20, 147, 147n24, 148, 152, 174n38, 177n53, 188n79, 188, 194, 207, 214, 215, 217n41, 220n57, 223, 234
see also repudiation 14, 14n58, 16, 71–73, 73n68, 74, 75, 77, 100, 128, 136, 137, 137n61, 138n61

Egypt 2, 3, 3n11, 3n14, 28n17, 146n20, 167n6, 168n8, 207n1, 229
El Shamsy, Ahmed 11n49, 15n60, 15n62, 16n66, 19n73, 144n9, 144n11, 167, 167n2, 167n4–6, 168n11

Fadel, Mohammad 10n44, 38, 38n76, 106n16
Fātima bint Qays 39, 175, 175n40, 217
al-Fawzān, Ṣāliḥ 7, 7n30, 8, 12, 12n51, 13
Fundamentalist Church of Jesus Christ of Latter Day Saints 2

Al-Ghazālī 4, 4n15, 55, 55n142, 56n148, 153n48
Guardianship 16, 30, 31, 51–53, 55, 57, 91n51, 92, 115, 132, 162, 169n17, 196, 210
see also *walāya* 51, 57
walāyat al-ijbār 210, 211

Ḥafṣa 88, 81n11, 87, 90, 129, 194
Hallaq, Wael 14n57, 15n61, 16n67, 17n67, 18n70, 19n71–72, 38n76, 38n79, 143n5, 147, 147n27, 178n54, 231n20, 236n31
Hammada, Faruq 8n37, 150n38, 158n65, 162n76
ḥaqīqa 50, 82, 189n84
al-Ḥasan al-Baṣrī 46, 46n114, 67n39, 73, 74, 110, 155, 176n48, 180, 183n64, 186n73, 187, 210235
Hishām ibn ʿUrwa 39n85, 43n101, 62n12, 122, 123, 202n134
Al-Hudhayfi, Ali 12n51
ḥujja 12, 40, 40n92, 41n94, 41n96, 49, 78, 78n1, 79, 79n5, 80n7–8, 82n11–12, 83n16, 83n20–21, 84, 85, 86n28, 86n30, 87n34, 87n36, 88n38, 88n42, 89n43–44, 90n49, 92n53–54, 93, 93n58, 93n60, 94n63, 95n66, 96n70, 97n73, 98, 98n77, 98n79–80, 100, 101, 101n86, 102, 107n18, 124, 124n7, 129n32, 130n32, 168n10, 168n16, 173n35, 178n55, 188, 188n78, 190, 190n90, 192n94, 199n126, 209n7, 216n33, 226
al-ḥulum 33, 33n48, 43, 47, 47n116, 47n119, 48

Ibn ʿAbd al-Barr 17n67, 41, 90, 103n3, 105, 109, 114, 146n22, 147, 152, 156n58, 164, 165, 168, 171n23, 173, 179n33, 178n55, 184n66, 191n92, 194, 195, 195n107, 196, 197n118, 198–205, 207n2, 208n4, 226, 227n7, 232, 233
Ibn Abī Shayba 17, 29n28, 59, 59n3, 63, 63n18–20, 63n22, 64, 64n24–25, 65n33, 66, 68–71, 71n60, 72, 72n63, 73, 73n65, 73n67, 73n69, 74n74, 74n80, 77, 83n18, 104n5, 137, 137n57, 168n16, 173n35, 175n43, 235n29
Ibn Hajar 12n52, 177n52, 185n68, 202n134
Ibn Ḥazm 113n47, 132, 133, 153n48, 187n76, 211n13, 225, 226, 226n2, 227–230, 232, 233, 233n25
Ibn Hubayra, Yaḥyā ibn Muḥammad 149, 150n35–36, 155n54, 233n22
Ibn Masʿūd 89, 89n43, 98n75, 175, 175n44, 191
Ibn al-Mundhir, Abū Bakr Muḥammad ibn Ibrāhīm 8n2, 8n37–38, 9, 12, 12n51–52, 13, 20n75, 39, 41, 72, 81n11, 88, 105, 109, 109n27, 147, 147n24, 148, 149, 150n37, 151, 151n43, 152, 154n48, 154n51, 155n54, 156n56, 157, 158, 158n64, 159, 159n69, 160, 160n71, 161, 162, 162n76, 163, 165, 167, 167n3, 168n8, 168n12, 169–171, 171n23, 171n25, 172, 172n29, 173–182, 182n63, 183, 185–187, 187n76, 192n97, 193n99, 194n104, 201, 202, 202n136, 203–206, 209n7, 216n38, 232, 232n21, 233
Ibn al-Muqaffaʿ 143, 236
Ibn al-Qaṭṭān al-Fāsī 8n37, 20, 150, 151, 151n41, 154n50, 158n65
Ibn Qayyim al-Jawzīya 54, 206, 210–212
Ibn Qudāma al-Maqdisī, Muwaffaq al-Dīn 6–12, 12n51–52, 13, 14, 17, 20, 38, 39,

43n101, 47, 56, 56n146, 76n83, 148, 151, 158, 160, 161, 161n71, 170n20, 171n23, 174, 174n31, 177, 178n55, 184n66, 198n124, 202n136, 204–207, 207n2, 208, 208n4, 209, 209n7, 210–212, 212n20, 213, 214, 216n33, 216n38, 217, 217n40, 223, 233
Ibn Shubrama 70, 155, 161n75, 162–164, 184, 184n66, 191, 191n91–92, 193, 199, 226, 227
Ibn Taymīya 34n54, 43n101, 63n17, 145, 145n15–17, 146, 146n 20–21, 147, 147n24, 206, 211, 211n14, 212, 212n17, 215n32, 223, 225, 228–231
Ibn al-Zubayr
  Al-Mundhir 88
  Muṣʿab 39, 39n84
  ʿUrwa 39, 39n83, 39n85, 41, 43n101, 62, 62n12, 122, 123, 129, 130n34, 182n63, 200, 202n134
ʿidda 9, 9n39, 9n40, 37, 48, 69, 73, 73n66, 74, 100, 118, 130n32, 136, 138, 212, 214, 215, 223
ijbār 9, 9n43, 210, 211, 222
ijmāʿ 5, 8, 8n37, 12, 12n51, 13, 13n53, 19, 19n71, 105, 146, 148, 148n29, 149, 149n34, 150, 150n35, 150n37, 151, 151n40, 152, 153n47–48, 154, 154n48, 155n54, 156, 157n58, 158, 158n64–65, 159, 160, 160n73, 162–165, 169, 170, 170n20, 173, 179, 197, 197n119, 198, 198n121, 203–205, 225, 226n2, 228, 229, 229n14, 230, 230n16, 231, 237
isnād 11, 74n80, 93n60, 111n40, 159, 171n23, 188
ius vitae necisque 31, 31n35

Al-Jaṣṣāṣ, Aḥmad ibn ʿAlī al-Rāzī 40, 40n90, 48, 48n120, 49, 50, 50n126, 51, 55, 56n146, 80, 82, 85, 122, 126n20, 155n54, 162n78, 164, 169n17, 187, 191n93, 192, 192n94, 212n19
Jeffs, Warren 2, 2n7
Jordan 2, 3

kabīra 8n36, 10, 50, 56n146, 201
kafāʾa 10, 14, 131, 150n36, 174–177, 193, 216, 217, 221, 222, 223
  see also, *kufūʾ* 8n38, 90, 93, 93n60, 130, 174, 176, 181, 217
Kamali, M.H. 148n29, 209n7, 237, 237n35
ketannah 25n3, 32
Kenya 4n16
khabar al-wāḥid 145, 169, 202
Khansāʾ bint Khidām 65, 66, 84–87, 90, 127, 173, 173n35, 184, 197n118
khilāf 8n38, 44n105, 45n112, 143, 153, 169, 229
khiyār al-bulūgh 11, 37, 215, 219n50, 220
kiddushin 32, 37

Laiou, Angeliki 28n22–23, 30n30, 32n47, 33n50, 38n77
legal capacity 10, 14, 18, 26, 43n56, 37, 56n148, 58, 65–67, 70, 71, 74, 75, 77, 84, 85, 87, 91, 93, 94, 101 103–107, 109, 111, 119–121, 123–128, 130, 132, 138, 139, 162, 165, 174, 188n82, 189, 189n84, 190, 194–196, 196n117, 204, 207–209, 221, 223, 232, 233, 234n27, 235
  of females 66–67, 85–91, 111–114, 127, 165, 190
  of slaves 18, 67–68, 93–94, 107–109, 128–132
  of the mentally deficient 91–92, 132–133
  of virgins 94–97, 109–111, 128–132, 132–133
  of orphans 107–109
Lex Burgundionum 35
Libya 2
Lombards 30
Lowry, Joseph E. 11n49, 13n53, 15n59, 19n71, 144n6, 153n47, 168n9, 168n14, 180n59, 197n119, 201n131, 203n137, 231n19

mahr 34n51, 42n97, 93n60, 119, 219
Mālik ibn Anas 17, 103n1, 165n87
al-Marghinānī 96n69, 169n17, 234n26
al-Marwazī 77, 105, 143, 143n4, 152, 154, 155, 155n52, 161n74, 165, 167, 178n55, 183–187
maturity 1, 10, 14, 16, 18n69, 25, 29, 33, 34, 37, 43–46, 48n123, 49, 51–53, 56n158, 57, 57n149, 63, 68, 70, 75, 80, 83n15, 85, 94, 97, 106, 108, 109, 114, 118, 122–124, 126, 133, 139, 149n35, 155, 174, 178, 183–185, 187, 190, 191, 195, 196, 197n117, 200, 207, 212, 214, 219, 221, 223, 233–235
mental deficiency 91, 91n52, 103, 107n17
Motzki, Harald 25, 25n1, 55n142, 59, 59n2, 59n4, 60, 70n52, 109n24, 117n64, 148n32, 185n70, 219, 219n49–52, 220, 220n58, 234
muḥallil 69, 69n49, 70
mukallaf 33
Muslim (hadith compiler) 11

Nadwi, Mohammad Akram 6n24
nafaqa 68, 93n60, 115, 118, 180, 181, 212, 214, 219
nikāḥ 4n15, 8n36, 8n38, 9n40, 18n69, 38, 44, 47, 47n117, 53n136, 60, 63, 65, 79n5, 81, 81n11, 84, 85n27, 86, 87, 89, 106, 114, 133n34, 156, 159, 160, 163, 165, 170, 171, 177n52, 178, 182, 186, 186n74, 198, 207n1, 215, 233n22

patria potestas 30, 30n30, 31, 51n131
Plutarch 27

Al-Qāsim ibn Muḥammad ibn Abī Bakr 105, 105n8
Qudāma ibn Maẓʿūn 9, 38, 40, 40n91, 42, 98n79, 100n83, 184, 184n66
Qurʾānic verses 54
  Q2:237 (who holds the marriage contract) 47
  Q2:232 (on divorce) 104n7, 188, 188n80, 189
  Q2:281 (on guardians, according to al-Shāfiʿī) 87
  Q4:3 47, 49, 50, 80, 80n9, 151n43, 162, 162n79, 191, 191n93, 192, 216
  Q4:6 (marriage age) 18n69, 44, 46, 53, 96, 123n5, 126
  Q4:34 (nushūz) 34n54
  Q4:127 (female orphans) 50, 78, 80, 212
  Q24:31 43
  Q24:32 (*ayyim/ayāmā*) 61, 195
  Q65:4 (non-menstruating women) 7, 9, 47, 212, 214
Al-Qurṭubī, 40n91, 46n113, 47, 48, 48n122, 50n127, 151n43

Al-Rabīʿ Ibn Sulaymān 15n59, 167, 263
rescission (see also *khiyār al-bulūgh*) 11, 16, 18, 38, 62, 68, 70–71, 73, 77, 79, 80, 82, 83, 93n61, 94, 100–101, 107, 108, 127, 128, 130, 131, 133, 155, 162, 164, 174, 177, 177n53, 178, 184–187, 191, 196, 200, 202, 215, 216n33, 220, 221, 224
repudiation 14, 14n58, 16, 71, 73n68, 75, 100, 128, 136, 137n61, 138n61
Reynolds, Dwight 54n140
rushd 18n69, 44–46, 51, 53, 53n136, 96, 96n68, 123, 159n69

ṣabī 47, 54, 55, 92, 107, 117
safīh/safīha 91, 91n51–52, 92, 106
ṣaghīra 8n36, 8n38, 9n40, 10, 31, 40, 47, 48, 50, 51, 53, 55, 56, 56n146, 70, 79n5, 92, 98, 98n79, 149n35, 156, 163, 170, 171, 189, 201, 215
Saḥnūn 15n59, 17, 70, 97n74, 103, 103n2, 105, 105n11–12, 106–110, 111n40, 112–116, 119, 120, 120n73, 121, 168n16, 173, 173n34, 192n96–97
Sālim ibn ʿAbd Allāh ibn ʿUmar 105 and 105n9, 110, 165, 198
Satlow, Michael, 18n68, 26n4, 30n29, 31n37, 31n40, 32n42, 32n44–46, 34n52, 34n56, 35n61, 36, 36n67–68, 37n74
Saudi Arabia 3, 3n10, 4, 4n16, 5, 5n19–20, 8, 148, 148n33, 206, 230
Al-Shāfiʿī, Muḥammad ibn Idrīs 11n49, 17, 122
Al-Shāshī, Aḥmad ibn Muḥammad Niẓām al-Dīn 189n87
Shatā, Muḥammad Muḥammad 150
Al-Shaybānī, Muḥammad ibn al-Ḥasan 17, 40, 40n92, 42, 48, 49, 77, 78, 78n1–2, 79, 80, 81n11, 82, 82n11, 82n14, 83–91, 93, 93n60, 94–98, 98n79, 99, 100, 100n83, 101, 102, 104n4, 107, 111n41, 129n32, 130n32, 168n10, 168n16, 192, 195n109, 199, 209n7, 216n33
al-ṣighar 33, 49–51, 62, 191n93, 210, 213, 227
Al-Subkī, Taqī al-Dīn 146, 146n20–21
Sonbol, Amira 206, 220n57
Spectorsky, Susan 7n28, 9n42, 88n41, 188n79, 210n12, 217n41
Sezgin, Fuat 11n49, 20n75, 103n1, 108n24
slaves 18, 36, 41, 41n96, 67, 79, 83, 88, 92–94, 96, 100, 101, 103, 107, 124, 128, 131n37, 159, 172n28, 181
Soranus 27
Sudan 2
Sufyān ibn ʿUyayna 123n3, 172n30
Sufyān al-Thawrī 59n2, 123n3, 183n64, 192, 216, 216n35
suitability 10, 14, 16, 18, 35–37, 67, 68, 75–76, 77, 93, 93n60, 127, 131, 131n37, 132, 139, 162, 163, 174, 175n43, 176, 185, 192, 193, 204, 205, 216–219, 221–224
Syria 2, 3, 35n59, 39n81, 41n97, 59, 102n87, 145, 146n20, 221n61, 229

Al-Ṭabarī, Muḥammad ibn Jarīr 47, 47n117–118, 48, 48n120, 50n127, 72n61, 81n10–11, 151n43, 153n148, 162n77, 212n19
Al-Ṭaḥāwī 40n89, 45n108, 80, 85–88, 90, 90n49, 104n7, 105, 111n40, 152, 155, 155n54, 156n55, 162n 77, 163n82, 164n85, 165, 168, 168n8–10, 168n12, 192n97, 193, 199, 205, 227, 227n6, 232
takkanah 32
Ṭāwus 82n14, 186, 199
Al-Thaʿlabī 45, 45n106, 46, 47, 96n68
thayyib 11n50, 31, 56, 61, 63–65, 65n34, 84, 109, 121, 124n9, 138, 149, 170, 170n21, 173n35, 183, 184, 191, 194, 195, 197, 197n118, 202, 235
  thayyib/bikr 11n50, 61, 63, 65, 183, 202, 227
Tucker, Judith 41n97, 54, 102n87, 120n73, 207, 218n47, 219n53, 220n59, 221, 221n61, 221n63–64
Toorawa, Shawkat 11n49, 15n59

ʿUmar ibn al-Khaṭṭāb 39 and 39n82, 39n86, 40, 60, 61, 71, 104, 146, 175, 188n79
Umm Kulthūm bint ʿAlī ibn Abī Ṭālib 9, 38, 39, 89, 191
Umm Salama 40, 50, 188, 189, 191, 191n93
United Nations Children's Fund 1
Universal Declaration of Human Rights 1, 4, 4n17

Violence Against Women Reauthorization Act 2
virginity 10, 10n44, 52, 52n133, 56, 56n147, 64, 66, 96, 102, 103, 106, 107, 109–111, 113, 114, 119, 120, 120n73, 121, 127, 150, 183, 184, 187, 191, 195, 197, 201, 204, 208, 210, 211, 218, 223, 234, 234

walāyat al-ijbār 210, 211
walī mujbir 9, 30, 62–66, 79, 106, 123–128, 169, 184, 187, 184, 203, 207–212, 218–219, 224, 234, 234n27
Weiss, Bernard 19n71, 19n74, 144n6, 169, 169n18, 236n32

Yazbak, M. 207, 219, 219n50, 220, 221n60
yutm 48, 49, 54, 80n8

zabrā *129*
ẓannī 169
zawāj 38, 192n93
Zayd ibn Thābit 39, 39n81.
Al-Zubayr ibn al-ʿAwwām 40, 39n83, 98n79
Zulficar, Mona 4
Zysow, Aron 11n47, 13n56, 19n71, 148n31, 203n137

Printed in the United States
By Bookmasters